Democracy as Problem Solving

Democracy as Problem Solving

Civic Capacity in Communities Across the Globe

Xavier de Souza Briggs

The MIT Press
Cambridge, Massachusetts
London, England

For information about special quantity discounts, please email special_sales@ mitpress.mit.edu

This book was set in Sabon by SNP Best-set Typesetter Ltd., Hong Kong.

Printed on recycled paper and bound in the United States of America.

Library of Congress Cataloging-in-Publication Data
De Souza Briggs, Xavier N.
    Democracy as problem solving : civic capacity in communities across the globe / Xavier de Souza Briggs.
        p. cm.
    Includes bibliographical references and index.
    ISBN 978-0-262-02641-3 (hardcover : alk. paper)—ISBN 978-0-262-52485-8 (pbk. : alk. paper)
    1. Political participation. 2. Democratization. 3. Community development. I. Title.
JF799.D42   2008
321.8—dc22   2007037630

10 9 8 7 6 5 4 3 2 1

For my students, who keep me puzzling

I speak the password primeval, I give the sign of democracy.
—Walt Whitman, *Leaves of Grass*

Contents

Preface and Acknowledgments

Many scholars and activists have tackled the question of how to make democracy work. Some have also asked deeper questions about what it is *for*—that is, as a recipe for collective life, since "what works" is very much a matter of perception. It depends on what one believes worth doing. And in the first decade of the twenty-first century, in high-conflict regions and elsewhere, we are once again engaged in tough debates about the social conditions under which democracy can best develop where it is, by any definition, a new and largely untested idea. But at the same time, democracy looks awfully stunted and stymied where it has reigned longest and to greatest fanfare, such as in my country, the United States, where my parents were among the millions of immigrants who believed in the democratic ideal, not just the ideal of equal opportunity, and who worked hard and benefited.

This book is an effort to extend ideas about democracy at work, in all its ambiguity, untidiness, and contradiction, and through those ideas to improve the practice of democracy. I focus on the concept of *civic capacity*, not merely a capacity to set directions collectively but also to devise and implement the means of acting together more effectively, with and beyond government. This blurring of the traditional divide between direction setting (policy making) and outcomes (implementation) is at the heart of the story, and the target problems it encompasses are universals, including: how to manage urban growth as populations expand and concerns about environmental sustainability grow, how to restructure the material basis of our lives (the job economy) where old industries are no longer competitive, and how to invest in young people—through social protections and human development, broadly defined—so as to make every other goal possible.

Across the world, this idea of democracy—as an imperfect recipe for problem solving that engages the public, private, and not-for-profit or "social" sector in collective action—is desperately in need of careful and creative attention. It is my contention that more of that attention should go to the tangible choices faced and strategies chosen by people and institutions as they problem-solve over time—that is, to the civic process that no longer stops at shaping official policy through advocacy but blends community agenda setting, strategy making, and productive action in a host of innovative ways, stretching institutions and the very idea of democracy in the process. The cases in this book are just that: not short-run episodes of conflict or resolution, of straightforward "participation" or "partnership" reforms, but sagas of multiple chapters and decision points, played out in specific local contexts on four continents: Africa, Asia, South America, and North America. While I am fascinated by changing governance in Europe, particularly as regional institutions evolve there, limited time and other resources led me to focus on less "state-centered" places—that is, where government does not consistently dominate entrepreneurial public action.

My direct interest in these themes began when I worked as a community planner, puzzling over how citizen participation at the street level scaled up, or did not, in the form of public policy and also major private commitments, such as corporate investments in distressed neighborhoods. That interest evolved when I began to design and lead training programs at Harvard University for senior practitioners struggling to make a difference while dealing with the contradictions and tensions in partnerships, participatory planning processes, and other popular ideas—ideas too often resting on weak practices and a resistance to scrutiny. But the experience that compelled me to research and write this book was working in America's federal government and visiting a terrific variety of big cities and small towns facing common problems and holding a remarkably common assumption about the key to progress, roughly: "Give us the resources, without the red tape (restrictions), and we will get the job done." Federal budget scarcity aside, this seemed to me a reasonable idea in places with a high capacity for creative collective action—that is, for not just pulling in one direction but managing to discover a *promising* direction and pursue it effectively. But the claim seemed much less reasonable in places with a long history of in-fighting and civic dysfunction, some of it exacerbated by the very resources "mailed in," from higher levels of government, to help.

Given that genesis over a decade of work inside and outside of the academy, I owe many debts in the production of this book and the more practice-oriented work products that evolved as part of the same project.

First and most importantly, I was welcomed into six far-flung places to poke, prod, and learn from those who are trying to make a difference. For opening doors and ideas, I am particularly grateful to: Sheela Patel and Jockin Arputham (Mumbai, India); Edgar Pieterse, Alan Mabin, and Joel Bolnick (Cape Town, South Africa); Jeroen Klink and Carlos Vainer (Greater ABC Region, Brazil); Margaret Brodkin (San Francisco); Robert Grow and Steve Holbrook (Salt Lake City); and Sabina Deitrick and Robert Stumpp (Pittsburgh). For key insights and introductions, I am also indebted to Sharit Bowmik and Sudha Mohan (India), Sue Parnell (South Africa), and Ned Hill, Hal Wolman, Richard De Leon, and John Parr (United States).

Next, many academic colleagues have been unstinting in their support. At Harvard University, Archon Fung, Christine Letts, Jenny Mansbridge, Mark Moore, Bob Putnam, and Christopher Winship read and commented generously on early iterations of this work. Celeste Benson, K. K. McGregor, Luiza Nanu, and Camiliakumari of Wankaner kept me organized and productive while I taught at Harvard, and a small army of research assistants, most of them students in public policy and management but also law students and undergraduates, tackled topics as diverse as the productive functions of conflict, impacts of devolution and "glocalization," trust and trust repair, game theory, urban political change, alliances and production networks, culture and group process, human rights as aspiration and as social policy, and participatory decision making. I am indebted to Iris Ahronowitz, Celeste Benson, Karen Bhatia, Nick Brown, Faisal Chaudhry, Jill Feldman, Evan Hochberg, Girija Kaimal, Silvia Kangara, Suzy Lee, Karen Mack, David Mihalyfy, Nidhi Mihrani, Dan Nicolai, Allan Oliver, Tim Reith, Shyamala Shukla, Jonathan Taylor, Ana Trbovich, and Derek Yi. In addition, hundreds of students in my Harvard course on negotiation and collaborative problem solving stimulated many new ideas. I thank them all.

MIT's Martin Luther King, Jr. Fellowship, which brought me to the Department of Urban Studies and Planning as a visitor in 2002–2003, provided financial support, wonderful students, and supportive colleagues who offered advice on the project. The latter include Lang Keyes, Balakrishnan Rajagopal, Martin Rein, Bish Sanyal, Larry Susskind, Judith Tendler, Phil Thompson, and Larry Vale, some of whom also commented on the book manuscript. They later helped me to make MIT a wonderful new home for my work, where Daniela Trammell kept administrative wheels turning in countless helpful ways. Jainey Bavishi and Dulari Tahbildar provided superb research support, producing maps and analyzing media coverage of ideas and events in this book. Students in my MIT courses on the politics of planning and collaborative problem solving encouraged me to push key arguments further without putting them out of reach to nonresearchers.

Other universities provided invaluable opportunities to get feedback on the work in early form, and for this I am especially grateful to Nicole Marwell (Columbia University), Lorena Barberia (Fundação Getulio Vargas in São Paulo), and Laura Evans (University of Washington).

The funders of this project were also partners in a host of ways, at multiple stages. Harvard's Hauser Center for Nonprofit Organizations provided seed funding at the early stages of concept development, as well as a stimulating and collegial work environment. I am especially indebted to Mark Moore and Shawn Bohen there, along with Tiziana Dearing, David Brown, Peter Dobkin Hall, Marshall Ganz, Sanjeev Khagram, Christine Letts, and Peter Frumkin. The Kennedy School of Government's Executive Education Program likewise provided challenging audiences of senior practitioners with whom I could develop and test key ideas in the classroom—in particular, the United Way of America/Casey Fellows and the NeighborWorks leaders in American community development—and a means of generating flexible funding for travel and other project needs. My colleague and friend Marty Linsky taught me through his unique training work with leaders, as well as his keen insights on the draft of the book.

Julia Lopez and Darren Walker at the Rockefeller Foundation, and Ralph Smith and Miriam Shark at the Annie E. Casey Foundation, also provided early financial support and endless encouragement, particularly as this study gave birth to a major online resource for practitioners and educators, now called The Community Problem-Solving Project @ MIT. Lopez also read and commented on the manuscript at a crucial stage. Miguel Garcia at The Ford Foundation supported vital fieldwork and offered critical questions about whether better civics actually leads to social innovations that matter.

To all these funder-partners: Your work, your personal examples, and your confidence in me have been tremendous gifts. Thank you.

Other colleagues and sources who commented generously and helpfully on the manuscript, some on very short notice, include Greg Behr, Joel Bolnick, Dexter Boniface, Tom Croft, Sabina Deitrick, Richard DeLeon, Mike Eichler, Kevin Fayles, Michael Funk, Christina Gabriel, Pat Getty, Robert Grow, Marie Huchzermeyer, Jeroen Klink, NTanya Lee, Nicole Marwell, Alan Matheson, Harold Miller, Mark Moore, Steve

Page, Robert Putnam, Harold Richman, Rick Stafford, Bob Stumpp, and Beth Weitzman.

Several of my teachers inspired an interest in these topics and whatever skills I have developed for analyzing them, including Pat Collins, Bob Crain, Daniel Iacofano, Anita Miller, Jonathan Reider, Malcolm Sparrow, and Jim Sebenius.

Finally, my wife, Cynthia, made more sacrifices to see this project through than anyone. She patiently proofread and reread drafts, too. For her love and support, I am grateful always.

I
Foundations

1

Introduction

The idea of democracy is a wider and fuller idea than can be exemplified in the state even at its best. To be realized, it must affect all modes of human association, the family, the school, industry, religion. And even as far as political arrangements are concerned, governmental institutions are but a mechanism for securing to an idea channels of effective operation. . . . Regarded as an idea, democracy is not an alternative to other principles of associated life. It is the idea of community life itself.

—John Dewey, *The Public and Its Problems* (1927, 143, 148)

The Pittsburgh city councilman wants a table at the rear of the café. He has squeezed this interview into a trademark busy day, but an obvious pride of place keeps him recounting changes in the city as we work our way to the back, navigating the laptop computers and other signs that Steel City is, at least in part, a city of "knowledge workers" now. "That's where we get developers together with community residents if we need to work out a conflict," he says, pointing to a glass-walled side room near our table. And the thought hits me immediately: the room is a metaphor for many of the civic changes underway in this former industrial powerhouse region, once the home of philanthropist-magnates such as Carnegie and Mellon and more than a dozen Fortune 500 companies, where more old-economy jobs were lost faster—in the restructuring of the 1980s—than anywhere else in America.

The room with glass walls is not big and it is not "public," not in the sense of belonging to government, representing everyone, or functioning according to formal rules of procedure. Nor is it a corporate boardroom where a few CEOs work out master plans with the mayor or governor and then steer them for decades or longer, like the fabled, elite-led "renaissance" plans that remade the physical fabric of downtown Pittsburgh and cleaned polluted air and rivers in the wake of World War II. Granted, conflicts over neighborhood development have never been the main target of centrally planned, regional master strokes made by a cohesive business-government elite. They always left the most local politics to the locals. But the glass-walled room is a mechanism nonetheless, a space for getting public work done when official channels fall short. Contrary to the conventional wisdom about the most democratic mechanisms being the most visible public stages, where everything is on the record, the backroom conversation is a key to exploring interests outside the spotlight of adversarial politics and gamesmanship. It is one element in a larger, emerging structure of decision making that is more democratic—more accountable to the public will—in part because *it gets things done.*

At their best, democracies confront important public problems. What is at stake in Pittsburgh, and communities in much of the rest of the world, is how to shift the economy, accommodate urban growth or decline as part of a more sustainable future, and invest in human development through institutions and leadership decisions that span government, business, and civil society. Wider demands for participation in decision-making, and much more robust expectations of transparency and accountability, help define the new civics of leading change—but with few clear roadmaps from place to place and situation to situation. Does more democracy mean less "development" (progress), for example? The glass-walled room is a place for informal consultation, for exchange and problem solving *out* of the official public eye, and so it has a place in the larger civic fabric of a changing industrial region. As an inversion of yesterday's hidden-from-view "back room" for elite decision makers, the new room is a place where, as negotiation analysts would point out, a costly public impasse can be reexamined without the need to protect reputations or go on the record. It hits me, as Councilman Peduto takes me to the heart of a changing Pittsburgh through his own story, that we can envision the glass-walled room—the figurative one, not the one in this coffee shop, that is—but not always get there, that when we get there, we often bring our own rules to the table, not a shared sense of how to act together to make our civic life more productive.

A world away, I am in Mumbai (Bombay), a major engine of the surging Indian economy and a city-region where almost half the population lives in slums. Here, a global bank recognizes that a unique network of nongovernmental organizations accountable to the urban poor offers the very best option for limiting the costly delays and conflicts that threaten housing projects. Meanwhile, smarter government subsidies trigger the market, regulation helps curb abuses that sap economic efficiency and also erode trust, and broader spatial planning ensures that efforts to give Mumbai a "world-class" airport and other needed infrastructure will not steamroll the poor who have yet to share in India's new prosperity. It all began about twenty years ago, when government and civil society organizations slowly threw out an older set of rules about who could be counted on for what. "We grew tired of protesting and then depending on government to deliver," the president of India's National Slum Dwellers Federation tells me as our taxi speeds past the city's countless construction projects, "so we decided to start creating our own solutions." Yet the slum dwellers did not surrender their political strength—India's slums have long been called "vote banks" in highly competitive political campaigns—in order to form a think tank, planning outfit, or hasty partnership with government. A rich sequence of learning and bargaining, cooperation and conflict, among civil society groups, local and state government agencies, and private developers and lenders has over two decades, brought new progress on slum redevelopment. This is no small thing since "slum-led" growth is how much of the world urbanizes, because Asia and other developing regions are urbanizing quickly, and because Mumbai has such huge and economically important slums. Much of the future of India's cities hinges on the kinds of arrangements that are redeveloping Mumbai's slums.

In Salt Lake City, an innovative organizing initiative for regional visioning and consensus building—one very carefully launched *outside* of state and local legislatures, with participation by businesspeople, environmentalists, and others—develops a broad-based constituency for sustainable "quality growth" and then helps the public sector develop new capacity to institutionalize and implement the vision.

Constituency and capacity—the will and the way—are much needed elsewhere, too. In Pittsburgh and the Greater ABC region (in the heart of industrial Brazil), public, private, and nongovernmental institutions work to install new foundations for competitiveness in a global economy, including regional leadership that overcomes a stubborn localism about important investment decisions. In Brazil, the Workers' Party helped lead a peaceful revolution to install more participatory local governance in the ABC and other regions, as the country emerged, in the late 1980s, from decades of military dictatorship. Brazil's experience illustrates how the transition to democracy and vigorous party competition can shape urgent economic restructuring, while greater Pittsburgh lacks both factors but has a long history of public-private cooperation enabled by philanthropic organizations and others that act as "civic intermediaries."

And in San Francisco and Cape Town, advocates leverage direct democracy (in the former case) and new constitutional rights (in the latter) to build a new commitment to the well-being of disadvantaged young people and their families. The change agents know that investing in people, the younger the better, is the most basic imperative in a changing world, and yet they struggle to define government's role in that effort alongside new and varied roles for nongovernmental or civil society organizations: as organizers of pressure politics for expanded forms of accountability, as conveners of policy discussions, as service providers and coproducers of change, and more. In both cases, strong support for government intervention contends with the limits on what government alone can accomplish to solve important problems.

In each of these cases to come, the players made significant achievements against the odds—in the face of division and complexity and the risk of "process paralysis" that has confounded other communities—to resolve important problems and to do so in democratic ways. How did they do it? The answer turns out to lie in how we think about democracy and what it means to make it work as a recipe for solving public problems.

A Puzzle: Democracy and Public Problems

This book is about collective action to address community problems and about what democracy actually entails as a recipe for such action. It is for scholars and other students of civic life and social progress, as well as those engaged in practical problem solving. Several big questions motivate the book: Do wide-ranging efforts to "make democracy work" around the globe promise to make democracy a more effective recipe for changing such social conditions or just an institutional machinery, a set of rules and routines, for fairer or more popular decision making? Does leading change in democratic ways require fundamentally different strategies and institutions in different places and situations, or do the same core dilemmas appear and reappear? Does the idea of democracy, as enacted by those who put it into practice, encompass a workable recipe for acting collectively, *with and beyond government*, on urgent community problems?

Traditional conceptions of democracy focus on how we elect those who "steer" government, how political interests and claims are voiced and processed and political conflicts resolved, how citizens are protected by right from abuses by the state, how the branches of divided government behave, and, occasionally, on how pent-up demands—the absence of evolution—can lead to revolution.

Out of these general questions, as I explore in the next chapter, powerful analytic traditions have crystallized for understanding democracy, including decision making at the local level: in cities, metropolitan regions, and neighborhoods or other small communities. The first tradition sees democracy as a *contest among interest groups*—a strategic process, mediated by some formal rules but decided by power, whether the model is one of structural conflict dominated by the elites (Fainstein and Fainstein 1979; Gaventa 1980; Logan and Molotch 1987) or pluralism through bargaining (Altshuler 1965; Dahl 1961; Stone 1989; Susskind and Cruikshank 1987). The second broad approach sees democracy as an instrument for *deliberation*—a collective search for better answers above and beyond self-interested bargaining, a "school" for developing citizenship, and a mechanism for expanding the public's faith in politics and thereby invigorating civic life (Bowman and Rehg 2000; Cohen and Rogers 1995; Fung and Wright 2003; Mansbridge 1980). The latter rarely explains what role deliberation versus bargaining plays in complex cases of political action over time—as opposed to in idealized "spaces" of dialogue or small, face-to-face workgroups. But the intersection between these approaches is important: political competition and conflict, for example, and not just the motivation to find better answers, help invigorate civic life. And the learning that deliberation can generate does not simply, or necessarily, lead to a convergence among disparate interests. That learning can also create new things to compete for, shifting the stakes of the "game" (the contest dimension of civic life) and sometimes the rules as well.

There is a third, hugely underdeveloped approach, which extends those two, helps reconcile their different emphases, and responds to their blind spots in vital ways. Nearly a century ago, philosopher John Dewey (1927) argued that democracy's potential is to be the fulfillment of "community life" itself, which necessarily includes progress on important community problems: not just authorizing a government to act but acting with it, and beyond it, if that is what it takes to have an impact on social conditions. "Governance" captures that general idea of managing collective life beyond the formal instruments of government. But unlike the approach I take in this book, most efforts to examine governance stop at illuminating the process for setting the political agenda and mobilizing resources, both public and private, to support that agenda. The political project and not the substantive task of changing "the state of the world," with learning and tinkering along the way, is the focus for the analyst, and this obscures vital civic lessons about producing change in the state of the world by treating implementation, in effect, as "noncivic": a largely technical process with inputs and outputs. Also, portraits of governance tend to focus (given a quest for stable, recognizable patterns) on the routine—and so overemphasize the maintenance of a status quo. As students of public leadership consistently remind us, significant problem solving is generally about doing the *non*routine (Stone 2001). And according to those who study civic apathy and *dis*engagement, the larger result—social impact, beyond the opportunity to participate per se—is precisely what citizens hope for. In fact, it may be the only reason they stay involved in public affairs (Barber 1984; Fung 2004; Putnam 1993, 2000).

These points convey the importance of *democracy as problem solving*. For Dewey (1927, 203), the challenges of using democracy as such are recognizable and debatable only because of prior transformations, one of which took power from "dynastic and oligarchic dynasties" in many corners of the globe and another that created modern nations with a professionalized government apparatus, with experts to respond to elected policy makers. But if the nation and its apparatus—the "mechanism" Dewey identifies in the epigraph to this chapter—are not enough to get our problems solved, then what? The theory and practice of what makes democracy work necessarily include the study of problem solving in action and of the collective capacity to problem-solve—not only to deliberate about the world and set directions for government, but to change the state of the world through collective action, not only to devise and decide but to *do*.

This is a conception of democracy as efficacious community, and community life as defined by effective joint problem solving, that echoes Alexis de Tocqueville's (1835) oft-quoted observation that "in democratic societies, the art of combining is the mother of all other human arts." It incorporates the insight that trust and reciprocal obligation in civil society are crucial to making the machinery of government work in democratic nations (Lipset 1994), to making public institutions "devices for achieving *purposes*, not just for achieving *agreement*" (Putnam 1993, 8).

But this conception of democracy also puts our debates about what community means well beyond the communitarian longing for closer bonds, sometimes labeled *social capital* (the usefulness in social connections, such as networks and norms). And it gets to the heart of the debates about social capital: how to create more of the kinds that generate collective benefits. A focus on problem solving also helps us avoid the risk of treating interpersonal connections as the cure-all for community problems. In effect, social capital has too often been promoted, by well-intentioned users of academic research on the concept, as though it *were* civic capacity—the larger-scale, more complex resource I examine in this book—rather than a useful ingredient.

Social and technological change notwithstanding, what contemporary community life can "supply," beyond feelings of belonging and affiliation, is a capacity to act together—on environmental problems, crime and insecurity, illness, educational failure, and more—in ways that are efficacious, rewarding, even irreplaceable. The urgency and promise of this "collective efficacy" (Sampson 1999), which implies developing both the will and the way to act effectively, are all the more clear in light of Dewey's portrait of a changing America—in what he and others called "the machine age," almost a century past. It is a portrait strikingly parallel to our own world, and many nations in it, today, a portrait colored by the potential and the strains associated with increased social diversity (a less homogeneous public, diversified need and frames of reference), more complex issues demanding public attention and decision, tensions between the global and the local (including more mobile populations, greater transience, a loss of traditional social bonds and stable cultures-in-place), and tensions between the need to institutionalize or regularize on a large scale, on the one hand, and the need to constantly adapt and experiment on the other (which typically happen fastest and best on a small scale).

Scholars have defined collective efficacy, a form of social capital, as resting on patterns of small-scale social organization, notably among neighbors in larger cities and societies, hinged on proximate trust (trusting in particular others who share one's neighborhood), social cohesion, and the expectation that others will act with you if the need arises (Sampson, Raudenbush, and Earls 1997; Sampson 1999). Acknowledging the risk in transplanting ideas without such strict limits, I have borrowed the term to suggest that collective efficacy also captures the core concept of democracy as a recipe for collective (or "community") problem solving. Scaling up obviously requires representation, in that we often do not represent our own interests in civic life, as well as accountable organizations that devise and carry out work, beyond the self-help that citizens can manage at the small scale. It is collective efficacy that Dewey warned *large*-scale, modern democracies—democracy in mass societies, not face-to-face, small-town ones—would lack, particularly with a divided or disengaged public facing more and more complex problems.

It is widely acknowledged that the requirements of civic life in democratic societies are changing and sometimes acknowledged that the erosion of old institutions does not automatically generate new ones that will work (Barber 1984; Fung 2004; World Bank 2000). The substantive problems our societies face are complex and shifting—in public health and safety, employment, housing, education, the environment, and more—but the rules of problem solving are changing as well, and these rules are at least as complex as the underlying problems. Expectations and roles are shifting dramatically with regard to who decides, who implements, and how. The public interest work of societies has been radically reshaped in less than a generation, with a widespread loss of trust in public institutions and expert-led bureaucratic approaches, a massive decentralization of decision making "downward" to local governments and "outward" to private and nonprofit contractors, the rapid transformation of civil society organizations and networks of innovation that span the globe, the diffusion of "empowerment" as an antihierarchical organizing principle for society, and more. As I explore in chapter 2, global debates about participatory governance capture one side of this sea change—the expectation of wider stakeholder participation in decision making that matters—and the "new public management" emphasizes a different expectation, centered on whether and how public institutions, which depend on our formal and informal "authorization" to be effective (Moore 1995), deliver acceptable results.

Business and nongovernmental organizations, informal citizen-led initiatives, "community-driven development" and "community building," and cross-sector partnerships are taking on much of the innovative work on urgent problems (Briggs 2003a; Warren 2001). And in some instances, citizen or community action has become a substitute, or shock absorber, for needed government and market action, for example to reduce inequalities in income or safeguard workers and the environment. National governments have devolved authority and responsibility, though not always resources, to local governments and also called on elected local leadership to make government more collaborative (Campbell 2003; Grindle 2007; Healey 1997).

Yet impasses are frequent, and civic action often seems rutted in adversarial stand-off or the vague mantra of "working in partnership" without genuine give-and-take and shared agendas. Inequalities in access and influence (power to act and to shape important decisions) persist, and yet governance must happen in spite of those inequalities—and not await massive social reform to eliminate them. Trust is hard won and easily lost, especially where a history of inequality and resentment across ethnic or other social borders casts a shadow. And government sends mixed signals about its responsibilities.

Much of the available insight and advice for navigating this rapidly changing environment is piecemeal, advocacy-driven, and developed in the context of a single country, if not a single locality, and a single domain of public problems (health *or* economic development *or* community safety). This book aims to address those gaps. It crosses problem domains and borders too. It is a journey from the rapidly sprawling suburbs of Salt Lake City to the crowded slums of Mumbai (Bombay), India—a city where the population in slums is larger than the entire population of Chicago—from the civic board rooms, City Hall, and social service providers of San Francisco to planning meetings in poor townships of Cape Town in postapartheid South Africa, and from the biotech centers of a former steel town, Pittsburgh, to the suburbs of São Paulo, in the industrial heart of Brazil. In all of these places, the concept of *civic capacity*, or the capacity to devise, decide, and act collectively to improve our lives, lies at the heart of this inquiry about making democracy work.

The Argument

Having outlined the book's aims, and before detailing civic capacity and its specific puzzles, let me preview my main argument, which is a fundamentally hopeful one, along with some of its sobering implications. I argue that it is possible to construct effective forms of civic capacity, under particular conditions and often against long odds, even where history has not endowed a place with a tradition of civic cooperation or widespread trust in public institutions. That is, there is nothing in these cases to disconfirm political scientist Robert Putnam's (1993, 183) finding, in his seminal study of civic traditions and government performance in modern Italy, that "the civic community has deep historical roots." Rather, there is much to corroborate and illuminate the idea that history need not be a curse.

To be sure, as Putnam (1993, 185) concludes, "building social capital will not be easy" in some contexts. But it is also the case, as he and others have highlighted, that it will not be enough to "make democracy work," particularly where a community faces important social or ideological divides and the need to adapt to change. Civic capacity is a shorthand for the ingredients that *can* make the machinery of governance effective: institutions that combine learning and bargaining effectively and constantly rather than divorcing dialogue from forging wise agreements; multiple forms of accountability—pressure politics, markets, negotiated compacts, codified rights, and more—to make "solutions" more broadly legitimate and sustainable; and space for the grassroots *or* the "grasstops" (authority figures and other influentials) to initiate important change, regardless of how broad participation becomes over time.

The core structures for creating and deploying civic capacity are stable coalitions that authorize things and implementation-focused alliances that get things done. Without wider civic strategies that connect to coalition agendas, alliance or partnership arrangements are "boutique" efforts—appealing miniatures—without the promise of significant impact on public problems. On the other hand, combining the coalition form with the partnership form responds to the two powerful logics of the age, which sometimes compete with each other and often get obscured in all the rhetoric: the logic of *empowerment* (which emphasizes changing political relationships and access to influence) and the logic of *efficiency* (which emphasizes measurable progress on social conditions).

This hopeful argument, with specifics about how civic capacity can be built and used, has some challenging implications, however. After all, autocrats, too, can get things done and even inspire collective action to achieve it, and popular movements can lead to "tyrannies from below." Breakthrough problem solving in democratic societies calls for more multidimensional forms of accountability, and more practiced, skillful combinations of learning and bargaining by civic actors, than most contemporary rhetoric about "acting in partnership" or "bottom-up" change has even hinted. Civil society organizations, for example, turn out to have important roles to play as brokers or civic intermediaries who help define problems and build capacity to tackle them, not just creative service providers, associations that articulate citizen interests, or professional advocates.

This is more than the standard researcher's conclusion that things turned out, on closer observation, to be more complex than someone had thought. As I outline in the next section and detail in the next chapter, our dominant conceptions of democratic participation, conflict and consensus, and "top-down" versus alternative approaches to tackling problems are misleading in several key respects—about what it takes to make democracy work—and uninformed in several others. One key implication is that we are sometimes misdirected, in the practice of politics and innovative change—out in the world, that is, beyond the seminar room—about something more fundamental: what makes our collective life democratic (or not). It is not just participation through the vote or the structuring of wider forms of participation but *structuring participation to achieve social progress* that makes for strong democracy. The book ends on this second, normative argument, considering whether we are compelled to trade away inclusiveness, at least in some instances, to achieve that progress.

The Heart of the Inquiry: What Is Civic Capacity, and Why Does It Matter?

This book focuses on questions about a vital resource for collective problem solving: *civic capacity*, including what it is, what it is for, and how political actors develop and deploy it in diverse contexts to lead change. Although collective action is an age-old concern, civic capacity is a relatively new idea as a target for systematic research. Based primarily on a study of education reform in eleven major American cities, political scientist Clarence Stone (2001, 596) has argued that "civic capacity concerns the extent to which different sectors of the community—business, parents, educators, state and local officeholders, nonprofits, and others—act in concert around a matter of community-wide import" (also see Stone et al. 2001).

But to some extent, that outcome-oriented definition ("the extent to which different sectors . . . act in concert") confounds the questions of "will" versus "way." Civic capacity might be thought of as the extent to which the sectors that make up a community are (1) *capable* of collective action on public problems (the resource dimension), given the norms and institutional arenas for local action; and (2) *choose* to apply such capability (the dimension of effort, will and choice, or "agency"). While it may be useful in principle to assess a city's latent capacity to act, even this tends to be based on past actions. It is my contention, then, that capacity per se can only be meaningfully assessed in the context of effort.

Stone adds that the tasks for which civic capacity are required include setting agendas of collective action, building coalitions, and mobilizing resources in a specific kind of context: *where expectations of stakeholder participation are relatively high and the power to get things done is decentralized and fragmented.* Those, then, are the broad "tests" of capacity for nonroutine civic action, and the notion of broad tests enables us to examine civic capacity in a wide variety of political and cultural contexts.

Stone posits, furthermore, that the development and effective use of civic capacity may be specific to a particular problem domain (education, crime, economic restructuring, and so on) in a given community: "Any civic consensus is far from stable, and therefore the process of building support for a program of action around one problem is not easily transferred to (or borrowed from) another exercise in problem-solving" (p. 615). He also hypothesizes that stable institutions, not looser coalitions—short-run "marriages of convenience," in the lingo of politics— are likely to be the "pillars" of civic capacity. Communities need civic pillars that withstand the contentiousness that tackling major public issues invariably triggers.

Judd (2006) replies that Stone's definition of civic capacity is too close to that of a public-private governing coalition or *regime* (Fainstein et al. 1983; Stone 1989; Stoker 1995; Stone 2005). Judd argues, based largely on the case of St. Louis in the latter half of the twentieth century, that "civic capacity may be assembled within specialized arenas that act quite autonomously from one another" (p. 45). Or it may be missing entirely, robbing a community, at least for a time, of the will and way to undertake "ambitious public initiatives" (p. 46). Going further, Gendron (2006) contends that Stone's use of civic capacity ignores the structural inequalities of power or influence that reformers often face, to which Stone (2006) has replied that confronting unequal power is very much at the heart of mobilizing communitywide support for change but that reformers, likewise, cannot forgo the work of institutionalizing their influence in "viable forms of cooperation" that sustain change over time. "Power to" accomplish that, argues Stone, and not just the question of which group has "power over" another, is critical, and "power to" depends on developing and deploying adequate civic capacity. I return to the issue of power in the next chapter, emphasizing that instead of revealing what democracy "is," much research merely reflects what particular observers choose to understand about it: influence or control, collective accomplishment, social learning, the meaning of citizenship, and so on.

The Focus and Contribution of This Book

There are several crucial possibilities in need of further inquiry:[1] that the potential to assemble and use civic capacity is fundamentally determined by the history of an area's institutions, resources, and culture; that civic capacity's major tests include a substantial array of collective-action tasks, from forging shared agendas to building support for them and mobilizing resources to enact them, that are relevant in diverse local contexts; conversely, that effective civic action rests on such a variety of institutional bases, differing so substantially across communities and country contexts, that no common patterns that can reasonably be labeled (or developed as) "civic capacity"; that several forms of democratic accountability may be at issue all at once given the variety of tasks and the variety of actors and issues in play; and that contrary to some hopes about social capital, civic capacity may be domain specific and limited to "specialized arenas," not an all-purpose communitarian resource to be applied to whatever problem "comes along." I have been able to examine all but the final one of these possibilities in depth.

Without closer analysis of these possibilities, carried out on a wider range of cases, we risk, in civic capacity, the community cure-all expectation that quickly attached itself to social capital in the 1990s, as well as a circular, you-know-it-when-you-see-it logic: where there is civic cooperation on a contentious problem, there must be durable civic capacity at work.

But several important process questions about civic capacity must be answered if we are to better judge the claims outlined above. First, what strategies do political actors use to create more capacity for communitywide collective action, not just to win influence (get their way) in a variety of contexts? Strategy is about resourcefulness vis-à-vis task, which implies understanding one's civic context well enough to make better choices. As I will show in the next chapter, where civic capacity is concerned, strategy includes a conception of democracy that is broader, more flexible, and more powerful than simply expanding "voice" for citizens—or holding more meetings to engage them. Second, to what extent are those strategies, which presumably reflect and respond to the dynamics of civic capacity, driven by deliberative learning as opposed to competitive bargaining? And third, beyond the power to forge and enact broadly supported agendas of change, how does the implementation of agendas of change relate to other dimensions of civic capacity? Put differently, should we consider implementation or "production," as distinct from policy agenda setting and support winning, another test of community civics?

Civic efforts at the local level obviously cannot control the range of factors that shape conditions in the world, not directly at any rate, so "successfully civic" places can produce disappointing results in terms of jobs, educational achievement, pollution, and more. But creative, adaptive collective action, the civics of change, includes steps to reduce risks, to gain more control over the causal factors ("drivers") that matter, and to try new and more promising strategies over time. Well-developed civic capacity therefore reflects resourcefulness or "the pursuit of opportunity without regard to resources currently controlled"—Howard Stevenson's rich definition of entrepreneurship (Sahlman et al. 1999). Put differently, entrepreneurial actors may have to create civic capacity as they go, and this means facing different kinds of strategic problems over different stages of action.

Impact studies of specific programs, and studies of democracy that center on contentious decision points, generally ignore or obscure this rich civic process (Healey 1997, 2003). We need better explanations of how change is managed over time, against the odds, to make useful innovation possible and to better fit "collaborative policy making" or other tools to the right contexts. As Grindle (2004, 2) puts it in a study of government reform in schooling,

Research to assess the efficacy of various policy alternatives . . . is a centrally important undertaking. But it usually takes the process of reform for granted— how improved education becomes part of the political agenda, how reform initiatives are developed, what interactions and negotiations shape or alter their contents, how important actors and interests respond to change proposals, how initiatives are implemented and sustained once they are introduced.

With this book, I seek to add in several ways to the limited body of research specifically about civic capacity as well as the much larger body of work on making democracy work and making institutions with a public mission, whether inside or outside of government, more effective. First, as detailed in the discussion of methodological approach below, the book centers on parallel analyses of pairs of cases, enabling analysis across borders and across different problem domains, unlike many studies of local governance that center, as I noted above, on a single domain or single context or both.

Second, by focusing on process, the book offers new insights on how civic resources are reshaped over time—that is, on "moves" and other dynamics, not just structures—as civic entrepreneurs build and abolish institutions, identify problems and change the ways in which they get defined, navigate key decision points, and deal with what decisions imply (the new "game" or strategic situation created by the latest outcome). The constraints abound, but the study looks closely at how people create and deploy new possibilities, not how things "turn out" for high-trust versus low-trust regions, say, over long periods of time, but at how trust is won, to particular effects, and then built on—or not.[2]

Third, since civic capacity without tangible results is merely broad-based interest canvassing and mobilization, the book offers more attention than most studies of urban governance to how policy aims get acted on collectively. The book is not implementation research per se, but I offer attention to implementation models and barriers to success, from root causes of problems (that may not be addressed in civic agendas) to institutional turf battles, from mistrust among ethnic or class groups to unfocused participation that sends mixed messages to the public, avoids resolving conflicts about priorities, and fragments the authority and accountability needed to make measurable progress on problems (Kadushin et al. 2005). I contend that these are not merely sources of "noise" on the back end of the focal policy-making process; they are central to the way reputations and strategies develop to set agendas, mobilize new resources, and more.

My focus in this book is on the local ("community") level, not because all the resources for solving problems are found there, not at all, but because societies cannot do without effective local systems for acting on public problems. As governments, aid agencies, and ambitious nation-building efforts increasingly acknowledge, developing more collective problem-solving capacity, closest to the citizen, is a worldwide imperative (Campbell 2003; Grindle 2007; World Bank 2000). City-regions are the building blocks of the global economy, the centers of innovation, and, for most of the world's population, an important source of distinctive identity (local culture).

I turn next to my methodological approach before outlining the plan of the book.

Civic Capacity Where?: The Cases and Approach

Problems in Cities within Countries

Cases are uniquely valuable for understanding how processes evolve over time; they tell us what large surveys, for example, cannot about how people make something of their history through their perceptions, choices, and interaction with each other (Mahoney 1999; Ragin 1987; Yin 1994). I examine efforts to tackle communitywide challenges in six cities in four nations. From the outset, my aim was theory building in an emergent conceptual domain, not hypothesis testing in a well-charted one. This required choices of challenges (problem domain), nations, and cities.

Each of the three *problem domains* is important worldwide, to cities and the societies they propel: restructuring the job economy, managing urban growth without ignoring sustainability and social equity, and investing in young people and their families (i.e., through social protections or programs that enable or develop human capacity). Beyond being vital and relatively universal, these problems share two other traits: They demand *cross-sector* action, and they demand concerted *local* action, regardless of how important larger forces, such as national policy or global markets, turn out to be. In simple terms, as I noted at the outset, civic capacity cannot determine all the "cards" that a local community will have to play, but that capacity shapes, quite directly, how well the cards get played—even if a community cannot change its weather, endowments of natural resources, proximity to export customers, or, to cite an adjustable but not-easily-adjusted type of structural factor, the larger nation's trade and immigration policies. Selecting the problem domains was the first crucial sampling, which led next to a sampling of country contexts and cases of local experience.

In well-designed studies, sample choices are suited to specific analytic objectives, and in small-N studies, with just a few cases examined in depth, purposive sampling is more common than the random sampling of large-N survey studies, which trade depth, and sometimes validity too, for representativeness (Denters and Mossberger 2006; Eisenhardt 2002; Ragin 1987; Yin 1994). Here are the analytic objectives that drove my sampling choices: the analyses are comparative, first with parallel application of theory (cases understood as revelatory bases for inference, in and of themselves, about civic capacity; see Skocpol and Somers 1980; Yin 1994) and then comparison across cases in a pair (cases positioned in a more global matrix of possible outcomes; see Ragin 1987). As detailed below, the latter are comparisons as to civic tasks to be accomplished, not as to outcomes (neither policy choices as outcomes nor "end" outcomes in social conditions, such as regional income levels, urbanization patterns, and so on).

Within each of the three problem domains, I have paired a U.S. city-region with one in the global South: San Francisco with Cape Town, South Africa (investing in young people and their families); greater Salt

Lake City with Mumbai, India (managing urban growth); and the Pittsburgh industrial region with that of industrial São Paulo, Brazil, specifically the Greater ABC region (restructuring the economy). My choice of countries was purposive, meant to enable close analysis of civic capacity in development and use in contexts of special relevance to wider global trends. Notwithstanding their contemporary differences or distinct historical paths of development, Brazil, India, South Africa, and the United States are all large, regionally diverse democracies with vibrant civil society institutions, liberalized markets, and important hopes about the market contributing to public problem solving. Civic capacity is particularly at issue in such contexts, less so in contexts where government (and the political parties that steer it) dominates collective action on public problems, as in most of Western Europe. These nations are also, in many domains of public decision making, quite decentralized: local policy making, public management, and resources matter, even if they often prove, or seem to prove, insufficient to the tasks at hand, and even if a particular kind of "muscular" local government is longer established in one nation (the United States) than the others. What is more, Brazil, India, and South Africa have all decentralized within the past twenty years, enabling us to assess relatively early efforts by political actors to pursue major public initiatives with new institutional mechanisms (rules, incentives, and tools) in place at the local level.

In the global South, Brazil, India, and South Africa are increasingly recognized as pacesetters of social innovation for Latin America, Asia, and Africa respectively. For their progressive constitutions of social and economic rights (Brazil's was adopted as recently as 1988, when two decades of military dictatorship gave way to civilian democracy, and South Africa's in 1996, with the transition from apartheid government), for their experiments in participatory local democracy, and for other contributions, these three countries are more and more the object of comparative study. Though different in important respects, such as the degree of decentralization or service delivery versus participatory democracy focus, all three nations reveal, in compelling ways, the tensions among democracy, "development" (economic and social progress), and global economic change. The United States represents a major reference point, not in the normative sense of being what other nations should aspire to become, but in the sense of being, for better or worse, a seedbed and standard bearer for an approach to public problems that emphasizes public-private cooperation and as much government decentralization as possible.

I detail the choice of cities, which reflect the theoretical sampling common in small-N case-study research (Eisenhardt 2002), in the three section introductions. To illustrate with a preview, Salt Lake City and Mumbai are exemplars of the distinct problems of uneven urban growth facing wealthy and poor nations: unsustainable sprawl on the one hand and inefficient and inequitable "slum-led" urbanization on the other. Beyond that task challenge, the two cases also exemplify the challenges of significant civic action in American and developing-country democracies, respectively. Finally, both are recognized by experts in that problem domain as having experimented in significant ways with new civic approaches—and even for being models to emulate. I wanted to know: models of what exactly?

In methodological terms, the theoretical bases for sampling these and the other local cases included maturity, affording a long path of decision and accomplishment through which to trace civic action on complex problems; a reputation, outside the locality, for accomplishment along that path, in spite of clear barriers and notwithstanding many persistent problems and gaps; and access to key insiders, critics, and an ample media and public record, making for what Pettigrew (1990), in his seminal work on how to research change, has labeled "transparently observable processes." This last feature is especially crucial for rich description and the careful inductive reasoning that can make small-N studies "big" in their value for theory and practice.

The cases in this book are defined by four things: a *site*, a *focal problem*, a *period* of time, and one or more key *episodes*. That is, cases are defined by boundaries not only of place and theme but of time. Like all social processes, civic ones are about how actors make sense of things, interact, make choices, and shape relationships, institutions, and ideas over time. Two features are crucial: each case in this book has clear and deep historical roots as well as distinct, contemporary starting points. Take the example of managing a growing population while promoting a more sustainable model of physical growth in greater Salt Lake City and other parts of the American West. This challenge has roots in the settlement of the frontier by Europeans and those of primarily European descent—in Utah, by the Mormon pioneers—as well as the displacement of Native Americans from much of the land, about a century and a half ago. As I explore in chapter 4, certain notions of community, the "good society" and good city as part of it, and core values of environmental stewardship can all be traced to the upheavals and the hopes associated with that settlement. So can the demographic patterns and political institutions that settlement drove.

But just as certainly, contemporary efforts to act on public problems feature much more recent milestones, including triggers as starting points for community action. In the Utah case, that point is a nongovernmental organizing and consensus-building effort, launched in the mid-1990s to respond to highly visible public concern about rapid and costly urban growth. In Kingdon's (1984) classic distinction, the *conditions* associated with rapid urban growth became a public *problem* that key players decided it was time to tackle with a significant investment of time, reputation, and more. Centered on an initiative called Envision Utah, the organizing effort brought to media prominence and public awareness the ideal of "quality growth" and mobilized resources to promote that ideal in a political context that outside observers consider extremely unfriendly to public planning. That surprising emergence of a big public idea, as well as some unconventional civic strategies to promote it, helped draw me to the Salt Lake region. But the larger point for now is that each case in the book features such a starting point, as well as historical roots that I try hard to keep in view.

To highlight a second distinction, studies of civic life, particularly at the local level, often focus on long-run institutional change *or* on action at decision points, less commonly on how the two together define progress on some agenda of action. A focus on capacity for conflict resolution and consensus building, for example, naturally centers on the decision points, where the effective or ineffective handling of conflict comes sharply into view. But a focus on the underpinnings of those processes calls for attention to structures—for instance, institutions that embody key ideas (such as a public-serving mission or cause), or that enable deliberation, decision making, or the provision of services. And accounts of decision points too often present cursory attention to how those structures evolved over time, who did what to shape them, or how key institutions operate beyond the decision point that is the center of attention.

I examine both structures and decision points. I do this mainly by analyzing cases within cases (i.e., significant *episodes*) and by closely analyzing in-between periods in which relationships, institutions, and/or the frames around public problems—how they get defined, who is thought to be responsible or capable of acting, and more—evolve in important ways. The episodes include specific decision points and the players and "moves" associated with them. These points matter directly because they shape resources and the action that follows and also indirectly for what those decision points reveal about the capacity of the players involved to bring divergent interests and views to bear and resolve conflicts (or not). Yet democracy is more than deal making or structured consensus building about well-defined agendas. If the intensive episodes deliver the goods, providing the proverbial "mortar," one must also attend to what lies between them—to the bricks and how they are made. To use the formal language of strategic interaction offered by game theory, we care not only about how the players play particular games but why those games, and not others, arise in the first place, why some players, and not others, get to play, how rules of engagement shift ("evolution"), and how players acquire the resources—both tangible and intangible—with which to play.

Theoretical Approach

My approach is importantly different from that of other small-N comparative case studies, which have evolved significantly in the research world over the past two decades (Denters and Mossberger 2006; Mahoney 1999; Ragin 1987, 2000). In those studies, the aim is *causal* analysis: examining how variation in one factor (predictor) explains variation in some other factor (outcome) of interest. That analytic approach, a foundation of hypothesis testing in both the natural and behavioral sciences, is appropriate where achieving a specific outcome is the target of study, whether that outcome is a social condition (a revolution, a threshold rate of divorce or suicide in society, a level of industrialization, etc.) or a policy decision (a particular policy for land use, education, wages, environmental protection, or some other domain). Causal analysis is feasible and appropriate where the analyst can confidently control on (hold constant across the grouped cases) a reasonable number of confounding factors, beyond the factor to be tested, that might be associated with the outcome of interest. This is not feasible where cases offer contrasts in context (by design), at least where specific institutional arrangements are concerned, rather than matched context, and in part for these reasons, causal analysis is not the aim of my study. An extreme example makes the point. In the domain of managing urban growth, Salt Lake City and Mumbai are hardly comparable as to social conditions or policy choices. The section introduction on managing urban growth, which provides an overview of the domain and introduces both cases, therefore does not center, say, on whether the two city-regions "arrived" at a consistent land use policy.

My aim, instead of offering causal analysis, is to understand the process of building and using civic capacity in specific, revelatory contexts that provide lessons for other contexts. In this book, then, civic capacity is not an explanatory variable for predicting the success of problem solving.[3] The reason is that I am not confident we know what civic capacity *is* in distinct contexts and what building and using it would entail.

The book offers a process study grounded in the dilemmas that decision makers faced, the roads taken and not taken, and the efforts to move agendas under conditions of imperfect information, controversy, and other messy features of "operating democracies" rather than idealized ones (Mansbridge 1980). The aim for Salt Lake and Mumbai, then, and for the other case pairs as well, is comparing "tests" of civic capacity vis-à-vis a community problem and whether and how actors meet those tests. The contrast (between the two cases) in background conditions and specific policy outcomes and social outcomes is a substantial source of theory-building power at that level of analysis, though it would be the proverbial kiss of death in an outcome-driven causal comparison (Ragin 1987).

Drawing heavily on the accounts offered by insiders, my approach to developing propositions about the data is grounded theory, which emphasizes "the discovery of the theory implicit in the data" rather than testing grand theory deductively (Eisenhardt 2002; Glaser and Strauss 1967; Glaser 1998). Beyond the literature on urban governance, and beginning in the next chapter, I draw on varied research—from negotiation and action learning to social movement theory, the politics of the policy making process, and, to a more limited degree, organizational behavior—rather than on a single tradition. In this way, I build accounts that fit the data, all with the aim of addressing key questions, outlined above, about the emergent concept of civic capacity.

Data Collection and Analysis

To study operating democracies, I relied on documentary evidence, scholarly and journalistic accounts of events, institutions, and organizations in these settings, some administrative and census data, limited participant observation of meetings or other significant gatherings, and—most importantly—face-to-face interviews with key informants, which I conducted in all six cities between 2002 and 2006. The noninterview components are classics of the case-study method, which relies on triangulation (obtaining multiple sources of data about the same subtopics) to make more valid inferences (Yin 1994). The key informant interviews also figure prominently in case studies that seek to understand how a process unfolded as the participants in that process understood and navigated it (or as informed observers assess it).

The interviews, with public officials (elected, appointed, and civil servant), journalists, businesspeople, academics, and civil society advocates, provide insider perspectives on events for which documentary and other sources typically offer "filtered" accounts or no specific, action-oriented information at all: How and why did the players make difficult choices? What controversies or other strategic issues did they consider then or later? I asked my interviewees for referrals, thus "snowballing" my contacts along networks, but I also directly recruited key subjects ("cold-called" by letter, e-mail, and/or phone), based on media accounts or other guides to reputation and role, as a way of seeking out divergent perspectives.[4] This sampling approach, together with specific interviewing techniques, helped me test for disconfirming evidence—for example, where insiders' hypotheses about events and ideas might contradict my own emerging efforts to build accounts that fit the data. Of the prospective interviewees I contacted in six cities, no one explicitly refused to be interviewed, though a total of seven could not be scheduled under the time constraints.[5] The final sample included 111 interviews or just over 18, on average, per case.

I asked interviewees about three things mainly: public *agenda setting* (who tries to do it, who succeeds or fails and why, what agendas include and exclude, how they shift over time), *planning* (how and through what institutional settings specific strategies are developed to respond to a given agenda, who does or does not participate and why, what is learned, what sources of knowledge are deemed legitimate and relevant by the players and why), and *implementation* (who acts and how, what results, how perceptions of success or failure drive subsequent action on problems). But I also asked about specific *organizations* (evolution, capabilities, reputation) and *problem analysis* (informants' own "theories of the problem" and its possible solutions).

Plan of the Book

The next chapter discusses distinct traditions for approaching the democratic process at the local level—as contest, deliberation, or problem solving—as well as major social and political changes that have radically shifted institutions and expectations in democratic societies in recent decades. I outline the implications of studying democracy, and also strengthening it, as a recipe for collective problem solving, examining both familiar and counterintuitive ideas about several core themes: participation, accountability, and the role of conflict versus consensus. Beyond juxtaposing the contest and deliberation frames of reference to help clarify problem solving as an important third conception, I review several literatures that rarely converse with each other but serve as key sources of insight for my case analyses, consistent with the grounded-theory approach I outlined above.

The subsequent three sections analyze the civics of change in the three problem domains, looking within and then across cases. In each section, an overview chapter examines distinctive civic features of the problem domain and outlines my rationale for selecting each case. Two case chapters follow, with case summary and implications at the end of each chapter. The second chapter in each pair adds implications developed across the two cases.

The final chapter presents the study's major lessons about civic capacity, returning to the question about "capacity for what," our understanding of what makes problem solving "democratic," and the central themes of power, participation, effectiveness, and accountability.

2

Democracy and Public Problems

Democracy is a device that ensures we shall be governed no better than we deserve.

—George Bernard Shaw

As a recipe for tackling public problems, is democracy mainly a self-interested contest for influence—a strategic game—or is it a hopeful search for better answers that meet a wider community interest? For decades, students of local politics working in distinct traditions have often talked past each other when it comes to this basic question. But it gets to the heart of the connection between democracy and civic capacity as a resource that can be developed—or destroyed—through the way we conduct civic life.

Extending that broad question to several more popular ones, given the decentralization and global competitive pressures that have put a renewed focus on governance at the local level, does effective public action require less government and more "community" action or just new roles and rules for new times? If that action is collective or "collaborative," does that mean, whether from a normative or a pragmatic standpoint, that dissent and contention should be put on hold? In this chapter, I address these questions, aiming to advance the debates over political power in cities, as well as "community-driven" development, reinvented government, participatory planning and decision making, and solving problems via "partnership."

As outlined in the introduction, juxtaposing the contest and deliberation perspectives helps clarify problem solving as an alternative that draws on both of those. And discussing the changing expectations for democracy and social problem solving highlights additional concepts that I employ in the case analyses to come. But the purpose of this chapter is not to preview a test, say, of whether causal theory A is more valid than theory B. Nor is it to resolve an important question I take up in the conclusion, after analyzing the cases: If democracy can be so varied and complex in its workings and ambitions, what qualifies any process, however efficacious at problem solving, as genuinely democratic?

Views of Democracy: Contest, Deliberation, or Problem Solving

Contest: Elite Control or Pluralist Bargaining?
The first major analytic tradition in the theory and practice of local democracy sees it as a *contest among interest groups* carried out under particular kinds of rules, which make the contest "democratic." While I focus initially on American scholarship and commentary in this vein, the chapter turns soon to more global debates about the same fundamental questions. In the contest view, civic action is a strategic, interest-driven process in which public decisions are riddled with competing objectives and the proverbial pie must be divided. This leads to a competitive quest for influence: the power to shape decisions and thereby influence the allocation of more tangible resources, such as money, land, or oil. If democracy *is* mainly this, then civic capacity becomes little more than a tool for gaining strategic advantage. Particular actors may invoke notions and symbols of a "community" or common interest, whether cynically (as a rhetorical tool) or, more generously, to remind civic actors that they have certain shared interests in addition to their divergent interests.

The contest view of civic life in cities includes two main schools of thought: *pluralists*, who see power as dispersed and decision-making arenas as relatively accessible (Judge 1995), and those in the *political economy* school, who conclude that local politics is largely about elite domination and deep structural conflicts among groups, usually rooted in class or economic interests (Harding 1995). Studies in the pluralist tradition are largely concerned with who decides and who influences both the policy agenda (what is up for official discussion) and formal policy outcomes (what gets decided). Political scientist Robert Dahl's influential *Who Governs?* (1961), a study of local-government decision making and interest-group advocacy in the city of New Haven in the 1950s, associates governing, for example, with the distribution of influence and a conception of local democracy as bargaining among interest groups to win elected office and set policy. The power that counts is the "power over" other groups seeking to do those same things (Stone 1989).

But as Altshuler and Luberoff (2003) note, any history of these ideas must acknowledge the fact that Dahl wrote in response to claims about elite control of politics. Most famously, sociologist C. Wright Mills's *The Power Elite* (1956) argued that a small group of elites held sway in local civic life, whether through direct pressure on decision makers or because those who command a disproportionate share of wealth, social status, and political power in society share a worldview and thus easily act in concert to advance elite interests and "reproduce" their power. Mills's title soon entered the public lexicon even as Dahl and others responded critically, arguing that Mills overstated the level of political consensus and conformity at the local level and that his approach, which relied on key informants to name community influentials, led to a tautology: those thought to be influential locally named others they considered influential, leading the analyst to treat perceptions of influence as objective indicators of the real thing (power).

Later work in the pluralist tradition, whether influenced directly by Dahl or not, emphasized that government planning and decision making, especially when driven by an expert-determined, "rational" ideal of the public interest and a reform-oriented agenda, may fail to confront the need for interest-group support outside the bureaucracy as well as the realities of intergroup conflict (Altshuler 1965). As I will show, this need to build wider support and legitimacy is at the heart of civic capacity's value and use.

More recent work has focused on *conflict resolution mechanisms* and *governing regimes*. I return to the latter below, since the regime concept goes beyond the pluralist tradition and its conception of "power over." As for conflict resolution, a rapidly growing theory and practice literature focuses on strengthening institutions and procedures for resolving public disputes, including facilitated public policy mediation or consensus building (Innes 1996, 2004; Susskind and Cruikshank 1987; Susskind and Hoben 2004; Susskind, McKearnan, and Thomas-Larmer 1999). This tradition is centrally concerned with the costliness of impasse in decision-making—which focuses the observer on how interest groups deploy their influence, not on whether they have any to begin with—and the potential to create more sustainable, mutual-gains agreements about contentious public issues. Inequities of power are to be handled by those who authorize dispute resolution processes, such as courts and executive agencies, and, to a lesser extent, by trained facilitators who design and manage the processes but do not decide the outcomes. The close focus on alternative decision-making processes and how to overcome costly impasse is crucial, and consensus building aims to straddle the categories of contest and deliberation by squarely recognizing and addressing conflicting interests in structured settings that promote learning among the parties who define a dispute or who face an opportunity to generate new policy. But as I outline in the next chapter in the context of managing urban growth conflicts, it is not very clear where formalized, facilitated consensus-building processes should fit into the larger fabric of civic life—for example, over the years of action and multiple decision points that significant community problem solving typically requires.

Pluralism is a diverse and still-evolving school of thought, much more so than critics have typically acknowledged (Judge 1995; McFarland 2004), but its points of departure differ significantly from those of the second "contest" school, *political economy*. The latter emphasizes structural conflicts dominated by economic elites, such as a city's major investors, employers, and real estate developers (Fainstein and Fainstein 1979; Gaventa 1980; Harding 1995). In their classic text on how physical growth is advanced politically in cities, sociologists John Logan and Harvey Molotch (1987) conclude that groups whose interests are defined by the *use value* of urban space (consumption value, such as in renting a housing unit) are invariably in conflict with those whose politics reflects the *exchange value* of that same space (its value at resale—that is, ownership rather than consumption interest). Under this conception, the civics of managing urban growth, whether in Mumbai or Boston, say, unavoidably pits owners (who gain financially when land values increase) against renters (who lose under that scenario). In this view, a regime is less the embodiment of a shared agenda and schemes of cooperation to advance that agenda than a recipe for dominating civic life—for example, through what Logan and Molotch identify as the pro-development "growth machine."

I return to this conception of gladiatorial, economic-interest-based conflict over growth in the next chapter, because it poses a serious challenge to any notion of more broad-based collective action. But in sum, until recently, political economists emphasized conflicting economic interests to the exclusion of all else that defines civic life and the possibility of change (Fainstein 2000; Healey 1996).

For the most part, pluralists and political economists do not ask the same questions using the same types of evidence and then draw different conclusions. Rather, they ask somewhat distinct questions using different kinds of data and not surprisingly arrive at very different emphases. The study of civic life, like all behavioral sciences that include elements of philosophy and practical knowledge, is partly portraiture or storytelling. Telling stories about a complex world includes editorial choices, which can lead to depictions that are very different but not incompatible. The larger question, however, is whether civic life, if it is often neither equitable nor efficient at resolving conflicts—as pluralists and political economists can agree—offers society a way to do any better. This hope and possibility motivates the second major tradition: democracy as a deliberative rather than competitive encounter.

Deliberation

In the second view, democracy is potentially a powerful instrument for *deliberation*: a collective process focused on dialogue, aiming for a broader understanding of interests, and open to learning, which may include new frames for understanding what is at stake in civic life (Fishkin 1991; Fung 2004; Gutmann and Thompson 1996; Mansbridge 1980). Plainly put, deliberation suggests a way out of pure competition. Hopes for more and better deliberation reflect considerable evidence that political interests are much more varied, open to interpretation, and even unconsciously held—and, for these reasons, much more subject to change through social interaction—than the contest model would have us believe (Bowman and Rehg 2000; Fung 2004; Healey 1996; Susskind and Cruikshank 2006a, 2006b). The larger hope is to invigorate civic life by creating a politics that attracts wider participation because both the process and outcomes are more satisfying.

Practices are particularly important: in the deliberative view, democracy needs a set of "schools" that teach deliberative rather than purely competitive behavior. Civil-society associations are frequently examined for this potential, along with the converse potential for instilling patronage and cronyism, reifying group prejudices and hostility, and encouraging a politics of exclusion and domination rather than power sharing (Cohen and Rogers 1995; De Tocqueville [1835] 2004; Fung 2003; Putnam 1993, 2000).

But as respected observers have noted, "pure" deliberation is liable to be impractical beyond the scale of small groups of trusting individuals (Mansbridge 1980). If not prudently timed and structured, deliberative exercises can also waste time and distract the community. As Shapiro (2003, 20) puts it, "Sometimes by design, sometimes not, deliberation can amount to collective fiddling while Rome burns." Furthermore, some powerful learning is not in real-time, face-to-face sessions or gatherings of a well-defined group but takes the form of shifts in the "distributed" sets of beliefs of members of a change-oriented coalition or larger public (Jenkins-Smith and Sabatier 1993). Finally, deliberation in practice can become one more tool for the best organized and informed to dominate the civic agenda while putting a legitimating mask on things.

Yet deliberative theorists and practitioner innovators, who often promote the value of consensus-based decision making following intensive dialogue, have offered powerful arguments about the kinds of political behavior and decision outcomes that alternative decision rules encourage (Carpenter 1999). While majority-vote rules can leave almost half the polity dissatisfied, resistant, and resentful, for example, consensus rules are subject to manipulation by minority blocs who can veto the will of large majorities. This risk appears to be more serious where interests are in sharp conflict (Innes 2004; Mansbridge 1980). These insights help us understand why different rules may suit different contexts and goals: the protection of minority interests, for instance, versus stable power sharing, efficiency, or other goals.

In spite of the openness to decision-making approaches, and even where deliberative democrats have adopted a focus on problem solving (notably, Fung 2004, 2006c), the deliberative tradition does not seek to explain what role deliberation *alongside* competitive bargaining plays in complex cases of political action over time. Furthermore, the intersection between the traditions seems important, but too often it gets overlooked. Political competition and conflict, for example, and not just the motivation to find better answers, help invigorate civic life. And the learning that deliberation can generate may not lead to a convergence among disparate interests, equality of influence, or the capacity to resolve remaining conflicts. Moreover, beyond expanding individuals' interests, learning may create new things to compete for and shift the stakes of the political contest, as well as the rules and incentives that structure competition. Beyond agreements on policy, such as those generated by formally facilitated consensus building over environmental resources, siting disputes, or contentious social issues such as abortion, learning can generate new institutions—including spaces such as the glass-walled room I described in the first chapter—for deliberating more informally. But it takes time, strategy, and some good fortune for these possibilities to be realized. I consider these factors in the cases to come.

Collective Problem Solving, beyond "Governance"

The study of democracy as a recipe for collective problem solving, which I introduced in the previous chapter with reference to John Dewey, owes an important debt to the theory and practice of local governance worldwide (Pierre 1999; Stoker 2002; Wolman 1995). This tradition distinguishes *governance* (the set of norms, institutions, and practices for managing collective life) from *government* (the official apparatus, which is authorized and steered by popular will in democratic societies, for acting on public concerns). Governance, which encompasses government as well as business and civil-society roles and alliances, opens up a much wider range of possibilities for civic action than either the contest-over-policy tradition or the deliberation-through-dialogue tradition. Because of its broad scope, governance can accommodate, even welcome, both purely deliberative and purely competitive behavior and the range in between—as elements of a multifaceted "social production" model of civic life (Judd 2006; Stone 2006). Governance can include "public entrepreneurship networks" that find value-added roles for the public, private, and nonprofit sectors in emergent fields (Laws et al. 2001).

But problem solving goes beyond the growing focus of scholars and advocates on effective governance, which has centered heavily, in America's influential research literature, on *regimes*. Regimes are governing coalitions that forge ambitious agendas of action, mobilize resources to enact those agendas, and develop and oversee productive mechanisms or "schemes" for public-private cooperation that put the resources to use (Stone 2004). Much research has focused on how regimes get constructed and sustained in various cities, as well as on the question of who gets incorporated, or not, into the governing coalition (Stoker 1995; Stone 1989; Savitch and Kantor 2004). The regime focus, and the governance perspective more broadly, emphasizes the distinction between "power to" (achieve purpose by mobilizing support for an agenda) and "power over" (controlling decision making) that defines the democracy-as-contest tradition. McFarland (2004, 2006) has highlighted a third concept—"power with"—as the component concerned with what motivates and shapes behavior among coalition partners.

The problem-solving focus inherits those distinctions but goes beyond the regime concept in three ways. First, while the formation of regimes that wield broad-based influence is important in and of itself, that formation is not necessarily vital to every effort at ambitious public problem solving—a point Judd (2006) makes about American cities that is all the more true in global perspective, since urban regimes do not clearly exist everywhere (Stoker 2002). That is, regimes are probably not the only road to civic capacity (collective efficacy vis-à-vis communitywide problems or opportunities), and regimes, where they exist, may not be interested enough in certain issues to incorporate those issues into a long-run governing agenda. Yet this need not rule out significant change: the regime, if it does not adopt, may also not oppose; and the regime's range of resources may not be essential for forward movement in a particular problem arena. The accomplishments of the slum dweller-based Alliance in Mumbai (chapter 5) and the San Francisco children's movement (chapter 10) are cases in point.

Second, while scholars have employed the term *regime* to analyze the civics of advancing agendas of change, much regime function is about routine politics. Stability and routine are important sources of a regime's support and thus of its influence and efficacy vis-à-vis long-run purposes. But like Stone (2001) speaking of education reform in American cities, I argue, based on an international sample of cases in a wider range of problem domains, that community problem solving is defined by *non-*routine politics. That is, it necessarily includes efforts to shake up the routine and the stable.

True, change agents must institutionalize their influence or mechanisms for public-private cooperation to advance an agenda. Stone's (2005, 2006) reminders, focused on U.S. cities, about the importance of such mechanisms are highly relevant outside the United States, despite cross-national differences in political history or government structure, as the Brazil, India, and South Africa cases in this book make clear. But the main point is that significant community problem solving, which may neither establish nor successfully replace a local regime, calls for out-of-the-ordinary practices that we all too easily overlook if building and sustaining a regime is the key test of civic effectiveness.

Third, scholarship on regimes and other instruments of governance has not grappled nearly enough with the range of possibilities for three closely interrelated pillars of effective governance, particularly when viewed in global perspective: meaningful and consequential *participation* in public life, including the multiple purposes of such participation and the role of conflict when participation expands in a given society; the *assignment of responsibility* for acting on public problems, which depends on history and appears to be at least as dependent on ideology as pragmatism; and *accountability* for such action, which, in spite of certain global trends outlined below, is likewise a function of each place and time.[1]

Whose Job Is It Anyway?: Legitimate and Effective Public Action

Civic, Governmental, Participatory, Accountable

Civic capacity's central concern is enabling effective public action, which is often necessarily broader than official (government) action. With notable exceptions, the study of democracy and the design of governance innovations, such as citizen committees and collaborative forums, have focused, to a great extent, on the issue of directing government or "steering the state" (Fung 2004). Steering well and justly is important for a host of reasons. But as any manager, implementation researcher, or governance expert knows, official policy does not equal impact.

Government policies may be largely symbolic, chosen directions may never get implemented, they may get distorted along the way, or, regardless of how tangible, complete, and faithful action is to the policies from which that action is supposed to follow, the intended results may never be achieved. This is particularly true where there is limited information or considerable uncertainty about the future (making the likely efficacy of policy tools more limited and harder to predict), where government alone has limited leverage over the forces driving the targeted problem (making "coproduction" with players outside of government a must), and where controversy and mistrust lead to informal "vetoing" of government rules and priorities.

Setting a nation's monetary policy is not a problem of that type, but getting the next generation educated in a fast-changing world, making urban communities much safer in the context of insecurity and inequality, accommodating growing populations while at the same time making cities more environmentally sustainable, tackling public health crises in the context of social taboos and complex and uneven medical guidance, restructuring the job economy of a local region after devastating decline, incorporating immigrant newcomers on a scale without precedent in history—these and many other public problems and opportunities *do* present with these challenging traits. Beyond conflicting interests, these problems often present with conflicts over values and identities—what defines people and their sense of what it means to belong to a community.

Some leadership gurus have taken to calling these "adaptive" rather than "technical" problems (Heifetz 1994), in that the former require significant learning and risk taking rather than the application of known technical solutions to well-identified problems: the perfect tutoring program to improve student learning, for instance. But most important public problems present with adaptive features as well as significant technical complexities. Dewey (1927) highlighted this complexity as one of the key challenges to modern democracy, and although he could scarcely have imagined the Internet, cell phones, text messaging, multimedia presentations, simulation modeling, e-mail, and other information and communication technologies that have the potential to strengthen democracy, he probably foresaw that new technologies would offer no panacea.

Information tools can help us tame complexity but also overwhelm us with it, enabling new forms of genuine deliberation but also projecting scaled-up versions of "ritual participation." The tools can mitigate conflicts over the "state of the world"—that is, conditions and prospects about which stakeholders may have very different and very ill-informed assumptions and beliefs—by providing more credible analyses and forecasts (Raiffa, Richardson, and Metcalfe 2002). But the tools can also enable each side of a polarized debate to dress up its preferred scenario or causal story with false precision and cherished symbols.[2] Rhetorical power is a key to civic mobilization and therefore to active citizenship, but this alone does not ensure civic capacity.

To understand what drives perceptions in a world where public is more than governmental, consider the accountability revolution. It is sometimes referred to as a "performance revolution" sweeping all three sectors—public, private, and nonprofit or nongovernmental (Behn 2001; Ebrahim 2005; Kettl 2000; Kaplan and Norton 2000; Letts, Ryan, and Grossman 1999; Stoker 2002; Weber 2003). This revolution is reflected in the "new public management," or the movement to "reinvent government," as it is more widely known in America (Osborne and Plastrik 1992). The new public management includes controversial cost-cutting, "merit pay" for government workers, outsourcing government services to the for-profit and nonprofit sectors through performance-based contracts, and other strategies.

But the revolution is broader, and its implications far more sweeping, than those stock managerial models indicate. In public and private organizations, and in efforts to team up across them in the cause of public problem solving, we see a dramatic break with older conceptions of accountability, a shift beyond *behavior that complies* (with rules) to *behavior that accomplishes* (promotes performance on crucial tasks). This shift reflects the recognition, in fact, that the former has often undermined the latter and driven talented people away from government service (Behn 2001). A shift is also occurring from direction setting by technical experts in traditional bureaucratic organizations to blended action and network-based communities of practice that draw on expert as well as "local" knowledge (Snyder and Briggs 2003; Wenger 1998) or public entrepreneurship networks that foster cross-sector, interorganizational cooperation around focal problems, such as how to advance "green technology" (Laws et al. 2001).

This is consonant with the argument that government organizations and entrepreneurial public managers exist, first and foremost, to create public value (Moore 1995), which demands discretion and learning, and not to blindly comply with the dictates of policy makers who steer government. Furthermore, it is consistent with the widespread finding that citizens are motivated to participate in public affairs not out of an abstract desire to strengthen democracy but out of the rational belief that their investment of time, reputation, commitment, and other precious resources should measurably change social conditions (Barber 1984; Bolan 1969; Fung 2004). That is, citizens are motivated by problem solving for results, not by process or by seminar notions of idealized democracy.

Even regulation, which we have traditionally associated with police powers that belong exclusively to government, can be "community driven" and at the same time performance driven—if the community extends the limited capabilities of government in crucial, mutually accountable ways. Citizen-driven "bucket brigades" and "grassroots ecosystem management" that enhance environmental quality (O'Rourke 2004; Weber 2003), plus the effort to leverage so-called street science (Corburn 2005), blending community knowledge and professionalized knowledge, reflect these developments.

Seen in this light, efforts to make public decision making more transparent, accountable, and inclusionary are many, varied, and enormously encouraging, whether in the form of participatory local budgeting in Brazil, parent-teacher councils shaping urgent school-level improvements in urban America, village-level economic development planning in India, or similar innovations. The aim is to hold public agencies more accountable and improve results, through what Archon Fung and Erik Olin Wright (2003) have termed "empowered participatory governance"— that is, reforms that go beyond citizen advice or review of policy and devolve decision-making power to citizen bodies. The new push is also for "compacts" forged in an "accountability environment" rather than the endless pursuit of individual scapegoats for performance failures, waste, fraud, or abuse (Behn 2001; Kearns 1996).[3]

But each of the public problems in this book, and indeed many of the problems that citizens, nongovernmental organizations, and public officials are deliberating in those innovative forums, demands that "communities" coproduce needed change with government (Ostrom 1996; Waddell and Brown 1997). This is not the same as saying that the urgent problems of our time demand smaller or less regulatory government, and it is not an argument focused on self-help or more social capital (useful social bonds) to substitute extensively for money and other types of capital, as in "more community, less public funding."[4] Indeed, as Edward Weber (2003) suggests in his exploratory study of emerging forms of governance in the environmental policy arena, for new approaches to survive, they must find ways to balance national policy interests and the security of government-backed rules with the enormous potential benefits of cross-sector local networks, collaborative learning, and transparent and widely verifiable results.

Nor is this an argument against reforming public agencies where such reform is clearly useful, even urgent (see Behn 2001; Fung 2004). Rather, this is a different conception of how much effective public action we can rely on the public sector to ensure. That distinction underlies an ambitious definition of what aspirations to democracy actually include, at least if democracy is to contribute to human progress and development. It is a definition that emerges not principally from democratic theory or from received wisdom about how official policy making should work—that is, from people's informal theories about how things get decided by "the powers that be"—so much as from the rapid diffusion of the concept of partnership and from a broader cultural logic of empowerment.

To focus on the first idea, effective partnerships are not always democratic in the way we have traditionally thought about the exercise of voice and shared power. Some declared partnerships are not the genuine article at all: they are unequal and limited contracting relationships dressed up as opportunities for the "partner" with few evident alternatives. But legitimate and effective partnerships that tackle some of the most important public problems of our time directly provide the twin ingredients of effective public action: *legitimacy* and *productive capacity*. Legitimacy confers vital informal authority to be heard in the public square, to act on public problems, and to have other players respond to one's actions. Productive capacity is the means for learning, adapting, and operating to generate visible results.

These essential ingredients, which help determine the effectiveness of mission-driven public organizations (Moore 1995), too often elude formal systems that rely solely on representative government, open and competitive elections, majority rule, interest-group bargaining, professionalized public agencies, and the other stock institutions of modern democracies. Most of all, the lack of legitimacy for public institutions robs collective problem solving of what international affairs expert Joseph Nye (2004) has termed "soft power." It is the magnetism and informal authority to influence the actions of others, and it comes from perceived integrity, trustworthiness, and values that resonate, not the power to compel or buy the actions one desires and—often—not from practices that clash with strong cultural expectations (Johnson, Dowd, and Ridgeway 2006).

Soft power helps explain why partnerships *may* be well worth it despite key pitfalls, such as a loss of control, and risks, such as the loss of reputation and tangible resources if things go badly. The reason is that some public problem solving demands a multilateral approach in order to be legitimate, not just because the partners involved complement one another—get different things done well—in the operational dimension. Public policy that lacks soft power is frequently—and more and more visibly—inadequate to solve key social and economic problems, from crime to school failure, environmental sustainability to economic restructuring, public health crises, and more.

In the United States, we have learned this the hard way, perhaps most dramatically in police-community efforts to make segregated and highly disadvantaged neighborhoods safer and more secure. Where a history of racial mistrust and perceived abuses of police power cast a long shadow, carefully constructed and respectful partnerships provide "an umbrella of legitimacy" (Berrien and Winship 1999) for public officials to act. This is important above and beyond the productive supports also provided by many partnerships, such as investigative evidence or deterrence through informal social control, which reinforce and extend what public officials can do to change social conditions.

Grassroots ecosystems management likewise reflects the wisdom of soft power, which supplements rule-bound traditional bureaucratic procedure with new forms of public participation. And the evolving practice of facilitated consensus building aims for problem solving—getting beyond the routine and the status quo—with specific principles for promoting legitimacy and trust, accountability through the selection of stakeholders and agents to represent them, and joint fact finding to overcome disagreements about the state of the world (Susskind, McKearnan, and Thomas-Larmer 1999; Susskind and Cruikshank 2006a).

In developing partnerships democratically, and this is a worldwide growth industry with too few guides or safeguards, one must be attentive to a range of interests and to the presence or absence of support for ideas—the principal things that political decision-making systems exist to test in democratic societies young and old. But one must also, quite consistently and vigorously, attend to the *quality* of ideas for proposed action (the likelihood that they can be implemented and that, if implemented, they will yield results) and the degree of *commitment* to help implement (take action jointly).

These imperatives separate effective coproduction, where there is a complementarity and synergy among the players' contributions, from the displacement or substitution of one productive community resource—be it public, private, or nongovernmental—for another (Ostrom 1996). The lack of attention to these different outcomes has dogged hopes for creating and applying more useful social capital, as a resource for solving problems, around the world (Woolcock and Narayan 2000).[5] It has also led critics to decry a legitimate concern for producing results as mere "managerialism" meant to exclude wider participation in decision making or to justify an abdication of government's rightful role (e.g., Heller 2001).

But the twin imperatives of legitimacy and capacity also imply a range of objectives for participation that debates about invigorating democracy, or promoting active citizenship, often obscure. To be sure, participation is important for shaping official policy (for guiding or steering government) and for developing legitimate support for government action. Not only is consulting those affected by decisions a must in democratic societies, but it is psychologically important as well. A large body of evidence in the field of procedural justice underlines the importance of fair hearing, for example. People are much more likely to be satisfied with decision outcomes when they feel they have been heard, even when the decisions are costly and unpleasant (Deutsch 2000; Raiffa, Richardson, and Metcalfe 2002; Schmidtz 2006; Susskind and Cruikshank 2006a).

Yet from the standpoint of problem solving, participation is crucial for two other reasons as well. First, the proverbial "two heads" can be, though they are not always, better than one. Managed well (and those are the key words), inclusionary groups and processes, which blend different sources of knowledge and disseminate knowledge too, can generate better, more actionable ideas than top-down, exclusionary, technocratic planning. The principle has been powerfully confirmed from studies of diverse workgroups and firms (Adams 1979; Amabile 1996) as well as social-movement organizations (Ganz 2000). Advocates of deliberative democracy often emphasize this rationale for wider and better structured participation (Fung 2004, 2006a, 2006c; Mansbridge 1980; Williamson and Fung 2005). And so do the critics who detail how and why the technocratic and typically bureaucratic "rational planning ideal"—an outgrowth of the Enlightenment belief that logic and reason should guide society—has failed so often in practice (Arnstein 1969; Friedmann 1987; Scott 1998). Efforts to replace planning by professional experts with something better must contend with that older model's mistaken but admittedly convenient assumptions: that professional knowledge is superior to other forms of knowledge, including local, indigenous, or "craft" knowledge born of experience (Scott 1998); that citizens will be persuaded by professional knowledge because technical superiority, according to objective standards of science, makes it more legitimate than other kinds of knowledge (Scott 1998); and that members of the public share a culture—norms of communication, decision making, and influence—so that encounters between experts and citizens, or among diverse citizens, will produce learning and trust under rules of fair play (in fact, this is often not the case; see Briggs 1998; Healey 1997; Sandercock 1998; Tauxe 1995). But the point, for now, is that well-structured participation *can* lead to decisions that are better in that they are substantively wiser, not just more popular or more legitimate, and this is crucial in the context of heightened demand for results.

Second, wider and better structured participation may enable coproduction: generating knowledge and commitment to drive private and nongovernmental action, not just government action, and the blending of actions by these sectors to produce a meaningful impact on public problems. This idea was well enshrined in the "small democracies" of cohesive, relatively homogeneous agrarian communities with limited government machinery to tackle problems.[6] But as Dewey recognized a century ago, the idea, not to mention its fulfillment, is elusive in big, institutionally complex, and socially diverse democracies. The field of management and organizational change, not political theory, has gone farthest to develop the idea that commitment gets developed through entrepreneurial collective action (Deming 2000; Ganz 2000). There is arguably more in teams of self-managed or "empowered" workers than in community visioning exercises, deliberative polling, or other self-consciously democratic civic experiments to explain how commitment to coproduce change gets built, sustained, and focused on what works. But certainly, as I examine in the chapters to come, there are promising examples in civic initiatives too.

Contentious, Collaborative, Consensual?

If civic capacity's purpose is to enable collective action, "collective" does not mean, and cannot mean, purely consensual or conflict free or even consistently "collaborative" in the sense that that term is often used. As many students of democracy have noted, but as the elastic rhetoric of "partnership" and "community building" frequently does not, collective action benefits from divergent as well as convergent thinking, from robust and flexible mechanisms for "getting to yes" as well as space and rules for "having a good fight." These plain-English labels are more than homage to a bestseller on the theory and practice of negotiation on the one hand, legal scholar Roger Fisher and anthropologist William Ury's *Getting to Yes* (1981), and a widely read management article on what makes teams or workgroups productive on the other (Eisenhardt, Kahwajy, and Bourgeois 1997). Rather, the two labels draw attention to what civic capacity is *for* in the realm of conflict, whether within or across the government, market, and civil-society sectors.

Potentially, civic capacity is for both having a good fight and getting to yes, for confronting and pushing on one hand (the traditional realm of pressure politics and "insurgent" social movements) but also for overcoming impasses that impede valuable agreements—each of these in its appropriate context and time. As any committed activist knows, the former can sharpen debates about important values and conflicts among them, mobilize people to act on their values and not merely spectate or complain from the sidelines, and force essential learning and changes in political opportunities (Coser 1956; Fainstein and Hirst 1995; McAdam, Tarrow, and Tilly 2001; Schattschneider 1960; Warren 2001). Well-organized contention includes values-driven "prophetic voice" and pressure politics that changes what gets bargained, by whom, and how—what scholars have termed "transgressive politics," in that the basic rules of engagement (the norms and institutions through which civic life happens) are transformed in the process (McAdam, Tarrow, and Tilly 2001).

Moreover, while civic life need not begin with the assumption that interests are in conflict or that voting is the only valuable means of arriving at just decisions, it is a reality of large democratic societies with diverse publics that the "unitary ideal," as political scientist Jane Mansbridge (1980) terms it, will be limited to selected, often ad hoc groups. That is, the "small democracy" of face-to-face exchange among trusted parties, to arrive at a common interest, has a place but cannot be treated as a template for democratic life as a whole. It is an impractical ideal where interests diverge and reasoned exchange among trusted others is limited or essentially impossible to construct. Real democracies, as opposed to idealized ones, contain elements both strategic (contested) and learning oriented (deliberative). And without mechanisms for conflict resolution and consensus building, "good" fights can quickly turn bad, further eroding the willingness to engage, deliberate, and even coproduce change.

There is evidence, for example, that the proliferation of participatory approaches to managing water and other vital resources worldwide has led to many unstructured negotiations, misunderstandings about the meaning of consensus, deeper impasses, and a fear of sharing power (Susskind and Ashcraft 2007).[7] But as leading scholars of transformative social change McAdam, Tarrow, and Tilly (2001) contend, with a focus on large structural changes over the medium to long run, researchers' efforts to understand the role of contention still do too little to illuminate how creative action in specific episodes *leads* to larger change. I aim to address this in each case, treating episodes as cases within cases, as outlined in the methods section of chapter 1.

The second feature—getting to yes or coming to workable agreements in the context of ongoing differences—helps "deliver the goods." It also helps keep conflicts, which can all too easily become shrill, self-serving, and unproductive, in check. In its pure form, getting to yes hinges on bargaining effectively where some interests are shared and others are not, and will *remain* not, as negotiation theorists and practitioners have emphasized (Fisher and Ury 1981; Raiffa, Richardson, and Metcalfe 2002; Susskind and Cruikshank 1987). Far from the image of "horse trading" for competitive advantage, punitive military deal making, or purely opportunistic gaming or claiming, "principled" bargaining, whether assisted or unassisted by professional mediators, is a core civic skill. It is also an underdeveloped and frequently misunderstood skill in democratic societies that expect more and more shared decision making.

But through learning and relationship building, and as small-scale unitary democracies such as deliberative "study circles" show, civic engagement can also change people's preferences, change the way problems are framed, bring new resources and stakes into view, and expand the menu of options under consideration. In this way, I use "getting to yes" as a shorthand for the element of civic process that is broader than pure bargaining (over fixed interests and values). Where getting to yes is concerned, the book aims precisely to examine how coming to agreement contributes to larger processes of civic action—that is, beyond the decision points on which negotiation, conflict resolution, and consensus-building theorists and practitioners have focused help-fully so far. This includes dialogue that leads to agreements and not just to the understanding that deliberative democrats prize (Susskind and Cruikshank 2006b). But it also expects, through formal as well as informal exchanges over time, the *achievement of purposes* that people value. This is the ultimate test of problem solving; it is more than devis-ing and deciding together. It includes *doing*—acting—to change the state of the world.

Both contention and agreement seeking, then, capture important dimensions of problem solving as strategic behavior,[8] grounded in part on guesses we make about what others will do, why they are doing what they are doing, and how to deal with uncertain outcomes (Ganz 2000), as well as disinterested learning, grounded in the commitment to new knowledge and capability. As I hinted above, the strategic dimension often gets obscured in the now-ubiquitous rhetoric of "community build-ing" and apolitical notions of acting in partnership (Briggs 2001; Chaskin 2005; Kadushin et al. 2005; Warren 2001). That dimension highlights key reasons why too much community initiative and grassroots "claim making" is not well integrated with formal policy making systems. Popular mobilization does not always lead to effective and essential bargaining, and the "grasstops"[9]—that is, a community's influentials or leaders, not necessarily the traditional political or economic elites—may need to be mobilized constructively, and their conflicts sorted out, too. Viewed from the so-called roots, the grasstops may *seem* always and everywhere to be organized and effective at acting in concert—and to the detriment of the disadvantaged group or the transformative idea—but the cases to come show why this view can be so misleading.

Civic capacity is not about some hoped-for evolution "from protest to collaboration," as popular reports on the rise of cross-sector partner-ships in American community development typically framed things in the 1980s.[10] Knowing when to emphasize conflict, consensus, or a bit of both at once, and being capable of managing both well, is a matter of craft, judgment, and a willingness to take risks. Moreover, the effort to influence others toward honest and productive conflict, constructive and timely agreement seeking in the face of conflicting interests or values, or a blend of the two also helps put flesh on the bones of that most ubiq-uitous and elastic of ideas about enabling change—"leadership"—to which so many scholarly treatments of public problem solving and politics seem indifferent, if not downright averse and suspicious.

The bottom-line implication is that civic capacity is not only, or primarily, about capping conflict. Nor is it universally about stirring up conflict to get new proposals heard, change the balance of power, or make decision making more inclusionary. Both contentious and agreement-seeking civic action matter. And both demand acts of leadership when people and institutions cling fervently to one at the expense of the other, whether because of ideology, partisan perceptions, or what psychologists term "defensive routines" that block learning (Argyris 1985).

In the case of chapters to come, I explore the strategic and deliberative elements that define collective problem solving over time in particular places, develop a more robust view of the forms and uses of civic capacity that might meet the changing expectations of democracy I have outlined in this chapter, and—in the process—show why acts of leadership matter as well.

II

Managing Urban Growth

3

Managing Urban Growth: The Problem and Its Civics

It ain't what you don't know that gets you into trouble. It's what you know for sure that just ain't so.
—Mark Twain

A proud schoolteacher, standing in her classroom, looks into the camera as the narrator begins, "There are people who are part of your community who can't find housing they can afford." Images of elderly citizens and police officers appear on screen next, as the narrator explains that these people include "your grown children, grandchildren, parents, public safety officers . . . ." The thirty-second video, made for television, then encourages "your community to allow its fair share of affordable housing," and the spot ends with a simple request: "Talk to your local officials."

The video is no human interest story prepared for the TV news, nor is it traditional interest-group advocacy on behalf of a policy position. Rather, it is part of a public education campaign led by Envision Utah, a self-described "partnership for quality growth" focused on the greater Salt Lake City region, which is home to nearly two million people—80 percent of the population of the state of Utah—and growing fast. The video is a small part of a big effort: to address rapid urban growth (an issue with as many challenging civic dimensions as technical ones) and, in the process, to change the role of public planning as a tool for problem solving. The video is also a small part of a big puzzle: How is it that one of America's most ambitious and influential initiatives to pursue more sustainable growth emerged and took root in Utah, in the heartland of local resistance to government planning and land regulation? Why there, of all places?

This section of the book tackles that puzzle and a related one centered in Mumbai (formerly Bombay), the economic capital of a surging India, one of the great megacities of Asia, with some twelve million in the city and eighteen million in the metro area, and also—less auspiciously—a global capital of slums. Mumbai may or may not be "the future of urban civilization," as writer Suketu Mehta claims, but it is one very important window on what it will take to create an urban civilization that works for much of the planet.

The Urban Age and the Problem of Growth

The human race is now mostly urban for the first time in history. By "urban," I mean living in metropolitan areas with urbanized economies, defined by local labor and land markets. Industrialization spurred rapid urbanization in the wealthy nations beginning about two centuries ago, triggering massive migrations from the countryside and creating the modern industrial city, the social and political structures that evolved with that kind of city, and most of the now-familiar tools for managing city form and sustaining urban life: land and building regulation, urban transportation systems and other vital infrastructure, environmental protection measures for urban living (as opposed to remote wildlife settings), and more.

Over time, the modern city gave way, first in the wealthy nations, to a postindustrial city dominated by services rather than manufacturing. In the past half century, partly in response to the mechanization of agriculture and to investment shifts toward countries with lower labor costs in manufacturing, urbanization has gained enormous momentum in Latin America and, more recently, in Asia and Africa, where many cities—dotted with construction cranes and often hazed over by air pollution as well—are straining with growth.[1] The United Nations projects that developing countries will add about two billion city dwellers in the next twenty-five years, many of them poor migrants and their children moving to cities that do not offer adequate housing or infrastructure for the residents they have now (UN-Habitat 2005).

I focus here on managing growth specifically, not the problems associated with the *loss* of urban population and economic activity—for example, through deindustrialization (the focus of part II of the book). Problems of human development have become, to a great extent, problems of sustaining life in urban areas, with all the complexities of achieving economic growth, social equity, and environmental quality that the broad aim of sustaining life implies: how to create a competitive economy without significant degradation of the natural and human environment, how to limit economic inequality as technological change and policy restructure markets, how to accommodate greater social diversity in ethnic and other dimensions, how to make room for cultural expression and shared social life—a "community of place"—and more. But the pressures leading to uneven growth take on a very different character in wealthy versus poor nations. This part of the book examines the role of civic capacity in innovative efforts to manage urban growth in both contexts, drawing on cases in the United States and India. I begin with the shape of the challenge in these two contexts, whose fortunes, thanks to globalization, seem ever more intertwined.

Sprawl and Slums

Births and deaths—the net of which demographers call natural increase—constitute one driver of population growth, and migration from one place to another is the other main driver. But neither of these factors, which dictate *how much* population will grow in one place or another, determines *how* those places will accommodate growth. Everywhere in the world, it is the issue of how to manage urban growth that poses the highest stakes, most complex policy decisions, and most vehement conflict in the public arena. Even among wealthy nations, managing growth is riddled with tricky choices and, contrary to the pure free-market perspective, growth patterns are not a simple by-product of market demand but of specific public policies that shape demand and supply, including consumers' preferences and mental models of the world around them—their sense of what is possible as well as what is desirable.

The contrast between Western Europe and America is particularly sharp and telling. In Europe, steep taxes on gasoline, investment policies that favor already built-up areas over undeveloped "greenfields," sustained investment in public transportation, and a host of other policies—not just a culture of urban living with deep historical roots—have produced a relatively compact and centralized metropolitan form (Nivola 1999). This form includes central cities that are economically healthy vis-à-vis their suburbs, if costly to live and buy property in.

By contrast, in the United States, cheap gas, government-subsidized markets for mortgage loans, massive postwar highway investment, policies that favor new construction on greenfields on the fringe of metro areas over "infill" development in built-up areas, huge public subsidies for roads and other new infrastructure in those areas, school assignment policies and fiscal policies that include heavy reliance on local property taxes to finance public schooling (twin features that concentrate poverty and disadvantage in inner cities and encourage more affluent families to keep their children out of these areas), and other policies encourage a much more car-reliant and "sprawling" decentralized form for metro areas, where eight in ten Americans now live (Altshuler 1999; Briggs 2005; Rusk 1999; Squires 2002). It is a model with myriad private benefits but huge social costs—inefficient use of water and other natural resources, overburdened infrastructure, pollution, disinvestment in older communities, a spatial mismatch between where many disadvantaged job seekers live and where jobs are growing, and more.

It is not a simple, policy-drives-form story, of course: many Americans have come to associate the good life with a lifestyle that sprawl has created. In plain terms, sprawl is a part of our culture, so consumers signal a demand for it, or at least for many aspects of it—spacious and cheap housing, abundant roads, and more—which the market, mostly encouraged by public policy, readily supplies. Sprawl is also a cause of culture wars, as high-stakes political struggles and competing visions of community and the good life cast advocates, variously, as heroes and villains in a great contest for America's future. As journalist Anthony Flint (2006, 5) argues,

This saga—smart growth, the backlash against it, suburbs-in-overdrive all the while—is uniquely revealing about who we are as a country. It's about our politics and our culture and our ability to think collectively. In the act of choosing where to live and work, every single one of us makes choices that lay bare the tension between our individual desires and our common purposes.

But the larger point for now is that major public choices, not just private ones, helped to create a dominant model for accommodating urban growth, a model that has come under more and more criticism in recent decades as environmental awareness has deepened. Imperfect and loaded as the term may be, *sprawl* is the shorthand for uneven or poorly managed growth in America. For the most part, sprawl *is* how we grow, and it is thus the target for most efforts to manage growth differently, and more sustainably, in the years ahead. As I will show, a key to developing and deploying civic capacity to deal with sprawl is framing this target problem effectively. The revelatory U.S. case in this section of the book is the Salt Lake City region, which in recent years has been home to one of the most innovative and widely cited efforts to confront the costs of sprawl and find an alternative—"quality growth," as local leaders call it—that can enjoy wide public and private support.

In the developing world, uneven growth takes on a quite different character, for which I will use the word *slums* as shorthand. Slum-led growth is how much of the developing world urbanizes: cities, acting as job magnets for rural migrants, do not accommodate population growth, especially that of the poor, through regularized systems of housing and basic service delivery, and so slums emerge instead. Because so much construction is informal and low cost, slum-led growth is generally across, not up. Linking the two concepts that frame this section of the book, then, many slums sprawl. According to public officials, most of Lagos, Nigeria's doubling in land area between 1985 and 1994, for example, was that kind of sprawl (Davis 2006).

An estimated 925 million people, or about one in six people on the planet, live in urban slums now (UN-Habitat 2005). And it is widely acknowledged that the future of slums is central to the world's linked challenges of economic growth, poverty reduction, and environmental sustainability. The United Nations Millennium Development Goals include the target of achieving "significant improvement" in the lives of 100 million slum dwellers by 2020 (UN Millennium Project 2005), and a joint initiative of the United Nations, World Bank, and eleven aid agencies seeks to take slum upgrading projects to scale and create "cities without slums."

Unlike older sections of cities in North America, Europe, or other wealthy regions, which may become home to the urban poor over time, slums in the global South are generally not "run-down" areas that were once well off, nor specifically segregated quarters (ghettos), where marginalized social groups are concentrated but that are still part of the formal legal and institutional fabric of the larger city. Rather, slums in Third World cities make up an almost parallel universe—a "shadow city," as journalist Robert Neuwirth (2004) has termed it—often with a large and diversified labor force that includes professional workers, a large informal economy lacking income security and benefits, poor sanitation, a host of improvised systems for accessing water and power and other basic services, unrecognized or informal systems of property ownership and land and building regulation, unofficial policing, organized crime, and related features (UN-Habitat 2005).

Generated and reproduced outside the formal systems, then, Third World slums are, in one sense, places separate and apart—all but invisible in the mainstream urban press except in stories about criminality, stigmatized in popular culture, unserved or underserved by government, and, in some places, unpoliced as well. Yet in economic and physical terms, these slums are inextricably linked to the larger cities around them. From Mumbai to Rio de Janeiro, from Karachi to Mexico City, Cape Town, and beyond, slums supply vital labor and consumer demand for bustling urban economies and shape their physical character and potential for development.

This dual reality, of vitality and marginality, is very much a part of the second story, centered on Mumbai, where no less than half the population lives in slums. This megacity—an economic engine of the surging Indian economy, a so-called New York of India[2]—also turns out to be ground zero of a new civic approach to the problems associated with slum-led urban growth. It is an atypical collaboration among government, global financial institutions, and a network of organizations accountable to the urban poor. This is why I selected Mumbai among many other cities that are home to slums as well as important slum redevelopment efforts.

Setting Up the Cases: What Kind of "Public Problem" Is This?

As students of policy change and learning have long emphasized, the civic and other challenges of problem solving depend in part on the attributes of the problem to be addressed (Sabatier 1993). Recognizing the links among land control, wealth, class identity, and political influence, many studies of local politics, particularly in America, have treated the civics of urban growth as a contest for the future of a place. As I noted in the previous chapter, the pluralist tradition focuses on which interest groups can influence government decision making through available channels. With this approach, managing urban growth, at least in American localities, becomes a problem of accommodating interest groups via the formal machinery of government land use management and public investment decisions—a machinery apparently driven by incrementalist agreements far more than by comprehensive "rational" planning by trained planners (Altshuler 1965). Simplified for the sake of discussion, managing growth is reduced, in this first approach, to a problem for government and those who would influence formal policy making through voting and lobbying.

In contrast, the *growth machine* model (Logan and Molotch 1987; Molotch 1976) emphasizes the role of powerful conflicts between those with only consumption ("use") interests in urban land and those with investment ("exchange") interests—for example, between renters who favor lower housing costs and property owners who benefit from rising values. Beyond drawing more attention to these structural conflicts rooted in economic interests, the growth machine approach also provides a compelling account of how a sustained coalition of public and private parties—often led by big business, the real estate industry, the building trades, and growth-favoring media—champions urban development in public *and* private arenas of decision making, mobilizing resources to compete with other localities for investment and status.

Still, the emphasis is on who champions or opposes growth and why, not on how civic action might change the way groups understand their own interests or accommodate others' interests. Though many have analyzed opposition to growth, for example by neighborhood groups (Altshuler 1999; Mollenkopf 1981; Richmond 2000), researchers in this vein have not yet focused on the quest for alternative *models* of growth, let alone on where the alternatives seem antithetical to the interests of a local growth coalition (or well-established "machine"). Also, it is not always clear how narrowly one should read the "economic growth" agenda, whether backed by a tightly coupled political machine or not. Does backing environmental protection, for instance, merely reflect enlightened self-interest on the part of business or also a genuine commitment, by business leaders as citizens, to community betterment?

The tradition of *regime analysis* has also examined "governing arrangements" that extend well beyond the machinery of government (Stone 2005; Stoker 1995). Regime analysts generally agree that governing coalitions in American cities are typically made up of business and government elites. But in general, regime studies have not examined significant policy change that runs counter to those interests, where frames of reference, the alignment of interest groups, and more must be restructured. Also, as I noted in the previous chapter, it is not clear that the regime concept, developed to understand local governance in a country that privileges private-sector initiative and strictly limits aid to cities from higher levels of government, applies well to other nations and regions, such as Europe or the developing world (Kantor, Savitch, and Haddock 1997; Stoker 2002).

Some careful analyses of the politics of urban growth have centered on policy reform at the national and state levels that influence local decision-making and growth patterns (review in DeGrove 2005; Richmond 2000; Weir, Wolman, and Swanstrom 2005). In the United States, the state-level focus is especially appropriate, since states grant municipalities the power to govern land use and shape local decision making with tax and infrastructure policy, in some cases with planning requirements, and in other ways. The weakness of mechanisms for interlocal or metropolitan governance is a constant refrain in this research: strong localism at the municipal level, a deep and perhaps unquestioned faith in "home rule" over land use, thwarts many efforts to shape regional solutions to growth problems. For example, when just 94 of the state of Wisconsin's 1,600 municipalities adopted "smart growth" laws requiring community master plans, political enemies attacked them as too costly, a violation of local control, and too threatening to private property rights. One local elected official even claimed, "This is the Soviet system" (Flint 2006, 189).

Acknowledging these central features of local growth politics in America, Weir (2000) emphasizes the pivotal role of state policy coalitions in the case of Oregon's landmark 1973 reform, which redirected urban growth away from sprawl, a coalition of "strange bedfellows" including farmers, urban advocates, and environmentalists. In a few states, but notably not others with similar political concerns, such interest-group allies turned to metropolitan approaches as a way of coordinating local decision making about new growth patterns, billing the new approaches as more sustainable than the sprawling status quo.

Weir notes the importance of mobilizing broad support, not only to win reforms (get them "on the books") but also to protect them against attack over time. Reviewing lessons of the 1960s and 1970s, she concludes, "Go-it-alone strategies do not work" (p. 150). Environmentalists have tried and failed to shape growth, concludes Weir, largely through more regulation, and urban advocates have tried to reverse central-city decline through campaigns for more aid to cities. Both approaches have led to dead ends, particularly as a strong property rights movement, opposed to almost any kind of land regulation, emerged—most forcefully in Utah and other parts of the American West.

These standoffs and the often costly legal battles that accompany growth-related conflicts have led some observers to advocate a much wider application of consensus-building approaches to policy making (Innes 1996; Innes and Gruber 1994; Susskind and Gensberg 2002). Such approaches, they stress, are supplements to, not substitutes for, representative democracy. That is, innovative approaches can extend democracy's capacity to forge valuable and sustainable agreements among disparate interest groups. Though the Utah case, as I will show, included key features of consensus building, such as a focus on wide outreach, neutral process, and careful fact finding to minimize conflicts over data (understandings of "the state of the world" and likely impacts of growth on its future state), consensus building was valuable as part of a much broader process of coalitional politics, public education, public sector capacity building, and shrewdly chosen demonstration projects. And contrary to the prevailing wisdom that elected officials should be the sponsors of "ad hoc" stakeholder processes to develop consensus agreements on important policy matters (Susskind and Hoben 2004), the Utah initiative I examine in the next chapter gained momentum and legitimacy by initially distancing its efforts from government authority and only later embedding them in a variety of government planning and policy making processes. Different emphases appear to be appropriate, on this axis of formal governmental versus informal nongovernmental authority, in different contexts, but clearly there must be a strategy for relating one to the other effectively.

Like Weir, Shutkin (2001) examines innovative efforts by environmentalists and social justice advocates to build broader coalitions, including efforts to curb sprawl and promote more sustainable development in New Jersey. Citing the importance of that state's example, Shutkin notes, "The pervasive and persistent environmental degradation that has brought the state so much notoriety has also motivated countless citizens, civic organizations, businesses, and governments across the state to engage in innovative experiments in social action" (p. 230). Shutkin links his work to John's (1994) call for a "civic environmentalism," but whereas John's emphasis is on more entrepreneurial approaches by government—providing market incentives, for example, beyond a regulation-only approach—Shutkin emphasizes "the *civic capacity* of communities to engage in effective environmental problem-solving" (p. 15). He documents efforts based on nongovernmental or civil society action, emphasizing advocates' aims and partial victories in legislatures or the courts. But Shutkin leaves the task of analyzing the challenges of developing and deploying civic capacity, as well as understanding its specific forms, on the agenda of future research.

Finally among the U.S. examples, DeGrove (2005) explores the political origins of state-level planning frameworks for growth management in nine U.S. states, as well as their implementation and political challenges. Most U.S. states have not shown the will to enact such state-level planning frameworks, in part because of the fierce protection of home rule outlined above, and even where planning requirements exist, they have shown a limited impact on growth patterns (DeGrove 2005; Logan and Zhou 1989). To plan is one thing, to grow according to plan is quite another. These two factors—local resistance to state "imposition" and the determination to shape growth patterns themselves and not just plans and policies—figure prominently in the Utah case.

Slums and State-Market-Society Cooperation

In the developing world, managing urban growth was initially treated, at least in formal analysis, as a social and economic policy problem for central government planners and policy makers, as well as for the aid agencies that influence and support them (UN-Habitat 2005)—a problem of inadequate services and failed promises to shelter the urban poor—for example, when slums were cleared without adequate replacement housing being built and provided. Critics of slum clearance schemes shifted attention, in the 1970s, to the microlevel problems of community groups and "self-help housing" advocates who were active in the effort to improve slums rather than raze and clear them (Sanyal and Mukhija 2001).

But the devolution of authority from national to state and local governments in many developing countries, an emphasis on market-oriented reforms and innovations, concerns about the competitiveness of city-regions in a changing global economy, and a greater interest in the role of civil society in the governance and implementation of policy change, have generated new approaches. Broadly, these approaches aim to (1) expand the efficiency and scale of slum improvement and, in some instances, to (2) integrate such efforts into broader development strategies for the economically important cities in which slums are found worldwide—from Mumbai, New Delhi, and smaller cities so vital in India's fast-growing economy to Rio, São Paulo, Jakarta, Mexico City, and beyond. The latter emphasis reflects the "new economic geography," in which freer trade flows, migration, and other aspects of globalization have, ironically, made local capacity for collective action more, not less, important (Yusuf, Evenett, and Wu 2000). Both emphases increase the variety, complexity, and importance of interactions among government, business, and civil-society groups in local problem solving.

Notably, the development studies literature on cities, focused as it has been on economic growth, public service delivery, and poverty reduction, has only more recently begun to explore, in an era of privatization, the wide range of business contributions to, and political interests in, managing urban growth (UN-Habitat 2005). Like regime analysis in America, newer research approaches to slums and urban growth in the developing world are focused on the interplay of public and private decision making, including the formation of knowledge and influence networks across organizations (Brown and Ashman 1999; Waddell and Brown 1997), as well as the institutional conflicts, accountability demands, and transformed roles that decentralized approaches invariably entail (Brown and Korten 1991; Sanyal and Mukhija 2001). But a strong tradition of studying implementation in development projects, like a counterpart tradition in American policy analysis, also sheds light on local capacity and small-scale patterns of governance—politics in action, as the actors develop strategies and act—in a way that the structural analyses of local politics typically has not. These studies emphasize the role of trust building and the challenges of designing and implementing incentives that respond to the diversity of interests in slum redevelopment.

More broadly, studies of development planning have also emphasized the abject failure of most bureaucratic or "modernist" planning systems to respect and incorporate local knowledge and enable adaptive responses by communities, especially vulnerable ones, over time (Scott 1998). The main response to the muscular "developmental state" was by nongovernmental organizations (NGOs), which criticized top-down government approaches and piloted their own development projects, often with the enthusiastic backing of advocates and some aid agencies (Sanyal 1994). Yet decades of failure mixed with success point to the need for a "synergy" and coproduction between state and civil society (Evans 1996; Ostrom 1996; Tendler 1997), as well as intersectoral cooperation (Kaleganokar and Brown 2000) or what Sanyal (1994) terms "cooperative autonomy" in the relationship between government and civil society. Cultivating this patiently, under adverse circumstances, is a central thread of the Mumbai case I examine in chapter 5—and an ongoing subject of debate among policy makers, practitioners, and opinion leaders worldwide.

Growth as a Problem of Civic Capacity

Creating alternative patterns of urban development that are not only popular but, by some measure, wise and that by definition challenge the status quo in important ways is far more daunting a problem than advancing a particular policy position or winning approval for a particular project. Beyond the structural conflicts over land and its value, there is a classic "tragedy of the commons": each user of urban space directly experiences the benefits of the extant, dominant model but only indirectly and inconsistently experiences its social and economic costs, which are often distributed very unevenly and which may lead, through overconsumption, to the quiet erosion of the shared resources that make community life possible.

In the language of systems thinking, metropolitan areas are indeed complex systems of interdependent parts, but the *feedback loops* (Holland 1995) that make natural systems so adaptive are often broken and obscured in urban life: by the tremendous diversity of private interests in urban development outcomes; by failures of representative politics (where elected officials do not represent the full range of their constituents' interests, where that range may be unknown, and/or where representatives prioritize their own interests); by fragmented decision-making authority or what McKinney and Harmon (2004, 19) aptly term "a briar patch of policies and institutions"; by the complexity of causes and effects (making it hard to read signals from the environment reliably or deliberate them meaningfully); by deep value conflicts that generate different conceptions of what is at stake; and by other barriers.

These barriers call for social learning—for deeper changes in the mental models, not just resources or influence, of many stakeholders and, as we will see, a reinvention of planning as an institution and process. But the barriers surely do not lend themselves to dialogue or consensual approaches to decision making in all instances. What is more, the many interdependencies that define life in urbanized areas also mean that it is quite easy for well-intended efforts, by government but also by private parties, to work at cross-purposes (Brown and Korten 1991; Shutkin 2001). It is also quite possible for distinct logics of decision making, each with a claim to legitimacy and usefulness—from the market-based exercise of private rights to public dispute resolution, so-called community initiative, and management by experts—to defeat, rather than complement, one another and thereby to leave the public less capable of confronting problems effectively over time (McKinney and Harmon 2004).

Civic capacity is no cure-all. Better governance of growth depends on efforts to shift both public and private action and to coordinate them as well, structural conflicts are to be expected—divergent groups will not "learn" their way to consensus on all fronts—and not all acts of public-private cooperation will reflect durable mechanisms of cooperation with long-run impacts. Key decision points will include games of influence—that is, plays for strategic advantage that "win-win" partnership rhetoric dangerously ignores or misreads.

As Weir, Wolman, and Swanstrom (2005) find in the U.S. context, encouraging elected officials and political influentials—across city and suburban jurisdictional borders—to redefine their policy preferences and explore novel coalitions is ever more crucial in an era of reduced federal aid to cities, devolution of authority, and institutional rules in state legislatures that thwart bold policy reforms. Likewise, Sanyal and Mukhija (2001) emphasize that progress on slum redevelopment in developing countries in an era of decentralization hinges on navigating important conflicts among institutions and interest groups in ways that produce new learning, durable mechanisms for conflict management, and wiser rules and incentives to guide private action, including that of businesses and civil society groups with varied agendas. But little prior research on the civics of growth has focused on how these tasks actually get accomplished.

Preview

In the case of urbanized Utah, the civic challenges were formidable: a long-standing and particularly deep-seated aversion to "planning from above," especially where perceived to limit local decision making about land use (home rule), as well as a broader resistance to the regulatory function of government as a limit on the culture of freedom and choice in the West, and as a threat to the logic of a supposedly free market. To elaborate on the puzzle I outlined at the outset: How did a movement for "quality growth" take root and take hold in this terrain, of all places, reshaping local development policies and decisions, spawning models of compact living in a region that seemed devoted to sprawl, contributing to a public transit boom beyond all expectations, changing the way thousands of citizens participate in planning the future of their communities, winning over a hesitant media and many conservative elected officials, and garnering top national awards in planning and real estate development in the process? The quintessential features of American governance and culture outlined in those questions make the Salt Lake region from the mid-1990s forward a revelatory case—that is, one of great conceptual and practical significance (Yin 1994).

In the case of Mumbai, a Byzantine politics of slumlords, real estate developers, bureaucratic incompetence and corruption, piecemeal policy reforms and incentive schemes, deep mistrust, and the day-to-day survival challenges facing slum dwellers all thwarted collective action on the problems linked to slums. Yet over the past two decades, an alliance of organizations accountable to the urban poor has worked with government officials and the private sector—including leading international banks, aid agencies, and philanthropic organizations—to pioneer new and sustainable models for slum relocation, housing development, and vital, community-managed infrastructure. With so many challenges and so many incentives *not* to cooperate across the divide between state, market, and civil society, how was it that Mumbai and the work of the pro-poor alliance centered there would be held up, by the United Nations, as one of the world's top exemplars of collaborative progress on slums— and the latter as the key to meeting global "millennium" goals?

4

Rethinking the American West: A Civic Intermediary and the Movement for "Quality Growth" in Utah

Beholding such an extensive scenery open before us, we could not refrain from a shout of joy . . . the moment this grand and lovely scenery was within our view.

—Mormon pioneer, entering the Salt Lake Valley, 1847 (May 1987)

Visions of the American West, both within the United States and around the world, invariably emphasize freedom, wide open spaces, and self-reliance. Yet the West is a paradox of competing themes: strong Native American and European settler traditions of communal life alongside rugged individualism, private initiative against a backdrop of large-scale public planning, and what the renowned Western writer Wallace Stegner once eloquently described as the need for "a society to match its scenery."[1]

Extensive government involvement in land management has been important in the region, from the sometimes violent acquisition of Native American land and the major federal land grants of the nineteenth century to federal ownership and management of protected wilderness and mineral reserves through the present day. More than 90 percent of all federal land in the United States is in the eleven westernmost states and Alaska, and the federal government owns about one-third of the West, including about 60 percent of the state of Utah. Native American tribal lands make up another one-fifth (Kemmis 2001; McKinney and Harmon 2004). In part because of the ongoing federal role and the patchwork of decision-making agencies that hold sway, the local politics of the West tend to frame government initiative, most of all if it affects the exercise of private property rights, as unwelcome interference. Local resistance to state-level land-use initiatives is a case in point. With a deep-seated tradition of localism and a strong property rights movement, the most conventional approach to managing growth—build a coalition for state-level reform, and shape local decision making through the state government—has gone nowhere in Utah and other states in the Mountain West.[2] Even the word *management,* it turns out, when linked to *growth,* has been a cultural turn-off for many, based on public-opinion surveys.

Utah's politics have been shaped significantly by the Mormon faith and its settler tradition, which centered on creating "an earthly Kingdom of God" in the Salt Lake basin (Larson 1989). In recent decades, the state's politics have been very localized and small-government conservative as well, particularly outside relatively "liberal" Salt Lake City.[3] In the mid-1990s, then, when rapid metropolitan growth helped turn the *conditions* associated with sprawl into *problems* that key civic actors wanted—somehow—to tackle, the conventional approach, understood as policy reform from above, was simply not in the cards.

Instead, a self-described "public-private partnership" followed another course. The key elements with relevance for civic capacity were: distancing planning from government and effectively framing the growth issue alongside the creation of a credible "civic intermediary" institution (Envision Utah), creatively framing alternatives for growth and carefully testing public support for these alternatives before addressing public policy, moving from vision to implementation strategy in ways that emphasized "choice" over "control" and that directly encouraged private-sector initiative as a validator and driver of change, and continuously adapting the functions of the intermediary to compensate for government's lack of planning and implementation capacity—rather than assuming an advocacy posture vis-à-vis particular government positions on policy. Using this sequence, a Utah coalition with important connections to established institutions, including the Church of Jesus Christ of Latter-Day Saints (hereafter, Mormon Church) and the governor's office, drew on preexisting civic capacity, extended that capacity, and put it to bold and effective use to tackle the strains of rapid urban growth. The coalition developed a broadly supported agenda and mobilized disparate community resources to advance that agenda significantly in a short time.

Responding to a Fuzzy Problem: Distancing and Framing

Coming out of the recession of the late 1980s and early 1990s, Utah's real estate market began an unprecedented boom, much of which took the form of suburban sprawl: large-scale new construction of single-family homes on large lots, as well as new shopping malls and other commercial development, at the metropolitan edge. Most of this new development took place in the ten-county corridor known as the Wasatch Front—literally, the Salt Lake City–facing "front" of the Wasatch range of the Rocky Mountains (figure 4.1)—where 80 percent of the state's population, and much of its population growth, is concentrated within "natural growth boundaries" of mountains and salt flats (figure 4.2). Political insiders recall news coverage and public discussion of how rapid growth threatened the region's prized quality of life as well as a concern to protect the renowned open-space assets that make Utah a favorite destination for outdoor sports—year-round tourism that is crucial to the regional economy. "The timing was magical," says a former state official of the political window of opportunity: "The economy and growth really peaked in 1994. Our economy was growing at twice the national average. A few years later [in a subsequent recession], the rug would have been pulled out from under us."

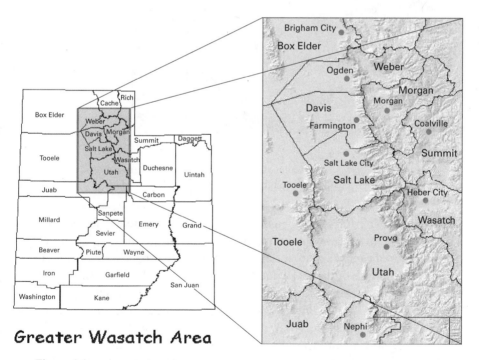

Greater Wasatch Area

Figure 4.1
Salt Lake Region, Utah, showing the Greater Wasatch Front (the Envision Utah focus area for regional visioning, 1997–1999). *Source:* Envision Utah

Figure 4.2
Urbanized area, Salt Lake Valley, 2000, showing "natural growth boundaries"
(computer-enhanced satellite image). *Source*: ESRI, Landsat ETM.

But earlier efforts to manage growth had been soundly defeated, and
leading environmental advocates in the region—traditionally, the sharp-
est critics of sprawl and its social costs—were widely perceived as extrem-
ist, out of touch with local values, and indifferent to local needs. So who
could address the strains of growth and how? In 1988, business leaders,
working with elected officials and nonprofit advocacy groups, had established the Coalition for Utah's Future. It was to be a mechanism for
dialogue on contentious policy issues, ironically with a major focus on
how to stimulate *more* growth (at a time of recession) but also with a
mandate to build consensus on environmental protection, child care, and
other issues of long-run importance to the state. Longtime insiders and

newcomers to Utah politics alike underline the importance of such quasi-independent consensus-building institutions in a state where the legislature is heavily influenced by conservative rural interests and by those in urbanizing areas who have a rural mindset that resists change. But as I will show, the character of consensus and the makeup of the institutions involved have been the subject of some debate.

By 1995, a Coalition-sponsored survey identified the strains of growth as the number one public concern. When members of the Coalition approached Governor Michael Leavitt about establishing a statewide growth commission, he declined, citing resistance to state land-use planning and facing a backlash from the right in his party but encouraging the Coalition to organize a broader effort, supported but not led by government, to build consensus. The Coalition quickly established a steering committee, made up of state and local officials, the state's largest housing developer, other business leaders, and "planning advocates," to address the issue of "quality growth" and recommend an approach for the state. At the Coalition's urging, the governor organized a public "growth summit" in November 1995. But the gathering focused narrowly on road building, showing just how much official perspectives lagged behind the reality on the ground.

"There was a real backlash [to rapid growth] emerging, people started to panic," says a prominent real estate developer who participated, "but the localities' first instinct was 'you need large lots to preserve the rural, exurban nature.' Many municipalities were headed toward larger and larger lot sizes and big shopping centers"—that is, toward a pattern that would have accelerated sprawl.

The quality growth steering committee presented initial findings on growth trends and risks to state legislators. The Coalition also worked with state-government staff to project growth trends in demographics, land use, transportation, and air quality in greater detail and organized a major effort to interview key stakeholders—about 150, from business, elected office, environmental advocacy, and other sectors—with questions about whether a process to "coordinate future growth" would be helpful, whether the interviewee would support such a process, and who should be involved. As one insider recalls, "Our study showed that there was a gap where the region's long-term future was concerned: The multi-issue groups were too local, the regional entities were too one-issue in focus." This wide canvassing returned political advice and support to move ahead.

Members of the steering committee also carried out a political "autopsy" of the one major effort to redirect growth in Utah—the effort to create state land-use planning guidelines, spearheaded by Democratic Governor Calvin Rampton in 1973. Though it cleared the legislature, Rampton's initiative was quickly overturned by the voters through public referendum. Rampton advised the steering committee on quality growth to engage those who led much of the opposition in the 1970s: real estate developers. "It probably took a couple of weeks for the real estate community . . . to kill that," confirms a developer with long involvement in Utah politics. Rampton had failed to engage the real estate industry in the policy making process and felt that had doomed his effort to address growth patterns and strengthen mechanisms for land-use governance in particular.

These steps led to critical early decisions about how to develop a consensus-building effort on growth: distance the effort from government but draw on the analytic expertise of government staff and the constituent knowledge of public officials; involve the likely opponents directly and proactively; emphasize a neutral stance on growth alternatives, at least until a broad process of community engagement had run its course; and frame assumptions about growth—including what "good growth" might include—as carefully as possible to keep diverse perspectives "at the table." On the last point, these early steps underscored the power of language, and savvy framing and public education would remain a hallmark of the Coalition's efforts from this point forward.

Whereas a variety of terms have been used nationwide to describe alternatives to sprawl—including "sustainable" and "smart" and even "sensible" growth—a senior state official observes, "Smart growth has some real strength in the Democratic party . . . for example with Glendening [a smart growth champion, the former governor of Maryland] . . . but a real stigma to it here. We have always used 'quality growth' very intentionally. We used to say that ours was 'homebrew.'" Over time, the Coalition's effort would give content to that label, emphasizing the power of local governments to plan with regional implications in mind and also the importance of market mechanisms to expand choices.

The public face of Utah's response to rapid growth was not simply a matter of message, though, but of messenger. As the steering committee recommended an extended process of public engagement and the formulation of credible alternative scenarios for future growth in the state, the Coalition's initiative—initially called the Quality Growth Public-Private Partnership but soon renamed, more simply, Envision Utah—focused carefully on the role of its lead representative, the chair. The Coalition's members focused on the credibility of the chair with the well-organized groups, such as real estate developers and local elected officials, most likely to oppose a critical discussion of the status quo model of urban growth. Defusing this opposition to open discussion early on seemed critical to sustaining any longer-run consensus-building effort.

The Coalition selected Robert Grow, president and chief operating officer of a major steel company, former chairman of the American Iron and Steel Institute, and a land-use attorney and trained engineer as well, to be Envision Utah's first chair. A successful businessman with a solid understanding of land development, he was also active in the Mormon Church—the state's largest faith institution by far and a major civic player and landowner in its own right—as well as on state advisory boards. Grow had chaired the Coalition's study committee.

In a state where so much politics is steadfastly local, Grow brought a rare statewide stature, as well as working relationships within the state's relatively small network of opinion leaders and civic insiders—mostly white, male, and Mormon. And as the early champions and critics of Envision Utah agree, Grow more specifically brought a keen understanding of how *not* to address the contentious issue of growth: certainly not by creating an elite group of "experts" to meet in closed-door sessions, render a detailed blueprint for growth, and then pitch the blueprint to the public or their elected officials. "I had been a land use lawyer," recalls Grow, "and so I went to national conferences on the planning tools available. It didn't seem that much was working. Environmental advocates were worried about trusting the public to choose well."

"Grow must have spent a year doing background work before he ever held a meeting of the partnership," says a state official who was closely involved. "The cross-section he got . . . of various stakeholders—civic, religious, business. The tent was so big that, in the end, when things got controversial, it was too hard to walk." Insiders confirm that Grow's behind-the-scenes recruiting of key stakeholders, including homebuilders and other potential opponents with significant political influence, was crucial before Envision Utah formally launched a long-range planning process. A prominent real estate developer explains the significance of this ground-laying work:

We [developers] had spent a lot of time fighting initiatives that we saw as unfriendly to the real estate industry and specifically affordable housing. . . . In my role with the homebuilders association through the 1990s, my job was to sniff out initiatives and kill them as quickly as I could, to keep [policy makers] from doing things that would further restrain homebuilding, impose taxes, costs. . . . Had we not been at the table early on, with an opportunity to make our feelings known and understood and found some willingness, on the part of really smart people, to listen to what he had to say . . . we would probably have been in that position again. . . . I don't know if Envision Utah would have ever found its legs. The real estate industry would have gone about the same thing [it did] in '73.

Though many in local government would need to be persuaded, a third of Envision Utah's announced "partners" were local elected officials from the region's Council of Governments. They were the authorities who would make most decisions over local land use; they also governed the metropolitan planning organization, which planned and allocated millions of federal transportation dollars each year for roads or transit.

The Mormon Church—known locally by its abbreviation, "LDS" (Latter-Day Saints)—also lent quiet but significant support.[4] In countless face-to-face meetings, Grow and others assured civic and religious leaders that having a "conversation" about the region's future was in the best of Utah traditions—an expression of congregational life in the form of reflection and action—and not a disguised effort to foist particular policy ideas on local communities.

Supporting Grow was a small core staff team that included former state legislator and environmental advocate Stephen Holbrook. Holbrook would be executive director from the launch of Envision Utah in 1997 until 2004, and a broad array of observers affirm that Holbrook's political judgment and nationwide contacts complemented Grow's contributions and those of chairs to follow. Honorary cochairs Governor Leavitt and Larry Miller, owner of the region's professional basketball team, provided additional public- and private-sector standing to Envision Utah at the outset, and state-government involvement included a major commitment of staff resources for demographic and economic analysis. Leavitt would later become one of the longest-serving U.S. governors of his era, bringing what one official called "a passion for the productive middle, acting as a moderate, bringing the right and left together."

Envision Utah's official kickoff, at a press conference and meeting of invited "partners" on January 14, 1997, reflected a savvy about local symbols that would become one of the initiative's trademarks. An actor, dressed as Brigham Young, the founder of Mormon Utah and the area's first territorial governor, addressed the gathering and, through the press, the public at large. "Young" reminded the audience of his strong support for community planning—support that organized the Mormon pioneers into well-defined settlements and produced the town plan and street grid that defines Salt Lake City to this day. This was the beginning of a long, and by many measures successful, campaign to reconnect planning—in the sense that Howell Baum (1997) has defined it, "the organization of hope"—to strong local traditions and values. Peter Calthorpe and John Fregonese, well-known architects and planners linked to a movement of designers known as New Urbanism, also addressed the kick-off gathering, outlining a nationwide interest in finding alternatives to sprawling urban growth. Participants were asked to sign a pledge card affirming that they would put self-interest aside and explore long-range solutions for Utah that reflected the common good—another symbolic act, to be sure, but one that signaled a determination by Envision Utah's lead organizers to quickly place their long-range planning process above the polarizing debates that specific development projects or policies often trigger.

Envision Utah decided to target the ten-county Wasatch Front, where projections placed most future growth in the state (figure 4.1); years later, it would expand to cover the entire state. The Front was vast (23,000 square miles or about the size of Ireland) and also a vast landscape of jurisdictions: 90 cities and towns, over a thousand elected and appointed officials shaping growth policy in those places, and 157 special-purpose agencies to manage water and other resources, transportation investments, and other needs as well. The initiative began official fundraising, gathering support from local governments, leveraging the state's in-kind contribution of analysis, and winning crucial major grants from local and national foundations, to cover staff support, research, and pubic education expenses.[5] The initiative also organized its core participants into steering, public awareness, and technical committees and commissioned a major "values survey" of the region's residents—a survey that would inform Envision Utah's approach to engagement, its public awareness campaigns, and later its focus on the provision of "tools" to support local-government pursuit of unfamiliar approaches to land use.

Observers of politics have long underscored the power of values, and of efforts to represent and "claim" public values, to shape voting, public comment on policy decisions, protest action, and other forms of political behavior. Over the past decade, the theory and practice of negotiation and dispute resolution have highlighted, more specifically, the importance of distinguishing values from interests (Forester 1999). While the latter represent our specific understandings of *what we want*, or think we want, in a given situation where a decision looms, and while interests may be shaped over time through framing and deliberation, values are deeper, more abstract principles that help define *who we are*. Because we experience values as part of our identities, perceived attacks on values, or perceived indifference to them, can all too easily be seen as attacks on, or denial of, our selves, our very worldview and sense of what is valuable or right.[6]

Envision Utah selected Wirthlin Worldwide, a firm with a track record of political research for major political figures in Europe and America, to conduct the values survey. "Their approach is 'persuade with reason, motivate with emotion,'" recalls Robert Grow. Envision Utah determined to make a campaign of public awareness building and engagement center on Utahns' most important shared values, which the survey identified, in a sophisticated hierarchy of concerns, as personal security, accomplishment, self-esteem, and freedom (figure 4.3). Not only would Envision Utah use this to build and sustain a constituency for planning on contentious issues, but this values framework would help tame the complexity of the issues by connecting planning discussions to concrete things that the region's inhabitants valued: time with family, community responsibility, personal safety, and so on.

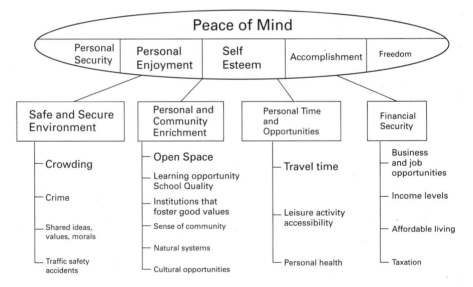

Figure 4.3
Envision Utah Values Survey diagram. The survey generated a hierarchy of public concerns that became the initiative's touchstone for public engagement and awareness campaigns. *Source:* Envision Utah, data by Wirthlin Worldwide, May 1997

Organizers quickly highlighted and repeated, at every opportunity, another special feature of the regional context: Utah has the nation's highest birth rate, and two-thirds of the Wasatch region's projected growth was natural increase.[7] Utahns would be planning first and foremost for their children's and grandchildren's future, not that of newcomer migrants to the area.

While raising funds and gathering these data to guide the process, Envision Utah began to actively pursue opportunities to put quality growth and the aims of the community engagement process in the news. The initiative's leadership was extraordinarily sensitive to the need to distinguish the process from "government planning" and "growth management," and yet the initial news coverage, which intensified later in 1997 when Envision Utah organized community workshops to engage the public in assessing growth alternatives, reflected uncertainties about the initiative's identity and its real aims. In a single month, for example— May 1998—the *Salt Lake Tribune*, the area's largest daily, described Envision Utah as a "long-term planning advocacy group"[8] on the one hand, emphasizing support of a process and of the need to plan, and as a "statewide growth management think tank,"[9] emphasizing expertise in, and perhaps suggesting a position on, the issue of growth "management," with its largely regulatory and negative connotation.

But as this first phase segued to the public process that would make Envision Utah much more visible and controversial, the initiative had accomplished several things: established itself as an intermediary (a convener and framer of important public issues), distanced the aim of planning from government authority yet ensured vital technical expertise and the active engagement of elected officials as experts on constituent concerns, and engaged the most likely private-sector opponents—the developers and homebuilders who, a quarter-century earlier, had snuffed out Utah's only other attempt to find an alternative to sprawling growth.

Framing Alternatives and Testing Support

Supported by professional architects and urban planners, the first round of Envision Utah workshops, launched and widely advertised in May 1998, used classic techniques in participatory design: employing visuals, including photographs, to gauge community preferences (Sanoff 1999). The strategy is to focus on end outcomes that people value, not particular development projects or technical planning concepts. The *Tribune* reported:

Figure 4.4
Political cartoon. Early criticism of Envision Utah focused on the legitimacy of
its approach. Reprinted with permission from the *Utah Standard-Examiner*

Envision Utah's first week of community workshops started with a question:
How should a Wasatch Front and Back with 5 million people look and feel in
2050? It ended with a more basic question: How to get the 1.6 million people
already here to agree? . . . If one truth emerged from the first round of community
meetings, it is that even if most people agree suburban sprawl must be slowed,
some folks still like living in suburbs with big yards and big garages.[10]

Public criticism began that Envision Utah was not a neutral convener
at all—that the organization preferred a compact and walkable form of
development and had begun, after two rounds of workshops in 1998, to
inappropriately attribute this preference to a divided public (figure 4.4).
The media highlighted a gap that would persist for years to come:
between support that residents might express in principle, at long-range
planning meetings, and what they would support in the near term in the
way of development specifics, especially in small towns on the metropolitan fringe. For example, when residents in the semirural town of
Farmington rejected compact development as the Envision Utah workshops continued around the region, the *Tribune* reported that

the theory that Utahns are willing to live closer together to preserve vast open
spaces from development is taking a beating in west Farmington. Neighbors who
loathed a [developer's] plan to build more than 500 tightly clustered homes in a
pasture . . . have persuaded the developer to spread the homes over more of the
property and increase the lot sizes. It is a triumph of horseback suburbs over
"walkable communities," which Wasatch Front residents are telling planners

they want. "Who says we need to cram everybody into one place?" asked Tonna Bounds . . . who led the push for larger lots. "People come here because they want a piece of U.S.A., and that does not consist of a 5-foot backyard."[11]

And the *Tribune* editorial commented,

Clearly, the jury remains very much out when it comes to views about how best to accommodate growth. Planners, urban engineers and citizens favoring alternative scenarios should continue to disseminate their ideas to as wide a public as possible, but at the same time, avoid making assumptions about what citizens prefer.[12]

Echoing what local elected officials would tell me in interviews some six years after the Envision Utah visioning process, Flint (2006, 191) writes about this opposition to more compact living that "density is all that is cramped and unhealthy and somehow un-American about urbanism. Being free from density is associated with moving up in the world. . . . Density even sounds like a bad word, to be said with distaste, like 'pollution' or 'congestion.' "

Robert Grow and the core supporters and representatives of Envision Utah continued to face suspicion from elected officials as well. Many remained wary, and some were vocal about it. Jerry Stevenson, mayor of Layton City and later a strong supporter and chair of the effort, was one early critic. "Maybe with Envision Utah, I haven't quite caught the 'envision' yet," he would tell the press in September. "I'm a firm believer in economics, and a lot of what's happening [in the region] is economics-driven."[13]

"The market determines how many homes get built," concedes Dan Lofgren, a real estate developer who has long been active in Envision Utah and served as its vice chair, "but the public gets to determine where they get built. The market wanted variety—starter homes, townhomes, affordability—but local land use policy wasn't letting it happen. So this [planning process] was a major opportunity for us to educate builders, elected officials, others." Lofgren also stresses the importance of a long time horizon: "The magic of getting me [a real estate developer] to sit down next to a conservationist and . . . find common ground because my livelihood and his position on a development project aren't at stake and we can talk about a future we both want—for these mountains to be available to everyone, for our kids to own homes and be able to find jobs in this community."[14]

Beyond the long time horizon, Grow, Holbrook, and the other organizers insisted on giving participants in the planning process concrete tasks: responding to images, using paper chips (like pieces on a game board) to determine development types, on a map, that would accommodate another million people in twenty years. "You have to give people something tangible to do," comments Holbrook, "not set up an abstract conversation. We tried to move from philosophizing to problem-solving." At the center of the process were the "table talks," wherein about ten stakeholders worked to generate consensus on how to accomplish these specific tasks. "A churchleader might be sitting next to a mayor, real estate developer, and environmentalist," notes Holbrook. The table talks reflect what researchers Cornwall and Gaventa (2001) have described as part of a larger shift, worldwide, from *information exchange* models of citizen engagement to *processing* models, wherein citizens deal directly with the tough trade-offs faced by policy makers. Based on a two-stage engagement process—the first stage focused on *where* to grow in the region (in built-up areas versus undeveloped lands), the second on *how* (form)—Envision Utah began to report strong community support for "infill" development over new growth on undeveloped lands, walkable neighborhoods over heavy reliance on automobiles, and strong protection of "critical lands."

Based on public input and a baseline growth scenario generated by state government staff, Envision Utah staff and its consultants also worked hard, in 1997 and 1998, to develop alternative long-range scenarios for the region, having studied scenario development in long-range visioning done by other city-regions, including Denver, Minneapolis, Phoenix, and Portland.[15] Like the citizen table talks, the scenario developers had a clear task: to show distinct ways that one million more people could be accommodated in the region by the year 2020. But unlike the intimate face-to-face gatherings, the scenarios had to earn standing as legitimate knowledge in the eyes of the public—a factor consensus-building experts have outlined as fundamental to policy making (Andrews 2002; Ehrman and Stinson 1999).

Envision Utah publicly released four long-run development scenarios, emphasizing the neutral and deliberative process followed by state planning staff to make crucial assumptions about the future, on November 14, 1998. The four included the status quo, highly dispersed growth pattern projected forward (Scenario A), slightly less dispersed development that would obtain if all existing local plans were followed (B), a compact alternative with significant transit expansion and more walkable neighborhoods (C), and a still more compact fourth scenario (D).

The state's projections showed that beyond significantly reducing new land consumption, C could save taxpayers and developers over $15 billion in infrastructure costs. The stage was set, and a major campaign of public education and unofficial voting, to test support for each scenario, began. The process had evolved beyond gathering preferences, informing people's intuitions about where unplanned growth would lead the region, and "crunching" numbers—into a discussion about choosing a specific vision of the future and figuring out how to realize it. Grow and others continued to avoid mention of near-term implementation choices, as skeptics—and some supporters—pushed for specifics on where the planning exercise would lead. He told the *Tribune*, "Once you say how you're going to implement this, you blow away two-thirds of the people who aren't involved." But a real estate developer argued, echoing other critics, "Envision Utah needs to be charged with coming up with specific legislation to implement their findings."[16]

The contention persisted, as the substance of the scenarios and the context for their use was debated. In January 1999, the *Tribune* observed that Envision Utah was "wading through public confusion and political name-calling in its quest for policies to curb urban sprawl" and that it "struggled to remind residents that if they want big yards and extra cars, the group would not stand in their way."[17] Community workshops, said the newspaper, gave residents a chance to vote on "hypothetical futures" but also "brought out the skeptics who fear the whole exercise is a government plot to end the suburban good life." At the national level, Vice President Al Gore, a well-known environmentalist and a Democrat preparing to run for president in 2000, had proposed a $10 billion "smart growth" initiative that drew attention in the region, in large part because of Envision Utah.[18]

Some 17,500 of the 580,000 newspaper inserts mailed by Envision Utah and also made available online—each providing a readable description of the four scenarios and a mailer to return the reader's unofficial "vote"—were completed.[19] The governor had called this voting a "citizen obligation," and local media editorialized on behalf of the survey as well. Some critics contended that the scenarios were oversimplified and also constructed to most favorably portray the compact alternatives. Meanwhile, efforts to demonize the "quality growth" concept, as well as the Envision Utah process, failed to gain momentum—even when a fierce national debate made "smart growth" and Gore's proposals a target for attack. "We had our run of the anti–smart growth people," recalls a state official, "and they flew in national speakers and so on. But Grow and the others had built too broad a base."

In March, Envision Utah released its survey results, announcing that Scenario C—a moderately compact alternative to sprawl—was the public favorite, chosen by about 56 percent of respondents on its own or in combination with D, an even more compact alternative that analysts projected would lower air quality.[20] The initiative acknowledged that the response rate was but 3 percent (not unusual for a mail-in survey) and the respondents a self-selected group who tended to be more affluent and educated than the regional average. But based on a carefully conducted, statistically representative follow-up poll of the region, independent analysis showed that the mail-in's preferred choice was valid and that adjusting for respondents' demographic traits did not change the result.[21] Envision Utah immediately signaled the importance of ongoing public engagement to choose specific growth strategies consistent with the new vision, and press coverage was positive.

From Vision to Strategy and Implementation

Thus far, Envision Utah had recruited skeptics and potential opponents, held off challenges to become an advocacy organization with a specific policy agenda, and completely upended the traditional approach to public planning in the state of Utah—distancing citizen engagement from government authority, challenging participants to make choices that reflected real trade-offs and competing objectives, shifting the focus from near-term development decisions to long-run outcomes and their implications, and emphasizing the relevance of long-range planning—and its literally "big" ideas—to the core values and everyday experiences of local people. As the U.S. Senate's Smart Growth Task Force began hearings in March 1999, Envision Utah became its first case study, and a senior staff member told the press that the initiative's "method of using resident involvement instead of government mandates is the type of solution the 23 senators are looking for."[22]

But what the task force may have missed was the initiative's extraordinary two-level strategy, targeting the grasstops *and* grassroots, so to speak: Envision Utah had not begun with broad public outreach. It had "political legs" because of its savvy recruitment of influentials, including likely opponents. The initiative had secured, acted on, and sustained a mandate to do grassroots community engagement for the purpose of consensus building, in effect to create a public for a bold public idea. Part coalition backing that idea (quality growth) and part civic intermediary enabling an atypical dialogue, Envision Utah had, more tangibly, developed well-researched scenarios (possible futures) and tested public support for them—a process that no elected body had been willing or able to do in the state's history.

The challenge now was helping the region's many interest groups and centers of influence to actually move in concert with a new vision—to outgrow sprawl. As a representative of the Utah League of Cities and Towns observed in March 1999, "Envision Utah has done a fine job of identifying the costs of sprawl and getting a consensus that people want something different for the region as a whole, but it is more difficult to get people to embrace change in their own neighborhoods."[23] In this final section of the case, I examine Envision Utah's challenges and choices beyond the regional visioning phase, including its reinvention as an intermediary: from consensus builder to capacity builder and public educator.

In April 1999, soon after results of the unofficial scenario "vote" were made public, Robert Grow, the initiative's charismatic and widely respected founding chair, stepped down and was succeeded by Jon Huntsman Jr. A businessman and former diplomat, Huntsman struck a reassuring tone, telling the press that Envision Utah was "an educational tool drawing on the views of thousands rather than a heavy-handed government program. This is one of the greatest exercises in democracy I've ever seen. No one can claim this is centralized planning or Big Brother stepping in."[24] Indeed, quality growth principles, though linked to the Envision Utah "brand" and supported by a broad base of the region's most influential people, had no force of law, for the organization had no formal authority. Voters and their local elected officials would accept or reject the application of new growth ideas to their communities, a feature that significantly strengthens the consensus-building effort's claim to legitimacy and accountability. Though skeptics and critics remained, in July, an independent, good-government policy research group hired by Envision Utah to assess its planning process defended its transparency, the quality of its scenarios, and the initiative's respect for market forces against claims of a regulatory heavy hand or predetermined solutions hidden behind a show of public participation.[25]

Huntsman would later campaign on his service to Envision Utah and win the governorship in 2004. Together with Envision Utah's staff director, Stephen Holbrook, and its steering committee of influential business and civic leaders, Huntsman reinvented the initiative over the next few years, launching a second major phase of community engagement and creating new relationships with government at both the state and local levels. The result of the first effort was a Quality Growth Strategy focused on six core goals: enhance air quality, increase mobility and transportation choices, preserve critical lands, conserve water resources, provide wider housing opportunities, and make more cost-effective public investments in the infrastructure to support growth.

As for the second effort, where previously the governor's support had primarily been that of the bully pulpit and data analysis, the state became a direct financial supporter of local-government efforts to pursue quality growth and exchange planning lessons. Governor Leavitt and allies in the state legislature had just won passage of the Quality Growth Act of 1999, which called for the creation of a state commission to study growth patterns, identify "quality growth areas," and make recommendations about providing state-level incentives to cities and towns willing to focus development in those areas. Notably, the act, though it specifically emphasized land conservation, "efficient use of land," and "housing availability," also expressly forbade regulatory action by the state.[26] The act offered the carrots without the sticks, and a range of observers credited Envision Utah with making it possible for state government to step forward on the growth issue.[27]

A newly formed state commission included several core participants if the initiative, and the commission would work closely with Envision Utah, in subsequent years, to recognize exemplary local-government efforts and fund local planning. Budget cutbacks during recession would soon eliminate the planning grants, and some observers worried that some of the grants had gone to "pet projects" of particular legislators and not to important planning efforts with broad community support. Yet the Quality Growth Act gave state government a politically safe way to promote quality growth as a viable and increasingly tangible alternative to sprawl.

Between 1999 and 2001, Envision Utah worked to develop a set of planning tools, drawing on national models for transferring land development rights, creating "transit-oriented development," and more. The tools were to suit the region's topography and politics, all within the quality growth framework. Envision Utah unveiled a planning "toolbox" in 2000 and promoted it widely. Still avoiding the role of policy advocate, the initiative targeted two crucial stakeholders—local governments and real estate developers—facilitating demonstration projects, assisting with analysis, leading annual public awareness campaigns focused on one or more of the component principles of quality growth, and running its trademark community workshops in key cities and towns facing growth pressure—but only when invited to do so by a local mayor.

In June 2001, the *Tribune* reported that the initiative had "completed its transformation from a regional agenda-setting group to a tool for cities and builders,"[28] citing the appointment of Greg Bell, a former mayor, to succeed Huntsman as the initiative's third chair. "Utah posted the nation's fourth-fastest percentage growth in the 1990s," said the newspaper, and "the shift . . . to a mayor and former planning commissioner signals the 5-year-old group's new emphasis on helping cities and developers implement new ideas about smart growth." But the effort had not abandoned public education, recognizing the need for a credibly independent, nonpartisan effort to continue building a constituency to encourage local-government experimentation with new approaches.

Envision Utah also moved quickly to pursue major demonstration projects, from innovative county-level growth plans to major housing or "mixed-use" developments (that combine housing, retail, and community facilities) to create more walkable neighborhoods. The region's historic role as a mining center would offer a new and unforeseen opportunity. An environmentally savvy, London-based multinational company directed its local subsidiary to form a land-development company and explore innovative options for developing the company's vast land holdings in the Salt Lake Valley—at 93,000 acres, an estimated 50 percent of the developable land in the area. Noting the consistency between Envision Utah's quality growth principles and the parent company's approach, Kennecott Land became actively involved in the pursuit of growth alternatives in the region. "In mining, we've learned that how you treat the land and the community gets heard around the world," the company's president, Peter McMahon, told me.

For its flagship real estate project, Daybreak, Kennecott asked New Urbanist designer Peter Calthorpe to return to the Salt Lake Valley. At buildout, Kennecott's holdings will comprise a new, planned city, with perhaps 160,000 homes—"the largest quality growth development in the world," says Robert Grow, or what the *Washington Post* called a "megasuburb, twice the size of San Francisco."[29] But as a long-run regional demonstration, the project faces the challenges associated with winning local clearances and responding to market demand. Observers cite Daybreak as a triumph and opportunity for Envision Utah but also as a window on the dilemmas intrinsic to its current role: When and how should it advocate, beyond educating and facilitating, to make things happen?

A local developer stresses the initiative's informal role as a catalyst of support in lieu of traditional lobbying: "Envision Utah even offered to come out for or against us [informally], whatever would help." He adds, "People in small towns [here] love coming together to do a vision. But they don't want it built if it seems to threaten the status quo." Old habits die hard, and Envision Utah had its new work—adoption of quality growth at the local level—cut out for it. But the effort had "broadened people's conception of what demand is here," says this developer, highlighting the need for a wider variety of housing types. He adds that the local real estate developers association had offered to "take the heat" on controversial issues to "help Envision Utah protect its brand." Other "demonstrations" have helped. Quality growth got a boost in 2002, when Salt Lake City hosted the Winter Olympics. The city offered visitors Trax, a newly built light rail system that quickly exceeded projected ridership levels. An effort to place rail funding on the ballot had failed in the early 1990s, yet after Envision Utah's planning process and public education announcements, the measure passed in 2000. Here, in the land of large lots and resistance to traditional planning, localities actually began to clamor for new transit stops, according to transportation planners and media observers.

In May 2003, a Wirthlin survey commissioned by Envision Utah showed that 62 percent of the region's residents remained unfamiliar with the initiative *by name*. However, 68 percent of those who were familiar with it approved of its efforts to "create walkable neighborhoods, expand mass transit choices, and preserve open space," and 72 percent of those who were unfamiliar with the initiative approved of the efforts when told of its goals.[30] Moreover, 76 percent reported a positive view of Trax, and 88 percent favored expanding it. Local media widely credited Envision Utah with the success of a voter-approved quarter-cent sales tax increase to support transit development. A large majority of survey respondents also favored a wider housing mix to accommodate different age groups (75 percent) and income levels (80 percent)—a domain in which Envision Utah had campaigned, as I previewed in the previous chapter, with images and a narrative emphasizing "your own children and grandchildren" and schoolteachers, police officers, and other public servants.

A linked survey of hundreds of local officials indicated that all had heard of Envision Utah, more than 96 percent were aware of its Quality Growth Strategy and planning tools, over 94 percent were in cities or towns that had sent a staff member to Envision Utah trainings, and over

60 percent said their jurisdiction had used the planning tools. Some were the "converts"—early critics of the effort, local elected officials in particular, that I interviewed about how and why quality growth proponents had reassured them (the skeptics) about the movement's goals and the promise of voter education and support. Envision Utah reported that over 2,000 local officials, developers, realtors, and others had attended the initiative's trainings on the use of quality growth planning tools.

Not everyone had come around. One small-town mayor on the exurban fringe of the Salt Lake Valley told me, for example, that he and his voter base still associated Envision Utah with the bane of density—an "urban" lifestyle—and with it a host of urban problems such as crowding and crime that they were determined to avoid. At the time, that town had dug in its heels in the face of new real estate demand, insisting on large, ranchlike lots for all new homes.

Yet as I completed my fieldwork in the region in early 2004, some seven years into the Envision Utah initiative, its staff was actively engaged in planning key growth corridors around the region and partnering with metropolitan transportation planners to better integrate long-range transportation plans and investments with land-use plans for quality growth. "Government fragments these functions," comments Robert Grow, who remains involved, "but we brought these 'silos' together." The initiative's positive reputation now made it a sought-after partner for public agencies with major planning responsibilities tied to regional growth. The Envision Utah leadership was supporting efforts to study growth effects of state and local tax policy—a very politically charged issue throughout America—and considering ways to respond to new top-of-mind public concerns about a weaker job economy and the challenges facing public education.

With its major philanthropic funding exhausted, the initiative was also working to become financially sustainable in its role as capacity builder for local governments without competing with private firms for government contracts. And some observers, particularly minority advocates, were calling for more attention by Envision Utah to the region's growing ethnic diversity—a diversity just starting to appear in the initiative's leadership, which remains centered on the region's top businesspeople and established civic influentials. A prominent real estate developer offered a broader assessment of the initiative's status vis-à-vis its original, ambitious goals: "We have to resist the temptation to declare victory. We need to institutionalize it somehow. We still have people to persuade."

As this book went to press, there were more and more signs of the quality growth movement's impact. Several large Utah counties have adopted, in their long-range plans, core elements of the quality growth strategies, including major land set-asides for conservation and transfer of development rights authority. And in 2006, the regional council that plans and allocates major investments of federal transportation dollars— now led by strong Envision Utah supporters, both elected and appointed— adopted an aggressive ten-year plan to add three light rail lines, as well as a major commuter rail line, to the popular Trax system.

Summary and Implications

Dilemmas of urban growth spotlight the essence of civic capacity as a resource: the capacity to solve problems together in a shared place. As respected Western environmentalist and former mayor Daniel Kemmis (1990, 7) writes, "The strengthening of political culture, and the reclaiming of a vital and effective sense of what it is to be public, must take place and must be studied in the context of very specific places and of the people who struggle to live well in such places."

In this case, I have focused closely on Envision Utah's origins, choices, and timing—not primarily to provide an account of savvy political management but to offer a view of building and using civic capacity that goes beyond very broad structural accounts, including overviews of the rapidly evolving collaborative forms of resource management that Kemmis (2001) and others have highlighted as hallmarks of a new politics in the American West.[31]

First, the Utah context represents an extreme illustration of how inadequate the popular vote and issue-based lobbying are to leading significant change on a contentious public problem. The coalition's early recruitment of political insiders, not its subsequent efforts to engage the grassroots public and those with private interests in urban growth, represents the first key to developing and acting on a shared agenda of change. This was achieved in spite of deep divides, mutual suspicion between opposing viewpoints, and a political culture unfriendly to regional planning. These features suggest an embedded view of the real promise of consensus-building approaches advocated for managing sprawling growth (e.g., Innes and Gruber 1994; Susskind and Gensberg 2002). Consensus-building approaches demand a wider civic strategy if they are to shift the agenda, constituent support, and results "on the ground"—and not simply resolve disputes over a single development project or forge a policy framework on a complex, multifaceted issue such as urban growth. As for significant learning, the broad approach to consensus building in Utah has a real claim to "dramatic changes over time in the distribution of beliefs" (Jenkins-Smith and Sabatier 1993), both of core coalition members, other influentials, and the initially change-resistant public at large. I return to this in the next chapter's comparative summary.

Second, an early willingness to do broad-based consensus building gave Envision Utah, a fledgling intermediary organization with ties to government but no formal authority, legitimacy as well as influence (reach). It is difficult to imagine that any business, government, or non-profit interest group, leading on its own, could have achieved so much "soft power," and with it political reach, in the Utah context. It was not clear, based on a wide range of interviews with elected officials, public and private planners, journalists, environmental advocates, and others, and on extensive media and report review, that Envision Utah had shrunk from any of the major challenges associated with regional growth and its implications—only that the group carefully managed public percep-tions, especially on the most controversial issues such as taxation, and constantly looked for ways to enhance its legitimacy and broaden its base of support through visible projects.

Third, the keys to agenda setting and development of a specific menu of policy choices included a determined early focus on long time hori-zons, an emphasis on public learning about growth choices, and atten-tion to the trade-offs implied in policy making—the more ambitious processing model of public engagement, not simple information exchange, to use Cornwall and Gaventa's distinction, and an essential part of active citizenship. But a consistent effort to link big ideas to traditional values, to the symbols of a Mormon pioneer culture, and to everyday life experi-ences was also key. This approach applied to structured public gatherings as well as to savvy and well-researched public awareness campaigns.

Fourth, having skipped back and forth across the public-private divide—a blurred boundary between quite interdependent institutions in this case—the movement for quality growth in Utah managed to reinvent itself, stage by stage, via the leadership and operational strategy of its influential intermediary organization. As a focal point of civic capacity, Envision Utah has shown an extraordinary commitment to achieving purpose, by adapting without surrendering trademark functions. The succession of chairs and focus of activities reflected this role shift, this evolving to meet priority needs as they emerged: retaining a consensus-building, leadership-level table for dialogue but also working "in the trenches" with local elected officials and planning staffs as a capacity builder and public educator as well.

This evolution went beyond agenda setting or traditional policy advocacy, then. It captures the coproduction of change that is a hallmark of effective collaboration, and this plays an even bigger role in the India case I examine in the next chapter. In Utah, this approach reflects a deep appreciation of the market's dual role as a *validator* of public support for growth alternatives (a cultural logic) and as a *production device*—in particular, a generator of demonstrations that connect abstract policy and planning ideas to tangible outcomes that can inform the next round of deliberation about the future.

Focused on the roles and capacities of intermediary institutions in public problem solving, table 4.1 captures these linked aspects of legitimacy, influence, and institutional reinvention or adaptation to changing circumstances. It poses a wide array of possibilities, as well as daunting choices, for civic entrepreneurs. With multiple roles come the risk of role conflict and confusion, of sending mixed signals or creating inappropriate expectations. But depending on how well key civic roles are being performed, if they are being performed at all, in particular settings, civic intermediaries have multiple opportunities to focus attention, forge relationships, and broker resources—and to win or lose support from other players.

Fifth, as for democratic accountability and legitimacy, local governments have retained decision-making authority over land use, making the pursuit of growth alternatives a sometimes adversary slog from the advocate's standpoint—what one insider terms "an evolution, not a revolution, of thought"—but providing the movement for quality growth with a very strong claim of accountability to voters. As Susskind and Gensberg (2002) note, this accountability is crucial if consensus-building approaches to contentious issues are to be more widely applied, and a common misperception is that multistakeholder consensus building is a substitute for, rather than an extension of, established institutions of representative democracy. As the next chapter will explore in greater depth, multiple forms of accountability underlie the Utahn and Indian efforts to tackle problems of growth with and beyond the instrument of government. Understanding these multiple forms is particularly important when one's focus is broader than small, face-to-face problem-solving groups or public-private ecosystem management institutions on which environmental researchers have focused (e.g., Weber 2003)—that is, when the focus extends to the very public that not only helps decide

Table 4.1
Civic intermediaries: Problems, roles and capacities

Civic problem or need	Potential go-between roles/niches	Capacities required
Civic process and knowledge problems: real or perceived conflicts among stakeholders, impasse, information breakdowns (data gaps and discrepancies, risk and uncertainty), missing or frayed relationships.	Facilitator and public educator. Educating stakeholders and the public (about other stakeholders, substantive issues and stakes, and options for action), being a data clearinghouse, building and mending relationships, mediating disputes, designing and managing joint problem-solving processes.	Group facilitation and public event management, stakeholder and issue analysis, negotiation and dispute resolution, strategic planning, data and information systems management, public communication, social marketing.
Operational capacity problems: missing capacity, poorly structured or deployed capacity (duplication, fragmentation of effort, "stovepiping").	Coordinator and capacity builder. Coaching and training, developing organizations, coordinating.	Operations management, training, organizational development, strategic planning, program design and evaluation.
Performance and accountability problems: inconsistent or underdeveloped standards, inadequate measures of what other players can do, lack of trust in their competence or approach, insufficient capacity to measure and report back.	Performance investor and monitor. Screening and validating resource seekers, matching donors with recipients, pooling and distributing funds, helping players to define credible performance targets and consequences for non-performance, as well as performance incentives.	Performance measurement and management, evaluation, operations management, management information systems, financial management.
Legitimacy and political support problems: missing or incomplete mandate to act, uneven support among diverse stakeholders, disenfranchised stakeholders.	Organizer. Identifying stakeholder groups and helping them to organize, facilitating coalitions and "building movement," persuasive framing of "the state of the world," engaging media and public figures, helping advocates to develop capacity.	Political organizing and advocacy, data analysis, policy and program design, public communication, negotiation and dispute resolution, training, organizational development.

policy and devise a collective strategy but also implements or undermines it through countless everyday choices about what to consume, where and how to live, and how to use the vote and other forms of pressure politics.

Sixth and finally, the case illustrates how the dialectic of learning and bargaining can be shaped and managed to do significant problem solving. As social learning, the process of using and extending civic capacity to manage rapid urban growth in Utah brought new values, institutions, and options to light, both through small-scale citizen engagement and leadership-level consensus building and through large-scale public education campaigns. The still-early signs are that the process may have shifted public preferences in the region, too, both for alternatives to sprawl and approaches to governing growth, as well as consumer choices about transportation, the physical form of communities and housing types, and more. As bargaining, the process built a broad coalition of interests to back and defend long-range planning (reassuring potential adversaries of their place at the table) and worked informally to deploy the influence of civic leaders in ways that made space for controversial ideas. The process also consistently defended the importance of local decision-making venues, where the details of urban development are still negotiated project by project—now with powerful new growth options, a quality growth frame of reference, and a broader set of growth-related interests in play.

The case suggests, then, not only how learning and bargaining strategies can be sequenced but how the two bring different forms of accountability into play in democratic politics—on the one hand a long-view adherence to deep values and the experimentation on task that is intrinsic to good problem solving, on the other the give-and-take of well-defined interests, in the context of electoral representation and interest-group lobbying, where shorter-run trade-offs must be faced and judgments rendered on particular policies or projects.

5

The Grassroots-to-Grasstops Dynamic: Slum Redevelopment and Accountability in Mumbai

There will soon be more people in the city of Bombay than on the continent of Australia. . . . Bombay is the future of urban civilization on the planet. God help us.

—Suketu Mehta, *Maximum City* (2004)

I am in Dharavi, Mumbai's largest slum and, with a population estimated at one million people, perhaps the largest on earth. I am seated on the floor of a one-story building near one of Dharavi's dirt entrance roads. So are the two women, in brightly colored saris, who welcome me, via an interpreter, right before pulling out their cell phones. There is a brisk order to the room, which is the local headquarters of the Dharavi Development Committee, a community group affiliated with the National Slum dwellers Federation and *Mahila Milan* (Hindi for "women together"), a network of small-scale "savings groups" now established in slums across India. On the walls are a chalk-written record of members' weekly savings plus a dozen or more news clippings. One clipping covers a recent visit to Dharavi by Prince Charles, another the city's booming real estate market, now—as of February 2004—more lucrative, in terms of return on investment, than the property markets of London, New York, or Zurich. I am in a city of stunning extremes. Sitting here, I calculate that it would take the average member of Mahila Milan some two months to save what I spent this morning, in my hotel's business center, for just two hours of Internet time to stay in touch with my office back in America.

I am here to visit the Rajiv-Indira Housing Cooperative, made up of slum dwellers who have, with help from a Mumbai-based nongovernmental organization (NGO), leveraged their own savings with debt funding from a global financial institution and an innovative international British philanthropy to obtain state government housing assistance to which they are entitled. But just before we leave this room and walk past the shanty homes and bustling home-based enterprises, I learn something more: the two women are building contractors. They are part of an emerging network that any corporate strategist would recognize and admire: a horizontally and vertically integrated chain that not only organizes slumdwellers to secure resources from public and private sources but pools and leverages their own funding, designs durable and functional low-cost homes with and for slum dwellers, shares financial risk with the public and private sectors, documents innovations with models transmitted worldwide, leads peer-to-peer trainings and exchanges on three continents, and builds as much of the new housing and basic infrastructure as possible with slumdwellers' own labor. The last point is the giveaway: *I have just been welcomed to Dharavi by two entrepreneurs, two "start-ups," on the move.*

Rajiv-Indira is a small but impressive part of a larger story, one rich in civic puzzles. In the public-sector dimension alone, the story combines a dramatic shift in the economic policies of the Indian government; fierce party politics that have—for more than a decade—centered on Hindu nationalism and xenophobia toward the city's Muslim minority and often led to violent conflicts; a political patronage machine with many slums targeted as "vote banks"; and a large and entrenched bureaucracy that fumbled at many of the tasks of slum redevelopment and struggled, because of graft as well as incompetence, to win trust from citizens, especially the urban poor.

In the civil-society dimension, the story belies simple assumptions about people's organizations, power, capacity, or links to government. Community groups organized as accountable "federations" by slum dwellers themselves have allied with NGOs staffed largely by middle-class professionals and even launched what some are calling a "transnational network" of federations—Shack/Slum Dwellers International—connecting local networks in Asia, Africa, and Latin America. According to many observers, the most highly developed arrangement here in India, and perhaps in the world, is a cooperative relationship of three institutions known to its members simply as the Alliance. For the Alliance, says anthropologist Arjun Appadurai (2001, 29), "The politics . . . is a politics of accommodation, negotiation and long-term pressure rather than of confrontation or threats of political reprisal." But it was not always so, and party politics, market shifts, and other shocks constantly challenge the Alliance and other civil-society networks working to tackle the uneven growth that has made Mumbai the world capital of slums.

Finally, in the private sector, as countless billboards around town remind visitors and residents alike, this is the era of "India Rising." With dramatic deregulation and other liberalization reforms coming out of India's late-1980s financial crisis, and with information technology, film, and other sectors booming from global as well as domestic demand, the Indian economy has, in recent years, enjoyed one of the highest growth rates in the world. This growth makes for frequent comparisons with neighboring China, the other "tiger" economy with a billion-plus population and rapid urbanization.[1] The Indian stock market is surging and so is consumer demand from the rapidly expanding middle and upper classes.[2] Yet more than 80 percent of the country gets by on $2 per day, according to UN statistics. Many hopes rest on Mumbai, India's largest city, the center of its massive media and entertainment industry ("Bollywood"), and a major financial, educational, and IT hub for the nation and the wider region.

In the early 2000s, Bombay First, a consensus-building and planning group of top businesses, worked with the prestigious international consulting firm McKinsey and Company to produce a high-profile report, *Vision Mumbai*, showing how poorly the city's infrastructure and land use lag behind those of competitor urban economies, such as Shanghai, and offering recommendations for "transforming Mumbai into a world-class city" over a decade of major targeted investments.[3] Now underway are projects to dramatically expand rail capacity and speed and to modernize the airport, part of what the British newsmagazine *The Economist* has described as a "$40 billion, ten-year make-over."[4] But in a long and linear Manhattan-like city built up across seven islands (figure 5.1), with outdated land and building regulations, a patchwork of poorly coordinated public agencies, and revenue and taxation troubles, the fate of such long-range economic plans are inextricably linked to prospects for the estimated half of Mumbai's population that lives in slums.[5]

This symbiotic relationship works on many levels, as the observation about vote banks suggests above. But in terms of the metro region's economic competitiveness, two of the most important levels are labor and transportation infrastructure. From the low end of the professional occupations, or of industrial and commercial enterprises, to the countless "toilers" who work the city's dirtiest and most dangerous jobs—often on a daily or piece-rate basis and without benefits or income security—slums supply the region with a vital workforce, as well as with thousands of small enterprises, inexpensively housed and often well located to buyers, job centers, and transit lines (Appadurai 2001; Bhowmik 2003).

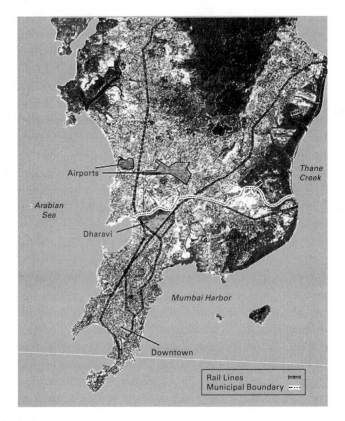

Figure 5.1
Mumbai, city and inner suburbs, highlighting urbanization and transportation
infrastructure, 2000 (enhanced satellite image). *Source*: Landsat ETM.

Infrastructure is, to some extent, the flip side of this coin: slums are
so well located for workers that they lie directly in the path of vital
upgrading and so find themselves in the crosshairs of the citywide make-
over. Until government reconsidered a failed policy of sudden evictions
and began to work with community groups and NGOs on relocation
and resettlement, almost all of the metro region's vital commuter railways—the world's largest, with more than seven million trips per day
(Patel, D'Cruz, and Burra 2002)—as well as many of its major roadways
and even the airport were ringed by squatters' shacks or other makeshift
dwellings. These "encroachments" constrict road traffic, force trains to
slow constantly to protect the encroachers, and also prevent reconstruction of facilities. Efficient railways are especially vital to the region's

future, since they enable the northward growth that is Mumbai's only physical outlet (Patel, D'Cruz, and Burra 2002; also see figure 5.1).[6] But the "noose" of squatter settlements has made any expansion of rail and other transportation lifelines a politically contentious, uncertain, and doubly expensive task. As *The Times of India* asked about one stand-off in Mumbai's near suburbs, "Will the interests of the three million commuters [per day] be able to rid the railway of its encroachers, or will the 20,000-odd hutments continue to hold Mumbai's productivity to ransom?"[7] Viewed simply from the standpoint of its infrastructure, Mumbai, the biggest engine in one of the world's great emerging economies, has been crushed by its lack of attention to the slums and their "place" in the city—literal and figurative—so much so that *Vision Mumbai* has even warned government and business leaders of collapse if the city continues to fall behind competitors.

So how did civic capacity to tackle uneven urban growth emerge here, in the form of extraordinary new cooperation among public, private, and nongovernmental players—cooperation singled out by the United Nations as a model for global progress on slums? And what are the prospects and limits of this capacity?

A History of Failure and Conflict

India urbanized rapidly well before the movement led by Mahatma Ghandi won independence from Britain in 1947. In Mumbai, at the turn of the twentieth century, British-backed growth in textiles, manufacturing, and other industries led to a population boom in what had been a relatively small city of fisherman and traders. Rural migrants fled their economic insecurity as landless tenant farmers and their political powerlessness as members of India's lower castes, and merchants and professionals likewise flocked to the city. Yet after independence, central planners, in what has been described as "four decades of quasi-socialism,"[8] focused on rural development—true to the Gandhian vision that the "real" heart of India lay in its villages and the drive to make them self-sufficient. This left cities to poorly planned and financed growth under a patchwork of public agencies and entrenched municipal commissioners (administrators), with no empowered elected governments in most cities and little capacity to finance or coordinate local development (Mohan 2001). Bureaucratic fiefdoms flourished under a rigidly trained and rule-bound civil service, so much so that discussions of how to revitalize Indian democracy routinely headline the concept of "sensitizing" the bureaucracy. Corruption and inefficiency thwarted government action and eroded public trust, and since local government had limited powers and little fiscal reach, citizens were doubly discouraged from participating actively in local governance (Appadurai 2001; Mohan 2001).

Worldwide, this post-independence period corresponded with a focus, initially, on clearing slums and constructing government-run housing that often functioned disastrously for a growing population of slum dwellers—if they secured units after demolition at all (Sanyal and Mukhija 2001). On a more basic level, demolition did not work: squatters quickly found and occupied other land or some of the same land, whether public or private. Strict limits on building density, price controls on rents, and poorly enforced property rights acted as huge disincentives to private housing investment. In lieu of accountable and responsive government and a well-functioning market, enterprising "slumlords" with patronage ties to bureaucrats and political-party insiders, became the brokers of space, housing, and services. These included, and still include, ration cards for food staples and prized voter registrations that give slum dwellers a small chit to play, as voting clients of their political patrons, in the slums of Mumbai and other cities. Explaining why she would not "pin her hopes on politicians," one slum dweller told the press, "They show up only before an election to tile a gully or repair a broken common-toilet door. And three days after the polls, they all disappear."[9] For all these reasons, the political economy of the slums is a web of advantage taking, side deals, and—for millions of the poorest—of scraping by on the margins.

In this context, the National Slum dwellers Federation (NSDF) was organized, in 1974, to fight for services and housing. Jockin Arputham, its president and cofounder and a slum dweller himself, remembers simply, "We would protest this and that, and win scraps from the table, but nothing ever changed." Yet a foundation for collective action by the urban poor had been laid, with its roots in India's vibrant social movements. New public programs for slum upgrading, rather than clearance, appeared, but outcomes were generally poor, and relationships between government and community groups remained contentious.[10] It was not until 1976, under newly elected Indira Gandhi, that central government recognized any slum dweller rights in India's cities, and her dictatorial approach included unpopular as well as counterproductive housing price controls. Except in the form of corruption and illegal service provision, there were no incentives for business to play a role in slums, certainly not in upgrading or redeveloping them, nor did government engage civil-society groups accountable to the poor themselves in problem solving. The explosive growth of slums in the 1980s meant good business for slumlords, who organized "weekend invasions" of land and sold basic services, through kickback deals with utilities and officials, to a thousand poor families at a time. Media coverage of slum life and upgrading programs generally focused on the stigma of illegality—the slums as a cancer on the city—and on failures of government planning and implementation.

Then, in the mid-1980s, almost everything began to shift.

Crossroads: Changes in Government and Civil-Society Strategy and Capacity

Studies of political change in democratic societies typically focus on the effects of major economic transformations, government restructuring to assume new roles or shift official authority, elected officials and powerful interest groups as "establishment" agenda setters, and periodically, on successful social movements that act as civil society insurgents outside that mainstream, shifting political will and public policy. All of these figure, to some degree, in the changes in Mumbai over the past two decades—the devolution and privatization of key government authorities, shifting competition among political parties for slum dwellers' votes, intensified business roles in urban redevelopment under a liberalized economy, and shifts in the character and disposition of key civil-society groups. Ground zero for these changes was the streets of Mumbai's slums, where I will focus on the emergence of the Alliance mentioned above before highlighting what turn out to be complementary shifts in official policy making and electoral politics.

By the mid-80s, government evictions of slum dwellers, and the even more insecure "pavement dwellers" whose makeshift huts were erected on the most irregular spots throughout Mumbai, were failing badly. Yet they continued. Shacks were bulldozed, and poor families often lost what few possessions they had. The next day, the shacks were rebuilt. From the standpoint of development progress, then, as well as accountability, government could confront the urban poor and enforce laws against occupation, but nothing tangible was accomplished. In 1984, a group of middle-class social workers began to change this through their work with pavement dwellers in Mumbai's Nagpada slum. "These were the poorest of the poor, the most marginal," recalls Celine d'Cruz, one of the social workers. "They were not complacent. And as for us, we had to unlearn all our training. Middle-class conceptions of what the urban poor needed were pointless." Registering that year as an NGO, the Society for the Promotion of Area Resource Centres (SPARC), the group developed a simple idea and carried it out with the poor: they would train pavement dwellers to collect data on their own (tenuously sited) communities and help them provide these data to government officials to facilitate the provision of services, including ration cards.

Over the next decade, "enumeration," as SPARC and its allies call the practice, would become a trademark tool, helping to make the city's invisible visible, engaging poor people in collective action, and offering something to an underequipped government bureaucracy.[11] SPARC launched the first "pavement census," offering a profile of the poor and their expenditures, with only the broad recommendation that the municipality needed help from higher levels of government. As observers inside and outside state and local agencies confirm, Indian NGOs had a reputation for confronting government with demands, and however justifiable, these demands rarely came with worked-out solutions or offers of partnership.[12]

"We took a list of families to the [ration card] bureau, for example," says D'Cruz, "and working with that was much better for them than dealing one-by-one with family claims." The social organization of the poor, in other words, could be a boon to government in terms of making pubic programs more productive. What is more, the unprecedented census showed, contrary to media depictions of the "parasitic" poor in our midst, that the city's poor paid more, on a unit basis, for basic services, than middle-class households. But government insiders remember that SPARC's census also threatened the turf of some public officials. SPARC began to consciously recruit allies in government who could vouch for it and negotiate inside the bureaucracy—what SPARC's founder and director Sheela Patel calls "picking off the state one person at a time."

The turning point, says Patel, was in 1985. The courts had ordered a new round of evictions, and typically, no one had consulted the affected poor or developed resettlement and relocation plans to address their needs—or their capabilities. One day, a group of pavement dwellers confronted a government official who had come to clear their settlement. "These were poor women saying, 'You will not move us. We will move ourselves.' We had done role plays [with the women], playing the government officials, letting the women practice how they would respond." The families took down their own homes, and the next day, they came back and rebuilt them. The women were thus able to save their valuables from being destroyed or stolen, and with everyone working collectively, there was less panic and fear.

SPARC then got the pavement dwellers legal help and established, through the courts, a principled ban on "wrongful" evictions, not an end to evictions per se. In dialogue with the pavement dwellers, SPARC decided not to argue a right to occupy space but to attack the inhumane *process* by which pavement dwellers were suddenly and violently uprooted, without recourse. SPARC argued, on behalf of the women, for a right (1) to be notified of impending eviction and (2) to be engaged in the process of developing shelter alternatives. In the process, SPARC began to establish two norms: that it would support poor communities in their efforts rather than develop policy and advocate on its own; and that it would work to generate new knowledge and better solutions, not just demands—"a politics of do first, talk later" (Appadurai 2001, 33)— and pitch those solutions to allies in the public sector.

In 1986, SPARC began to work with Jockin Arputham and NSDF, which brought the less visible pavement dwellers into the slum dwellers movement. Together, SPARC and NSDF helped poor women organize *Mahila Milan*, initially in small-scale savings clubs. These clubs likewise "federated" upward into larger networks, eventually across the country.

India is the world's largest democracy and among its most diverse in language, caste, religion, regional culture, and other dimensions. But the Alliance's leadership cuts across Hindu, Muslim, and Christian lines and is steadfastly secular in outlook. In a city of fierce party competition for slum votes, moreover, it is strictly nonaligned, willing to work with representatives of any party that will address the interests of the poor but refusing to barter slum dwellers' interests through the machinery of the vote bank (Appadurai 2001).

But something else has shaped the capacity and strategy of each member of the Alliance, each leg of the tripod. As organizational researchers worldwide have come to recognize, organizations that are so functionally intertwined coevolve (Polodny and Page 1998): SPARC, with its staff of professionals and grant-winning skills, contributed technical knowledge, financial management, and connections to public- and private-sector decision makers; NSDF brought deep experience in grassroots political organizing, including pressure politics, but the focus of that pressure began to shift; and *Mahila Milan* began to provide a steady link between the Alliance's policy agenda and family-level assets, as well as the hard-won experience of poor women who had learned to navigate a precarious life in slums.

There were many tests. Having set a precedent by negotiating a policy against forced evictions, between 1988 and 1990, the Alliance organized its first community-led resettlement of a railway slum, negotiating with government for a plot of land to occupy permanently. Government officials recall it as the first significant engagement, by government, of an NGO in slum redevelopment. "Within government," recalls an official, "we had to sell it to the industrial development department and the Railways as the best alternative. The other choice was impasse, because the [slum dwellers] wouldn't move."

These multilevel negotiations aside for the moment, as interviews and up-close observation confirm, two pillars—*federation* and *savings*—would come to define the Alliance internally and also guide its work with government and later the private sector. Appadurai (2001, 32) observes of federation,

This innocuous term from elementary political science textbooks has special meaning and magic for the Alliance. At its foundation is the idea of individuals and families self-organizing as members of a political collective to pool resources, organize lobbying, provide mutual risk management devices, and when necessary, confront opponents . . . it emphasizes the importance of political union among pre-existing collectives (thus federating rather than simply uniting, joining, and lobbying). . . . The idea of federation is a constant reminder that groups (even at the level of families) that have a claim to political agency on their own have chosen to combine their political and material power.

In other words, within the Alliance, federating provides a direct way to link up small-scale groups defined by shared struggles, trust, and reciprocal face-to-face relationships—all sources of social capital (Evans 1996; Putnam 1993; Woolcock and Narayan 2000). These are linked in larger collectives that practice deliberation and work to keep leaders accountable to a grassroots base while pursuing political and operational objectives. Veteran organizers, including Jockin Arputham and SPARC staff, invest in the face-to-face member education, cross-site exchange, and other tactics that help the federations mature and learn to resolve conflicts. And as for the second pillar, savings, Appadurai (p. 33) argues,

When Jockin and his colleagues in the Alliance speak of savings, it becomes evident that they are describing something far deeper than a simple mechanism for meeting daily monetary needs and sharing resources among the poor. Seen

by them as something akin to spiritual practice, daily savings—and its spread—
are conceived as the key to the local and global success of the federation
model . . . in putting savings at the core of the politics of the Alliance, its leaders
are making the work of poor women fundamental to what can be achieved in
every other area. It is a simple formula: without poor women joining together,
there can be no savings; without savings, there can be no federation; without
federating, there is no way for the poor themselves to enact change in the
arrangements that disempower them.

But over two decades of evolution, that empowerment would also rest
on durable networks of information, finance, and influence that stretch
far beyond the slums and indeed beyond India—on the development of
what scholars have termed "bridging social capital" (Briggs 1997; Gittell
and Vidal 1998; Putnam 2000). By the late 1980s, the Alliance was
poised to go global. In 1988, activists in several nations set up the Asian
Coalition for Housing Rights, based in Bangkok, and it enabled the
Mahila Milan savings practices to be replicated and adapted beyond
India through exchanges.

Later that year, on a visit to England, SPARC's Sheela Patel developed
another relationship that would prove pivotal. Ruth McLeod had just
taken the helm of a small UK-based philanthropy, Homeless International (HI), which was looking for a more strategic role in meeting the
shelter needs of the urban poor. McLeod was the sole full-time employee
of an organization in search of direction. "Several of us with shared
interests formed a group to explore them," recalls Patel, "and because
the Alliance was organizing our first learning exchanges beyond Mumbai,
we asked Homeless International to support them."

Some early exchanges failed badly, Patel acknowledges, yet these had
evolved, by the mid-1990s, into Shack/Slum Dwellers International, with
support from HI and other NGOs in wealthy nations. This transnational
network's approach to governance stresses peer accountability and
review: Indian slum dweller federations visit and critique South African
ones, which visit Kenyan ones for two-way exchange, and so on. SPARC
learned from HI how to frame its work and needs for other philanthropies and aid agencies in Europe, while HI gained an invaluable connection to street-level innovations led by organizations actively practicing
accountability to the urban poor. In retrospect, it seems crucial, for both
organizations, that the heads were choosy about new projects, mindful
of the need to work within their emergent capacity to manage operational details and learn through reflection at regular intervals. Like the
partners within the Mumbai-based Alliance, then, SPARC and HI found

that their organizational strategies and capacities coevolved, a point to which I return below.

A final crucial aspect of the Alliance is seen in SPARC's more local intermediary role: that of a mediator between the internal functions and styles of a grassroots people's movement—including the well-documented challenges of practicing participatory decision making within such a movement (Polletta 2002)—and the demands of external bureaucracies, with their complex budgets, project schedules, and technocratic mindsets. SPARC mediates what critical observers worldwide have recognized, at least since the 1960s, as a tension between "democracy" and "bureaucracy" when political-action aims are joined to tangible development ones.[13] This is a crucial tension in the context of democracy as a recipe for problem solving, which implies defining action aims vis-à-vis problems and mobilizing resources to support action—both through creative politics—but also making the productive arrangements required to then *act* together on the problems. Appadurai (p. 31) observes of the Alliance and its gatherings:

The coalition cultivates a highly transparent, non-hierarchical, anti-bureaucratic and anti-technocratic style. A small clerical staff consciously serves the needs of the activists, and not vice-versa. Meetings and discussions are often held with everyone sitting on mats on the floor. Food and drink are shared during meetings, and most official business (on the phone or face-to-face) is conducted amidst a tumult of other activities in crowded offices. . . . The leadership is at pains to make its ideas known to its members and to the residents of the slum communities, who are, in effect, the coalition's rank and file. Almost no internal request for information about the organization, its funding, its planning, or related matters is considered out of order. Naturally, there are private conversations, hidden tensions, and real differences of personality and strategy at all levels. But these are neither validated nor legitimized in either bureaucratic protocols or organizational charts.

As for external approach, Appadurai (2001, 29) comments, as I noted at the beginning of this chapter, that the politics of the Alliance emphasizes accommodation, negotiation, and long-term pressure "rather than of threats and reprisals." It is a "politics of patience," he argues, and one that emphasizes long-run mobilization of the poor and demonstration of their capabilities over the short-run reporting and accounting emphases of the dominant "project model" of social development.

This twin strategy, of internal and external negotiation and consensus building, affords me a transition to how major changes in government and traditional party politics, and not just creative grassroots mobilization or philanthropy, helped define the civics of managing urban growth in Mumbai. It is in the context of this broader change in politics and policy that the Alliance's role would sharpen and begin to transform the impasse over slums in the 1990s.

Government Shifts, the Impasse Yields

Above, I described the rural bias and lack of authority for city governments that defined India's approach to urban problems after independence. Only in the 1970s did the central government set up a Ministry of Urban Development, as well as a National Commission on Urbanisation to study problems and offer recommendations, a number of which were adopted in the Seventy-Fourth Amendment to the Constitution of India, enacted in 1992 (Mohan 2001).[14] That amendment required local elections, gave local government new powers and arranged for fiscal transfers to them, and mandated representation for women and historically marginalized groups, such as members of lower castes.[15] But housing and other development needs in slums remain the purview of states, not local government. And throughout the country, say close observers in government and academia, shifting bureaucratic mindsets to create more responsive local government, as well as an engaged citizenry and civic media to demand responsiveness, has been slow and fraught with setbacks—beset with opposition by politicians, bureaucratic turf wars, and, in some regions, a lack of organized and politically literate citizen demand.[16] In John Dewey's terms, India's landmark constitutional reform called for a shift in powers but could not, by itself, produce the active and conscious public needed to ensure a real shift in governance or public management.

In the early 1990s, however, an aggressive strain of Hindu nationalism took form in the Shiv Sena political party, shaping the politics of Mumbai and the state of Maharashtra in significant ways. As Mukhija (2003) notes, a key element of the Shiv Sena platform, in coalition with another opposition party, was "free housing" for all, with land giveaways, a proposal to go beyond the basic subsidies for slum upgrading put in effect by the long-dominant Congress party, the party of India's independence movement, in the 1980s (Mukhija 2003).[17] While the giveaways mean that the housing was not, in fact, free but rather subsidized by the taxpayer, the party emphasized that slum dwellers would not have to contribute their own cash resources to obtain newly built housing or lots, though they would pay for services, such as water and electricity. Controversial though the policy was—some claimed it legitimized illegal encroachments and inappropriately rewarded the encroachers—it was a popular move among slum dwellers. It came with a divisive and xeno-phobic campaign, in the state and local elections of 1994 and 1995, against the city's Muslims and "outsiders," as rural migrants to Mumbai's slums are often labeled (Appadurai 2001).

At the national level, liberalization had begun to eliminate the socialist command economy, reducing regulation and creating new monetary policy and incentives for private investment. In Maharashtra, state government began to experiment with an approach that helps define affordable housing and community development finance in America and other nations: using land-use policy to leverage private investment in housing for low-income people and leveraging public grants and other subsidies with private debt and equity capital (Mukhija 2003).

Under the new incentive scheme, in exchange for building compact flats in the slums, developers would receive "transferable development rights" to exceed density limits in other parts of the city. A developer who builds slum housing at, say, a cost of $10 per square foot, can build market-rate housing for middle- and upper-income households elsewhere in the city, perhaps at $80 per square foot. When the real estate market is healthy, and even more so when it is red hot, as Mumbai's has been for much of the past decade, this is an enormously profitable proposition. But to win development rights in the first place, 70 percent of slum dwellers in a given community would have to agree to participate. The rule cut both ways: it could be a mechanism for generating productive deliberation and consensus among slum dwellers or, effectively, a license to steal, with developers buying up the support of vulnerable slum dwellers to ensure the required ratification.

At last, though, government had created a significant incentive for private-sector investment and real estate development to address the city's enormous housing shortage—a shortage most acute for the very poor. In the process, it had also created new regulatory challenges and new financial risk in that slum upgrading and redevelopment were now subject to price swings and changes in capital availability. When the real estate market waned in the mid-1990s, local media described the slum redevelopment policy as "stillborn" and "floundering," for example. Plus, there were a host of new possibilities for conflict as well as cooperation among government, business, and nongovernmental organizations engaged in slum upgrading and the redevelopment of housing in the slums (Mukhija 2001; Sanyal and Mukhija 2001).

Divisive as it could be, party competition had helped to spur these new policies. And structural reform of local government had cast new light on government nonperformance and the need to engage civil society as well as businesses in building solutions to stubborn urban problems. As a veteran Indian civil servant who has held senior posts at the local as well as state levels observes, "Government was realizing its limits. We had always acted as a regulator, but social development requires a capacity that we did not have. We needed to delegate a part of our authority [over projects] to NGOs. . . . We needed support and logistics from the NGOs. And from the private sector, we needed financing and more." It is this context, and the bumpy evolution of coproduction hinted at in that observation, that defines the current chapter of tackling urban growth in the city—and the particular form of civic capacity that organizers have developed in this adverse context.

Grassroots to Grasstops: The Models Mature

Two episodes, as cases within the case, vividly capture the evolution of a collaborative, cross-sector approach to governance as well as implementation, both of which I mean to encompass with the term *coproduction*. Between them, the two also illustrate the range of challenging tasks that define slum redevelopment, from policy formulation to community consensus building, from data gathering to the operational details of humane resettlement and financially viable bricks-and-mortar construction. It is this range that demands the dialectic of learning and bargaining I outlined in chapters 1 and 2.

I will continue to focus on the Alliance and, in particular, the role of SPARC as a critical intermediary organization. Over the past decade, it was the most visible among a small group of respected NGOs active in slum redevelopment or upgrading in Mumbai, as well as the most regularly engaged in government task forces and other consultative bodies; the work of SPARC and the Alliance repeatedly garners labels such as "unique" and "precedent-setting," meaning that the network is respected but also that it has opened doors for a wider array of NGOs and community groups to collaborate with government.[18] At the end of this chapter, I will turn to limits and criticisms of the Alliance's approach–for example, from some housing rights activists.

Overcoming the Stalemate on Railways Slums
The first episode includes the relocating and resettling of families in large railway slums, which form part of the much-maligned "noose" around Mumbai's sagging transportation infrastructure.[19] This megaproject

followed a census of railways slums conducted by SPARC, the subsequent formation of the Railway Slum Dwellers Federation (RSDF), and small-scale but important demonstrations that railway slum dwellers would voluntarily cooperate with the powerful Indian Railways, one of the largest public enterprises in the world, if treated humanely and offered viable alternatives. The large-scale relocation and resettlement of the late 1990s engaged the Alliance with state government, the World Bank, and the Railways. This multiyear project, which resettled a staggering 20,000 families—without coercion—from beside the rail lines to make way for a massive transportation expansion, was a landmark for the city as well as for the work of the Alliance.

For the latter, the 1990s had seen notable progress on innovative, community-driven sanitation projects in the slums—which cost less and performed better than municipal's government's notoriously inadequate toilet blocks—as well as complex housing redevelopment, analyzed below, in which SPARC had, for the first time, taken on financial risk as the developer and even found itself competing with a private developer for slum dwellers' support. The transnational work also continued to evolve. But locally, SPARC, run on a small budget with a few core staff, was seen primarily as a housing advocate, an adviser on government policy toward slums and slum dwellers, and a manager of small service upgrading projects. The massive railway resettlement success put SPARC and the Alliance's contributions to the city in a whole new league. Government's top slum redevelopment official describes it simply as "a breakthrough."

The project was unusual in both process and outcomes—for Mumbai, for India, and indeed for "megaprojects" of infrastructure development worldwide—argue SPARC staff leaders Patel, D'Cruz, and Burra (2002, 159):

First, it did not impoverish those who moved (as is generally the case when poor groups are moved to make way for infrastructure development). Second, the actual move was voluntary and needed neither police nor municipal force to enforce it. And third, the resettled people were involved in designing, planning, and implementing the resettlement programme and in managing the settlements to which they moved.

Recall that SPARC, in its earliest work mediating between pavement dwellers and government, had focused on a policy against forced evictions, with provisions for humane and consultative resettlement, rather than a "right" to occupy illegally occupied lands. Also, the organization had, in a series of projects, respected government's need to set limits on eligibility for new land and housing units—a perennially tricky issue when handling squatters because it arbitrarily set cut-offs based on the date each squatter household had arrived on the land. Both decisions were strategic and pragmatic, though unpopular with some NGO advocates. Nonetheless, they were taken, say government insiders, as "acts of good faith" on the part of the NGO.

Informal networks mattered, too—for information, influence, and the trust needed to resolve conflict. SPARC had cultivated allies within government from its earliest dealings with the bureaucracy, but it later took the additional step of hiring former officials and welcoming motivated civil servant retirees, who volunteered as troubleshooters in the NGO's dealings with the public sector—working out decision makers' data needs, coaxing along slow payment offices, resolving regulatory or other hurdles, consistently underlining a sense of shared purpose even where conflicts persisted.[20] These are ongoing challenges, not discrete tasks accomplished once and for all, in part because of the structure of the Indian civil service: key officials cycle in and out among posts, robbing their agencies of valuable institutional learning-by-doing as well as productive working relationships with potential partners, including the increasingly important NGOs. Finally, SPARC's international networks had grown, and it had been a part of the task force developing the state government's resettlement and rehabilitation policy for the project, a requirement of the World Bank.[21] This was a significant role, since a World Bank loan covered approximately $57 million of the railway expansion and the Bank could thus shape key rules and incentives, withholding funds if government (or its partners) failed to comply.

Before the slum dwellers asserted their interests, resettlement had been treated as a side issue for the metro area's massive railway upgrading effort, the Mumbai Urban Transport Project. But commuter protest and vandalism in the early to mid-1990s made clear that resettlement was, in fact, the project's central issue. When the Railways criticized RSDF, the railway slum dwellers organization, for being "all talk," the latter made an unprecedented act of good faith, relocating families on a critical western line so that trains could improve their speed.[22] RSDF then took a firm position: slum dwellers would voluntarily relocate only if offered secure land serviced by basic infrastructure. Staying put was a fairly strong "no-agreement alternative" (Fisher and Ury 1981), since forced relocation had so often failed and the costs of deferred modernization to the Railways would be enormous.

The offer worked. By 1997, when a deal was struck, SPARC had been working with the Government of Maharashtra—actually, a cabal of distinct state agencies—for more than five years on the challenges facing railway slums. The two now found a site and created an institutional structure for receiving the land to which railway slum dwellers would be relocated. When the Railways needed to speed up its project (or forfeit its grant from central government), the slum dwellers agreed to move to a transit camp before permanently resettling.

"The resolution went back and forth for 6 to 8 months," recalls Sheela Patel, in part because of the range of distinct agendas, the lack of a clear template in past projects, and the fingerpointing between the Government of Maharashtra and the highly centralized Indian Railways (an arm of central government)—over who was responsible for what. Roles were settled: SPARC would work with RSDF to organize the slum dwellers into cooperative societies, the state's Slum Redevelopment Authority, set up several years before, would coordinate on behalf of government, and SPARC would receive development rights, not ownership, of the land.

In bargaining this division of labor, SPARC and its allies inside government convinced a string of government officials that there were no better alternatives; the slum dwellers' voting power certainly helped as well. But from a conceptual as well as practical standpoint, the crucial point is that the bargaining did not happen across a binary "government-NGO" divide but across multiple levels and institutional boundaries (figure 5.2), as agency officials debated proposals to meet their needs and

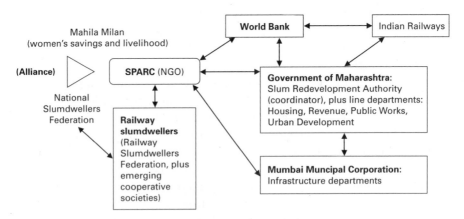

Figure 5.2
Railway slum resettlement and relocation, showing SPARC as intermediary

joined a gradual consensus in favor of a proposal negotiated with SPARC, acting for the Alliance on behalf of the railway slum dwellers.

Then came the construction and relocation phase, which posed significant financial challenges as well as conflicts over how to sequence relocation. Government wanted to dictate the sequence, while the slum dwellers federation wanted communities themselves to work it out, based on their readiness to uproot and move. There were many community-level disputes as well, whether because someone wanted to relocate a store as well as a home or because of disagreements over, say, placement of religious statues or other objects. "There are many tricks within communities over these projects, too," says Patel, including "falsifying documents, making allegations, and more ... Jockin wanted the government to understand that working things out openly, dealing openly with conflicts, was a *good* thing."

At the next phase, the World Bank reentered the picture to review the project workplan and financing. SPARC contended with Bank reviews and rules over a number of pivotal issues: the size of transit (temporary) housing units, the provision of infrastructure, and the prospect of SPARC handling not only the slum enumeration and resettlement process but also the new land and housing development at the point of relocation. The Bank doubted the capacity of an NGO to handle the large-scale development. "We will negotiate almost anything," says SPARC's Sundar Burra of the organization's overall disposition to conflict and of the range of conflicts in the resettlement project, "except the fundamentals . . . When the Bank proposed hiring a private contractor to handle relocation, that was absurd. We threatened to walk. But we said, 'It's not personal.'" And Patel recalls,

They forced us to compete with private marketing firms. The Bank tried to put us together with such firms. We spoke to everyone we knew at the Bank, and we lobbied [on the points of disagreement]. . . . [World Bank President] Wolfensohn had visited the railway slums with us in 1997 when he first took office. We showed him what it was like to try and avoid the trains, to avoid the shit [on the ground]. . . . It was now the year 2000. The World Bank project leader came for a site visit. He said, "Convince me." And we did. They changed the Bank's procurement guidelines. He became our champion. The WTO protests in Seattle had just happened. He invited us to present to the World Bank Board on community-led initiatives. We hadn't done what NGOs traditionally do: protest, threaten to block. . . . Procurement for goods and engineering equipment was different from procurement for managing communities. RSDF wanted to undertake this process using SPARC as a legal entry point, and the Alliance demanded they be given that right.

SPARC and its allies moved 900 families in the first year and a half but 10,000 more in the next two years. It went on to resettle slum dwellers near the airport—also a high priority for the region's infrastructure upgrading. The final phases of these projects were prolonged: working out loan repayment and helping with the permanent relocation of families, including the effort to help them build new lives and livelihoods in new, serviced housing locations. "It includes trying to create community jobs that contribute, even sweeping," says Patel, "and Jockin is running around telling people not to be complacent, to want more, to continue developing their [new] communities, not to become passive. Even 'cheaters' can redeem themselves. Jockin says that there is a fine line between cheating and entrepreneurship. You have to channel all that, let communities sanction their own, give people work to do, ways to contribute."

It is clear, from agency interviews and media sources, that SPARC proved itself on an entirely new level with the railway resettlement—and with that accomplishment had a significant impact, as well, on government and aid agency (World Bank) perceptions of the capacity of NGOs and their grassroots allies to organize and manage complex slum redevelopment projects. The state housing agency director described it, for example, as a "breakthrough," not only for the Alliance but for his agency's approach to NGOs and their role in shaping regional policy. This new credibility, in turn, opened up new possibilities for partnering across sectors. The *Times of India* reported in March 2002, "For years, government dawdled as squatters gobbled up the land. . . . Suddenly, thousands of such squatters were relocated and rehoused in permanent, legal dwellings, raising the hope that slums may not be such an insurmountable problem after all . . . [Sheela] Patel says that solutions to the slum problem can emerge only through a partnership between government and the slum dwellers."[23]

The effort also brought new financial and organizational strains for what had been a relatively small support organization—SPARC—that focused on "soft skills"—technical assistance, research and policy analysis, and informal mediation. But from the standpoint of civic capacity and coproduction, what roles did this new level of work imply for public and nongovernmental actors?

I take stock here to preview contrasts between the railway resettlement and the second, briefer episode below, and I draw on Barbara Gray's (1989) framework for interorganizational collaboration. It is a process framework in three stages: *problem setting* (defining problems for shared attention); *direction setting* (developing strategies that address the problems); and *implementation* (jointly acting on the strategies).

First, the Alliance and government jointly defined an agenda for planning and action that included the institutional structure of the project (its governance), not just flows of funds or program operations. Recognizing that fragmentation in government would stymie resettlement and relocation work, for example, the parties agreed to have the Slum Redevelopment Authority coordinate disparate agencies, while SPARC offered itself as counterpart coordinator for the Alliance, which was working with organized railway slum dwellers to create new, small-scale cooperative housing societies. Arguably, the complex and demanding stages that followed could not have been navigated without this clarity about agreed-on, sensible roles and functions. Yes, it was project-specific governance, but it also established a precedent and a template—a crucial "scheme of cooperation," as analysts of urban regimes term it (Stone 2005)—for government and NGO roles in future efforts to resettle slum dwellers.

Second, and contrary to a scenario in which government "plans" and civil society responds, the players jointly identified data needs and entrusted SPARC (for the most part) with gathering data in and around the slums. Developing specific strategies for the on-the-ground work thus drew on data that had been cooperatively defined and developed.

Third, as for implementation, following further negotiations that engaged the World Bank in rewriting its contracting rules—SPARC's allies at Bank headquarters, not just the field offices—SPARC won the role of contractor, meaning it would be involved in all operational phases of the work and would certify to government that rules about housing eligibility and more had been strictly followed. In lieu of other organizations both willing and able to manage the street-level conflicts and aspirations of the slum dwellers, SPARC and the slum dwellers federation completed the chain of coproduction, bringing distinctive capacities to bear on the task challenges at hand—in areas for which government has shown little competence and in which it holds little legitimacy in the eyes of the most affected public, the urban poor.

In the process, government and the civil-society groups, along with the key multilateral agency (the World Bank) piloted a new approach to governance and to the operational aspects of collaboration, not just policy reform. The approach offered accountability for tangible results. Slum dwellers resettled from dangerous rail passages to functional homes in permanent locations, in time with basic infrastructure to serve them, and vital upgrading of the world's highest-volume metropolitan transit system proceeded.

"The Only Thing You Can Sell Is Success"—Redeveloping Slum Housing

Many of Mumbai's slums are not precariously squeezed alongside rail lines or other untenable sites but instead occupy public or privately owned land that is well suited for permanent settlement. The issue is how to make them more livable and sustainable. Over the past decade, government, the private sector, and civil-society groups in Mumbai—again, most notably the Alliance partners—have developed progressively more complex partnership models for demolishing inadequate housing and financing and constructing functional replacement housing (thus, slum *re*development). These models are vital—and are of great interest to policy makers worldwide—since slum redevelopment cannot happen at the needed scale without private capital.

Reviewing the stage-by-stage evolution of each major project, let alone the series, is beyond my scope here. What is more, the core elements of the Alliance's interaction with government, founded on cooperation as well as conflict, follow the contours of the railway episode examined above. But the substantial involvement of the private sector and the role of financial risk and risk sharing distinguish slum redevelopment from the relocation and resettlement case above.

Recall that competitive elections led an opposition alliance to propose trading density bonuses for housing construction in Mumbai's slums, beginning in 1995. For the first time, this policy gave the private sector—real estate developers and potentially lenders as well—a role in slum redevelopment and also expanded the range and complexity of interactions among institutions in the public, private, and NGO sectors. For local players in all three sectors, working out durable schemes of cooperation over a series of precedent-setting projects has centered on two closely related issues: developing capacity and sharing risk. Capacity helps dictate who plays what role in the complex and contentious process of redevelopment. It also affects how well partnerships can limit various forms of risk (overall) and share that risk among the partners involved.

For the real estate industry—Indian banks, developers, and construction companies—the slums represent an important emerging market, thanks to the policy reforms of the mid-1990s and the city's generally robust demand for space. My interviews with senior officials in private

Indian banks, as well as World Bank analysts of the sector, underscored this. But until the Alliance's entrepreneurial entry into the world of complex, market-oriented housing deals beginning in the late 1990s (Mukhija 2003), banks were unfamiliar with these deals and wary about the unpredictable risks they posed.

Typically, banks dealt with established real estate developers who bring a known or verifiable capacity to manage large fund flows, deploy their influence to secure approvals from bureaucratic and sometimes corrupt public agencies, market to customers, and of course oversee the physical work of design, site prep, and construction. Yet few of these developers have ever had reasons to develop products in Mumbai's slums, and so they lack knowledge of slum dwellers as customers, as well as skill at handling conflicts at the community level. From a social development perspective, most developers and banks also lack a public-serving mission. Except for the interest in generating a stronger brand through community goodwill or "citizenship points," the banks and developers have every incentive to maximize profits even if this means compromising benefits for slum dwellers.

NGOs potentially bring skills and forms of knowledge that are missing in the business world, as well as experience in appropriate housing design and integrated planning—thinking about slums holistically, as places to live and work, raise children, and so on. As social development agents, NGOs, unlike for-profit firms, also have access to grants and "patient capital," such as loans at reduced interest rates or less aggressive repayment terms than conventional private loans. As for the social equity mission, most observers agree that NGOs are a mixed bag. In India and elsewhere, many NGOs lack reliable forms of accountability to communities they claim to serve, and in the worst cases, they can become "rent-seeking" patronage machines, like corrupt public agencies, for siphoning money and other resources meant for the poor (Sanyal 1994; Tendler 1997). Moreover, until this episode in the mid-1990s, NGOs had little or no experience, anywhere in India, with the financial, construction, or regulatory aspects of real estate development in slums.

Government, for its part, lacked experience assessing the capacity of NGOs or of private developers as candidates for work in the slums. As my agency interviews detailed, the public sector also lacked experience structuring complex finance—for example, to leverage private capital with public funds in the form of loan guarantees or subsidies. Some public officials were also eager to protect their turf, including side deals with slumlords. But slum dwellers' voting strength, and the ruling Shiv

Sena party's promise to build housing, created real incentives for government to deliver on its new policy. And as Mukhija (2001) shows, the need for predictable and streamlined project approvals and for stricter oversight of building standards and density bonus awards under the new slum rehab policy would lead not to a shrinking of the government role but to a blend of decentralization and centralization of authority, of deregulating in some areas and sharpening regulation in others.

The Alliance's initial foray into this tricky terrain was at Markhandeya, a project in which SPARC helped to secure a loan guarantee from a European aid agency in order to secure a local loan from an Indian financing agency. SPARC clashed with a real estate developer and leaders of the slum dwellers' local housing cooperative, and—midway through— became the developer, assuming the bulk of the project's financial risk at a time when demand in the market outside the slums had slackened considerably (Sanyal and Mukhija 2001). The project was bruising and slow, but it showed that the multiple risks faced by most market-oriented housing deals could be shared creatively. As the lead NGO working in Mumbai's slums, SPARC, in particular, demonstrated the capacity to handle the community conflicts and legitimacy crises that can lead slum dwellers to walk away from public and private demands, and these represent an important part of what bankers treat as *project execution risk*. Likewise, a deep knowledge of slums, including their largely unrecorded economic transactions and assets, gave SPARC and its Alliance partners better information on the *commercial risk* (market demand risk) born by these projects, which are fueled not only by the sale of housing but also of transferable rights to build more housing. Government developed a new institution, the Slum Redevelopment Authority, to coordinate reviews and approvals by disparate agencies and to act as dispute resolver and final arbiter among the many parties involved: the NGO, cooperative societies, and private lenders and builders.

In its next project, launched in 1996 at Rajiv-Indira in the Dharavi slum, SPARC landed a very big partner: CitiBank, the global financial giant, agreed to finance the housing project as part of the company's aggressive move into the Indian market. Controversially, SPARC, which was invited into the project by the local slum dwellers' Rajiv-Indira Cooperative Society, agreed to lend its name to CitiBank's marketing material and to participate in press conferences. Sheela Patel and other leaders in the Alliance saw the relationship as one of mutual benefit within certain bounds. Homeless International, the UK-based philanthropy that "grew up with us," to use Patel's description, provided a crucial loan guarantee.

Like the large-scale railway slum resettlement, this precedent-setting project—the first time a bank, let alone a global giant, had played any role in slum redevelopment in India—was fraught with conflicts and delays. More than a year into the project, for example, CitiBank balked at the shifting market risk and complained of the barriers created by Mumbai's awkward environmental regulations, which limit development near the coastline.[24] By 2003, with most of the building done and sales apace, the project was performing well, the Alliance had upped its credibility once more and also stretched its organizational capacity into new domains of risk analysis and project management, and government had another visible success with which to tout its slum redevelopment policy. Acting again as an enterprising intermediary—not a true neutral but what I will call an "interested facilitator" advocating for slum dwellers' interests while actively supporting a process larger than those interests—SPARC had once again demonstrated a reliable capacity to perform. The organization also strengthened its networks. As government officials readily acknowledge, SPARC reconciled disparate priorities and time frames, keeping the players focused on purpose. It also blended the invaluable knowledge of professionals, in engineering and finance and other domains, with the unique skills and knowledge of the urban poor. Government's Slum Rehabilitation Authority had likewise developed vital experience at critical oversight and public finance functions.

By the early 2000s, while local media warned of rapacious developers and local mafia intimidating slum dwellers into applying for the program elsewhere among the city's slums[25], observers could also see what the combination of private capital, accountable NGO project management and risk mitigation, and reasonably responsive government could accomplish. For the Alliance, it was another turning point. SPARC and its partners created a fourth organization, *Nirman*, to act as the Alliance's real estate development arm. And Nirman launched a program to help enterprising slum dwellers—like the ones I met at the beginning of this chapter—start small building companies, helping them win a share of the profits in redevelopment.

Epilogue

The year 2004 saw continued interest in Bombay First's call, in its vision report of the prior year, to make Mumbai a "world-class" city, including a major upgrading of some slums and resettling of others—to allow for vital infrastructure improvements. But fiscal shortfall and complaints about the city's costly and inefficient administrative structure dominated these debates, leading the media and opinion leaders to call for a strengthening of transparency and accountability.[26] "Slumbai" is what the papers called the city, and they warned of dim prospects to move on any collective agenda of transformation.[27] During the record-breaking monsoon rains of 2005, as the city flooded, hypercompetitive party politics triggered another major wave of forced evictions, with officials declaring that new arrivals would make it impossible to make any headway on slums. By the time the National Slum dwellers Federation and its partners negotiated an end to those evictions, an estimated 60,000 families had been displaced, while thousands more continued to resettle from railways and the airport ring under the Alliance's "people-managed" resettlement approach. This, multiple observers confirm, also represents the slum dwellers' most direct source of political leverage: that encroachers stand—or squat, as it were—between Mumbai's political and business elite and the infrastructure upgrading that a would-be world-class city so desperately needs.

The challenges to becoming such a city were underscored on July 11, 2006, when a series of coordinated bomb attacks on Mumbai's trains, allegedly carried out by jihadi insurgents angry over the India-Pakistan conflict in Kashmir, killed hundreds and paralyzed the massive rail system. Encouragingly, Indian Prime Minister Manmohan Singh urged calm and restraint, and the city infamous for Hindu-Muslim conflict in the 1990s—a place routinely depicted in the international media as "chaotic" and "steamy"—did not erupt in more sectarian violence.[28]

No governing citywide coalition—no dominant regime—ensured an equitable future for urban growth in Mumbai. The finger-pointing and foot-dragging tied to the new vision was enough to try even the most pragmatic and well-rooted "politics of patience." And my investigation left several important questions on the agenda of future research: How exactly does the Alliance manage its relationships with Mumbai's fiercely competitive political parties, and how exactly does the Alliance manage to successfully avoid Hindu-Muslim sectarianism in its work?

But a twenty-year history of experimenting, of cooperation and conflict, had left the capital of slums with new capacity to act collectively on the problems as well as the opportunities in those slums, which will help determine the wider area's success as a global city-region—and to do so without the patronage politics and mafia coercion that represent a much more familiar structure for getting things done.

Summary, Implications, and Comparison

This part of the book examined the forms and uses of civic capacity, well beyond the politics of the public policy process alone, to tackle serious problems associated with rapid urban growth. In Utah, the new civics of urban growth demanded savvy grasstops organizing to reassure potential adversaries before a broad outreach to the grassroots. This meant a concerted effort to recruit influential political insiders as validators and advisers, to reframe growth management as "quality growth," and to distance planning from the perception of government imposition. The resulting process, an extended campaign for change led by a nongovernmental intermediary collaborating closely with government and the private sector, compensated for the failures of electoral institutions and professionalized public agencies to meaningfully address the strains of rapid, unplanned urban growth. But the end outcome, in terms of local land-use policy and development patterns, depends on many negotiations, locality by locality, with elected officials, private development interests, and the citizen-consumers whose everyday decisions also shape the landscape. The Envision Utah process has made a different future visible and achievable, not guaranteed. These features define civic capacity—its forms, uses, and limits—in the Utah case.

In Mumbai and other cities in the developing world, the problems associated with slum-led growth present a largely distinct set of civic challenges, in part because empowered local governments and cross-sector development partnerships are typically much less established than, say, in the United States, but also because slums exist as "shadow cities"—often neglected, precariously and often illegally sited, preyed on by slumlords and politicians, and generally denied opportunities to collaborate strategically with the public and private sectors. Market-led efforts have a poor record of reaching the poor, and government-led ones often lack legitimacy as well as competence. Nongovernmental organizations frequently compete with each other or fall into narrow, policy- or project-focused advocacy roles, foregoing opportunities to build broader coalitions with each other and with business interests. Sometimes, NGOs also lack accountability to the poor who live in urban or rural communities. These features—the potential for complementarity and the incentives for abuse, neglect, and impasse—frame the opportunities and challenges confronting those who would build significant civic capacity and deploy it to change conditions on the ground. The context is different, but civic capacity in the dimensions I have described is a key resource for tackling growth, just as it is in the Salt Lake Valley and other sprawl-ing regions in wealthy nations. At stake are the fortunes of the nearly one billion people who live in the world's growing slums—and countless more whose cities are made less livable, competitive, and environmen-tally sustainable as long as slums are neglected.

Though no governing coalition or regime has emerged in the economic capital of the world's largest democracy through the grassroots-to-grasstops dynamic I examined in this chapter, a remarkable version of what political researchers call a "scheme of cooperation" (Stone 2005) certainly has. This evolution, rather than building will around a shared regional vision of change à la Utah, is pivotal in the Mumbai case. Cooperation has hinged on key changes in how government, civil society, and business relate to each other. Yet broad invocations to "partnership" reveal relatively little about these changes. There are several lessons, and telling contrasts with the Utah case, here.

First, democratic problem solving demands accountability, but as increasingly observed, its forms must extend beyond the model of profes-sional agencies answerable to elected officials, who in turn answer—at least in principle—to the voters (Fung 2006b). Table 5.1 outlines a blended model of accountability that is well illustrated in the case of

Table 5.1
Sources and uses of accountability in democratic problem-solving: A blended model, using the Mumbai case

Source	Use (function)
Electoral politics	Party competition for slum dweller votes drives reforms to high-level rules and incentives, as well as accommodation of disparate interests in the city.
Institutional bargaining and learning	Acting as agents for collectives, organized slum dwellers and "interested" intermediaries, such as support NGOs, negotiate rule changes and discretionary decisions of public and private players as well as operational roles in development, ensuring that policy particulars reflect local knowledge about problems and promising solutions. Bargaining and learning require demonstrations and risk taking, blended capacity (or coproduction) to produce measurable results.
Markets	Price signals lead to more efficient resource use (demand-led development), compel an accounting of private benefits and costs, and attract for-profit firms to extend productive capacity and scale.

slum redevelopment and resettlement problems in Mumbai. Yes, the direct source of tangible new results in and around the slums is coproduction or partnering. But project-level frameworks for accountability miss the larger lessons about its multiple forms in a wider civic context. It was not savvy project-level negotiations that led to market-oriented policy reforms in the mid-1990s, for example, but rather the imperatives of election campaigns. For its part, the market helps drive a more demand-led approach to meeting critical housing needs. But it is institutional bargaining from a base of (1) political strength and (2) organizational capacity that shapes roles and outcomes in complex and often contentious partnership projects.

This is one way that historically marginalized groups can be empowered beyond shaping official policy, which has been the central focus for many students of participatory governance: *People can govern through projects in which they are actively involved as coproducers of change,* not just through shaping government's rules or resource-allocation decisions. In lieu of poor people's organized political capacity and clout, though, the rhetoric of partnerships can mask efforts to trim budgets or hand off work, with little accountability to the poor (Miraftab 2004; Warren 2001). Or it can turn such projects into one-off successes, not breakthroughs that create a durable scheme of cooperation. Such schemes must include rules of productive engagement between elites and nonelites, and between government and other sectors. Finally, innovation and learning are produced through organizations and their interactions, not simply revealed as aggregates of consumer demand (for product innovation) or voter-induced response by policy makers and bureaucrats (for policy innovation).

The form of social learning as shifts in policy-relevant beliefs (Jenkins-Smith and Sabatier 1993) may be limited to the "policy subsystem" (in the analytic shorthand) of slum redevelopment for now, rather than wider learning by the public or by public officials. But learning has also taken the forms of: deeper knowledge of counterparts' interests—the railway slum dwellers and the massive Indian Railways, for example—at the bargaining table (Fisher and Ury 1981; Susskind and Cruikshank 1987, 2006). Other outcomes include shifts in where and under what rules bargaining, coproduction, and other forms of engagement happen—in other words, transgressive politics (McAdam, Tarrow, and Tilly 2001) that begins to shift the institutions and rules of the game in key ways and not just people's ideas about the particular public problem at hand. An example is letting slum dwellers resolve for themselves what a public agency or World Bank regulation might have tried to direct in the past; this is a major shift for all three groups (agency, Bank, slum dwellers organization). The slow shift in practices that follow from such learning may be very difficult to replicate by support from above, since it surely rests on unsettling and shifting the players' ingrained mental models about how things should happen, and as students of organizational behavior stress, mental models do not shift simply by directive or by monetary or other rewards (Senge 1990).

To sum up this first major lesson, the need to develop and deploy multiple forms of accountability distinguishes civic capacity in the context of Mumbai slums from the dominant focus, in U.S. research, on the construction of citywide regimes that can forge and drive an agenda of collective action—and rarely one that engages the poor or addresses their interests in a significant way (Stone 2005). On the other hand, the cases share a focus on coalition building to achieve purpose.

The second main lesson is that accountability must be organized and sustained in several directions at once: between agents who learn and bargain together; between the interest groups those agents represent; between elected or appointed agents (or selected ones in the case of some civil-society groups) and their constituents; and between organizations that partner, sharing various kinds of risk and reward. Yes, accountable relationships help curb corruption and other forms of opportunistic behavior, but as I noted in the introduction, accountability is, more than ever, not just about *compliance with the rules*—of fair play, say, or equitable distribution—but about *accomplishing the purposes* for which one has been given support. Blended accountability and a vigorous focus on purpose also offer a much better brake on bad behavior than long-tested and seldom proved reforms that isolate powerful bureaucrats from the public (Behn 2001; Ostrom 1996). As Pritchett and Woolcock (2004, 207) observe,

It is in the tension between the interests and incentives of administrators, clients, and front-line providers that the solutions (plural) lie. . . . These tensions—between specialists and the people, planners and citizens, authority and autonomy—cannot be escaped. Rather, they need to be made creative rather than destructive.

Like Envision Utah, SPARC is a respected intermediary that has shown a pragmatic willingness to play multiple roles over time, organizing and focusing divergent interests, mediating conflict, generating better evidence to center debates and improve planning, and more. Within the Alliance, SPARC helps win victories for federated members, not for broader classes of persons as some human rights advocates would prefer. But it would be a big mistake to treat SPARC or the wider Alliance as apolitical or easily satisfied dealmakers. Moreover, debates about the roles of civil-society organizations and the need for pressure politics too often obscure the dynamics of accountability "up" and "down"—for example, the influential acts of good faith that SPARC and slum dwellers' organizations have made to signal a respect for government rules and policy priorities or the efficacy of street-level deliberations and social control to curb opportunistic behavior and disputes among the slum dwellers themselves.

These community-level capacities reflect social capital at work, both in its individual-good form of linking people to resource-providing institutions and its collective-good form as a source of reciprocal trust and the enforceable sanctions that buttress that trust (Portes 1998; Putnam 1993). Observers of similar local organizing in America have coined the phrase "community development system" to describe some of these arrangements and their multiple benefits for actors at the grassroots and grasstops (Keyes et al. 1996). For the Alliance in India, the accountability among peer federations in a transnational network spanning three continents represents yet another level of scrutiny and pressure to be transparent as well as pragmatic.

The third lesson is that beyond political agenda-setting, coproduction is a very important cause and effect of civic capacity. This lesson builds on a key insight from earlier research: under the coproduction model, each partner surrenders some control in exchange for the potential advantages offered by their partners' distinctive capabilities (Wood and Gray 1991). As with any approach to producing an outcome, partners face three overall tasks: defining work to be done, dividing it well, and coordinating their work effectively. Often, this calls not only for synchronizing preexisting capacities but for developing and integrating new ones, through the strains and stretch of demanding projects. In Mumbai, it has gradually drawn government into more deliberate and agile roles as a "smart" regulator—not slavishly procedural but responsive and flexible, problem-focused, as needs evolve (Mukhija 2003; Sparrow 2000)—and as a judge of prospective partners in the private and non-governmental sectors. These changes are central to making "community-driven development" work, with reinvented government as a part, but they are not the standard fare of civil service training.

And while coproduction in the context of urban slum redevelopment may be more institutionally complex than the rural service delivery and resource management that have received more attention from development research, Mumbai illustrates why such coproduction represents an essential element of local capacity to act on important problems. As Ostrom (1996, 1083) observes,

Prior efforts aimed at improving the training and capacity of public officials have frequently had disappointing results. Efforts at increasing citizen "participation" in petitioning others to provide goods for them have also proved disappointing. Efforts directed at increasing the potential complementarities between official and citizen production or problem-solving activities may require more time at the initial stage of a process but promise a much higher long-term return.

Or as SPARC's Sheela Patel puts it, "Some advocates are not comfortable with it, dismissing 'self-help.' But poor people are just better at doing some things for themselves. What they need and deserve is the support to leverage those capabilities."

Beyond these largely instrumental aspects, which focus on the operational interdependence among partners, there is the need for legitimacy or so-called soft power, which rests on informal norms and expectations about who should act on what kinds of problems, how, and when (Moore 1995; Nye 2004). Legitimacy is important for trust, and trust, as I have explored, flows from a web of accountable relationships, typically backed by contractual agreements to deliver X (good) or else Y (consequence)—not from a simple transfer of powers and resources. *Multilateralism*—the need to signal a shared, jointly sanctioned approach for reasons of legitimacy—captures this intangible yet important value of partnering effectively to create change. It is a large part of both cases, though the specific civic "tests" in Utah and Mumbai were distinct.

Slum redevelopment in Mumbai is not a case of governance and coproduction by blueprint. On the contrary, learning by doing is at the center of the case. What is remarkable is how intentional key actors, most notably the Alliance partners, have been about continuous learning and institutional innovation. That culture of learning is surely a contributor to Mumbai's civic capacity to act on the huge challenge and potential of its slums—and thereby make itself worthy of the label "world-class city."

III

Restructuring the Economy

6

The Civics of Economic Restructuring

I've been rich, and I've been poor. Believe me, rich is better.
—Sophie Tucker

Give a team a task to accomplish, and several outcomes are possible, depending on the nature of the task, the supports given the team, and the character of the people you choose. First, the team members may not manage to work effectively together. They may not, for example, generate an effective, shared understanding of what is to be accomplished. In civic terms, there is a broad sense of the problem but no shared and actionable agenda for tackling it emerges. In fairness to the team, the problem may be so complex that it is hard to generate more than a broad understanding, and so the problem remains clear (in outline form) but intractable. Or an inability to manage conflict may impede the team's effectiveness, whether because healthy conflict is missing and the group "dumbs down," settling on comfortable but wrongheaded ideas (the phenomenon known as groupthink) or because conflicts among team members boil over and threaten relationships as well as the accomplishment of tasks.

A second outcome is possible, however: the team becomes effective as a group but does not deliver what has been requested, whether because key ingredients are not available or because a failure in the production process—perhaps one team member is called away, and no adequate substitute can be found in time—leaves the group with a great plan and effective working relationships but no work product at the appointed hour.

Finally, the team may become an effective unit and "deliver the goods," but the goods may not secure the outcome desired. Perhaps some change in the wider world, beyond the team's control, has made what would have been an impressive work product a mere demonstration item: shiny and elegant but not, in the end, viable.

The challenges associated with turning around a local economy—not merely generating economic activity but *transforming* its character and value in significant ways—pose all of those risks. Increasingly, observers agree that the changes demanded of local city-regions as competitive units are beyond the authority and capacity of any one player or sector— making economic restructuring more a matter of joint problem solving than smart policy making in the traditional sense. Countless studies, speeches, and news stories call for "partnerships" and "cooperative networks." Yet the cooperative approach, as some have learned the hard way and others seem yet to discover, is riddled with hurdles and risky bets. If business, government, and nongovernmental players can manage to jointly define an agenda, overcome conflicts about priorities and worthy investments, and deliver the goods—literally, in the sense of goods or services for sale, and figuratively, in the sense of the local arrangements that enable productivity—global competition may render the output nonviable or essentially noncompetitive. Somewhere else, they have done it better, faster, and/or cheaper.

These challenges are especially serious in the many communities across the globe where an older industrial base must be updated, replaced, or otherwise transformed, and for these reasons economic restructuring represents a high-stakes test for a community's civic capacity. Restructuring also poses a significant boundary question for the concept: If a community does not secure the desired economic outcome, given how much lies outside the community's direct control or even its sphere of influence, to what extent can that be considered a *civic* failure?

The job loss associated with significant economic decline, and the physical and social signs of that decline, are ubiquitous and well known. But the raw material for recovery may not be so obvious to the outside observer: built-up institutions with established mindsets and allegiances; human capital (skilled workers and would-be entrepreneurs) whose skills must be transformed and/or deployed in entirely new ways; outdated rules imposed by firms as well as public agencies; and what experts on long-run industrial cycles diplomatically refer to as "inherited" labor-management relations (Markusen 1989).

Older industrial regions with those traits face daunting challenges to mobilizing and focusing collective action. Many of these challenges are associated with information or control. For example, multiple "best guesses" about the economic future may be appealing, but all will be challenging to prove convincingly to other players. For a time, the needed sense of urgency may be missing, or it may be diffused across disparate priorities, not focused on a few things that collaborators can support and pursue consistently. Except in small industrial towns—which are truly one-industry places—the differentiated quality of the local economy is such that elements of an old economic base often persist for decades, and perhaps quite productively, alongside elements of a newer economy— a phenomenon that economist and planner Sabina Deitrick (1999) has referred to, in the context of Pittsburgh's frequently misunderstood economic evolution, as "layering." Layering means that there is no one overarching economic challenge for local leadership but several, corresponding to the several different economic sectors that need attention: manufacturing *and* software, for example, financial services *and* advanced food processing.

Finally, not only does a still-evolving global marketplace add risk and uncertainty to the picture, but a number of the crucial policy levers— most business tax policies, say, or the availability of significant public financing to leverage vital private investment—are managed at higher levels of government than the city. This structural feature is especially important in the United States, where local governments receive significantly less aid from higher levels of government than do counterpart localities in Europe or other parts of the world (Savitch and Kantor 2004). And because important elements of the local problem reflect a much bigger strategic game—meaning that our outcomes depend not only on what we choose to do but what our competitors choose to do and how they update their choices to reflect ours—some important information for our decision-making is beyond our reach.

Like the members of our metaphorical team, the actors in a local economy begin with a clear, if intractably broad, task. It is a task with both political and technical dimensions: to make their city or city-region more competitive—that is, not only to generate local business activity, which may merely redistribute the limited economic pie, but to expand the pie—to enable economic growth.[1] While a large literature has considered the new pressures and opportunities that come with globalization, I will focus on key questions about what kind of civic or public problem economic restructuring represents for local democracy, given the inherent need to "team up" but also the institutional barriers, risk, and uncertainty that reflect legacies of earlier times on the one hand and a changing global future on the other.

In this chapter, I examine three distinct perspectives on what kind of public problem economic restructuring is—a problem for government decision-makers (making and implementing public policy), a problem of public-private collaboration or partnering, or a problem of shifting institutions and norms to create an economically innovative and adaptive "milieu." Each perspective offers important insights for those who would understand the character, use, and limits of civic capacity as a resource for transforming the economy. But each perspective has important blind spots as well. I discuss these and then outline key questions about the pair of cases to come.

Restructuring as a Public Policy Challenge

Many observers have examined economic restructuring as a problem for public policy makers, the process of policy making, and the work of implementation by public agencies. The "politics of local economic development," in particular, has often been treated as such. Economic restructuring is seen as an object for analysis and response by elected officials and expert staff. For much of the twentieth century, local governments in the United States were much more reliant on their own resources, usually from property taxes, than local counterparts around the world; this reliance deepened in the 1970s and 1980s with major cutbacks in federal aid to cities. But devolution has brought many of the same expectations and resource dependencies to subnational governments, including municipalities, in the developing world (Campbell 2003), while Europe and other wealthy regions continue to make localities relatively subordinate to national planning but offer significant fiscal transfers in the form of aid to cities and towns.

Those who have examined economic restructuring from this perspective, particularly in U.S. cities or city-regions, have several central concerns (review in Wolman and Spitzley 1996): How much leverage do local policy makers and officials actually have over business decisions, for example to locate or expand in a given jurisdiction, as well as business outcomes? Who acts to influence local policy, what are their interests, and how do they act? In particular, what do businesses seek from local or state government, how, and with what policy outcomes? To what extent are business-led coalitions (Stone 2005) able to enroll public officials in carrying out an overall economic agenda or drive a politics focused on growth, even at the expense of social welfare or other public concerns (Peterson 1981)? Much local economic-development policy making has been criticized as "corporate welfare" or imprudent monument-making by mayors and others who back stadium deals or convention centers with deep public subsidies. How do distinct industrial cycles of expansion, relocation, and decline shape the politics of economic growth—most immediately, the business and labor problems that actors need to solve in the political arena and the kinds of institutions that develop to solve them (Markusen 1989)? Within government, what do elected officials decide or influence (what scope of issues), and how important are the priorities and discretion of administrators? How much do they shape and carry out programs that meet their interests or reflect their understandings of economic challenges and opportunities, as opposed to adhering to elected policy makers' intent? How much is government policy making driven by a jurisdiction's rational economic interests and prospects versus a concern for city image and the need of elected officials (the agents) to claim credit for "doing something"? How do aid from higher levels of government and the strength of a city's market position (the "driving factors") affect city governments' bargaining leverage with the private sector (Savitch and Kantor 2004), and given their room to maneuver ("steering" factors), how much does the character of local politics itself—who is active, with what values and preferences—shape government strategy? Finally, what tools does the local public sector have for promoting more equitable development, in light of the limited evidence that the most common growth-oriented economic strategies benefit the poor and working class (Krumholz 1999)? The last question is far more than a technical matter of what policy measures are efficacious. In policy debates, this question often pits organized labor and poor and working-class residential areas against the "downtown" business class (banks, big corporations, trade associations) and their allies.

The restructuring-as-policy making perspective holds several crucial insights. The public sector is not a monolith but is made of up myriad interests, roles, and understandings of the economy (e.g., as a problem to be solved or an opportunity to forge one's reputation or gain influence). Policy makers are not mere subjects of some predetermined economic fate (i.e., they have discretion), but structural constraints beyond the city limits matter for local decision making, bargaining leverage, and more. Public-sector decision making faces huge information problems, not just conflict rooted in divergent interests. That is, policy making does not and cannot occur in a vacuum, with planners drawing up and employing rules and incentives that may lack business sense. Businesses and other nongovernmental players have multiple opportunities to shape policy but cannot necessarily ensure the efficiency or equity of policy outcomes. Well-intended policies may fail, effective policies may be scrapped as unfair or less important than other policies, and so on. Real or apparent conflicts between economic growth and equity are common in the struggle to make policy an effective mechanism of change. Finally, what the political process demands of government economic policy may shift dramatically depending on where local industries lie in a life cycle of expansion or decline.

On the last point, as Markusen (1989) argues persuasively, political conflict and cooperation in the context of mitigating decline—often by negotiating more competitive wage rates and external aid for local producers—is quite different from the politics of ensuring continued rapid growth early in the industrial profit cycle, where land scarcity and infrastructure are typical priorities. As context for civic action and sources of civic capacity—for example, in a city's institutions and built-up relationships and reputations—this life-cycle emphasis suggests a complicated set of agendas in relatively large and diversified cities, such as Pittsburgh, that were once industrial powerhouses. They retain important remnants and champions of the old economy yet aim desperately to grow the new.

Finally, and perhaps most basic of all, the literature on restructuring as local economic policy making highlights the curious invincibility of tax incentives and other favored policies in the face of negative evaluation. A nineteenth-century European diplomat famously observed that "there is nothing so tragic as an elegant theory ambushed by a gang of facts." But particularly at the local level, much economic policy appears to resist any such ambush, underscoring how strong the political incentives are for elected officials and others in public roles to reassure constituents by doing something with the tools at hand.[2] Under the once-dominant and still common approach to policy, state and local governments compete for footloose companies and capital. Under this approach, the lack of confirmation about what works leads to a "shoot anything that flies, claim anything that falls" strategy by economic development agencies and their political bosses—at least based on candid conversations with the insiders (Rubin 1988). Careful observers have offered the same caveat about economic planning by state and local governments in developing countries (Meyer-Stamer 2003).

What the policy making perspective does not tell us much about is whether and how political interests and policy strategies evolve through interaction (making it possible to transform a transactional game of influence, at least in part, into powerful joint problem solving), how particular approaches to the problems of economic restructuring allow some players to gain influence while others lose it or are kept out, what factors shape agenda setting that engages public officials with the private sector and other stakeholders who bring important information and capabilities to the table, and what enables or disables the feedback loops or other mechanisms through which policy makers learn what economic rules and incentives would, in fact, be smart and helpful. This learning is crucial to good problem solving, but it is beyond the narrow question of who influences public policy or how much.

In the developing world, as I hinted above, these kinds of public policy problems were long positioned structurally, and framed politically, as national or central-government challenges. Addressing the challenges often involved big, long-range plans to develop domestic industries (with special protections against foreign competitors and large public investments) or, more recently, deregulation and other efforts to liberalize economies, lower trade barriers, and attract foreign investment more aggressively. Because national governments did have significant leverage over business decisions, the politics of economic development in an era of classic industrial policy revolved more around avoiding the "capture" of policy by corrupt officials or colluding corporations and managing the failures associated with making bad guesses, regulating economic activity in cumbersome ways, or offering an ineffective set of incentives. As Rodrik (2004) laments, this has led to a skewed focus on developing country governments' "sins of commission" (too much government intervention of the wrong kinds) rather than its "sins of omission" (what government did not do but could and should have).

A large literature on the politics of economic policy making in developing countries suggests how important the risk of capture is, underscoring that public-private partnerships run this risk of collusion against the public interest, and underscoring how much policy outcomes may diverge from economic realities—for example, because decision makers are ideologically attached to particular policies, because aid agencies or foreign governments pressure policy makers into sticking with particular choices, or because policy makers think the evidence incomplete or inapplicable to their economies (Amsden 1989; Stiglitz and Charlton 2005; Wade 1990). But this body of work also includes a more recent emphasis on learning-oriented engagement by government with other actors—in other words, a problem-solving approach distinct from the design-and-retreat approach of classic bureaucratic policy making. Rodrik (2004, 38) argues that "the right image to carry in one's head is not of omniscient planners who can intervene ... but of an interactive process of strategic cooperation between the private and public sectors which, on one hand, serves to elicit information on business opportunities and constraints and, on the other hand, generates policy initiatives in response." A widely respected observer of the determinants of economic growth across nations, Rodrik goes so far as to argue that enabling this process of learning-while-doing is probably more important than choosing any one-best policy.

What this mainstream literature on the politics of economic growth in developing countries does not examine closely is the dynamics of local economic policy making, which is more and more important—again, not in isolation from higher levels of government or the pressures of the global marketplace but very much in tandem with them. In a review of local economic development planning by the public sector in developing countries, Meyer-Stamer (2003) concludes that there is thus far little clear evidence of success (as is the case in the wealthy nations), a mismatch between the skills in government and the planning requirements of typical strategies, a tendency to work much harder at creating plans than implementing them, and a tendency to take on overly ambitious projects—inspired, perhaps, by storied urban redevelopment projects in Europe that evolved over decades—rather than to start with simpler ones and make public-sector engagement part of a local learning process.

As I explore below, in an age of devolution and globalization, policy makers and researchers in the developing world (or those focused on it) have paid increased attention to regional competitiveness, the imperatives of adaptation and learning, and the nature and limits of policy making by subnational governments, leading to some convergence of thinking—between the wealthy North and global South—about what government can and should do to spur local economic growth as well as equity. This observation includes growth in the context of restructuring. Much of this newer perspective has avoided the U.S.-style emphasis on local officials' scope of decision and focused instead on how networks and collaboration are embedding policy making in broader programs of action.

Restructuring as Partnering

Many observers have emphasized collaboration or partnering—across organizations and across the government, business, and nonprofit sectors—as the key to restructuring urban economies. In the developing world, this emphasis has accompanied a larger shift toward public-private partnerships and privatization as mechanisms for development—a shift some have championed for its flexibility and scale potential and that others have sharply criticized as threatening public benefits, as well as returns for the poor (World Bank 1997). Likewise, in the United States, Europe, and other wealthy parts of the world, partnering has been championed as source of information, finance, and other resources that the public sector, on its own, cannot marshal (Austin and McCaffrey 2002)—and more broadly as a tool for governing, where diverse resources must be mobilized (Beauregard, Lawless, and Deitrick 1992; Stone 2005). But partnering has also been criticized as an appealing label for arrangements that allow business to capture an ever-larger share of economic growth at public expense (Krumholz 1999; Stoker 1998; Squires 1989). It is no accident that the interest in state and local governments partnering with the private sector soared when massive industrial decline met with an ideology of laissez-faire, smaller government, led most notably by Margaret Thatcher and Ronald Reagan in the 1980s. The shift in ideology and policy left many cities, especially in the United States, to fend for themselves (Beauregard, Lawless, and Deitrick 1992).

At issue, then, is not just the means of forging partnerships but the questions of what specific tasks or aims are suitable for cross-sector partnerships, especially those that commit significant public resources, and of what the terms of partnership should be—in other words, questions about appropriateness, the relative influence or vulnerability of partners, and accountability.

Forms, Labels, and Participants

Partnerships come in three main forms: organizations, projects, and coalitions. The first may have expansive agenda-setting and project-initiating roles, as I will illustrate in the case of Pittsburgh, while the second represent the most visible face of coproduction, with its features of joint implementation responsibility and shared risk. That is, organizations or interorganizational "strategic" alliances generate projects, and projects allow a team-based approach to specific economic restructuring tasks, such as clearing blight or developing business start-ups in a new industrial sector. More controversial are direct business finance projects, billed as "partnerships" though the public sector is rarely more than a source of money and perhaps infrastructure, in which large public subsidies lower private risk. Third and finally, coalitions, reflect the long- or short-run arrangements through which partners mobilize political support for their agendas.

At all three levels, the term partnering is so elastic that it reveals little about the depth or degree of integration and interdependence in a two-party or multiparty relationship. In strategy terms, prospective partners can answer the question, "*How* partnered should we be?" in a variety of ways, from limited "parallel play" to much more integrated arrangements, wherein resources are shared, accountability is more extensive, and activities are coordinated or even completely redesigned under a shared management approach (see Briggs 2003b for a review).[3]

The 1970s and 1980s saw rapid growth in the number of economic-development partnership organizations, many of them regional or metropolitan in scope—by some survey measures, a threefold growth in the United States between the late 1980s and the late 1990s alone (Olberding 2002). Beyond chambers of commerce and other traditional business-promotion organizations, these partnerships engaged private- and public-sector decision makers in a range of planning and implementation initiatives for economic growth. In America, in general, these organizations appear to be business-led, with a changing cast of elected officials playing support roles or serving as points of contact for specific projects (Olberding 2002). This raises the possibility that the label "partnership" is meant to signal two very different kinds of actors (business and government) working together in common cause, for reasons of legitimacy—what I have labeled *multilateralism*, noting how nations may act on controversial problems on the world stage—as much as operational interdependence or complementarity. But under some circumstances, a forceful mayor or other elected official can shape the agenda and approach of these partnerships in pivotal ways. Chicago Mayor Harold Washington did so as part of a new progressive coalition he assembled in that city (Giloth and Mier 1989), and Pittsburgh's assertive Mayor David Lawrence was the crucial partner for industrialist Richard King Mellon in the postwar environmental cleanup and partial reconstruction of that city (Lubove 1996). By comparison, Europe's business-government partnerships generally feature much more prominent government roles and direction setting by public policy as much or more than nongovernmental "policies" informally negotiated by and with business leaders (Savitch and Kantor 2004).

The business activities and interests in play, as well as the role of individual business leaders as civic entrepreneurs, are much more varied, argue some business experts, than the "monolithic" business world portrayed by much research on urban politics (Austin and McCaffrey 2002). In the United States, partnership organizations report place marketing, regulatory reform, and financial incentive packages as defining their major operations (Olberding 2002). But some organizations have engaged in more ambitious restructuring of local government authority and finance to make their regions more competitive. For example, triggered by a major consulting firm's strategic assessment and recommendations, the business-led Cleveland Tomorrow partnership famously supported a major overhaul of city government finances and management in that economically and socially distressed city, beginning in the early 1980s. Though the group has been criticized and though its role diminished over time, the partnership undoubtedly helped a city broken by industrial decline and deep racial divides and mistrust to achieve a partial renaissance (Austin 1998). Likewise, greater Pittsburgh's Allegheny Conference on Community Development, whose expansive and often reformist agenda lies at the center of the next chapter, was, for decades, regarded as the model for close engagement by business in civic affairs—this in the context of a city undergoing significant economic restructuring.

Coalitions and Conflict

The coalitional view of industrial economies in transition highlights the role of conflict and competing ideology that the language of collaboration tends to obscure or downplay. Beauregard, Lawless, and Deitrick (1992) show, for example, how two coalitions competed to frame the problem of restructuring and win resources in greater Pittsburgh in the 1980s and beyond. The well-funded dominant coalition, centered on big corporations, financial institutions, middle-class professionals, and prominent elected officials asserted the urgency of pursuing Pittsburgh's postindustrial future in healthcare, finance, services, and high technology. A poorly funded subordinate coalition of organized labor, churches, and elected officials from the old manufacturing towns hit hardest by industrial decline championed "reindustrialization"—for example, through turnaround plans and financing for steel mills. This conflict included a spatial dimension as well: the central city and growing, new-industry suburbs of professional households favored the dominant agenda, while fiscally weak, working-class small towns held out hope for the marginalized reindustrialization agenda. "In sum," say the researchers, "regional collaboration is unlikely to be as regional or consensual as the name implies" (p. 428). Despite the differences in political context, their study found the same stubborn divides at work in Sheffield, England, which had likewise sought to replace a once-dominant industry through "collaborative" strategies.

The Developing World

Intensive public-private collaboration and extensive business engagement in reform or other activist policy making at the local level is newer and far less common in the developing world. As I outlined above, this is in part because local governments have neither been as "muscular" there, historically, nor as reliant on business-driven tax revenues to finance local services. But closer engagement, with the attendant risks and opportunities, is clear over the past two decades—because of both decentralization and ideological shifts toward market-friendly approaches (Campbell 2003)—and so are a set of patterns that largely parallel the U.S. experience I outlined above.

A growing body of research and commentary underscores the importance of entrepreneurial government engaging business in learning, carrying out demonstration projects, and sharing the risks as well as rewards associated with new sources of economic growth. In some cases, this work also underscores surprises about the capabilities and commitments of nongovernmental organizations (NGOs) that take on economic development roles, such as in workforce training programs (Tendler 1997). Much like a counterpart literature in the United States, this body of work highlights the role of personal networks and trust, public-sector fragmentation, the responsiveness of higher levels of government (or lack of same), entrenched habits of thought and behavior in both business and government organizations, a climate of risk and uncertainty, and still-evolving market pressures as the defining features of local business-government partnership (Boniface 2001; Guimarães and Martin 2001). As I hinted early in this chapter and explore in the two chapters to come, these features appear to be endemic to restructuring as a civic problem—in the broad sense of being a problem for collective action within and across risk-sharing organizations and networks.

The interrelated problems of equity, efficacy, and representativeness are also inflated by the huge information problems in this area of public life, as highlighted by Giarratani and Houston (1989, 556):

Strategies for growth based on the partnership model may not address a region's problems with the full choice set in mind, and therefore, the opportunity costs of policy initiatives may never be given a fair hearing. The actual choice set considered will usually be limited by the interests of the partners. If significant elements of the community are excluded from the partnership, it is unlikely that the full costs are being considered.

Partnering as Limited Cooperation under Uncertainty

A final perspective on partnering emphasizes the decision dilemmas that players face under conditions of risk and uncertainty—that is, economic development partnering as partially competitive and partially cooperative gaming (Axelrod 2004). This perspective is most concerned with the conditions under which cooperation arises and endures—or fails to. Grounded in stylized rules—in part because big, simplifying assumptions and computer simulations rather than complex real-world cases are used to test many hypotheses about cooperation—this approach nevertheless highlights a variety of practical problems worth testing against the two restructuring cases I examine in the chapters to come. I will focus on four central problems: reputation, information quality, trust, and norms. Each structures the local "ecology" of cooperation.

First, because efforts to develop and advance collective agendas involve repeat interaction ("iterated" or multiround games), strategic actors must generate and work hard to protect their reputations (Gamson 1966; Long 1958; Axelrod 1984). This means, for example, that reputational considerations can become a central aspect of political self-interest, not an afterthought or a mere reflection of personal integrity or community-mindedness.

Second, under conditions of incomplete, contested, or ambiguous information, other players' actions (or "moves") can easily be misinterpreted, so mechanisms that improve transparency and the reliability of information, for example with careful communication and monitoring standards or third-party facilitation or review, can help secure otherwise elusive or unstable cooperation among parties (Axelrod 2004). Yet key players—such as those with information advantages—may not see such transparency as being in their interests; there are incentives to distort information. Also, where access is concerned, it is a truism of political life that the advantages of carefully cultivated networks erode when information is more widely available through less exclusive channels (Knoke 1990).

Third, because trust is often hard won but easily lost, a host of stylized experiments and real-world analyses alike confirm the wisdom of "starting with small stakes and raising them as the relationship develops" as a way of avoiding, and enabling one's partners to avoid, having to make "leaps of faith" (Axelrod 2004, 17). This also means that players work to embed exchanges that involve risk in durable relationships, which buttress trusting "leaps" (Granovetter 1985).

The fourth point is closely related to trust and its sources: while individual players can exploit uneven access to information (asymmetry) or ambiguity and complexity, effective multiparty cooperation hinges on a shared understanding of the rules of engagement or rules of the game. Without this, players cannot reliably signal each other or prevent and manage conflicts. But much local civic life revolves around informal exchanges and coalitional arrangements, not specified contracts. Thus, assumed rules and expectations—norms that define local political culture (Coleman 1990; Elazar 1966; March and Olsen 1996), not explicitly stated legal rules—can shape behavior and the interpretation of behavior in important ways. Changes that rupture norms can, in turn, reverberate widely and for prolonged periods, as the system finds a new equilibrium. And culturally diverse communities appear to struggle more with conflicts and confusion over norms, precisely because different expectations about behavior may be strongly held and yet unstated, taken for granted (Briggs 1998).

On a final note, game theory and its relatives have been much better at explaining how established games are played than how new ones develop or how games are transformed by learning—in which interests, stakes, rules, and more can be rethought and modified.[4] These themes are central to the third and final perspective on the civic dimensions of economic restructuring—how to change the local game, in a sense, and what players aim for.

Restructuring as the Cultivation of an Innovative Milieu

The first perspective—restructuring as policy making—privileged the role of the public sector, with business as a key interest group and also a claimant of public resources and attention. The second—restructuring as public-private collaboration—weighted the balance toward business and its problems but, at least among critical observers, with a core concern for varied public interests and public sector constraints. The third and final perspective—restructuring as the cultivation of an institutional milieu capable of ongoing adaptation and productive innovation—focuses squarely on business determination of the economic future, with government and civil society as support players. This perspective emphasizes business economics, organizational dynamics, and the functions of interpersonal and interorganizational networks to a degree that is rarely explored, say, in the mainstream literature on the politics of local economic policy making. This school of thought is centrally concerned with how to promote a distinctive local blend of competition and cooperation, with government and civil-society groups acting as enablers. The economic context for this aim is the transition in high-value economies from traditional models of standardization in mass production to a model of flexible specialization (Piore and Sabel 1984). Much work in this vein reflects the influential work on economic *clusters* carried out by business economist and strategy guru Michael Porter. As Porter (2000, 15) defines them, "Clusters are geographic concentrations of interconnected companies, specialized suppliers, service providers, firms in related industries, and associated institutions (universities, standards agencies, trade associations) in a particular field that compete but also cooperate."

Porter's genius was to take a long-familiar concept in economic geography and marry it to principles of microeconomic theory and competitive strategy that concern the role of business location. The message to businesses is fairly straightforward: You survive and thrive in part because of the interconnected sets of firms and other organizations around you; those entities and the links you share are part of your competitive advantage, especially where the information and capacity vital for risk taking and flexible, innovative production are concerned. Since Porter's work has generated a cottage industry of cluster studies and consultancies worldwide, as well as warning bells from critics, it behooves me to briefly explore the major recommendations he makes for policy makers and political action.

First, Porter identifies "cluster upgrading," not subsidizing favored sectors, as the proper target of economic policy. Second, he emphasizes "removing obstacles, relaxing constraints, and eliminating inefficiencies to productivity and productivity growth" (p. 28). But third, he encourages public investments in education and training, sponsored fora that convene cluster participants (government as social catalyst), public data sources organized around clusters rather than outdated (he argues) industry-sector categories, and subsidized research and development for cluster-related technologies. Highlighting city and metro-level cluster initiatives from Bogotá and Charlotte to Rotterdam and Christchurch, Porter's enthusiasm for private-sector leadership is unreserved, as are his hopes for broad-based political mobilization (p. 31):

Active government participation in a privately led effort, rather than an initiative controlled by government, will have a better chance of success. Companies usually can better identify the obstacles and constraints (as well as the opportunities) in their paths than can government. Letting the private sector lead also reduces the initiative's political content while taking advantage of the private sector's often superior implementation ability. Cluster initiatives should be as nonpartisan as possible and should remain independent of any party or administration's political agenda. Legislators and the executive branch, the opposition parties, and those in power must all be involved.

Leaving aside Porter's arguments about appropriate private- versus public-sector roles for the moment, some observers have cautioned that the cluster concept has been marketed well beyond the evidence base, as a "policy panacea." This is an important notion, and not just for economic outcomes, since fuzzy problems and complicated evidence make a community (or region or nation) ripe for politicking around such concepts. Martin and Sunley (2002, 5) conclude, for example, that "the cluster concept should carry a public policy health warning." They note how elastic the concept has become and how the association between high-growth industries and certain patterns of geographic concentration does not prove that it was the local pattern that enabled the growth.

Meanwhile, the best available evidence is that clusters in developing countries are much more heterogeneous than the "stylized role models" that have shaped discussion in Europe and North America, say Altenburg and Meyer-Stamer (1999). The researchers add that policy measures to strengthen this range of clusters—from "survival clusters" that are competitively weak but create important employment opportunities to "mass-producer clusters" that require significant upgrading and innovation once exposed to free trade—vary widely. And so, presumably, do the particular tasks for which effective collaboration among the business, government, and civil-society sectors (including unions and training organizations) may be vital.

A second vein in the restructuring-as-cultivating-a-milieu perspective focuses on the nature of local institutional culture and mechanisms for adaptive learning. This work emerged from research by European geographers and others on the widely admired systems of flexible production evident in Italy and Germany by the 1970s. But it crested with an influential book on the world's most famous and wealthy cluster, the high-technology Silicon Valley, and its main domestic rival across the country. In *Regional Advantage* (1994), AnnaLee Saxenian compared the Valley's success with the partial stagnation of America's second most important technology cluster, the Route 128 corridor around Boston. Each cluster evolved around a research university "anchor," noted Saxenian—Stanford and the Massachusetts Institute of Technology, respectively—but Route 128 organized according to a traditional, hierarchical model of independent and secretive firms succeeding or failing in "silos," whereas the Silicon Valley, she concluded, had flourished under a decentralized system that allowed for both close cooperation and intense competition. This system and its pro-learning, pro-innovation culture extended from the corporate boardrooms and university R&D labs to the informal social life of the Silicon Valley. It led the Valley to outcompete Route 128 by a significant margin by the early 1990s, despite the latter's enormous early advantages, in R&D contracts and access to private capital, in the decades after the Second World War.

In Saxenian's formulation, the collective-action problems that government and other broad-based community institutions can address to create innovative milieus are of two kinds: pooling risk and resources to help start-up companies excel; and, as Markusen (1989) noted about profit cycles, managing the physical and social demands of growth— ideally on a regional basis that reflects the real geography of the emerging economy rather than on a parochial, town-by-town basis. A recent study of "enterprising places" in the United States and the United Kingdom, such as the Research Triangle region in North Carolina, suggests that credible intermediary organizations can be important for tackling such needs. Like Porter, the researchers emphasize a "measured connection" to government to ensure access to resources and decision-making clout as well as an independence (buffering) from political cycles and leadership swings (Baxter and Tyler, 2007; Smilor et al. 2007).

These ideas, along with the much-publicized success of high-technology clusters in media worldwide, have led to several interrelated trends in how economic restructuring is conceived, and these trends are important for understanding the problem that local leaders *believe* they must solve as well as the *process* of problem solving. First, the conventional wisdom is that innovation per se is the key to success. On the one hand, this can lead to such an emphasis on new products that basic productivity, transportation costs, and other competitiveness factors are given short shrift. On the other hand, the focus on adaptation as an ongoing imperative suits today's more turbulent economy and the built-in risks and uncertainties I highlighted at the start of this chapter. Second, universities and the commercialization of university-based research and technology have become much more central to the concerns of policy makers and public-private partnerships. Universities are complicated, decentralized institutions with civic as well as business-minded priorities of their own, as the Pittsburgh case reminds us. Third, while economic policy makers and agencies still court companies and apply incentives for which the impact evidence is skimpy at best, learning and risk taking get more attention than under the old "smokestack-chasing" model of locational incentives.

Learning, in fact, becomes a defining purpose of partnerships in the milieu perspective. Like Rodrik, some observers have gone so far as to reframe economic development, including restructuring, as a process of learning and knowledge management in network-based "communities of practice" (Snyder 2002). Others have emphasized the conditions under which adversarial relationships, between workers and managers, for example, or among competing firms, can be transformed through institutions that allow "studied trust" to emerge (Sabel 1992). Disparate players, in this view, do not surrender their interests. But they have the opportunity to rethink those interests in the context of deeper learning about the problems and opportunities they confront. Sabel (2004) has characterized business and government organizations that take this pragmatic, searching approach as "experimentalist."

It remains to be seen whether and how the civic life of a community can shape the conditions under which such organizations emerge and make a difference. Also, the innovative milieu, and its cousin concept, the cluster, are essentially apolitical ideas whose realization hinges, to an extraordinary degree, on politics. I mean politics not in the narrow sense of contesting elections and formal policy decisions, though those are certainly important at times, but in the wider sense of building constituencies for ideas and agreements that take a chance on those ideas. This includes the appealing ideas and the less inviting, change-demanding ones underneath: cultivating new institutions or adapting old ones and reorganizing authority (and thus turf) to mobilize resources, assign work, monitor it, and make midcourse corrections as needed. To stick with the authority issue and the experimentalist model for a moment, no laboratory for experimenting ever functioned well, let alone accountably, without an authority structure. But reorganizing authority is a notoriously unpopular business, making it very tempting to adopt the language of the innovation economy wholly out of proportion to the reorganization actually accomplished. And the politics of economic restructuring tends to call for psychological ownership and credit claiming to a degree that proponents of the cluster concept seem to think unworkable.

A final disconnect in the call for transforming economies into innovative clusters concerns social equity, both in terms of what happens to those most dependent on the older skills and job types and what equity requires as a public-sector responsibility. On the first score, it is not clear, under the milieu model, what is to become of workers or other who cannot adapt to the high-skill and often unstable employment that comes with emergent sectors, such as start-ups in the technology sector. Except for the thoughtful but still limited body of work applying cluster concepts in a balanced way to poor countries, there seems little acknowledgment of the huge problem of dislocated workers or the possibility that some workers can hope for little more than the low-wage service rungs of a new local economy (though Porter, Saxenian, and others do call for smart public investments in workforce development).

On the second score, government is, in the economic realm, surely more than a productivity-enhancing device, in part because even the most productive economies do not automatically provide an adequate safety net or other sources of economic security. Government may not be the source of the social contract—that comes from civil society itself—but it is an important keeper of the contract, not just a catalyst for economic prosperity. A focus on productivity, adaptation, and innovation does not simplify these questions of who gets left behind or how far government's obligations extend. But perhaps a balanced consideration of that popular focus will allow decision makers—in all sectors—to ground these tougher questions in real prospects and needs instead of feel-good commitments, campaign slogans, and seminar debates.

Summary and Preview

The three perspectives I examined in this chapter respectively emphasize public-sector authority and decision dilemmas related to economic rules and incentives (the *restructuring-as-policy making* perspective), the potential and also the complexity of blending public and private sector agendas and organizational capacity on behalf of economic change (the *restructuring-as-partnering* perspective), and business productivity and innovation imperatives for which nonbusiness organizations can provide useful supports (the *restructuring-as-cultivating-an-innovative-milieu* perspective). Together, these perspectives offer a much richer and more balanced set of insights into what problems public, private, and nongovernmental players believe they need to solve in the realm of restructuring than does the policy making perspective alone, which has absorbed most of the attention on how the democratic process relates to restructuring. The three perspectives also illuminate the range of interests, constraints, and opportunities that are likely to define the moves those players make, relationships they form, and resources they are able and willing to mobilize over time—whereas each of these perspectives, on its own, treats some important player on the landscape as a puzzling or predictable monolith inside the proverbial black box.

From the standpoint of understanding a community's civic capacity, these three perspectives suggest more problem-specific questions about the two cases of economic restructuring. These focus the general questions about governance I outlined in chapter 1. First, what understandings, interests, and relationships lead key players to the strategies they choose to pursue? Second, how does joint agenda setting by partners, if it obtains, happen? In particular, what moves or shifts in the environment create conditions that favor cooperation or noncooperation by potential partners, and how is formal policy making or partnering integrated, or not, into a larger process of restructuring? Third, given the inherently multifaceted and decentralized nature of the problems associated with transforming a local economy, what barriers and decisions do actors face as they try to mobilize resources on behalf of an agenda of change? And fourth, what institutional mechanisms, if any, seem to allow learning while doing, which, to varying degrees, underpins all three models of restructuring reviewed in this chapter?

The next chapter examines economic restructuring in greater Pittsburgh, arguably the birthplace of the modern public-private partnership in a major industrial American city, now a "hyperorganized" region seeking to create the recommended milieu of high-technology and high-wage innovation, and for both reasons an important and revealing case. The subsequent chapter looks at efforts to revive and redirect Brazil's industrial powerhouse, in the manufacturing suburbs around São Paulo collectively known as the Greater ABC region. Unlike Pittsburgh, where the decline of unions tracked the collapse of the city's traditional base in high-wage manufacturing, the ABC remains the heartland of organized labor in Brazil, and for much of the past two decades, local government was led by the Workers' Party that grew out of the industrial unions. The Greater ABC case highlights the meaning and use of civic capacity in the context of democratization, the devolution and economic decline that spurred activist local government, and the special competitive challenges that face many developing countries in a global economy. Also unlike greater Pittsburgh, the ABC region lacked any history of public-private cooperation before the wave of mobilization and institution building that marked the rebirth of democracy in the area. The Brazil case is of special conceptual and practical import, both within and beyond the developing world, for those reasons.

7

The Hyper-organized Region: Leading the Next "New Economy" in Pittsburgh

What is economic restructuring? It's turning around an aircraft carrier in a pond.
—Pittsburgh elected official

Enter the city of Pittsburgh, and you cross water. The Allegheny and Monongahela Rivers carried the products of heavy industry from here, Steel City, and the many mill towns in the surrounding region to humming factories and growing towns across the world. The panorama of downtown, seen from the river bridges, also conveys the legacy of the region's industrial economy and the great wealth it produced from the mid-nineteenth to the late twentieth century. There is the cleaned-up and redeveloped downtown driven by a postwar coalition of powerful banks, manufacturing corporations, and public officials—the fabled partnership of the 1940s and 1950s known as Renaissance I. There is the rehabilitated housing and the newer office towers associated with another major land development and quality-of-life improvement effort in the late 1970s and early 1980s, Renaissance II. And turning to the west, there are the newest jewels in the crown, all completed in the late 1990s or early 2000s in the interest of economic competitiveness: two major-league sports stadiums, a high tech convention center, and—miles back, behind us now—the ultramodern airport (figure 7.1). These are part of a third chapter, wherein the claim to "renaissance" remains unclear.

To the well-informed observer, there is the equally important institutional legacy behind this stage set downtown: one of the most extraordinary concentrations of philanthropic wealth of any region in the world, renowned research universities and a linked medical complex, all of which grew out of the industry-university nexus more than a century ago, and the large and hierarchical corporations that remained after the

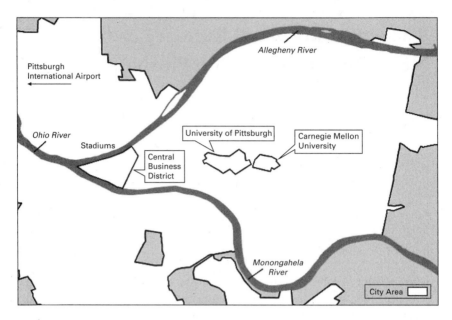

Figure 7.1
City of Pittsburgh and environs. *Source*: ESRI, 2005.

collapse of "big steel" in the early 1980s. Enter the city, and you also cross a patchwork of affluent suburbs and struggling small towns, many of them bankrupted by the loss of an industrial job base and the failure to find a viable replacement. The physical landscape, in other words, bears the indelible imprint of the institutional one—and vice versa. The landscape is a marker of the region's capacity for collective action as well as the strategies of physical redevelopment on which that action was long focused.

Historian Roy Lubove (1996) has argued that Pittsburgh has the unique distinction, among major industrial cities in America, of having been reborn not once but twice through public-private partnerships. In this chapter, I examine what might be considered round three of a regional, not just city-centered, saga: the effort by key interest groups and organizations—some old, some new, and some reconfigured—to develop and implement an agenda of economic restructuring that is broadly supported as well as substantively effective. The latest chapter demands a much more fundamental transformation of the city and region's competitive edge than redeveloping land or adding amenities, though projects in those domains may certainly play a part.

Inevitably perhaps, the latest chapter includes a tension between the old Pittsburgh and the new—in a place that is "layered" with economic engines, no longer propelled by heavy metals or any other one driver of growth, and with myriad economic development and civic organizations and their agendas (thus the label "hyperorganized"). The central puzzle is about how to organize and carry out this most ambitious of collective-action agendas when (1) the old, top-down recipes for civic capacity no longer suffice and (2) the character of the problems to be solved make it difficult to figure out what works and who should be responsible. Even among U.S. industrial regions, greater Pittsburgh stands out for the degree of complexity and fragmentation in governance compared, say, to greater Cleveland, which has also aggressively pursued public-private partnerships since the 1980s (Austin 1998; Austin and McCaffrey 2002).

Paradoxically, greater Pittsburgh suffered the greatest loss of industrial jobs of any U.S. region over the course of deindustrialization in the late 1970s and 1980s at the same time that it garnered top awards for "livability" and projected an image of comeback and innovation, of transforming itself from Steel City to a high-tech "knowledge city" (Deitrick 1999). I begin with a brief look at how far the region fell economically and why, how much it in fact bounced back, and where the economy has been headed. This assessment of markets, partnerships, and policy choices frames the analysis of the latest decade of local organizing and reform, in which I look at what it means to develop and use civic capacity for economic restructuring in a former industrial region.

The Fall, Rise, and "Layering" of the Regional Economy

The 1970s and 1980s brought massive and well-publicized employment loss to all of America's old industrial regions. But the Pittsburgh region was especially hard hit given the job losses in heavy metals and the area's concentration in that sector. Between 1980 and 1986 alone, the manufacturing job base shrunk by 43 percent—a loss of some 115,000 high-wage, unionized jobs, nearly 50 percent of them in the steel industry (Deitrick 1999, 12). Most of this job loss was to domestic competitor regions that offered more efficient production and distribution (Giarratani and Houston 1989).

The 1963 *Economic Study of the Pittsburgh Region*, a landmark in the field of regional economic analysis that local leaders in business and government largely ignored, had warned of overspecialization in heavy industry (mainly coal, iron, steel, electrical machinery, and glass), over-concentration of the labor force in large firms (which had the side effect of making many small manufacturing towns entirely dependent on one or two big employers), and the region's failure to keep up with changes in technology and world markets (Lubove 1996).

A long cycle of production peaks and troughs, going back as far as the 1920s, culminated in a bottoming out after 1979 (Clark 1989). With the massive loss of employment and income came a loss of private investment, corporate headquarters, and a way of life built around seemingly secure, high-wage employment—in many cases from generation to generation—in Pittsburgh and the mill towns along the major rivers (Lubove 1996). The nation's most fragmented region in terms of units of local government per person—Allegheny County alone is home to Pittsburgh as well as 130 small towns and cities—became a patchwork of municipalities struggling, one by one, with economic distress, without the regional government or revenue sharing arrangements that help small jurisdictions in other regions to balance the books while providing essential services (Hamilton, Miller, and Paytas 2004). A longtime civic insider observes,

Everything references that [loss of heavy industry] . . . I think that it was a real body blow to the region in terms of their seeing themselves as one of the important regions of the country. That's still a very defining thing. It is a source, in a very significant way, of the resistance to change, a fearfulness about change, about giving up the region's roots, the connections to the past . . . *Interviewer: Why not just the opposite: a crisis to spur change?* [Because] it sapped their confidence.

From the mid- to late 1980s, however, at least to outsiders, Pittsburgh garnered the reputation of a comeback city in a region determined to transform itself. Growth in banking, business services, healthcare, higher education, and other service jobs roughly matched the national average, a public-private partnership called Strategy 21 emphasized the potential of technology and the importance of quality-of-life upgrading, and top research universities took center stage in the search for economic revival. Like other declining regions, greater Pittsburgh hoped to bounce back transformed—as a high-skill, twenty-first-century "knowledge economy" (Giarratani and Houston 1989; Mitchell-Weaver 1992). And in 1985, Rand McNally named Pittsburgh the nation's "Most Livable City"; the area was touted as a model for other regions coping with industrial decline (Deitrick 1999).

The latest partnerships seemed to echo the successful postwar environmental cleanup and downtown rebuilding achieved during Renaissance

I, an effort of the 1940s and 1950s led cooperatively by banker Richard King Mellon and Mayor David Lawrence and heavily supported by the Allegheny Conference on Community Development. The Conference, a roundtable of the largest corporations founded by Mellon and leaders of the Pittsburgh Regional Planning Association in 1944, engaged big business in large-scale, well-focused civic efforts (Mershon 2000). In the terms favored by students of urban regimes, the Conference was to anchor the governing coalition in the postwar years, forge and sustain a shared agenda of change, and develop the "schemes of cooperation" with government and other players to achieve that change (Stone 2005). In its organization, and some would say its outsized influence, The Conference fit the hierarchical, heavy industry model around which the region's economy and social institutions were organized.

As Beauregard, Lawless, and Deitrick (1992) emphasize, however, while outside observers imagined a consensual regional agenda in the 1980s "comeback" period, and while this fit with the laissez-faire, market-led approach to deindustrialization in the United States at the time, the reality was one of conflict and increasingly divided fortunes—that is, between those tethered to the old economy of greater Pittsburgh and those developing and riding the new. The old regime was evolving. A strong coalition made up of large corporations, major regional banks, Pittsburgh elected officials, philanthropic foundations, and the newcomers to the scene—the universities and research-based medical center—focused on building toward the hoped-for postindustrial economy. A weaker coalition of labor, activist churches, and small-town elected officials tried desperately to win support for reindustrialization. The newly founded Steel Valley Authority, for instance, critiqued the Allegheny Conference and its core membership of big companies for focusing on downtown property values while the same companies continued to shift jobs and capital away from the region (Mitchell-Weaver 1992).

The well-funded public-private partnerships focused on a vision of continued growth for the region's population—struggling, in the process, to convince surrounding counties that the region meant more than Pittsburgh and Allegheny County—and not the challenges associated with managing decline or helping displaced industrial workers adjust (Giarratani and Houston 1989). Hundreds of thousands of workers and their families who had been a part of the old economy stayed, hoping for a return of big steel and other heavy industry. The postindustrial agenda assumed that new sectors of job growth would automatically spur workers to gain new skills and better incomes. For its part, the Allegheny Conference came under increased criticism for the failure to take risks, for devolving into a largely promotional device unable to find its footing.

This division aside, the area's comeback as a service-driven economy was, in fact, partial and misleading. Most new service-sector jobs were at a fraction of the wage levels of lost manufacturing jobs, and much of the new growth served local, not export, demand (Giarratani and Houston 1989). As anchor for the region, said one analyst, Pittsburgh had seen the "transformation from an internationally oriented industrial city to a regionally oriented service economy" (Clark 1989, 63). It was smaller, too. Pittsburgh's population was cut roughly in half between 1960 and 2000. Inauspiciously, it led major U.S. cities in population loss in the 1980s, and the surrounding region likewise suffered significant decline and persistently high rates of poverty and unemployment. Between 1980 and 2000, Pittsburgh slid from sixty-sixth to seventy-seventh among major central cities on a distress index combining poverty, unemployment, population loss, and household income (Furdell, Wolman, and Hill 2005). According to census figures, the Pittsburgh metro area was home to 2.7 million in 1970 but only 2.3 million by 2006, with significant domestic outmigration continuing and very little immigration from overseas.

What is more, some elements of the apparent comeback were short-lived. In the 1990s, manufacturing jobs began to grow again but service job growth slowed dramatically, and it became clear that the region lacked strong connections to new growth sectors, such as the much-hyped technology sector (Deitrick 1999). For example, important concentrations emerged in the biomedical, software, and robotics fields, but these remained small and struggled to retain the firms with growth prospects. Lycos, a renowned web portal company spun off by Carnegie Mellon University, became an iconic case in point. As it began to grow rapidly, the company moved to join the greater Boston tech cluster, its founder and CEO citing better access to creative talent and ideas. The firm became a multibillion-dollar giant—but not in Pittsburgh.

Meanwhile, the large-scale real estate projects identified above—the airport, convention center, and sports stadiums—generated temporary booms in construction employment. But these projects represented an effort to upgrade the region's amenities in order to retain companies and, if possible, to enable new growth; the projects were not sources of economic growth in and of themselves. And the new airport failed to meet projected traffic levels by 1995, eventually losing US Airways, one of the region's largest employers (Deitrick 1999).

Finally, the local manufacturing sector was evolving, belatedly to be sure, through reorganization, technological advances, and diversification (Deitrick 1999). Yet the competitive dynamics of these evolving clusters remained largely invisible in the effort to define and advance an agenda for economic growth centered on software, robotics, and biomedical innovation. The successful manufacturers "help pay the largest single tranche of the area's total wage bill," noted Mitchell-Weaver, Deitrick, and Rigopoulou (1999, 24). Yet they were all but invisible in the reigning 1990s rhetoric about a new high-tech economy.

Together, these trends produced a "multilayered" restructuring (Deitrick 1999), in which old industries were evolving in ways difficult for the body politic to track and perhaps to shape, many popular new "development" projects redistributed rather than created wealth (representing a platform for future growth), and newer tech sectors began to garner headlines, as well as public and private resources, but represented a small share of the region's jobs or job growth. The local press and elected officials, say longtime observers, remained focus on the "big-bang theory" of economic growth: wooing big employers, rather than ensuring the basis for sustained growth in a variety of sectors and from various types of firms.

Clear spatial divides emerged as well, in the 1980s and 1990s, among: The central city with its universities and rebuilt housing and office complexes, the newer suburbs popular with young firms and middle-class professionals, and the fiscally failing or bankrupt old industrial towns with high rates of unemployment, poverty, and associated distress (figure 7.2; Beauregard, Lawless, and Deitrick 1992). In the context of a declining core and inner industrial ring, rapid new suburban development means that greater Pittsburgh is sprawling while also "hollowing out" (Brookings Institution 2003; Mitchell-Weaver, Deitrick, and Rigopoulou 1999). These class divides, compounding jurisdictional ones, complicate the civic landscape in significant ways.

These trends defined the restructuring problem to be solved, as well as the civic momentum and fault lines that emerged in greater Pittsburgh after the "body blow" of heavy-industry collapse in the 1980s. Contrary to the facile image of successful comeback through broad-based partnership, the region came into the 1990s with no clear driver of economic growth to count on and cultivate and no shared (let alone institutionalized) sense of itself as a region. Other problems included deep divides between the fortunes and commitments of blue-collar workers and old-economy communities on the one hand and the new economy still

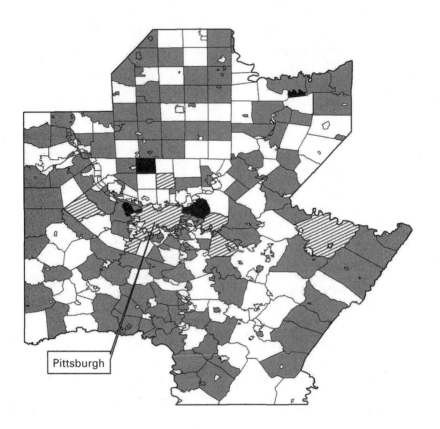

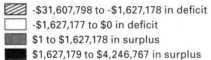

Surplus or Deficit by Municipality

- -$31,607,798 to -$1,627,178 in deficit
- -$1,627,177 to $0 in deficit
- $1 to $1,627,178 in surplus
- $1,627,179 to $4,246,767 in surplus

Figure 7.2
Economic inequality in the Pittsburgh metropolitan area, 2004
Sources: "Financial statistics, 1998–2004," Pennsylvania Department for Community and Local Economic Development, Pennsylvania State University, Pennsylvania Spatial Data Access.

emerging on the other, a skills mismatch between the work of the old economy and the promise of the new, a discredited business leadership organization that nevertheless represented the area's only influential civic catalyst—and potentially an antidote to fragmented local government—and a contest to define a viable economic future and then mobilize resources effectively to achieve it.

It was in this context that a new effort to forge a collective agenda and organize change would emerge in the early 1990s, just when—unbeknownst to most—the storied Allegheny Conference, the only influential mechanism for coordinated public-private action historically, faced a clear choice: reinvent fast, or shut down. Before I pick up that part of the story, I need to briefly explain how the Conference came to be.

Evolution of a Civic Force: The Allegheny Conference and Its Partners

In one sense, the Conference was, by the early 1990s, a prisoner of its fabled past, not so much resting on its laurels as propelled by an outdated recipe for mobilizing civic cooperation, struggling for a focus in uncharted economic terrain. As Muller (1988, 39) notes, the Conference's founding initiative, Renaissance I, not only accomplished massive physical revitalization in and around the region's urban core but kept major corporations, whose CEOs mostly lived in Pittsburgh or nearby communities in Allegheny County, committed to the area, "kindled a spirit of optimism throughout the region," and defined the approach to public-private cooperation on big civic problems for decades to come. Two towering figures—Richard King Mellon in business and Pittsburgh Mayor David Lawrence in government—led the effort to shape the redevelopment agenda and mobilize public and private resources. Some historians of the period have argued that as the mechanism for collective action by big businesses, the Conference supplied the ideas (hired planning consultants) and the public sector responded to the plans, "largely with acceptance" (Sbragia 1990, 58). But other analysts, along with some civic insiders, contend that the Conference largely responded to the goals of Mayor Lawrence, who masterfully created a political machine in the postwar years (Weber 1988). Throughout the 1950s and early 1960s, the construction trades and other arms of organized labor welcomed the jobs but did not shape the high-level decision making. Likewise, neighborhood groups were not consulted. The agenda was orchestrated by a small circle of influential business and government officials, through cross-sector boards, lobbying, and the movement of loyal staff from key private-sector to public-sector positions or vice versa (Mershon 2000).

This period also cemented the Conference's ties to state government. Traditionally Republican economic interests transferred their support to the Democrats, who dominated the city's politics after the 1930s. Party competition would not define the local civic landscape, not even when the industrial economy hemorrhaged jobs. In the context of such fragmented local government—the region's patchwork of jurisdictions—this lack of party competition made the role of big business in policy innovation even more important.

The late 1960s brought the first serious challenges to this business-government partnership for physical redevelopment, which was not yet driven by any recognized need for economic restructuring. Neighborhood groups now fought "slum clearance" funded by the federal urban renewal program and driven by the local redevelopment machine. In 1969, Peter Flaherty, a newly elected small-government mayor, put redevelopment projects backed by the Conference on hold. He focused on cutting the cost of local government and directed the city planning department to listen, for the first time, to neighborhood groups (Lurcott and Downing 1987). Sbragia (1990, 59) argues that these steps "laid the basis for the strikingly consensual nature of redevelopment in Pittsburgh in the 1980s."

Beginning in 1977 under Mayor Caliguiri, Renaissance II again focused on redevelopment, now expanded to include housing and other neighborhood development projects, not just new office towers and cultural facilities. Robert Pease, executive director of the Allegheny Conference from 1969 to 1989, expanded the traditional focus on big downtown projects to include equity-oriented initiatives, such as public education reform and loan programs to strengthen minority-owned businesses. Through Renaissance II, the long-established local government partnership with big business was revived downtown, but another partnership, with nonprofit organizations and banks, was born to promote small-scale redevelopment neighborhood by neighborhood (Lubove 1996).

Meanwhile, the industrial economy had entered its free fall, and the attention of corporate leaders shifted to the prospect of a postindustrial knowledge economy. In 1985, with the support of city and county agencies and state legislators, the Allegheny Conference presented *Strategy 21: Pittsburgh/Allegheny Strategy to Enter the 21st Century*. Consistent with expectations in the wider region, which would later be recognized as ten counties, Strategy 21 limited itself to the central city plus Allegheny

County. It identified cultural assets as key to the center's competitiveness. Though area universities and hospitals had long been members of the Conference, they had not been high on the economic development agenda before. Now, they were officially central to the vision of a "knowledge-based" Pittsburgh to lift the region's economy.

The process minimized conflict: Strategy 21 set no rank-ordered, collective priorities, leaving each participant to pursue its favored initiatives (Sbragia 1990). The prevailing wisdom was that a loss of homegrown industrial corporations meant that leadership and commitment to change had to "come from many sectors," as a university official told the local press.[1]

The major research universities, though they would be slow to commercialize research, were poised to become civic players to an unprecedented degree, as well as economic assets that helped set Pittsburgh apart from many less successful deindustrializing cities. Starting in the early 1980s, Carnegie Mellon and the University of Pittsburgh had begun an aggressive effort to secure more sponsored research funding—the seed money for America's first innovation and technology-driven regional economies: California's Silicon Valley and Massachusetts' Route 128 corridor (Saxenian 1994; Smilor et al. 2007). Elected officials, philanthropic leaders, and other gave new attention to the universities as sources of spin-off technology companies and to a research-based medical complex, the University of Pittsburgh Medical Center, which would grow to become one of the region's largest employers. The year 1986 included a symbolic turning point: The Pittsburgh Technology Center opened on the site of an abandoned steel mill not long after the city's largest industrial employer filed for bankruptcy.

The Allegheny Conference remained the only large-scale vehicle for coordinated private-sector participation in civic initiatives. There was no go-to regional statesman or power broker analogous to Mayor Lawrence in the years of Renaissance I, local government in the region was highly fragmented, and state government was not organized to recognize the economic region as such but controlled most of the public investment vital to economic restructuring. Nonprofit groups were focused on street-level neighborhood projects rather than the complexities of regionwide economic strategy. The one well-defined alternative to Strategy 21's focus on high technology—reindustrialization—failed to gain traction, as I noted earlier. No broad-based coalition developed to focus on the precarious place of dislocated workers in the new economy or to marshal evidence that a myopic focus on "tech," which took decades to become economically significant in other regions, would lead local leaders to overlook important opportunities for economic growth.

For its part, the Conference was oddly positioned and viewed by some insiders as a shadow of its former self—in danger of becoming a "lunch club," as one observer put it. Its board would soon expand to better represent the universities and add some women and racial minorities, and the Conference championed the dominant vision of the region's future. Yet its active core membership, the big companies whose CEOs had both the motivation and the means to lead civic initiatives, continued to shed jobs or leave the region altogether, highlighting the divergence between major corporate interests and the regional interests, as well as the need for major investments, including massive upskilling of the workforce.

How, then, would civic action contribute to real economic growth in a region that had, by the early 1990s, begun to recognize that the postindustrial future was neither as assured nor as straightforward as the leading coalition—and the public at large—might have hoped?

Reinvent or Perish: Agenda Setting, Reform, and Reorganization in the 1990s

The Allegheny Conference entered the 1990s with the clear need to reinvent itself but few well-developed ideas about how to do so. Robert Pease retired as executive director in 1990, after nearly a quarter century in the role, and the Conference approached Rick Stafford, a management consultant who also had senior experience in state government policy making, to replace Pease. Stafford remembers vividly that the Conference did not seem to be a force for change, but incoming board chair Vincent Sarni, who ran one of the region's largest manufacturing companies, convinced Stafford that the next few years could serve as a crucial test. Stafford met with other board members—corporate CEOs, many of whom came from outside the region, and the heads of major philanthropies—who felt, unanimously, that the Conference needed to become a much bolder and more focused force for change and that an outdated approach to governance was holding the region and its economy back. "I signed up," Stafford recalls.

Following months of consultation and strategic planning, the Conference articulated a new focus at its annual public meeting, in November 1991. The longtime business partner in the politics of physical revitalization—the Allegheny Conference of Renaissance I and II—would have a new focus on regional governance, including more equitable taxation, as well as policy reform in education and workforce development. But this called for a fundamental shift in the staff-centered culture that had come to dominate the Conference and the function of its board. The new formula was to decide on a well-defined policy goal and then attach a key leader (engaged board member), very personally, to advance it. It became this person's role to build the needed constituency for the idea and mobilize and direct resources to achieve it, backed by the staff of the Conference.

The litmus-test project under this new approach was to create a regional asset district, based in part on a working model in greater Denver, which would fund major region-serving facilities that were in decline, such as the zoo, arts organizations, major parks, and (later) sports stadiums from an Allegheny County–wide, rather than a Pittsburgh-only, tax levy. A linked reform, modeled after the Twin Cities' metropolitan revenue sharing policy, would offer property tax relief to poorer municipalities by redistributing county resources under a new formula. Considering the region's tremendous government fragmentation and the resentment of Pittsburgh in many small cities throughout the county, some CEOs thought it could not be done. But thanks to coalition building beyond the city limits, it was done, approved by the state legislature in 1994, and this meant the Conference had regained some legitimacy as a capable, broadly focused civic actor.[2] The Conference had also passed the test defined by its leadership. On the other hand, the effort to make the asset district "truly" regional—multicounty— failed, say insiders, because relationships with the outlying counties were weak, and the perception in those counties that Pittsburgh and Allegheny County only looked out for themselves remained strong.

Next, the Conference turned to the structure of county government, engaging local experts to assess its services and management structure. Within a few years, voters would approve a fundamental restructuring, replacing a divided commission with a strong county executive to enhance management and accountability for public services, including the coordination of government's economic development functions. The office of Allegheny County Executive would become one of the most important in the state—and later figure prominently in efforts to organize regional strategy. This change is widely hailed by knowledgeable insiders as one of the region's most important governance reforms in decades.

To make the region attractive, recalls Stafford, area leaders needed to think in terms of the incentives and legal structures that produced great assets, such as modern stadiums, a convention center, world-class arts centers, and more:

The complexion of the Conference changed, if you will, from bricks-and-mortar redevelopment projects and sort of accepting things, structurally, the way they are.... The emphasis through the 70s and 80s was on ... projects. We didn't totally forsake projects. But over here [in the 90s], it was on policy change.... Concomitant with that, we merged the civic agencies.

Reorganization

Merged is a small word for a big and multifaceted task. Fragmentation—the patchwork of small jurisdictions confronting big, shared, regionwide problems—was not unique to the public sector in greater Pittsburgh. It also afflicted the sector of private not-for-profit and quasi-public agencies with significant responsibilities in policy analysis, market research, business recruitment, marketing, technical assistance, and other key economic development functions. By various counts, there were, by the 1990s, some 200 to 300 economic development organizations active in Allegheny County alone, with overlapping boards, missions, competencies, fundraising appeals, and lobbying or civic outreach efforts. Open a business in the area, and you might be approached by half a dozen or more uncoordinated organizations: one to market the firms in your sector or industry to national and international customers and investors, another to lobby state government for tax concessions or R&D dollars, a third to study local governance issues, and so on.

In November 1993, a panel organized by the Allegheny Conference and headed by Carnegie Mellon University President Robert Mehrabian, released a provocative report on the state of the region's economy as well as its prospects. Known simply as the White Paper, the report made a pointed case for sweeping civic reorganization. It was harshly critical of the area's "layer cake of competing organizations," offering what the *Post-Gazette*, the area's leading daily newspaper, described as a "chilling look at the region's recent economic history." As the report observed, "Once the source of visionary strategies and solutions that could unify our region, our economic development civic structure is beset today by increasing factionalism, fragmentation, and overlapping agendas which divert attention from solving real problems."[3]

To some observers, the region's civic culture, accustomed as it was to a language of consensus and cooperation among established entities, did not respond positively to the White Paper's pointed assessment, nor to Mehrabian's public assertion that "some organizations must merge with others, share a common agenda, or be abolished," as the *Gazette* characterized the view.⁴ A former government official recalls that

[Mehrabian] published this report saying that we were very ineffective, that unless we shaped up and started thinking regionally that we weren't going to make it in the global economy. Well, they were furious, "they" being the Allegheny Conference people. Mehrabian was from California. He wasn't from here, and this wasn't the way business in Pittsburgh was done.

But those closely involved in the assignment argue just the opposite: Mehrabian was chosen because he was an outsider, but his report stopped short of recommending consolidation of the economic development agencies—an idea the Conference leadership was keen to focus on—and instead suggested a regional visioning process with strong public input.

The aftershocks of the White Paper led—very visibly and publicly—to a new and more consensus-oriented strategic planning process, which produced the aptly titled Working Together strategy for job growth. I examine this below as one in a series of efforts to grapple collectively with the challenge of nurturing new growth drivers for the economy. But as for what Mehrabian's report had termed "civic structure," business and government leaders privately acknowledged the need for more coordination and, more controversially, for reorganizing that included consolidating organizations and/or shifting their functions.

A popular management cartoon shows the boss meeting with a harried employee, who sits across the desk. Knowing that the employee is about to ask him something difficult, the boss has pulled out his foolproof guide. It is a spin-wheel with three outcomes only: yell, hide, and "re-org." Reorganization is messy but sometimes essential to getting significant change accomplished. The details, however, can make one cross-eyed. The challenge of civic *re*organization, and the process of accomplishing it, has not been a major focus of prior research on local economic restructuring, but in the Pittsburgh region and other "old" economies with a dense concentration of organizations active on development issues, reorganization—rather than mobilization of established entities—may represent one of the most significant roads to greater civic capacity. Reorganization in the nongovernmental sector would comprise the second major civic shift in greater Pittsburgh in the 1990s (i.e., alongside the reorganization of local government). Here again, the Allegheny Conference was at the center. As then executive director Rick Stafford recalls, this represented another important shift from the Allegheny Conference of physical redevelopment campaigns:

Before the 90s, the policy of the Conference was quite clearly: Don't take responsibility for any of these other agencies. I think the theory was . . . [in spite of overlapping membership and funders] we don't want to clutter up the Conference agenda with a lot of concerns about stuff the chamber [of commerce] worries about—parades and things like that. On the other hand, what was clearly evident when I started was the competition among these groups and lack of coordination among these groups. When I ran around and interviewed everyone about [top-of-mind concerns] . . . one thing they all talked about, along with tech jobs, was . . . civic organization.

With Sarni as chair of the Conference, the organization now looked for opportunities to bring other leading agencies under its umbrella. This required a significant investment of time and leveraging personal relationships. One structural upside to "overlaps" was the interlocking boards: the same few dozen top CEOs made up a critical mass of board seats at all of the top economic development agencies. Re-org worked, argues Stafford, because of the commitment of the area's business and nonprofit leaders to a civic reorganization agenda and also because key windows of opportunity opened up through staff turnover.

Several examples of the practical politics of re-org are revealing. First, Sarni, who also sat on the board of a longstanding, good-government research organization known as the Pennsylvania Economy League (PEL), suggested to Stafford, when PEL's staff director left, that perhaps he (Stafford) should head PEL. PEL had been chartered by state government decades before, with support from the region's major manufacturing corporations, to provide financial analysis and basic research to small towns in the region. It offered analytic capacity that the Allegheny Conference lacked in house, but PEL was struggling financially. Moreover, PEL's bylaws were complex, and it had its own board. A merger would not work. Given this structure, Stafford suggested that Sarni meet with the CEO who chaired PEL's board to personally make the case for affiliating the two organizations under a single staff director. A favorable reception there led to a small working group, comprised of board members from each organization, to devise a transition. PEL's board approved Stafford as its new director, under a complicated process structured by PEL's state bylaws—effectively making PEL an affiliate of the Conference.

The next "affiliations" included the Pittsburgh Regional Alliance (PRA), also when its executive directorship turned over, as well as the regional chamber of commerce—all as part of the multiyear job growth campaign, Working Together, to which the Conference had committed itself publicly. In each instance, the absorbed organization had to be confident that this was not simply a project of "empire building" by the Allegheny Conference.

The gains were hard won, in part because each carefully negotiated re-org added complexity. Absorbing PRA, for example, required the votes of no less than four boards of directors. And PRA was itself a loose umbrella, struggling with limited success, by the late 1990s, to coordinate disparate quasi-public agencies with overlapping marketing and international promotion functions. Founded by merger in 1995 with the encouragement of the Allegheny Conference, PRA was to be a "one-stop information clearinghouse for companies seeking to expand or move to the region" and to "devise a unified marketing plan" for the area.[5] It was greeted with cautious optimism.[6] But several years later, insiders viewed PRA as a failed experiment—the would-be "superagency" that could not overcome turf-mindedness.

Hundreds of the economic development agencies in the White Paper's infamous "layer cake"—from separate tourist promotion boards for each county to countless enterprise development and advocacy organizations—were still in business as the decade came to a close, and privately, foundation officials report that they receive many requests for funding, from varied agencies, to carry out similar activities. So when Stafford agreed to jointly direct PRA and the Allegheny Conference in 2000, this was, in effect, a decision that putting a shaky umbrella under a bigger umbrella was better than reverting to myriad autonomous agencies or closing down agencies altogether.

This was hardly the seamless, cross-functional integration that business-minded CEOs had hoped for at the initial suggestion that the Conference should be "together" with service-providing economic development agencies. It also implied the risk of role confusion—the drift toward "chamber of commerce stuff" that an earlier generation of Conference leadership had so strictly avoided and the possibility that the Conference would now be obliged to promote the interests of individual member companies or industry sectors rather than focus on broadly supported policy change. In addition, the reorganized Conference represented a more complicated animal for the press, the public, elected leadership, and prospective partners to respond to. What would this mean for its reputation, in particular for the legitimacy needed to influence opinion and mobilize resources on challenging issues? As one close observer assesses the series of consolidations,

The merger of the Allegheny Conference and the Pennsylvania Economy League made a lot of sense. . . . The League had problems, and there was a long-standing symbiosis between the two. . . . The Greater Pittsburgh Chamber [of Commerce], it made a lot of sense to bring that in, too. There were three chambers [one for older firms, one for small manufacturers, one for technology companies], and that was nonsense. . . . Cleveland has one regional chamber. . . . To bring together business climate and quality of life in one place made sense. [But] the PRA [acquisition] I have always had concerns about. . . . The PRA was performing a lot of the economic development strategy function for the region. It wasn't doing it particularly well. I think a lot of [that] did need to be pulled in to the Conference . . . but it was also an operating agency. It ran programs, ran marketing campaigns, worked with businesses. . . . When that came under the Conference, the Conference was no longer an independent leadership-strategy-think tank advocacy [group]. It was now a service provider. . . . All of a sudden, the Conference lost its ability, I believe, to be a neutral broker, which [it] had done a lot of. . . . A whole class of issues which were relevant to the PRA [the Conference] was no longer neutral on. . . . It's not important when you're working on quality-of-life issues, like fixing a park. But when you're dealing with business taxes or environmental rules, it now looks like business versus everybody else. . . . It looks like you're . . . speaking from a special-interest need.

Organizing the Region Politically

In the parallel move that defined a decade of reorganization, the Conference organized a regional alliance—an advocacy coalition called the Southwestern Pennsylvania Growth Alliance to represent the ten counties surrounding Pittsburgh (figure 7.3). It developed from a loose lobbying coalition of county officials[7] in 1989 to an organized body with public and private leadership, including officials at several levels of public office. It built on the foundations laid by the countywide asset district that the Conference had helped to secure in 1994. The original proposal was multicounty, and the clear lack of support for that outside of Allegheny County signaled the need to build a constituency for action on a genuinely regional basis.

The Growth Alliance was to counter what locals perceived to be state government favoritism toward the Southeastern region of the state, centered on Philadelphia. State-level and cross-county political advocacy "in one voice" were the aims, and the near-term objective was securing $150 million in state government aid for major industrial and tourism development projects. A local referendum to raise tax dollars for stadium construction in Pittsburgh and industrial upgrading in outlying counties had failed badly in the November 1997 elections. In spite of heavy campaign spending by the Conference, opponents successfully labeled it "the stadium tax." The press called the dramatic defeat an "upending" of traditional politics, a backlash of the working class against the corporate elite,[8] and this defeat led the Conference to focus

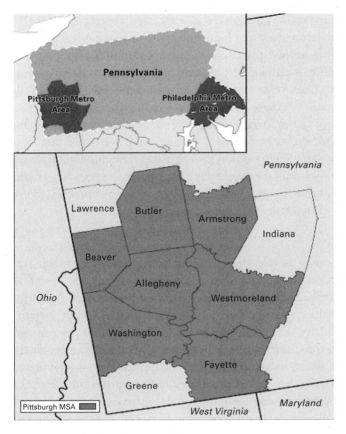

Figure 7.3
State of Pennsylvania, ten-county southwestern region and Pittsburgh metropolitan area. *Source*: ESRI, 2005.

on multicounty coalition building to garner state aid. The press did not fail to point out that launching another new entity begged the question of its role and the need to coordinate it within the existing "puzzle" of agencies:

> The political idea behind the Growth Alliance is to form solidarity among the 10-county area's 47 members of the state House and 13 state senators. Members of the delegation said this part of the state needed a bloc of votes to offset Philadelphia.... As to where the Growth Alliance fits into the puzzle of other local economic development agencies ... the niche ... was described as one of political advocacy.[9]

Among its key accomplishments, the Growth Alliance developed a ten-county consensus plan on priorities for economic development assistance from the state. Two governors expressed appreciation for this regional priority-setting bloc and funded projects in all ten member counties, building trust among the counties and momentum, says a former Conference staffer, for thinking and acting as a region. As one local reformer puts it, "Ten years ago, every conversation began with, 'Well, what's the region?'" Perhaps that barrier was now overcome, and the new geography of the most important long-range government planning organization and the corresponding business-led agenda-setting and advocacy group—the Southwestern Pennsylvania Commission (SPC, on which more below) and the Allegheny Conference, respectively—both reflected that. Given the region's patchwork of local governments, many of them fiscally distressed, that was something to build on.

Taking Stock

As the 1990s came to a close, the Allegheny Conference was a larger and more multifunctional organization—"The Allegheny Conference and its Affiliates," formalized as a parent organization with subsidiaries in 2002.[10] It had helped to win a sweeping restructuring of county government and a multicity taxation and revenue sharing plan, unprecedented in the area. And the Conference was beginning to connect to a genuinely regional base of firms, universities, and elected officials even if its image and core membership was still concentrated in Pittsburgh and Allegheny County. As for legitimacy and reputation, the Conference was still viewed as the voice of business, perhaps more "big business" than was reflected in the board and membership makeup. But it also got credit for expanding its leadership ranks, building on the addition of the universities and hospitals ("eds and meds") in the 1980s, in an effort to be more inclusive. The press sometimes described the group as made up of the region's top corporate, university, *and* civic leaders. A small number of women and people of color sat on the board, and bigger-tent, more transparent agenda setting was its new challenge. The press previewed the Conference's annual public meeting in 2004:

Not only have the players changed but so has the game. The Conference no longer is a clique of good old boys—an all-white gathering of corporate honchos crafting city policy. . . . The scene tonight will have its share of rich and powerful, but more prevalent will be scores of private sector leaders from around the region who years ago would not have had a foot in the door.[11]

As for capacity to act on agenda items, on the up side, directed by the board, a single staff director could now—at least on paper—coordinate research, marketing, and policy development on behalf of economic development for the region's core, adding multiple functions to the multijurisdictional perspective that the private sector often brought to public issues. As a case in point, analyzing and restructuring county government engaged the Allegheny Conference, with the PEL as a coordinated support function, for more than seven years. "Without an organization like the Conference," says one business leader, "the region would have no leading group to push it along the way. It would be fragmented like our government." This notion is strongly supported by research on the role of governing coalitions in American cities (review in Stone 2005). But it was not clear that the Conference could play that leading-group role well and be a service provider and advocate for member companies' special interests. Diversion and internal division were issues, too. Speaking of its current status, one close observer compared the Conference of the early 2000s to a "big corporation that made a lot of acquisitions but has not successfully integrated them" and added, expressing a more widely held view, that the Conference "suffered severely from a lack of focus." To assess the significance of these organizational changes, I revisit next the underlying task at hand.

Is There a Strategy?: Cultivating Growth, Building Stadiums, Chasing Companies

As I noted in the previous chapter, not all "development" is economic growth, and not all growth follows easily from policy. Cultivating a milieu of innovation—rather than trying, against the odds, to "pick winners" (future business successes) via official planning—is the strategy recommended for knowledge sectors, in particular. But cultivating can mean many things, from improving public infrastructure and strengthening the workforce to changing the way companies network, share knowledge, and choose to compete with other local firms. And then there is "the culture thing": how to create entrepreneurial habits and a willingness to take significant risks, not just the formal structures that support business start-ups or transfer university research into the marketplace. Important as it is, culture rarely seems amenable to policy orchestration—in economic restructuring or any other domain.

In greater Pittsburgh, the controversial White Paper, released in 1993, had not only spotlighted a need for civic reorganization. It also highlighted the region's rudderless and notion-driven approach to economic growth. Though big steel had collapsed, advanced manufacturing and materials science still made up an important share of employment. Yet the companies in this sector were largely overlooked, concluded the report, in the eager drive for tech jobs and "place-making" real estate development that defined the late 1980s and early 1990s. The service sector had replaced many of the industrial jobs lost but at a fraction of the wage levels. Most service jobs were in retail and healthcare, not the high-skill, high-wage software development or robotics jobs that celebrated university-based research in those fields seemed to promise. Furthermore, *every* region seemed to be pursuing a tech-focused "Silicon Valley strategy," and there were few clear signs that the Pittsburgh region, in the context of such competition, could grow and retain the companies that the area's strong research universities might spin off.

But the White Paper faced harsh criticism, not only from those who disliked its blunt attack on turf-minded economic development agencies but from those who saw more hope on the economic horizon. In response, the Allegheny Conference quickly organized a broader working group to rethink regional economic strategy, offer a more cooperative frame for the tasks ahead, and pursue an ambitious target of job creation by the end of the decade. As one longtime observer puts it, the eagerness to outline a broad agenda without doing truly broad-based constituency building was still a problem for the traditionally top-down Conference board and its working groups: "They'd get together and *declare* a regional strategy." So what was the strategy, and how did the Conference and its allies propose to implement it?

At its annual public meeting in November 1994, the Allegheny Conference unveiled *Working Together to Compete Globally*. It called for 100,000 new jobs by the year 2000, which would require doubling the pace of job creation. In place of rhetoric celebrating high technology, quality of life, or other notions of the good economy just around the corner, *Working Together* called for a strong focus on the fortunes of existing companies, many of them small or medium-sized, in key export industries. In essence, it was a "cultivate" strategy rather than a plan to chase new companies. The press underlined this focus, which was significant in a region attached to "landing" big companies and their jobs.[12] The action steps included policy reforms to improve business climate (such as through state tax reform), improved workforce development in targeted sectors, stronger links to shared suppliers, and demonstration projects to accelerate the commercialization of new technologies developed by university researchers or corporate R&D labs. To signal inclusiveness, the report also called for setting aside 20 percent of a new $50 million development fund for "inner city neighborhoods and other struggling sectors of the region's economy."[13]

Over the next six years, two aspects of the new blueprint were constantly in the news: the effort to foster a shared regional vision and more
effective collaboration among public and private agencies; and progress
against the 100,000-job target. In April 1995, for example, the Conference created the Working Together Consortium, a group of 85 business,
government, and civic leaders charged with monitoring progress on the
strategy and ensuring that it would not become "just another grandiose
report that collects dust." The *Post-Gazette*'s editorial page noted that

there is more and more evidence that the Allegheny Conference on Community
Development is making a successful transition to a new mode of leadership. . . . Conference representatives made the point Wednesday that economic development
in this region is going to involve more than 37 big-corporation CEOs.[14]

As for measuring progress on economic growth, the task itself is notoriously tricky: Should we count net job growth only? Should we focus
on the number of jobs rather than their wage or skill levels? How do we
attribute credit for gains (or responsibility for losses) when so many
factors drive economic change? These features lend themselves, in the
field of economic development, to claiming credit for anything good, one
half of the field's hunting-derived adage: "Shoot anything that flies, claim
anything that falls" (Rubin 1988).

Local observers and the press acknowledged these challenges but generally applauded the effort to foster more cooperation on behalf of smart
economic change, as well as greater optimism about achieving it—even
when Working Together eventually declared that it had fallen about
15,000 jobs short of its target.

In the latter half of the decade, as the practical projects associated with
"cultivating" evolved, the Allegheny Conference, as I noted above,
worked successfully with allies to restructure county government, partially restructure local taxation, and consolidate major economic development agencies. The Conference also organized a new regional political
lobby to offer a unified message to state government. This was crucial
for major capital projects as well as sustained funding for research and
development innovation funds. But in spite of the shift to policy issues
and civic reorganization, the politics of big real estate projects dominated
any strategic focus on changing the region's appetite for risk or establishing the institutional infrastructure—venture capital firms, tech lawyers,
and more—crucial for job growth through high technology. In the public
eye, the Conference and other business-led groups were most visible as
supporters of twelve-year Pittsburgh Mayor Tom Murphy's land redevelopment program, at one point pitched as "Renaissance III."

To some, Renaissance III was, as one business insider put it, a "build-it-and-they-will-come" strategy for revitalizing downtown housing and retail and completing two new major-league sports stadiums as well as a convention center. To more generous observers, the initiative was crucial for retaining firms and workers in a region still losing population. Backed strongly by major banks and the building trades and other arms of organized labor, the mayor made aggressive use of tax incentives that effectively mortgaged future public revenue, all on the bet that growth would bring new income to the region's urban core. The core would offer the "world-class" facilities needed to compete globally. The familiar public-private partnership model for real estate development got most of its projects approved and built. But the region's job growth remained weak against the national rate, lacking a major growth sector through the 1990s and into the new decade. Plus, the image of Pittsburgh as a gritty city of smokestacks endured, according to those who polled recruiters and corporate location consultants worldwide. The facilities got built, but when the recession of the early 2000s led to a sharp drop in tax revenues, Mayor Murphy's bet was called, and the city fell into bankruptcy.

More importantly for the economic strategy, such as there was, in the region, foundations, advocacy groups, and other civic players began asking pointed questions about whether the many economic development agencies that managed to stay in business actually knew how to cultivate growth in the hyped tech sector. They were also asking whether the region yet had the ingredients to generate a genuinely broad-based, participatory vision of the economic future that incorporated values, such as environmental sustainability and social equity, that were easily overlooked in the focus on business promotion. These questions define the two final sections of the chapter.

Tech Guys without Ties: Courting the New Economy

Two events have passed into local legend. In the first, the CEOs of the Pittsburgh region's biggest corporations—the core leadership of the Allegheny Conference—decided that it was time to build bridges to technology entrepreneurs. It was the late 1980s, and the tech sector was much hyped, thanks to Strategy 21 and other efforts, but still quite small. So the big companies invited the small ones to the fabled Duquesne Club, the prestigious and exclusive club of the city's business elite since the late 1800s. But on the appointed night, none of the "tech guys" were let in: they were not wearing ties as the Club required.

In the second clash between the old or established Pittsburgh and the new, a board meeting of the Allegheny Conference featured a presentation in which a technology entrepreneur criticized the region's culture as hidebound and insular. The CEO of one of the area's biggest corporations reportedly barked back, "We built Pittsburgh. You need to show us more respect!"

The stories are told and retold, along with the fact that the Conference has invited tech entrepreneurs to join its board but never to chair it. That seat, or so the perception goes, remains the rightful place of the big banks and manufacturers that have dominated the region's business leadership for a century or more.

There are other stories, of course, some more grounded in economic data than culture clashes and pains of adaptation, many of these forward looking and hopeful. Carnegie Mellon University doubled the number of start-up companies it spun off between 2005 and 2006, from robotics to gaming, medical devices, and software. By 2005, the University of Pittsburgh Medical Center was the second largest academic medical center in the country. Meanwhile, the University of Pittsburgh ranks in the top ten universities in federal funding for medical research. Based on labor statistics, between 1999 and 2005, continued population decline (which depresses the large retail, construction, and government sectors) and the loss of some 8,000 jobs at the US Airways hub dented employment. Yet over the same period, the Pittsburgh region created more new jobs than greater Boston or the Silicon Valley—two "knowledge economies" that suffered badly in the tech recession and two with which Pittsburgh's tech fortunes are frequently compared.[15] The area lends itself to the textbook glass-is-half-full or half-empty comparisons side by side: a lower volume of company spin-offs by research universities than benchmark regions but a healthy rate of growth in spin-offs; and rapidly improved university policies for technology transfer—from "being nowhere" on that front as recently as 1999, say experts, to being among the best in the nation, based on recent research on how leading universities practice technology transfer.[16] How did civic leaders pursue such changes?

Targeting Tech

Pittsburgh's leading business groups had begun to consciously target technology-led growth in the early 1980s. The 1990s brought something of a balancing act and, some say, premature celebration of the region's competitiveness in technology-led growth. By the mid-1990s, the honeymoon with *symbols* of innovation—tech incubators, for example, on the sites of former steel mills—had run its course. Promotion and lobbying by trade groups were likewise appreciated but clearly insufficient to ensure change. By the late 1990s, technology transfer by area universities remained bureaucratic and slow, well behind competitors nationwide. Researchers failed to find the indicators of an "innovative milieu" at work in the region (Mitchell-Weaver, Deitrick, and Rigopoulou 1999).

Pittsburgh was—and is—no Silicon Valley. The Pittsburgh region lacks the enormous pool of venture capital firms, technology lawyers, and technology-friendly regulation that helps keep the famous Northern California cluster at the forefront in information technology and the life sciences. Greater Pittsburgh likewise lacks the giant companies that anchor technology clusters in city-regions without a long history of university leadership in technology, such as Austin and Seattle. Yet contrary to popular belief, the Silicon Valley was not simply born of the market. Decades of Cold War research funding by government to the area's top universities laid the technological foundations, and the mix of markets, institutions, and an unusually unguarded entrepreneurial culture appear to have done the rest (Saxenian 1994). Silicon Valley did not emerge via grand plan, but it did not "just happen" either.

So how might the Pittsburgh region create enabling conditions and accelerate the process of turning ideas into growth companies? Clearly, the quality-of-life and business climate improvement agendas led by the Allegheny Conference and other established economic development groups could help. But institutions also shape the ideas-to-companies process at the core of new economic growth. This civic dimension of the "new economy" story involves entrepreneurs in government, the private sector, the top universities, and the area's influential philanthropic foundations. Quite unlike the public-private partnerships of physical rebuilding or even local government restructuring, it is a story of grappling for answers in a climate of risk, uncertainty, and, yes, a layer cake of economic development agencies: not one new technology transfer intermediary, for example, but half a dozen, each with different rules and requirements. Accountability is elusive: some agencies are funded to be boosters in a context wherein progress is debatable and every promoter has incentives to "claim anything that falls." This is a story about the power and limits of civic cooperation as a tool for achieving economic growth.

By the early 1990s, Pennsylvania's Ben Franklin Partnership, which funded technological innovation through cross-sector partnership projects, was touted as a national model of transformation from the old industrial economy to a high skill, high technology future. It was the first mechanism that brought public-sector financial incentives and promotion—government as "bully pulpit"—to bear on behalf of new technologies, new manufacturing processes, and less adversarial labor-management relations as well (Sabel 1992). Yet by the end of the decade, its Southwestern regional center was mired in scandal, regarded by entrepreneurs, university leaders, and other insiders as cronyistic and corrupt. The Partnership folded in the Pittsburgh region, leaving a vacuum into which entrepreneurs and philanthropies stepped.

These were institution-building entrepreneurs out to develop the support infrastructure that the Pittsburgh region lacked. With market research in hand, they convinced the area's well-endowed philanthropic foundations, the largest source of risk capital in the region, to invest. Between 1998 and 2003, this created an important new crop of nonprofit technology intermediary organizations to facilitate the commercialization of university research in tissue engineering, microchip enhancement, robotics, and other fields. State government had returned to the induced innovation game, replacing the troubled Ben Franklin Partnership in the Southwestern region with the similarly positioned Innovation Works. The foundations blended their funding with state dollars to support that quasi-public agency and the new intermediaries. They were to focus on early-stage business development in one or more specialty areas. The foundations also helped fledgling university technology transfer offices, Carnegie Mellon's most of all, to overhaul their intellectual property policies and ramp up enterprise creation. The universities also asked for some $125 million to hire new faculty and create a life sciences cluster.

From the standpoint of problem solving, the so-called support infrastructure was growing, but its performance was unclear. The intermediaries had proliferated, and so had a dizzying array of organizations competing for funding. The foundations had acted together to create a large and vital pool of risk capital, the region's first, but philanthropies lacked reliable mechanisms for ensuring accountability. How useful was the technical assistance provided by the intermediaries, for example?

Where funding expanded rapidly, so had objectives for its use. As one longtime insider notes, the mix of players in the technology transfer and business development game—business entrepreneurs and their managers, university researchers and administrators, technical assistance providers, and public and private investors—may share a vision of technology-led growth but face quite different incentives day to day. One "enterprising" university department head famously redefined the focus of one intermediary mechanism, the Digital Greenhouse, to include new specialties, recalls an observer, in order to hire faculty in those areas:

[He] really wanted to hire faculty in cyber-security, and the Digital Greenhouse had funding for faculty start-ups. . . . And so then the Digital Greenhouse . . . its mission [became] system-on-a-chip, circuit technology *and* cyber-security *and* advanced electronics *and* micro-electronic mechanical systems and maybe even nano-tech and all this stuff, because that's what people wanted it to be. It's a good thing that it was able to change, but it changed because people used the money in ways that it wasn't intended, and then no one stopped them from doing that.

Complicating the accountability issue in this new-economy domain, market windows opened and closed more rapidly than multiyear strategic plans could respond. And in some areas, such as hiring topflight researchers to "staff" a target cluster, there could be a decade or more lag between investment and payoff, *if* it paid off. A university might proliferate patents and spin-off companies, but the "success environment" might be insufficient to help those companies survive and thrive in greater Pittsburgh.

Lacking reliable ways to measure progress and setbacks and to attribute them to particular players, mutual skepticism and disappointment seem endemic. What is more, in a context where information is complex and diffuse, bright spots go unrecognized. One important example is the emergence of cooperative R&D between the region's established manufacturers and scientists and entrepreneurs in cutting-edge fields such as nanotechnology. Another notable example is the growing, high-wage, "legacy-based" cluster of high-tech steel suppliers "lost to policy makers" because of outdated industry classification systems.[17] These oversights undermine useful collective action to focus on growth prospects.

From the entrepreneurs' standpoint, moreover, the young nonprofit intermediaries are no substitute for a well-developed venture capital (VC) industry and the capital and customized business development aid the VCs bring. Civic cooperation has not yet changed this, nor has it yet secured reforms in the state's dated tax structure, which, business analysts argue, signals that the region is not quite ready to compete. Then there is the workforce needed to propel ideas from concept to revenue and job growth: the talented product managers and other non-science-based workers on which company growth depends so heavily. Efforts to consolidate and focus workforce development in the region—a field that, since the 1980s, has divided its energies between retraining older workers and equipping the young for jobs in emerging sectors—have not yet resolved this skills gap. Nor has the very public debate about how to attract a "creative class"—Carnegie Mellon researcher Richard Florida's (2000) catchy phrase for the relatively mobile, high-skill workers who seek out appealing places to live—shifted practices significantly.

Nor is it obvious how the region's civic collaborators can change ingrained habits. In the category of the Duquesne Club fiasco is the recent story of a tech entrepreneur who put together a proposal to attract new VC investors to the region. Unbeknownst to him, the staff of a local economic development agency that sponsored a meeting with prospective investors had added a cover in black and gold, with a football—symbols of the Pittsburgh Steelers football team. "I was deeply embarrassed," he recalls, "yet they thought this was savvy marketing. I see that kind of thing weekly, that parochial mentality." In the early 2000s, the Allegheny Conference made a major push to rebrand the region to attract investment, ideas, and skilled workers. But observers agree that this is an uphill battle, and the marketing language of "brand promises" may not suit the mobilization that is required. The region of limited immigration, deep family roots, and impressive civic commitment, a wide array of local observers agree, is also risk averse and deeply attached to hallmarks of the old Pittsburgh identity.

As I noted in the previous chapter, effective teamwork does not guarantee hoped-for outcomes, not when so much about the new economy is outside local control. But if a movement for change is to affect the makeup and skills of the workforce, public attitudes, state rules and incentives, openness to new cultures, and other keys to economic restructuring, that movement may need to embrace a more participatory approach, one even further removed from the top-down civics of yesteryear's redevelopment. The prospects of such an approach define the final section.

The Other Legs of the Stool: Public and Nonprofit Partners in Regional Strategy

Economic restructuring means placing regions "layered" with older and newer economies on a path to sustainable development and shared prosperity. This broader focus, though harder to define and pursue than, say, narrow industry promotion is also an antidote to the one-best-strategy mindset, which overlooks growth opportunities that fall outside the "formula." In 2003, *Back to Prosperity*, a widely publicized report on Pennsylvania by the Brookings Institution,[18] concluded,

Pennsylvania's economy is drifting as it responds incoherently to continued industrial restructuring. . . . Few states possess either greater potential or a more troubling history of recent underachievement than Pennsylvania. . . . The state is spreading out—and hollowing out. Population and jobs aren't growing so much as shifting from close-in places to farther-out ones. . . . Pennsylvanians are rightly proud of a system that has kept government "close to the people" and fostered a deep sense of commitment to place. However . . . Pennsylvania possesses one of the nation's most labyrinthine systems of state and local government— and that has exacerbated unbalanced growth and undercut economic competitiveness.[19]

In the first half of this chapter, I showed how the Allegheny Conference emerged in the postwar period as the civic instrument of big corporations and assertive public officials—all in the context of fragmented local government. But as the functional and spatial demands of restructuring expanded rapidly toward the end of the twentieth century, the region's one "muscular" mechanism of public-private cooperation was inadequate. More to the point, it was less and less authorized (informally) to lead change, as the image of an "old boys' network" and decision making by a corporate elite engendered suspicion that what was good for big companies, especially in Pittsburgh and Allegheny County, was *not* in the regional public interest and that restructuring had followed a narrow, self-serving mindset.

Where are the new instruments for civic cooperation in this divided context? Beyond the Allegheny Conference, which remains an important and controversial player, three actors stand out. First, the area's wealthy, influential, and credibly neutral philanthropic foundations, which have a history of working together on important problems, have become a more assertive force for change and accountability. Second, the only interlocal government body, the ten-county Southwestern Pennsylvania Commission (SPC), which directs a billion dollars per year in infrastructure investments, is slowly being energized by elected officials, new staff, and nonprofit gadflies as a force for regional agenda setting and action. Third, the region's nonprofit charities and social equity advocates are being organized as a collective force to work with *and* challenge both business and government on the vital issues the region must tackle.

In this final section, I look briefly at each of these developments, the challenges that remain, and how the strategies of key civic players have evolved. There is a striking contrast between the sweeping wish lists of regional governance reformers and, as seen in this section, the strategies of indirect influence, persuasive framing, patient "inside-outside" pressure on agencies, and cross-sector coalition building that leading controversial regional change actually requires.

Philanthropies: From "Maintenance" to Civic Leadership

As I noted at the outset of this chapter, the Pittsburgh region is home to one of the highest concentrations of philanthropic wealth in the world, much of it focused on local rather than global needs. The foundations are crucial backers of the Allegheny Conference along with a wide array of nonprofit and government-managed initiatives in the region. While knowledgeable insiders credit the foundations with fundamental contributions to the region's gradual restructuring, the past half-decade has seen notable new activism and civic influence by foundations. These patterns are consistent with the framework of civic capacity that I outlined in the first two chapters of this book, reflecting risk-taking community leadership beyond "arms-length" grantmaking to worthy projects or organizations. One foundation leader terms it a shift from "maintenance" to making waves—but from a stance of constructive engagement and multilateral, not unilateral, action.

Some features of this activism are traditional for Pittsburgh, such as lending the weight of philanthropies and their family founders to worthy causes (validating or conferring legitimacy on issues) and connecting a region that otherwise turns inward to global sources of knowledge and expertise (enhancing productive capacity in the form of new knowledge and skills). But some foundations in the area are playing a vital, if still emergent, role in restructuring by marrying those traditional roles with bolder risk taking in the public arena—from contentious urban school improvement, which the *New York Times* called "a stunning and rare example of philanthropy publicly flexing its muscles,"[20] to government restructuring, from high-tech entrepreneurship (examined above) to more participatory regional governance. Recent efforts suggest the potential and the risks inherent in keeping challenging ideas on the public agenda, encouraging players to work through conflict rather than bury or deny it, offering pressure—not just support—to demand greater accountability from government as well as nonprofits, and validating a vanguard (important new voices) in the face of an established old guard. The shift, by some area foundations, toward bolder civic leadership parallels a trend in American philanthropy toward performance-oriented social investment. But "performance" has a deceptive and comfortable managerial ring. The issue here is risking conflict and disappointment in order to spur significant change.

Was the recent case of "muscular" philanthropy in public education reform—in which area foundations suspended funding of the public schools but supported a mayoral task force to build consensus on the most controversial education policy issues—an instance of unelected, "third-party government" or responsible, risk-taking leadership to overcome an unproductive impasse in public problem solving? The policy decisions on public education were retained by elected officials and their appointees, not imposed by unelected interest groups. The task force's role was advisory, for example, though there was considerable political pressure for school district leadership to take the group's recommendations seriously. But influential nongovernmental actors, the philanthropies as funder-intermediaries, did play multiple roles in problem solving, exerting pressure for organizational performance, more constructive stakeholder participation, imaginative analysis and policy design, and conflict resolution, when the established system of governance led to a costly impasse. Along the way, the foundations risked alienating important publics and subsidizing new "pet projects" that might become the focus of tomorrow's standoffs or new, parochial agendas.

The same potential and risks, and the same questions about legitimacy and accountability, apply to philanthropic leadership on regional development and economic restructuring, which has intensified in the past few years. The early signs, as I elaborate below, are that philanthropies are turning several crucial civic levers: bridging the patchwork of government jurisdictions with long-range thinking; validating new voices in the discourse about the region's future, what is at stake, and who should have a place at the decision-making table; subsidizing experimentation with new tools of planning and governance, including "e-democracy" innovations; and exerting external pressure for change on established organizations—pushing for transformation, accountability, public dialogue, and learning over business-as-usual, bureaucratic decision making.

For some, the shift is welcome and long overdue. Some insiders publicly praise foundation support for critical initiatives while privately chastising grantmakers for subsidizing mediocrity, duplication of effort, and the proliferation of organizations competing for funding and turf. Regardless, the region's philanthropies are among its most important investors in new thinking and uncommon civic cooperation.

Regional Planning by Government: Moving in from the Margins

Observers have long lamented the apparent misalignment between the geography of important public problems and the geography of government authority vital to tackling them. Economic restructuring, for example, usually hinges on shaping land and labor markets, which are primarily regional (metropolitan), in order to compete in consumer and capital markets, which are increasingly global—but doing so across the little kingdoms that municipal "home rule" defines in America's very localized system of government. As I showed in the chapter on Utah, state government is in principle the overarching authority, yet localities strongly resist state-imposed leadership on many issues, and to further complicate matters, some economic regions span state borders.

As Brookings' *Back to Prosperity* report highlighted, for a state with a slow-growing population and multilayered economy—still-restructuring older industrial regions, emerging high tech, agriculture, and even major mining operations—this fragmentation of official decision making is a major barrier to progress in Pennsylvania. So is a structure of public investment skewed to favor newly built communities over declining older ones. In this context, localities hunker down to protect themselves and safeguard their home-rule prerogatives rather than risk losses through dramatic reform. Older and newer localities regard each other with suspicion.

A large literature documents the cyclical efforts to design and launch meaningful instruments of regional government in America to address these problems. There are general-purpose regional governments, most famously in metro Portland and Minneapolis/St. Paul, to which constituent municipalities are partially subordinate; special-purpose governments that manage selected services (e.g., metropolitan transportation authorities); restructured city-county arrangements; and planning bodies composed of local governments that allocate a shared fiscal pie in a particular policy area (Henig 2002).

The latter category includes *metropolitan planning organizations*, such as the Southwestern Pennsylvania Commission (SPC). Designated by the federal government and recognized by state governments to allocate public investments in transportation and other region-serving infrastructure, these organizations offer a unique capacity and potential legitimacy. They are governed by local elected officials, they often double as economic development planners under additional state or federal designations, and they control a region-shaping scale of public infrastructure funding (Katz and Puentes 2005). Yet these organizations are exemplars of today's governance challenge: their effective scope for direction setting and action on regional problems, beyond the narrow role of budget allocator, is defined by what other governments, as well as important civic organizations, voluntarily authorize them to do on behalf of the region. Well-supported metro planning organizations *could* break down "silos" of fragmented land use, transportation, environmental, and economic development planning, become consensus-building mechanisms for cross-sector commitment, and, in older regions, ensure a broader approach to restructuring. But few of these organizations manage to do so. And recall that the Allegheny Conference pushed hard in the 1990s for a regional coalition of elected officials, the Growth Alliance. The Alliance may have dented the hyperlocal outlook of some elected officials in the region. But it also signaled, for others, more politics as usual: logrolling and deal making, by corporate interests, in the halls of the state legislature.

In 2000, the SPC, long viewed as moribund and technocratic with a highway-focused, divvy-up-the-dollars-by-county approach to governance, announced the search for a new chief executive. Civic entrepreneurs seized on this as an opportunity to push for significant change. Sustainable Pittsburgh, a fledgling sustainable development research and advocacy group and self-described "civic forum" backed by Heinz and other leading philanthropies, indicted the SPC's status quo approach in a *Post-Gazette* op ed, arguing that SPC simply allocated road construction dollars to chase sprawling development rather than helping the region chart a more sustainable future. "This is putting our region in a competitive disadvantage," wrote Court Gould, director of Sustainable Pittsburgh, and he called on SPC to organize a less technocratic, more inclusive planning process.[21]

Though SPC pushed back publicly, Gould's bold op-ed, which emphasized how the Pittsburgh region lagged behind Seattle, Austin, and other competitor regions, was given to the candidates for SPC's top job. What is more, says Jim Hassinger, who soon accepted the post, a mandate for change was central to his informal job description. But so was the warning that he would need to work hard with his board of local elected officials to change ingrained mindsets and practices. Hassinger brought experience in some of the country's best-known regional visioning initiatives, in Chattanooga and Richmond, where industrial turnaround was front and center.

Thus far, institutional change, which is all too easily misunderstood as a project of either internal reformers or outside critics demanding accountability, reflects both. Elected officials who have a regional vision, together with a staff director seasoned in regional consensus building, are instrumental, on the inside, for nurturing new perspectives and experimenting with new practices. They manage the pace of change and the SPC projects that both spur and reflect that change. On the outside, a pragmatic engagement with SPC by nonprofit advocates—spearheaded by Sustainable Pittsburgh and backed quietly by influential philanthropies—is pressuring for bolder change, framing possibilities for action (often by mining lessons learned in other regions around the nation and around the world), and helping a bureaucratic organization gain the capacity needed to act in productive new ways. The latter includes a push for bolder regional visioning, propelled by, but not limited to, SPC's conventional planning to meet federal requirements.[22] Influence networks linking advocates to funders and elected SPC board members, networks which privately channel concern and options for action and publicly praise SPC for new steps it takes, are crucial to this process of enabling change. For its part, Sustainable Pittsburgh has gone from delivering the indictment to supporting the reform.

Some reforms may happen slowly or never at all. But next-stage discussions of consolidating city-county government services in the Pittsburgh/Allegheny core, along with signals of gradual but steady change in SPC's focus and leadership role, suggest encouraging movement against the grain of old habits and structures.

Organizing Nonprofit Voices for Social Equity and Environmental Sustainability

As Henig (2002) notes, social equity has been the weak link in every wave of "regionalism" seen in America since the 1920s. The place of the poor, racial minorities, and other historically marginalized groups gets tabled all too easily in large-scale planning and reform efforts, which have typically been carried out by the most established political players, defined by a mind-numbing excess of technical detail and "planner-ese" language, and structured to provide few public opportunities for generating and deliberating meaningful policy alternatives. Environmental sustainability, meanwhile, is still struggling to win a place in mainstream thinking about economic competitiveness.

These patterns call for well-organized stakeholders able to represent and pragmatically advance minority interests in regional restructuring, particularly if that process aims to be become more participatory, as reform at SPC suggests. The final civic development I highlight, therefore, is the increased organization, at the regional level, of the equity and sustainability-oriented nonprofit sector. I include advocates such as Sustainable Pittsburgh, the philanthropic foundations, and a host of service providers and advocates who work with racial minorities, the poor, and dislocated workers, most under the growing umbrella of the Greater Pittsburgh Nonprofit Partnership (GPNP). Where business has long had the Allegheny Conference and government the SPC, both of which are still evolving and repositioning themselves, the nonprofit sector had no regional umbrella association until GPNP emerged over the past few years—nothing, that is, beyond the eighty-plus consortia for particular fields of practice or ethnic groups or geographic subareas.[23] Whereas I included, in the previous two sections of the chapter, an account of nonprofits as agents of reform and accountability, my focus here is on agenda setting and mobilization in the organized sector as a whole—the missing leg of the stool, in terms of the region's civic structure.

GPNP emerged in the context of fiscal distress in the state and region, recall organizers. Nonprofit charities, in particular, were blindsided by government complaints that since nonprofits paid no taxes, they did not contribute appropriately to a bankrupt city in a severely distressed region. "This raised the question of who speaks for the nonprofit sector and why we were caught so off guard," says Gregg Behr, former head of The Forbes Funds, a nonprofit support organization. Summit gatherings, media efforts, and surveys reinforced the sense of a gap between the public's limited awareness of poverty, hunger, and racial inequality problems in the region and what nonprofits saw "in the trenches" everyday. Likewise, nonprofit leaders, including sector support organizations such as the Funds, wanted greater Pittsburgh to have access to the innovative, technology-supported tools for participatory planning and governance— from "electronic town hall meetings" to decision support tools that make complicated planning decisions more accessible for nonspecialists—that they saw counterparts nationwide employing. But the main issue, says Behr, is representing missing issues and their constituencies in the dialogue about the region's future:

I certainly don't have the sense that the nonprofit community ought to have its own separate agenda for the region's future—economic or social or otherwise. I think what you've seen . . . is an expression on the part of agencies who are working everyday, in the trenches, to help vulnerable populations or to advance the quality of life in this region, to press business and government to put certain social and economic . . . issues on the public agenda that have just been missing . . . It's in this way that the nonprofit sector is developing a sense of itself as a sector and trying to contribute to the public dialogue about particular issues.

Nonprofits in the region face the familiar challenges of handling crisis needs and keeping their often overextended organizations afloat, both of which make it hard to invest significant time in large-scale planning and agenda setting. But GPNP, with 251 members as of 2007 and annual summit gatherings, cosponsored by the region's grantmakers, of over a thousand participants—a scale on par with the annual meeting of the long-established Allegheny Conference—represents a pathbreaking effort to organize a voice for the sector and for the sidelined "restructuring" issues it tackles in the region.[24] As this book went to press, GPNP was at the table with SPC and the Allegheny Conference discussing how a participatory regional visioning process, modeled after those of Boston, Chicago, Lyon, Turin, and other city-regions but unprecedented for the Pittsburgh region, might work.

Time will tell whether, beyond having basic support resources, GPNP becomes highly resourceful: building broader coalitions, developing policy solutions that respond to critical windows of opportunity in the agendas of business or government, and otherwise focusing resources to encourage change.

Summary and Implications

I have examined barriers, opportunities, and choices faced by actors trying to lead restructuring in an old industrial region—a place layered with multiple economies in transition and structured by a dense concentration of civic institutions (including business associations) and of local governments as well. Prior research offered three main ways to think about the civics of local economic restructuring: as *economic policy making*, in which nongovernmental groups help shape government policy, with or without (usually without) "hard evidence" on policy effects; as *public-private partnering*, in which organizations in different sectors blend their agendas (the coalition form) and sometimes their productive capacities (the operational project or alliance form) as well; and as *cultivating an innovative milieu*, in which the premium is on learning and technological innovation, with government and other sectors creating a success environment for new growth and enterprising firms leading that growth. Building trust is central to the latter two projects, and this can be especially difficult in old industrial regions with established habits, roles, and decline-induced strains (Sabel 1992). All three models are important in the Pittsburgh region, and the three help us understand how civic capacity can be developed and used.

First, origins matter: efforts to tackle restructuring through civic cooperation build, especially in older regions, on a foundation of earlier efforts at regional development, which embody rules of engagement, organizational reputations, images of transformation, and more. In greater Pittsburgh, a textbook version of the business-government partnership, embodied by the Allegheny Conference, helped clean up the environment and rebuild downtown after the Second World War, reorganizing land use and tackling fairly straightforward problems. But significantly, restructuring per se was never on the agenda. This was a master-builder coalition shaped by determined corporate leaders and a strong mayor. For a long time, it was also the only developmental partnering that the region knew—sadly, since restructuring has required a much more decentralized, experimentalist, learning-intensive approach and at least as much attention to institutions as to land. More recent efforts have taken the elite-led model of planning and doing to a larger (regional) scale, with notable success in key domains, such as government restructuring and priority-setting for state government assistance, and much less in others, such as cultivating an innovation-friendly economic milieu or winning popular support for key projects.

Second, nongovernmental civic intermediaries have been important throughout the last century, especially for the learning-while-doing dynamic I cited as missing in much earlier research. But this case underlines (1) how a region can be productively served by more than one such intermediary and (2) how varied the challenges facing these institutions can be. In the 1990s, for example, the Allegheny Conference was revived and refocused as a force for policy deliberation and politically savvy reform. The Conference spurred widely praised government restructuring as well as a more controversial physical rebuilding agenda to improve the area's "quality of life" as a competitive asset. Engaged business leadership was well suited to both tasks, notwithstanding the fiscal strains and political conflicts that government-subsidized stadium building and other megaprojects engendered. The Conference also highlighted the need for a more balanced economic strategy—not abandoning manufacturing strengths, for example, in the all-out pursuit of a postindustrial service economy—and for much more coordination among the hundreds of economic-development agencies in the area.

But neither the Conference, the important philanthropic funders, newly empowered county government, or anyone else has made a big dent in that fragmentation. And several organizational "absorptions" later, the Conference, now a conglomerate of service providing and lobbying agencies rather than simply a business roundtable for civic action, may have lost legitimacy—the claim to being a neutral broker when difficult distributional (win-lose) issues are at stake (see Stone 1989). In adding functions while diversifying its base, the Allegheny Conference has yet to find a strong new position from which to claim that it represents the broad public interest in creating a more competitive region. For better or worse, and perhaps because it is a complicated animal for interest groups and the media to make judgments about, the Conference has not shed its reputation for being a big-business interest group. Also, the Conference clearly lost focus after reorganizing itself, a loss for which the massive civic challenges of economic restructuring do not offer much slack.

Leading philanthropies in the area have been vital intermediaries in other ways, buffering the area in hard financial times and straddling the patchwork of political jurisdictions to encourage regional thinking in lieu of capable regional government. Only more recently have philanthropies taken bolder political and financial risks, pressuring for change at the Pittsburgh public schools—through a kind of coalition-led financial brinksmanship that risked backlash in order to overcome factionalism and standoff—and at the metro planning organization, deploying influence networks, global knowledge, and other tools of agenda setting and persuasive framing. Foundations have also partnered with state government and the universities to try to induce innovation (by commercializing research), but the results of this, which include a new proliferation of organizations and projects, are difficult to assess.

Newer intermediaries, such as Sustainable Pittsburgh, have likewise blended "gadfly" strategies of pressure politics with supportive moves to help the metro planning organization and other agencies to rethink their agenda and reach out more, making decision making less technocratic and more participatory. Influence networks—which tie such groups to the credibly impartial philanthropies and them to elected officials—are the structures along which the inside and outside dimensions of institutional reform are evolving. Networks that join reformers inside the institutions with those on the outside are pacing and directing needed change.

Third, as for accountability, each of these intermediaries can claim, rightly, that they are *not* "third-party government" in sense of making policy—that elected officials retain all the formal powers of policy making. But consistent with the regime perspective on urban politics, these unelected groups do much to shape public agendas and put them into action as well. No simple or shared set of rules—for promoting more transparent or deliberative decision making, protecting minority interests, or safeguarding other democratic values—ensures the accountability of these in-between players. Each responds to a set of constraints and opportunities, obligations and sources of support, that place checks on the institution's behavior. These structures do not always encourage results: what I outlined in the opening chapters as accountability in the form of accomplishment rather than mere compliance (for example, with procedural rules of fair play).

Leadership style and alliance relationships are big issues for intermediaries given the fluid political context in which, and indirect channels through which, the intermediaries have to operate. Formal and informal structures aside, it is striking how important individual leaders—resourceful people who promote useful change—are in each instance. Also, it remains to be seen whether these multiple brokers can cooperate to help the region develop a sustainable, inclusive vision of its future and then act on that vision. The temptation to focus on the short run—the politics of deal making rather than of civic mobilization—is strong in such a turf-minded region. Thus far, the nonprofit sector has been much more patient than business in this regard.

Fourth and finally, because locals (and even government higher-ups) lack control over important economic outcomes, civic capacity has important limits as a resource for economic restructuring. This is most evident in the region's stutter-step progress on cultivating a so-called innovative milieu—a project for which there are, to be fair, some mature models but few roadmaps to guide the way. Consider the distinction between *necessary* and *sufficient* conditions for competitive success. Where authority and resources are dispersed, civic cooperation is vital for achieving many of the conditions necessary for significant restructuring: reorganizing governance, crucial infrastructure and public services, and systems of public finance (an extensive work-in-progress in the Pittsburgh region); securing investments and regulatory reform from higher levels of government (the region has had more success on the investment front);[25] pooling and focusing public and private investments in education and workforce development (two important areas on which the region lags); encouraging a more global, outward-looking focus where turf wars and tradition push the gaze inward and pushing for new attitudes and norms ("entrepreneurial culture"), also works-in-progress; and more. If participation is broad and creatively structured, civic cooperation may have information payoffs, too. It can improve the information needed for "placing bets" on particular economic sectors with the so-called wisdom of crowds (more actors, more frames of reference, better decision making under uncertainty).

But none of this is sufficient to *ensure* economic growth. This point may seem obvious, since nothing guarantees business success in a competitive global marketplace. But the more specific point is that some growth-determining problems are very discrete business problems, such as the absence of a critical mass of venture finance, product managers, or legal services appropriate for the tech sector in a particular region. Arguably, these problems should not wait for cross-sector coalitions and policy initiatives, which tend to be diffuse and politically contested. They call for laserlike focus, dedicated resources, and agile response. Relationships and reputations developed in the civic arena may affect such "spot" problem solving, but civics per se is not everything. And the Pittsburgh region's long penchant for organization may, paradoxically, have made this more difficult to see.

8

Progressive Regionalism and Entrepreneurial Government: Democratization and Competitive Restructuring in the Greater ABC, Brazil

If creating jobs and distributing money were easy, someone else would have done it.
—President Luiz Inácio "Lula" da Silva, of the Workers' Party, to the press, 2004[1]

Sometimes it is an unlikely messenger who announces the need for change. The year was 1978, and the call for greater democracy in Brazil appeared, curiously, in a leading business magazine. Calling itself a "democratic manifesto," the open letter to Brazil's military dictators was signed by eight of the country's leading industrialists (Kingstone 2004, 163–165). For five decades, the strategy of import-substitution industrialization, defined by high import tariffs and large-scale government intervention in prices and production, had gone hand in hand with highly centralized and autocratic government (Fishlow 2000). This produced one of the most extraordinary economic expansions in the world in the twentieth century, capped by the so-called Brazilian Miracle of the late 1960s and early 1970s—albeit with some of the worst economic inequality in the world as well.

The industrialists' manifesto called for an end to military rule and a partnership between business and government to pursue a new economic strategy for Latin America's largest country. The world economy had changed, observed the letter, and the miracle was over. Heavy external borrowing in the 1970s had left Brazil deep in debt, and its economy was bifurcated on a deep, structural level. A lower tier of "premodern" producers was utterly unprepared to compete in export markets, while the modern sector developed under import substitution was losing ground globally thanks to an antiquated tax system, excessive government control, a lack of capital investment, and too little attention to quality—all hallmarks of a closed economy that had reached its limits.

Later that year, massive strikes hit the industrial heartland in metro-politan São Paulo, the epicenter of a state (by the same name) that gener-ated more than a third of Brazil's gross domestic product. The "new unionism" soon gave birth to an extraordinary political party, the Partido dos Trabalhadores (PT) or Workers' Party, which would transform Brazilian politics over the next quarter century, claim the mayorships of more than a thousand cities and towns, launch innovations in local democratic participation acclaimed around the world, and eventually win the nation's presidency—an event with few if any precedents in the history of the political left in Latin America (Baiocchi 2003a). President Luis Inácio "Lula" da Silva, elected in 2002, was born dirt poor in Brazil's drought-stricken Northeast, and his rise was all about the marriage of economic and political change. He and the Workers' Party had grown up together. If not rags to riches, his story was certainly rags to influence. He had migrated, like so many poor Northeasterners, toward the indus-trial jobs concentrated in the Southeast, near São Paulo. He became an industrial worker, then a union organizer, cofounder of an important opposition party, and later candidate for governor and president.

But I am getting ahead of the story. By the late 1980s, the social move-ments that were energized under military rule—organized labor, progres-sive Christian base communities, students, landless rural workers, and more—helped to create new room for dialogue with Brazil's political elite and its military rulers. Entrepreneurs founded new organizations that joined a pragmatic economic reform agenda to the budding ethos of democracy and participation (Gomes and Guimarães 2004). Movement organizers helped shape a new constitution, ratified in 1988, which enabled decentralized government, as Brazil prepared for its first demo-cratic elections since a military coup had established the dictatorship in 1964.

Meanwhile, as the 1990s began, the economy was a disaster: Inflation had run at more than 100 percent per year for the most of the prior decade, and a "spectacular series of failed stabilization plans" brought no fewer than six major monetary reforms (Cardoso 2004, 29). Not until the mid-1990s did Brazil's central government, now democratically elected but still headed by a strong chief executive, begin to achieve sta-bilization, curbing inflation and capital flight. The federal government likewise shifted the role of government in the economy: selling off dozens of massive public enterprises in mining, energy, telecommunications, and other sectors in one of the world's largest privatization initiatives; cutting tariffs; and encouraging exponential growth in foreign investment. "In the spell of only a few years," observed Rodriguez-Posé, Tomaney, and Klink (2001, 462), "Brazil has gone from being virtually ignored by foreign investors to becoming the second most important destination— after China—for FDI [foreign direct investment] in the developing world." With the shocks came major gains in productivity and output quality indicators, as well as the large-scale loss of industrial employment. As in the United States, these losses hit hardest in the industrial belt, in São Paulo state, beginning in the 1970s but accelerating rapidly in the 1980s and 1990s as the Brazilian economy opened at last (Rodriguez-Posé and Tomaney 1999).

This chapter is the story of creating an open society—founded on participatory democracy—and an open economy at the same time. More modestly, it is a uniquely revealing local chapter in that larger story. Compared to the saga of restructuring in the Pittsburgh region, this is an alternative story in the category of democracy as problem solving. It features a political party—the Workers' Party, young and ideologically pluralist—in a much more central and transformative role, trying to build democracy and address economic problems with deep roots all at once. Tied to that, the story features activist, entrepreneurial local governments at the helm of local restructuring: accommodating conflicting demands, redistributing resources to tackle acute social needs, and fighting the incentives to simply chase companies with tax abatements locality by locality—the so-called fiscal wars that intensified when the federal government devolved responsibility for industrial policy.

Given the different roles of the party on the one hand and the government it came to (re)direct on the other, this story includes the special dilemmas of "radicals in power," as Gianpaolo Baiocchi (2003b) has phrased it, including that of reconciling the Workers' Party's progressive social aims with the realities of an increasingly competitive and open (deregulated) economy. But unlike most research on the Workers' Party's ascendance or of concurrent political developments on Brazilian democracy, I focus not on the process of institutionalizing participatory budgeting or similar democratic innovations in the conversation between citizens and their government. Instead, my focus is on whether and how progressive governance at the local level, alongside dramatic policy reform at the national level, has enabled economic restructuring that can claim to be both democratic and effective.

I examine civic capacity—what it means, how it is built, why it may matter—in this context, which differs dramatically from the Pittsburgh region in terms of recent political history and the nature of the local civic landscape but no so much in terms of the underlying competitiveness problems facing an historically high-wage industrial region. These problems include fragmented local government authority, competing political claims on economic priorities, complex demands for innovation and learning, and problematic tax policy, labor regulation, technological disparities, and other factors that often lie beyond direct local control.

In this context, conclude expert observers, the wide array of responses seen in an era of Brazilian decentralization and economic reform—from unproductive, "low-road" efforts to chase footloose companies to strategic, value-added regional growth strategies—is at least as much about "the nature of processes and local institutions" facilitating learning, bargaining and other interactions among the market, government, and civil society, as it is about the formal policy making process or the content of economic development policies (Tendler 2000, 55; also see Guimarães and Martin 2001). On a more sobering note, the Brazilian government's policies were once dated and protectionist, but they had a clear and strategic purpose: to build a large industrial economy in a developing country. Devolving economic development to state and local governments has added all the perils of more localized economic development policy that I reviewed in the section introduction, such as limited local bargaining power and a mismatch between the short-run interests of politicians and established companies on the one hand and the community and workforce on the other. "What has emerged in Brazil in the aftermath of [central-government] withdrawal," warns Boniface (2002, 25), "is a sort of 'do-it-yourself' development approach with no overarching strategic framework." That approach may not be economically efficient or equitable, particularly where parochial political interests dominate strategic thinking and the public good—or, conversely, where good government and creative civics safeguard against that but do not manage to overcome the global pressures that depress local wages and technological upgrading.

I focus, in this chapter, on the epicenter of Brazil's industrial heartland and trade union movement: the Greater ABC region, in the industrial suburbs of the mega-city of São Paulo (figure 8.1). The area is named "ABC" for three of its seven large, abutting municipalities, the three with the largest industrial complexes: Santo André, São Bernardo do Campo, and São Caetano do Sul. The seven-city region has an aggregate population of 2.3 million persons, according to the 2000 census. I begin with a look at the area's unique evolution within Brazil before examining the special challenges of experimenting with new forms of governance and

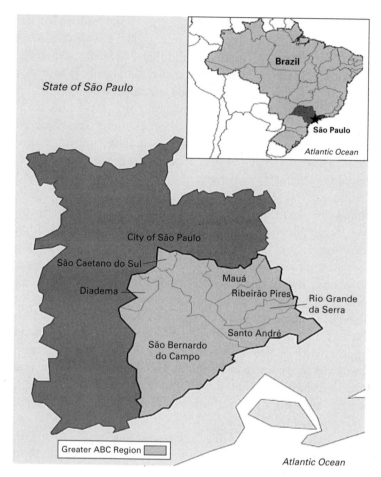

Figure 8.1
Greater ABC region within metropolitan São Paulo, Brazil. *Source*: ESRI, 2005.

restructuring a large industrial economy once shelters from global competition were suddenly removed.

Land of Industry, Immigrants, and Protectionist Growth

Brazil's economy, organized by Portuguese colonizers, relied largely on agricultural exports, first of wood and sugar and later of coffee and natural rubber, until the early twentieth century, when weak commodity prices worldwide dealt a severe blow (Skidmore 1999). Meanwhile, political elites favored a policy of population expansion to grow the economy, leading Brazil to encourage large-scale immigration. To the Portuguese, African, and indigenous base were added Italians, Spanish, Germans, Middle Easterners, Japanese, and others. Most flocked to the South and Southeast of the country, the most economically prosperous region thanks to coffee exports and nascent manufacturing focused on Brazil's domestic market. The slowdown in agriculture planted the seeds of intensive industrialization. Meanwhile, the immigrants from Western Europe brought with them union experience from industrializing cities, and so not surprisingly, the first unions appeared in Brazil in the 1880s, as São Paulo and other cities incorporated the newcomers into jobs and civic life.

Three things changed through the first half of the twentieth century and its two World Wars (Skidmore 1999). First, foreign immigration dropped significantly and was replaced by domestic migration from the poorer Northeast and Center of the country to the rapidly growing Southeast. Second, manufacturing gained strength after the 1920s, as national government began, for the first time, to pursue a strategy of import-substitution industrialization. Brazil was the pacesetter for Latin America, in fact, in combining protectionist prohibitions and tariffs on targeted imports with generous credit and large-scale public ownership of production in targeted sectors (Fishlow 2000). And São Paulo was the pacesetter within Brazil, combining rapid industrial expansion with much larger investments in public infrastructure and human capital, including public education and health services, than other regions of the country. Metropolitan São Paulo saw "the fastest long-term rate of city growth in the human experience," mushrooming from 31,000 in 1870 to over 18 million by the year 2000.[2]

The third sea change was creating, from the relatively decentralized federation in which Brazil was constituted in 1891, strongly centralized government "viewed as a necessary condition for social and economic modernization" in a vast, regionally diverse country (Rodriguez-Posé, Tomaney, and Klink 2001, 461). Elected presidents began this project of political and administrative centralization, which had enormous implications for the national economy and for regional development, in the 1930s, and the military dictatorship begun in 1964 extended it.

In this context, by the mid-twentieth century, the state of São Paulo represented more than half of Brazil's industrial output, as well as an important source of political pressure to continue building a literate, industrial, urban nation from a largely illiterate, agricultural, and rural one. Between the mid-1950s and the 1980s, the Greater ABC region within the state, which offered inexpensive land strategically located between the city center of São Paulo and the industrial port of Santos, became the center of Brazilian mass production (Klink 2001; Scott 1999). Between 1960 and 1980 alone, its population more than tripled, from just over 500,000 to more than 1.6 million (Klink 2001). A large automotive sector, seeded in the 1920s, matured and expanded rapidly in the 1950s, as foreign multinationals—Ford, General Motors, Mercedes, Volkswagen, Saab—established plants in the area, attracting suppliers of heavy machinery and auto parts (Rodriguez-Posé, Tomaney, and Klink 2001). A major government-owned petrochemical plant attracted other large petrochemical processing units and spawned a "downstream" plastics and molding industry (Scott 1999). Compared to other regions of the country, the industrial heartland offered high wages and so continued to expand under domestic migration. By 1970, almost 40 percent of Brazil's national income was in the state of São Paulo (Rodriguez-Posé, Tomaney, and Klink 2001).

But economic strength led to a more "muscular" civic life as well. Unions born on a corporatist model that limited bargaining power and constrained the right to organize became more assertive and independent over time (Sandoval 2004), leading to the landmark strikes of 1978–1979, the establishment of Brazil's trade union confederation, and the birth of the Workers' Party in 1980—all in the Greater ABC region (Rodriguez-Posé, Tomaney, and Klink 2001). The so-called new unionism also contributed to the movement for democracy, which I return to below. That movement culminated in a new Brazilian constitution in 1988, followed by the first direct elections of the nation's president in over two decades and an intensive period of local government reform and innovation that is still unfolding.

But as for the economy, by the mid-1980s, like Pittsburgh and other industrial counterparts in North America and Western Europe, the ABC region was shedding jobs fast and struggling to remain competitive.

The Decline

High land and labor costs, along with federal policies meant to dilute São Paulo's economic and political strengths, were pushing some producers to other regions of the country, including the impoverished Northeast, and the lower-cost interior of the state. The opening up of the Brazilian economy—under neoliberal reforms in the early 1990s—brought intense international competition and a final structural blow to local mass production. In the ABC region, total employment fell by almost 15 percent between 1986 and 1996, while manufacturing employment dropped by over 39 percent; like greater Pittsburgh, the ABC saw employment growth almost exclusively in healthcare, education, retail, and other service sectors with large numbers of low and moderate-wage jobs (Scott 1999, 8). Unemployment rose to more than twice the national rate, topping 20 percent, and while the region as a whole continued to add population, key production cities, such as Santo André and São Caetano, saw a net outmigration of workers and families for the first time (Klink 2001).

Technology was outdated, and industrial employment in the region remained concentrated in hierarchical, semiskilled "fordist" production units rather than the high-skill, flexible production and networked arrangements of suppliers and producers that were revolutionizing industrial economies in Europe, Japan, and elsewhere (Rodriguez-Posé and Tomaney 1999). Where productivity gains were achieved, it meant "jobless growth": the automotive sector doubled production in the 1990s, for example, even as employment in that sector continued to decline sharply (Scott 1999, 6). The region's many small firms correspond to what the leading industrialists of the late 1970s had identified, in their open letter to the national government, as Brazil's noncompetitive sector: low-skill, small-scale producers, paying only a third, on average, of the wage levels in large plants. Boniface (2001, 18) adds,

The "backward linkages" and economies of scale that had made the region attractive to investors in the 1960s and 1970s gave way to the so-called *custo ABC* (ABC cost). Reflecting the region's deteriorating industrial infrastructure and relatively expensive production costs, the custo ABC was apparent in the region's periodic flooding and horrific traffic jams (a worst-case scenario for modern just-in-time delivery methods), the high cost of land and water relative to other parts of Brazil, the high cost (and organized militancy) of labor relative to other areas . . . and mounting violent crime.

Economic "wars" between the Brazilian states, now experimenting, under decentralization reforms, with policies to attract foreign direct investment, put even more competitive pressure on the ABC region and other prosperous parts of Brazil. Brazil's tax system, which offers federal revenue transfers to the states and municipalities according to value-added economic activity, directly enforces this territorial race (Rodriguez-Posé, Tomaney, and Klink 2001).[3]

As Tendler (2000, 2) observes of the policy wars, advocates of U.S.-style incentives to recruit foreign companies and their investments emphasize not only immediate employment commitments but the promise of upgrading through "the transformative impact of large, outsider firms on the local economy." Drawing on interviews with senior public decision makers, she continues, "Governors and their recruiters say the outside firms provide immediate relief for problems of unemployment. They herald the outsiders as bringing new production technologies and organizational cultures, mentoring large and sophisticated customer firms . . . and contacts to export markets."

Tendler's interviews with business leaders, meanwhile, highlighted the very regional inequalities that twentieth-century industrialization produced in Brazil as a source of "push" and "pull" factors. Those factors now favor regions outside the industrialized Southeast and South. The higher-income, higher wage, and more saturated consumer markets there have begun to push producers away from the ABC and nearby regions, while the consumer potential in long-poor but faster-growing regions, such as the Northeast, pulled firms to set up major operations in those regions—a mirror image of the U.S. pattern, in which the South and Southwest drew producers away from the industrial Northeast and Midwest, including greater Pittsburgh, in the latter half of the twentieth century. Not only did foreign direct investment mushroom in the 1990s, as I noted above, but it was now much less concentrated on the São Paulo region (Rodriguez-Posé, Tomaney, and Klink 2001).

Yet even before the "bottoming out" in the 1990s, an extraordinary wave of regional organizing in the ABC, spearheaded in large measure by good-government reformers from the Workers' Party, had begun to develop ambitious new institutions for deliberating economic challenges and coordinating economic restructuring. Increasingly, the region adopted the language of the "new regionalism" and "associational economies" to define its problems and prospects. Restructuring in the Greater ABC, unlike other struggling industrial regions worldwide, was unfolding in the context of one of the most transformative democratic movements in the world.

Transitions: Democratization, Reform, and the Evolution of the Workers' Party

Born under authoritarian rule, the so-called new unionism of greater São Paulo was one important strand of the social mobilization that began to transform Brazilian politics, government, and civil society in the 1970s. "Base" communities founded by the progressive arm of the Catholic

Church, student groups, neighborhood associations, and groups focused on the status of women, racial minorities, landless farmers, human rights, and other causes led an unprecedented effort at grassroots organizing and coalition building to press Brazil's military dictatorship for democratization and greater social equality (Abers 2000; Baiocchi 2003a; Keck 1992).

Political openings began in the early 1980s. But As Baiocchi (2003a) recounts, social movements achieved a particularly visible victory in 1988, when the federal government invited delegates of these major constituency groups, though unelected, to be "consultants" to the writing of a new constitution. The constitution restored electoral democracy, enabled the political and fiscal decentralization of government—reversing a fifty-year shift in the other direction (Montero 2000; Stepan 2000)—and outlined a progressive charter of social and economic rights unknown in the United States and other established democracies (Power and Roberts 2000).

Beyond the immediate reforms, which did not resolve so much as shift structural problems in the design of Brazil's federal system (Power 2000), social mobilization had two far-reaching effects. First, it created enduring patterns of active citizenry and civic institution building that are widely associated with "deep democracy" and good governance (Barber 1984; Putnam 1993). This helps define the context for mobilizing business, government, and important civil society groups around economic competitiveness and social inclusion. Second, the mobilization that pushed the transition to democracy created a broad base for the Workers' Party, the most transformative political party in recent Latin American history. Ideologically pluralist, the Party expanded, initially from the massive strikes of 1978–1979 and then through local campaigns, with a core commitment not only to greater social equality in Brazil but also to broad participation and good governance—transparent, corruption-free, and effective.

This is not to say that the party always managed to govern effectively or that its governments succeeded in promoting greater equality as fast and far as progressive activists had hoped. As Baiocchi (2003b) observes, the Workers' Party, once it moved from incipient movement to legitimate opposition and then to being a governing party, faced classic dilemmas of "radicals in power." These dilemmas included the need to accommodate a progressive base as well as competing, sometimes diametrically opposed, interests, in order to get things done; the difficulty of translating visions into operational programs in the context of scarce resources and overwhelming "inherited" social needs; and—more basic still—the problem of competing factions within the party, some pushing for more radical change and others advising gradual reform and coalition building with the moderate center of political life. For all these reasons, some observers have chronicled the evolution of the Workers' Party and its achievements in office as part of "the rise of the pragmatic Left" in Latin America (Boniface 2003).

Beyond the dilemmas and the relative pragmatism they compelled, the party managed to strengthen civil society and organize institutional innovations—most famously local "participatory budgeting," in Porto Alegre and other cities. Contrary to the idea of participation as a straightforward empowerment project, the preparation of local government budgets through multitiered elections, public meetings, thematic working groups, and cross-neighborhood deliberations and bargaining is highly structured in Brazil. Plus, the design of that institution reflects significant learning and adjustment over time to "make participation work," in the literal sense of making it sustainable and *functional* vis-à-vis its purpose, not just *popular* vis-à-vis its ethos (Goldfrank 2003).

Not only did broader citizen participation, for which the Workers' Party has become famous worldwide, necessarily force new behavior from local government managers and elected officials, but it gave civil society groups new arenas in which to practice grassroots organizing, deliberation, and interest-group bargaining. As Baiocchi (2003b, 21) observes, "procedural innovations" emerged not simply from a commitment to broader, more democratic participation in public life but as a solution to a very specific political problem: How to achieve and sustain more equitable public investments in the face of conflicting political demands:

What emerged from the first large cohort of [Workers' Party] administrations was that some had successfully implemented participatory programs as a strategy for the negotiation of demands and legitimation of platforms with the population at large, in ways that helped avert some of the conflicts. . . . By bringing the conflict to be resolved into participatory settings, administrators found ways to generate consensus around redistributive platforms. . . . Successful programs were ones that relied on broad-based participation that went beyond social movements, unions, and neighborhoods associations.

Put differently, by carefully structuring and managing new mechanisms for participatory planning and decision making, Workers' Party-led local governments learned not only how to negotiate with organized political interest groups but how to compel such groups to negotiate with each other—and thereby provide government the kind of mandate to act that reflects a broad social consensus, however imperfect it might be.

But there was a downside to closer engagement with civil society institutions and influence. In some cities, party loyalists appeared to co-opt civil society groups, in effect making the apparatus of government, as well as civil society groups and networks, function as extensions of the Workers' Party and its policy program (Nylen 2003). Less ominously, participatory institutions have struggled to perform in cities with weak or disorganized civil society (Silva 2003).[4]

Moreover, the road to influence was not smooth and unbroken, at least in terms of electoral track record and reputation for accomplishment. Though the party was born in the Greater ABC, Workers' Party mayors struggled to retain office in that region and others, across election cycles, throughout the 1980s and 1990s, and subsequent administrations—which included governing "ungovernable" São Paulo, the world's second largest city—reflected hard-won lessons about defining and carrying out coherent policy agendas and adapting to political conflict (Keck 1992). Overall, however, observers widely credit Workers' Party governments with measurable achievements in participatory government, social policy innovation, and public infrastructure investments to benefit the poor and working class. The gains are especially impressive when viewed against Brazil's grossly unequal history of elite-driven government focused on the needs of the wealthy and their neighborhoods (Baiocchi 2003a).

More recently, the election of Lula to Brazil's presidency in 2002 signaled the Party's full maturation, in one sense, in the country's political life. So did the response by global markets and financial institutions and by other nations to the Lula government's economic strategy, which sustained much of the previous (Cardoso) government's commitment to a stable currency, stable capital markets, and an open economy.[5] But at midterm less than three years later, a major federal corruption scandal had tarnished the Party's squeaky clean image and damaged Lula's efforts to push through needed reform.[6] And returning to the core of our story, it is not yet clear how to rate the economic performance of local and state governments run by the Workers' Party given the serious structural challenges these governments face in the areas of competitiveness, income, and employment.

My concern here is not the fortunes of the Workers' Party per se but rather the era of experimentation and innovative governance that the Party helped to usher in, first and most intensively at the local level.

Recall that political and fiscal decentralization were hallmarks of the transition from military rule to electoral democracy in late-1980s Brazil. So was dramatic reform of macroeconomic policy, which added stability and encouraged foreign investment but also removed protections that had sheltered Brazilian industry from global competition for half a century. These trends produced a steep decline in the Greater ABC and a territorial race among the regions for employment-generating investments and upgrading. As Rodriguez-Posé, Tomaney, and Klink (2001) observe of these intertwined political and economic changes, decentralization was the major factor enabling local and state governments to become more activist on behalf of their economic prospects. But what compelled such activism and shaped it in concrete ways was the imperative of economic restructuring.

Like greater Pittsburgh, the Greater ABC was in crisis, and that crisis led to change. But what course would it take? Where the evolution of civic capacity is concerned, the case richly illustrates the development of new institutions to foster cooperation and the importance of political context for new practices of stakeholder engagement.

Building Regional Institutions, Tackling Competitiveness in the ABC

Urgency aside, in several key respects, the recent history of the Greater ABC region did not bode well for constructing a broad-based, collective approach to the area's challenges. As Boniface (2003) observes, for example, partisan elections were fiercely contested and class relations highly antagonistic in the Greater ABC, particularly between industrial workers and the big, multinational firms.[7] The struggle of organized labor against authoritarian rule "often failed to cut across class lines or across the public-private divide" (p. 15). As such, "Developing the potential for real synergies . . . had to be a political process in which regional leaders mobilized divided constituencies toward common purposes, despite their differences." The process, argues Boniface, had four basic elements:

(1) A systemic crisis . . . prompted reflection on the need for cooperative and regional solutions; (2) regional leaders engaged in a learning process of institutional trial and error; (3) effective political leadership emerged and was reinforced by the growing strength of the Brazilian Workers' Party and renewed citizen mobilization; and finally, (4) labor-business relations shifted to embrace tripartite negotiations [that included government], fortifying a cross-class alliance. (pp. 15–16)

This is a rich and multifaceted argument, summarizing a host of complex trends. Before examining these developments and tracing their recent effects more closely, I will reorganize and reframe the four elements somewhat to highlight distinctions among them and to facilitate comparison—at the end of this chapter—with the case of greater Pittsburgh.

First, Boniface highlights the shocks in the external *economic* environment that triggered a "systemic crisis." This was not a function of the local civic landscape or pathways of recent political change. It was about the territorial impact of massive industrial decline—a set of externally driven challenges—and it triggered local response but did not direct its course. Second, the political environment offered new openings, thanks to democratization and decentralization, and a repertoire of ideas and practices thanks to the social mobilization that both influenced the transition to democracy and fed on that transition. So there was new authority, especially for local governments and their constituents, to act, as well as an appetite for experimentation and a menu of ideas and procedures in play—a sketch of possibilities, really, at the outset.

That menu, in turn, was shaped significantly by the Workers' Party's agenda of economic opportunity, good government, and expansive democratic participation. But it built on the nascent recognition of regional problems *as* regional by organizations as diverse as the Catholic Church, labor unions, the major news daily (*Diário Grande ABC*), and research organizations (Daniel 2001). The menu acted to guide experimentation. The point of these distinctions is that the enabling conditions of external crisis and political opportunity did not, in and of themselves, steer local action. The repertoire of ideas and practices played a key role in steering.

As for specific processes and their immediate outcomes, Boniface's compelling thesis highlights two additional developments that follow from the first two. One, given the task, which included the complexities and risks intrinsic to economic restructuring, political leaders followed a path of trial-and-error learning that included experiments in institution building. This is significant in the economic growth dimension, since, as I noted in the previous two chapters, the incentives are great to offer public benefits indiscriminately to businesses ("shooting behavior") rather than pursue a slower and more strategic learning-oriented path. Put differently, in the narrow-but-essential public task of encouraging business, it is all too easy for "tool-driven" bargaining—deal-making defined by the familiar economic development tools in hand—to drive out learning, which implies unfamiliar actions, ambiguous roles, and uncertain outcomes. But institutional trial-and-error means fashioning new relationships and modes of decision making, not just new or innovative technical programs of change (programmatic interventions). So this learning orientation is potentially significant as a factor determining how much civic capacity will develop in a community and how it will be deployed, as well as the "end game": how successfully a community will adapt to changing global markets.

Second among the process developments that Boniface highlights, the bilateral and conflict-ridden business-labor relationship in the region was transformed somewhat into a trilateral and more cooperative engagement of government, business, and organized labor. A crucial feature here is the recognition, by labor leaders, that greater bargaining strength would not guarantee economic security in the face of massive industrial change (Guimarães, Comin, and Leite 2001). This tripartite engagement enabled innovative production arrangements (restructuring industrial work), wage concessions exchanged for greater job security, and more. In broad terms, this reflects the kind of public-sector-assisted "competitive integration" that the industrialists' "democratic manifesto" had asked of government in 1978. It also reflects a more global shift from the largely competitive, and often conflict-ridden, labor-management relations that characterized stable, mass-production economies to the blended interactions—both competitive and cooperative—that define joint problem solving by labor and management in an era of flatter authority structures, technological innovation, and flexible production arrangements (Sabel 1992).

Closer to the task of accomplishing change at the local level, and as any negotiation analyst will attest, turning a two-party game into a three-party one multiplies the possibilities for valuable trades, as well as learning; it may also reflect the value added by one or more of the parties as a facilitator of joint problem solving. In other words, changing the game not only has positive social spillovers if it reflects more effective cooperation between groups that were locked in confrontation. Changing the game can also produce measurably more valuable agreements in the short term: Government can concede on an issue to benefit labor, which concedes something else to government and looks to business to reciprocate in turn, and so on. Such multilateral, value-creating concessions, or sources of "joint gain," can be transformational—especially where the public and private dimensions of a community problem would otherwise lead to stubborn impasse (Susskind and Cruikshank 1987).

Even if interim developments are encouraging, do the combination of these enabling and steering factors ensure competitive success? No, they do not, but they do enhance the odds. Moreover, the particular conditions that shaped response to industrial decline in the Greater ABC should not be treated as prerequisites for collective action to encourage economic growth everywhere. Indeed, Montero (2001) has argued persuasively that interagency collaboration (within the public sector) and effective ties between economic development agencies and their clients in the business world produced important industrial advances in Minas Gerais, a state adjacent to São Paulo, in the 1970s and 1980s. This process, too, required significant learning and programmatic experimentation, which in turn demanded that the public sector be flexible in one sense (to address changing conditions and contingencies) and consistent in another—not abandoning a strategic, problem-solving engagement with industrial sectors in favor, say, of patronage-driven rents, or "pork," tying politicians to particular companies or union bosses. But the political process and institutional structure was far different from that pursued by government, civil society, and business in the Greater ABC starting in the 1990s. First, the task was different in Minas: new industrialization to compete with the industrial giant next door (São Paulo), not industrial restructuring. And second, given the new political moment, the much stronger union base, and the flourishing of the Workers' Party in the Greater ABC, the civics of restructuring demanded that initiatives focused on economic growth include a specific commitment to social equity and environmental sustainability—two values that had rarely been at the center of Brazilian industrial policy, or even on the visible margins, in Minas or any other part of the country.

Thus far, I have previewed conditions triggering the local response to industrial decline and the course that response followed, in broad terms. That course took tangible form via five important new institutions, outlined next.

New Institutions Develop

The regional approach began with a very immediate crisis—waste management, with the associated risk of environmental contamination—that spilled over municipal boundaries. As Boniface (2001, 19) notes, the expansion of municipal government autonomy that accompanied the transition to democracy did very little to create effective *inter*governmental mechanisms. But in December 1990, motivated by the need for political and technical cooperation on the waste issue first and foremost, mayors of the seven municipalities of the Greater ABC region—three of whom represented the Workers' Party, thanks to major local gains by the party in the 1988 elections—formed the first Intermunicipal Consortium (*Consórcio Intermunicipal*). Focused on joint research, planning, and investment, particularly in the area of public infrastructure, the Consortium generated interest in broader cooperation on issues of regional development. According to insiders, the Consortium development process also marked the start of a shift from the "out-dated and rigid technocratic planning model that had guided the region during the 1970s and 1980s, a period of rapid urbanization" (Boniface 2001, 20).

A series of follow-on successes developed the twin themes of regional cooperation and cross-sector collaboration among business, government, labor and other civil-society groups. In 1991, the city of Santo André, under the charismatic Workers' Party mayor and economics professor Celso Daniel, organized a multisector Forum on Local Economic Development. The following year, a regionwide "ABC 2000" Forum produced an even more public discussion of the region's challenges, a vision of the future, and a set of broad commitments by government and nongovernmental players (Rodriguez-Posé, Tomaney, and Klink 2001).

While many other regions of Brazil were "demobilizing" following the transition to elected democratic government, the vibrant social movement organizations in the Greater ABC, closely tied to the Workers' Party, organized a massive and successful get-out-the-vote campaign in 1994. Notes Boniface (2001, 23), "The movement succeeded in electing a record level of federal and state deputies [legislators] from the region . . . so successful was the movement that organizers decided to institutionalize their efforts into a large regional body," the Greater ABC Citizen's Forum (*Fórum da Cidadania do Grande ABC*), starting in March 1995.[8] The Forum would come to gather and represent more than eighty civil society groups from the region to discuss the area's problems and possible solutions. When a state government official approached local leaders in 1996 with the idea of creating a strategic regional development body with implementation capacity on economic development in particular, the Citizen's Forum "promptly convened to debate the subject" (Boniface 2001, 24) and joined with elected officials, the following year, to help found that new body.

Initially, however, the proposal was "shunned by local mayors who, at the time, were preoccupied by the forthcoming elections" (Rodriguez-Posé, Tomaney, and Klink 2001, 466). As such, observes Celso Daniel (2001), the Citizen's Forum was doubly important. It helped to sustain discussion of regional needs in the 1993 to 1996 period, after a series of electoral setbacks for the Workers' Party slowed the process of regional reform and institution building. The new Greater ABC Regional Chamber was established in March 1997, just two months after the election of seven new mayors, who sought quickly to revitalize and build on the Intermunicipal Consortium. Local Workers' Party leaders invited guests from Detroit, Barcelona, and other cities to share their economic and social goals and challenges, and this seminar set the stage for "letters of agreement" to formalize commitments by local players.

The new Chamber involved, through its founding charter and ongoing engagement practices, the public sector (state and local governments), civil society (the Citizen's Forum), business, and organized labor. The institution's design clearly distinguished the latter from civil society more broadly, including, for example, groups representing women, slumdwellers, education, and environmental concerns. Alongside government and civil society, then, business and organized labor together constituted a third pillar in this scheme: the local economy (Daniel 2001).

Looking back on the antecedents of this bold new experiment, Boniface (2001, 24) argues, "Developments in the automobile manufacturing sector were also decisive to the formation of the Regional Chamber and largely explain the decision of state and local leaders to adopt a tripartite design." This design was the core of an intensive effort, between 1991 and 1994, to experiment with a new approach to industrial relations in the all-important automotive industry—a "sectoral chamber"—as Brazil began to open its economy (Martin 1997). The tripartite sectoral approach represented a new era in labor relations, as the intensive period of strengthening organized labor (1978–1990) had secured greater union autonomy and wage concessions and also valuable bargaining experience but, with a focus on distributive bargaining—winning better terms through concessions by management—was not positioned to achieve much-needed restructuring to make the region competitive again (Guimarães, Comin, and Leite 2001; Leite 2002). The tripartite effort, in which government acted as a resource provider and mediator, also promised to mitigate the kind of interfirm conflict that has thwarted efforts to upgrade industrial clusters elsewhere in Brazil and around the globe. Boniface summarizes the impact of the automotive industry chamber:

The chamber resulted in a series of negotiated accords between labor unions (particularly the Metalworkers Union of ABC), businesses, and the federal gove rnment. . . . The accords were essentially a three-way compromise amongst labor, business, and the federal government: unions agreed to accept some "flexibilization" of production but were guaranteed job security; companies agreed to trim profit shares in exchange for production gains; and the federal government agreed to cut automobile sales taxes and delay full tariff liberalization in the manufacturing sector. . . . By all accounts, the chamber successfully contributed to the recovery and modernization of the Brazilian automobile manufacturing industry—a sector that, especially in the ABC region, was marred by outdated factory technologies. (pp. 24–25)

The success of these negotiations and the gradual withdrawal of the federal government led business and labor to look for other partners, including state and local government, whose engagement was increasingly important in the country's economic development (Boniface 2001; Leite 2002). Following the loss of a major new Volkswagen investment to neighboring Rio de Janeiro state in 1995, the São Paulo state government announced a plan to create a set of sectoral chambers on the federal model. This led in turn, a year later, to state government's proposal to local leaders in the ABC region for a regional chamber likewise designed to enable cross-sector deliberation and negotiation.

Constituted in 1997, the Greater ABC Regional Chamber is led by a Deliberative Council made up of the region's seven mayors, five representatives of organized labor and five of the Citizen's Forum (elected by those groups), the state governor and his or her appointed cabinet members, local city councilors (*vereadores*), and the area's state and federal legislative delegation (*deputados*). These Chamber's constituent groups do not participate with uniform vigor or visibility. Participant-observers argue that local government mayors and their staffs have been "the backbone" of the Regional Chamber (Daniel 2001) and that business participation has been uneven, in part because business associations are "not especially well organized at the regional level" and because the large, multinational manufacturing companies must answer to corporate decision makers across the globe (Rodriguez-Posé, Tomaney, and Klink 2001, 466). But the key manufacturing sectors—automotive and petrochemical—have consistently reaffirmed their support, and more localized businesses, including retailers, are well represented.

As Daniel emphasizes, the founding charter assumed that a diversity of players would work to build consensus agreements in the context of diverse interests and perspectives, not by denying those differences. The charter further aspired to a participatory model of "development with citizenship" and the possibilities of enhancing the region's competitiveness through systematic upgrading—in direct opposition to top-down, low-road development strategies defined primarily by bidding down the cost of local labor and offering public subsidies to attract or retain major firms (Daniel 2001, 466).

Moreover, the presence of multiple levels of government as well as organized civil society makes the Regional Chamber an exercise in "horizontal" as well as "vertical" authority relations (Daniel 2001, 465). It is not local civil society in lieu of multitiered government but the one engaged with the other—to define priorities and negotiate around interests. Finally, the Chamber is not a new level of government. It is a regional planning and consensus-building mechanism wherein multiple sectors participate voluntarily. This is significant, as I will explore in a moment, from several vantage points, including political sustainability (vulnerability to electoral shifts, for example), financial sustainability (since the Chamber has no claim on dedicated revenue streams from any sector), and leverage over members' actions. Nonetheless, the Chamber is a major development in regional governance in Brazil and significantly different from the nascent regional bodies of greater Pittsburgh or other American industrial regions.

In its first year of meetings, the Greater ABC Regional Chamber created an overarching agenda (scope of issues and priorities) and a set of working groups to tackle them. The priorities encompassed economic growth concerns, focused on the concept of competitiveness, as well as important elements of social and economic equity. Following a large gathering, the Chamber approved a list of proposals covering the need for sectoral policies to improve the region's comparative advantages, including critical workforce development initiatives; establishing a "movement" to eradicate illiteracy; implementing environmental protection; investing in regional infrastructure; providing more incentives for economic activity, including credit and incubator programs for microenterprises and small and medium-sized businesses; and creating a nongovernmental regional development agency focused on research, business development, and marketing (Rodriguez-Posé, Tomaney, and Klink 2001, 467).

In June 1998, the ABC Economic Development Agency (*Agência Desenvolvimento Econômico ABC*) would become the area's fourth important regional institution and the principal operational arm of the Chamber. With a board of directors that is 51 percent private sector (business and labor) and 49 percent local governments, the agency has attracted greater interest in regional cooperation on the part of large companies in the area. It has commissioned market research, organized a massive retraining program for industrial workers, and participated actively in the effort to develop clusters through vital supplier agreements in the region's petrochemical sector, as well as other initiatives to create "value chains" between small and medium-sized enterprises founded in the region and large companies based there, including multinationals (Guimarães, Comin, and Leite 2001; Rodriguez-Posé, Tomaney, and Klink 2001).

In a study commissioned by the fledgling economic development agency, economic geographer Allen Scott (1999, 15–16), a champion of the new regionalist perspective, framed the problem and a broad strategy for local leaders,

Clustered complexes of flexible industrial activities are often sites of intense innovative change. As such, they constitute the mainsprings of what are now referred to in generic terms as "learning regions." The spatial concentrations of firms and workers out of which these regions are composed, *notably when they are accompanied by certain combinations of enabling political and institutional arrangements*, are the essential building blocks of the new economy and the new regionalism. (Emphasis added)

By all accounts, the Chamber, the Agency, and the Citizen's Forum, having built on earlier foundations, have contributed to regional solidarity and multiplied the opportunities for learning and bargaining focused on the region's need to adapt. But regionalism was perceived by some of the area's decision makers as a project of the Workers' Party. And while the party's dominance of local governments in the ABC during 1997 to 2004 produced a kind of golden era of regional institution building, it produced a cooler reception at the national level, since the presidency was held by another party. Furthermore, say insiders, turnover in mayors and their staffs led the momentum for regional risk taking to wax and wane. The Chamber had signed more than seventy voluntary agreements by 2002, yet by the time of my second visit, in 2005, the area still lacked a regional business plan and a corresponding set of public policy priorities to focus action in the face of very limited fiscal resources. The regional institutions endured, but their development slowed markedly, after the tragic assassination of Santo André Mayor Celso Daniel, a respected "good government" innovator, under a cloud of conspiracy later linked to a major corruption scandal within the Workers' Party, in early 2002.[9] The incident was doubly significant since the Party rose to power in part by denouncing Brazil's historically murky campaign financing and high-level government corruption. Below, I explore the factors that help explain the limits of regional action after such a promising period of institution building.

Over the late 1990s and into the new decade, meanwhile, civil society groups and local governments developed new programs of social inclusion, from upgrading basic infrastructure in the poorest slum communities to sustaining microcredit, training, and other investments in the area's small enterprises and human capital (Somekh and Klink 2001). The Workers' Party spearheaded the process of local government transformation, though key programs, such as participatory budgeting have achieved such support that rival political parties have protected them once in office (Baiocchi 2003a).

Having concluded the previous chapter with the reminder that "civics is not everything," in this chapter's penultimate section below, I examine more closely the effort to *use* the new institutions, in specific ways, to promote competitiveness through industrial upgrading and equitable development.

Problem Solving in (and around) Young Institutions

Regional problem solving in the Greater ABC rested, by the late 1990s, on a new and unprecedented set of institutions that were, at once, multisectoral (business, labor, civil society, and government) and multijurisdictional (crossing municipal boundaries and "bridging" vertically to the state government). These institutions, centered on the Regional Chamber, emphasized voluntary participation and consensus decision making, both of which contributed new civic capacity in a region long dominated by adversarial labor relations, outward-looking manufacturing firms, and relatively passive and technocratic local government.

But the region continued to face the familiar challenges faced by governments who must negotiate with "mobile" capital. So the capacity of local actors to bargain effective development agreements, for example, with multinational firms, not just to foster local policy innovations or campaigns for social investment, had become very important. Moreover, as Tendler (2000) notes, state and local governments must all too often enter these negotiations with little information on what has been secured by governments elsewhere, in agreements that are typically confidential and closely guarded.

A second factor shaping the capacity of local reform and collective action to meaningfully affect industrial competitiveness is the competitive position of local firms and (entire) sectors of firms: in particular, the nature of their insertion into supply chains, whether local, national, or global (Humphrey and Schmitz 2001). Leite (2002) found, for example, that companies in the ABC's plastics sector participated actively in working groups established by the Regional Chamber from 1998 forward. These mostly small firms, whose clients are diverse and whose access to outside support for technological upgrading is limited, saw real payoffs in regional efforts to enhance worker skills, modernize technology and production methods, and secure more bargaining power through joint sourcing (bulk purchase) agreements with their suppliers. I examine these developments briefly below, as an episode (case within the case).

In sharp contrast to the plastics firms, Leite observed, the larger automotive assemblers and auto parts producers did not participate long in the Chamber's relevant working groups—for the sector, tax policy, or infrastructure. Explaining why their participation was initially enthusiastic but short lived, the firms told researchers, first, that the key government decision makers, from the vantage point of their competitive bottom line, were not present: They needed tax concessions or infrastructure investments mainly from federal and state government, and the few concessions they requested of local (ABC) governments were rejected. (Recall that the local governments were out to avoid fiscal "giveaways" to firms.) Second, upgrading in this sector appears to be driven by relatively hierarchical and centralized global chains, and the large clients (buyers) in those chains with whom local firms entered into joint improvement projects, not by participation in upgrading initiatives launched by local actors through the Regional Chamber. In other words, as compared to the plastics firms, automotive companies could not count on the discussions organized by the Regional Chamber (1) to provide them with key benefits that were within the purview of government, nor did the companies (2) rely on local initiatives to upgrade their production. As in the tripartite sectoral developments of the early 1990s, automotive competitiveness continues to be driven largely by federal concessions, such as tax breaks or large-scale financing for plant upgrading, and labor-management negotiation that has generally reduced employment but enhanced productivity in the sector.

Beyond these competitive constraints on important sectors, as I previewed above, regionalism had clear limits from the start, and after the initial period of institution building, the limits of consensus decision making and voluntary agreements became more clear—a sign of what one media insider criticized as the ABC's "triumphalism"—declaring victory much too soon. The elections of 2004 brought Lula, the Workers' Party candidate, into national office, which in turn brought the ABC new support from above. But those elections also undid the Party's six-year electoral majority of the ABC's municipal governments. Santo André, which suffered more employment loss and fiscal decline than any city in the region, remained a champion of interjurisdictional strategy. So did the area's major petrochemical plant, the Regional Chamber, and the federation of unions, which organize by sector and not town. Arguably, these were the area's only "natural" or consistent regionalists, say insiders (the Citizen's Forum no longer plays an important role). On the opposite end of the civic landscape were business associations still organized by municipality rather than sector, and smaller and less industrialized cities in the ABC that saw their needs as diverging from the rest.

By 2005, the pact against luring companies via a "fiscal war" had frayed, with at least one city defecting to lure a major firm, and despite having commissioned study after study, the region had no consensus on a business strategy (defined by competitive niches) or set of public policy priorities to support that strategy. Some business leaders grew frustrated with the long time horizons implied in many regional development schemes, and by the major focus on research early on, wanting to see faster action. Consensus decision making had produced many agreements on paper and some major accomplishments in infrastructure, but bolder moves—regional revenue sharing, for example, or aggressive pursuit of technology upgrading to benefit plastics and other sectors—languished in discussion.[10]

Furthermore, the proliferation of regional agreements led some to complain of a lack of focus in light of scarce financial resources. The regional agencies had no direct claim on local-government revenue, state government—in spite having encouraged the formation of a regional chamber to which it officially belonged—remained a conservative and limited investor, and the federal government was likewise a limited source of funding, though its tax policies, subsidized credit for industrial development, and control of quasi-public enterprises made it a key player in the regional economy.

Two cases within the case illustrate the power and limits of civic capacity developed in the ABC and so widely celebrated by outside observers. The first episode concerns the effort to expand the region's hugely important petrochemical plant, the *polo petroquímico*, which is the foundation of the region's competitive strengths in plastics. The second episode covers two municipalities' negotiations with a multinational company, Britain's Rolls Royce, over the development of a new power plant to serve the evolving petrochemical hub—and the firm's linked negotiations with civil society groups, in exchange for political support, over the terms of that development. These developments are especially crucial for the region in light of continued upheaval, and the threat of major layoffs and plant closings, in the large automotive sector.[11]

Reformist goals aside, then, how have new civic machinery and comparatively new norms of problem solving actually functioned to promote economic restructuring?

Case 1—Expanding the Petrochemical Pole and Upgrading Its Customers

In the late 1990s, a business-government-labor working group organized through the ABC's regional economic-development agency identified the expansion potential of the area's petrochemical production and plastics sector as a high priority for regional growth. The working group likewise identified important structural barriers constraining any expansion. "Downstream," the molders and other plastics producers were mostly small and medium-sized enterprises with uneven skills, access to credit, and production quality. But even larger structural barriers were upstream, at the Polo Petroquímico itself, run by the firm Polietilenos União: plant expansion was prohibited thanks to a state law passed during Brazil's dictatorship (when national politics worked to constrain São Paulo's further growth as an economic power), and the supply of raw materials was likewise blocked. The key supplier of petroleum products, the quasi-public corporation Petrobras, was now a competitor—and one still governed by the federal government.

The local discussion led to a solid coalition of business and labor focused on changing state law to permit the expansion (under promises to safeguard the environment), a reform achieved in 2002, and later compelling Petrobras to supply raw material. After the elections of 2002 that brought Lula into the presidency, the Polo went to Brasília, with strong backing by the region's Workers' Party mayors and its unions, to convince members of Congress and the President, to direct Petrobras to sell petroleum products to the Polo at a price set by the market. The strategy succeeded, thanks in large part, say insiders, to the Regional Chamber's role as a catalyst. Early union support, as well as lobbying by elected officials—all nurtured through working-group deliberations about how to expand the sector—delivered vital state and federal support. This support, in turn, secured the most important expansion of the region's vital petrochemical industry in decades.[12]

"Downstream" progress has been more gradual but nonetheless marked and directly shaped by the region's relatively young cross-sector institutions. Though discussions of the need to upskill and upgrade—to pursue "high-road" economic growth—marked the earliest dialogues about regional competitiveness, dating to the early 1990s, the plastics producers are many (making decision making highly decentralized), production skills and methods are lagging, and the sources of investment for significant upgrading are few—as I highlighted above in the comparison of the plastics and automotive sectors' participation in regional restructuring groups. Also, the ABC region has been slow to cultivate a plastics cluster—a set of linked firms whose competitiveness is pursued as a collective endeavor, with government in a support role. Yet in recent years, through working groups convened by the Economic Development Agency and supported by the local branch of Brazil's small business support service (SEBRAE), plastics firms have pursued bulk purchasing of supplies and healthcare, R&D planning, and quality improvement initiatives. Though firms were initially reluctant to share ideas with their local competitors, as a participating entrepreneur explains, "We build trust through exchanges—visits to each other's plants—and discussions about common needs."

Changing mindsets and labor-management relations is slow work, as studies of industrial upgrading in Europe and North America have consistently underlined (Sabel 1992). Furthermore, Brazil's tax policies offer disincentives to the smallest producers to modernize and expand. Many remain in the undercapitalized informal sector. Finally, affordable land and credit (risk capital in particular) are ongoing barriers in the ABC region, say entrepreneurs and business assistance experts. The most promising R&D development in years—the decision to open a new federal university in the ABC—promises returns in the medium to long term, not in the immediate time horizons that most concern owners and managers. But the sector shows concrete signs of moving from the rhetoric of upgrading to much-needed transformation, and revenue growth has been steady.[13]

Case 2—Engaging a Big Multinational: Deliberation and Bargaining

In the second episode, the cities of Santo André and Mauá negotiated with Rolls Royce over the development of a $130 million, state-of-the-art power plant (Martes and Macedo 2004). The process began in 1998 when the British multinational won the bid to produce a cogeneration plant for the local Petroquímica União, which was privatized in 1992. Rolls Royce faced a classic multiparty, multilevel negotiation, with a regional twist thanks to the ABC's rather unique civics.[14] The company needed an environmental permit and license to operate from state government, as well as site permits from the two affected localities. Within these three governments, multiple agencies pressed specific interests— from environmental protection and economic development to social equity—and then there was organized labor and civil society to deal with: environmentalists, neighborhoods associations, and more. In 2001, there were multiple public hearings, planning committee sessions, and even the call, at one point, for a popular referendum to rule up or down on the new plant. The concerns were technical as well as social and economic. But as a consultant retained by Rolls Royce told Brazilian researchers (Martes and Macedo 2004, 9),

[In the ABC region], the groups are very organized and are already prepared for popular debate on every issue to do with the city . . . and so this helped the process a lot. These are channels that have already been set up by the [municipal] administration itself. . . . so it's very easy to work. . . . The process there was on a very interesting level, both from the technical point of view and as far as getting closer to the community was concerned. . . . After, we worked with various segments: those that deal specifically with community organizations, neighborhood associations, religious groups, these formal regional discussion channels already exist, the regional discussion Chamber, councils . . . the Rotary Club, lawyers associations, and engineers—our dialogue is with all of them.

Ultimately, Rolls Royce won its approvals, state government won a fee to offset any environmental impacts, and the two municipalities won significant concessions for infrastructure upgrading, as well as new jobs from construction and plant operation. To win broad support, the company had negotiated directly with well-organized neighborhood associations (including associations of slum dwellers who lived near the proposed site), environmentalists, and others, agreeing to provide very localized benefits. These actors then lobbied government officials on behalf of the project. It is not clear, in the accounts available, what problems the deliberators might have failed to solve or how the deliberations were structured to allow weaker parties to make themselves heard. Nor is it clear how much the parties involved altered their preferences as opposed to bargained the best win-win deal possible at the time.

The company relied on public officials to line up support within government, across disparate agencies—all in the context of an established regional framework for pursuing industrial upgrading as long as it came with strong environmental protection, socially responsible corporate "neighboring," and good jobs. The outcome was a sign not only of market leverage but of the way complex, multiissue, multiparty dialogue and negotiation can be handled where local institutions and norms favor agreed-on principles for economic growth, mobilized civil society groups who know how and where to press their claims and deliberate with each other, and reasonably transparent government to act as regulator, referee, and occasionally coinvestor.

Summary, Implications, and Comparison

Brazil's premier industrial region, racked by a long decline in competitiveness and the new pressures generated by the opening of the national economy to world markets, entered the 1990s with civic strengths and weaknesses that differed profoundly from those of greater Pittsburgh. On one hand, the Greater ABC subregion of São Paulo had no history of large-scale public-private cooperation along the lines of Pittsburgh's politically potent "renaissance" partnerships. The ABC also lacked the Pittsburgh region's extraordinary concentration of wealthy and politically influential philanthropic foundations. Furthermore, as the 1990s dawned, the seeds of economic transformation in industrial Brazil were about to unfold in the context of one of the most remarkable transitions to democratic government anywhere on earth. Nothing similar happened in and around Pittsburgh as "big steel" collapsed.

The Brazilian transition included significant political and fiscal decentralization, which spurred state and local governments as never before and also left them largely on their own to tackle regional economic problems and opportunities. (Only in recent years, after I completed my fieldwork, has the Lula government, in a turn away from the Cardoso approach, provided new supports in the form of incentives for university-firm collaboration and subsidies for target clusters.) The transition to democracy, because it rested on significant social movements that included an assertive "new unionism" born in the ABC, also came with a powerful new ethos of public participation, transparent government, and equitable and sustainable development. These ingredients, including the practices of deliberation and democratic bargaining, were nurtured significantly by the Workers' Party, whose rise was especially rapid at the local level, and at the same time complicated by the party's political and administrative challenges as a network of "radicals in power," to use Baiocchi's phrase, and by structural barriers to cooperation among local governments that are common to Brazil, the United States, and many other countries.

Given such different starting points, it makes little sense to render a sweeping judgment about whether the ABC's more inclusive, government-initiated approach or greater Pittsburgh's elite-led, private, and still more exclusive approach to restructuring is better overall. Both are replete with the rhetoric of partnering and the challenges that sustained partnering entails.

But in terms of the three perspectives on restructuring that I highlighted two chapters back—restructuring as economic policy making, cross-sector partnering, or cultivating an innovative milieu—the contrasts between the Greater ABC and greater Pittsburgh are all the more striking. Government has played a far more central role, in the Brazilian case, in building new institutions—most notably across jurisdictions (intercity agenda setting and policy coordination) and across sectors (deliberation and negotiation between business, government, and civil society)—and also in articulating a balanced economic strategy. As Evans (1995) notes, mainstream economic development thinking, most notably by the World Bank and other lead institutions, long denied the importance of an activist or "developmental" state in fostering economic growth in such ways.

But in the ABC, and most of all in Santo André and other cities most consistently governed by Workers' Party mayors, entrepreneurial local government has been influential at least as much through building new administrative capacity and cross-sector coalitions as picking smart industrial policies. That is, the government role in restructuring is notable for its adaptiveness *as to role*, which implies a broad series of activities and standards of accountability, and not just for discrete *policies* on industry upgrading, retention, and so on. For this reason, the role of government is as much a part of the restructuring-as-partnering dynamic as it is of policy making in the narrow sense of "getting rules and incentives right."

In terms of the latter, the most dramatic and the most indisputably regional accomplishment was building a consensus to fight what scholars have termed "shooting behavior" by local economic development agencies (pursuing companies with costly public inducements). It has been a fragile consensus in some ways, and it may not survive as the ABC's widely admired Regional Chamber and Regional Economic Development Agency evolve to deal with the diversity in member cities' interests and needs. But that policy consensus is combined with a regional vision grounded—unlike Pittsburgh's—on broad-based engagement of citizen's groups, businesses, and local officials across many old social divides. The voluntary agreement, by local governments in the ABC region, to avoid raiding each other through "fiscal wars" has kept a focus on upgrading and upskilling—that is, on so-called high-road strategies of economic growth. The most self-critical local observers, inside and outside of government, acknowledge that the region has a long way to go in terms of walking that road. (Creating the milieu to support that strategy appears to be the toughest challenge in both cases, regardless of the one being elite and private-led and the other government-initiated and more inclusive.) But this is strikingly different from the fiscal politics of greater Pittsburgh, with its extremely localized economic policies, very limited revenue sharing across jurisdictions, strong beggar-thy-neighbor habits, and extreme fiscal inequality. Brazil's inclusive approach has gone much farther to mitigating the fiscal wars.

Another striking difference is in the "smart strategy" dimension of competitive restructuring: the decision to fight hard, in the Brazilian case, to strengthen industry from the start of the restructuring drive rather than focus narrowly on a postindustrial future—a tendency in Pittsburgh that was driven, admittedly, by strengths in high technology that the Greater ABC and other Brazilian regions lack, but which Pittsburgh-area decision makers came to regret as overly narrow and flawed. In Santo André and other ABC cities, nurturing the service sector reflects a strategy to diversify the local economy and enhance quality of life. But policy makers recognized early on that the region would not retain its high-wage character if it simply added shopping centers and hospitals. Thanks in part to the region's civics, sustainable development and social equity have also been much more prominent in the Brazilian context, as seen in the case of securing community benefits and environmental commitments from Rolls Royce when it sought to build a state-of-the-art power plant. Public and private leaders, through regular interaction, also recognized quickly that particular service sectors, such as logistics and communication, would be essential complements to industrial upgrading.

It is not surprising, in the context of entrepreneurial and activist local government, that nongovernmental intermediaries are correspondingly less important in the ABC than in greater Pittsburgh. One would have to acknowledge the powerful brokerage role of a political party in the former; parties, as I showed, are remarkably marginal in the politics of restructuring Pittsburgh's regional economy. Plus, nongovernmental groups have been engaged policy advocates, and the Greater ABC Citizen's Forum was the vital early organizer of the normally diffuse and diverse civil society sector. But where government is actively convening stakeholders and elected officials are shaping innovative policy agendas with those stakeholders, the need for "compensatory brokerage" by purely nongovernmental intermediaries appears to be more limited.

As for the high-road, manufacturing-intensive strategy in the ABC, the strategy may be enlightened, but the road itself has not been an easy one to walk. One reason is industrial structure. The prospects of some major sectors, such as the region's all-important automotive production sector, appear to be driven much less by localized cooperation than by the global structure of supply chains, technological upgrading financed by powerful multinational firms, and federal concessions on taxes and subsidized credit (again, Lula's government has made some headway, and as of this writing, local auto part supply chain members are collaborating, albeit belatedly, in upgrading). The potential of one of the pillars of high-road strategy—collaborative industrial networks nurtured by local government, unions, and other locally based institutions—is much more evident so far in the region's other sectors, such as petrochemical processing and plastics.

Moreover, the character of local civic life has clear enabling properties in a fluid environment wherein Brazil's state and local government and civil society groups must negotiate more and more with business, including large multinational companies (Tendler 2000)—but not simply through "hard bargaining" or pressure politics rooted in having leverage. The Rolls Royce episode richly illustrates what it means to use leverage effectively, deliberating local priorities in a climate of active citizenship and greater transparency without subjecting public decision making to costly, unending debate or impasse.

To be sure, the ABC still faces major barriers to restructuring. Scarce financial resources, the perverse tax and other incentives that help keep small firms small, informal and "basic" in production process rather than expand and modernize them, and the absence of effective and widely accessible R&D in the region still act as significant barriers to industrial upgrading, for example. Also, the ABC, like the Pittsburgh region, needs more strategic cooperation from the state and federal governments—cooperation at which European nations excel (Savitch and Kantor 2004). But local leaders, together with their federal partners, are pinning high hopes on a new federal university campus in the ABC region. And there are signs of progress on upgrading, which has been fostered by regional networks. Those networks were established by cross-sector civic leadership, and cultivated by engaged elected officials within that broad leadership, rather than by business entrepreneurs themselves.

By the year 2005, when I completed my fieldwork in the area, regionalism, and the regional character of economic restructuring, had retreated in some respects. There were clear signs that the ABC's cities were going it alone again in economic development. In the context of limited resources, the Chamber, said close observers, struggled to set clear priorities. And performance in civics, it turns out, is much like performance in comedy: timing is fundamental. Some eleven associations left the Regional Development Agency, frustrated with slow progress in 2002, only later to return. The scandal-clouded shooting of Workers' Party Mayor Celso Daniel—a charismatic organizer, economist, and good-government guru who was central to the flowering of regional institutions and cross-sector cooperation in the 1990s—explains some of the stalling. So does the Workers' Party's loss of key mayorships in 2004. Regionalism was closely associated with the party's leading political figures, including Daniel.

But I believe that another important part of the story is the need to evolve, to consider further transformations of the civic institutions and operational agencies that served one stage of regional restructuring but may not adequately serve another. Regional institutions thrive on a sustained sense of mutual advantage. Institutions founded on uniform membership and consensus norms of decision making suited the first phrase, in which foundations of trust and experiments in cooperation—both the learning and doing aspects—reinforced each other. This was in a region with a history of fiercely competitive class and party politics and adversarial labor-management relations. But the region's institutions and its individual risk takers have the opportunity, as well as the need, to innovate yet again.

The ABC's Regional Chamber might be more effective, for example, under a structure of tiered membership of the kind proposed by some observers of the European Union and its recent struggles to gain support in key member countries. That is, some agreements for regional cooperation or policy alignment—the boldest and often the riskiest, or at least the policies perceived to be so—would apply to core member municipalities and business sectors only, while other agreements would apply to all members. Likewise, the Chamber and Economic Development Agency have long made some decisions by majority vote rather than consensus, and flexibility on this front could be a significant determinant of future effectiveness—in particular, effective priority setting, which tends to sharpen conflicts when resources are limited and stakeholder interests are diverse.

It is not that the presence of a broad-based regional forum grounded in the ethos of democratic participation and dialogue is a weakness by any stretch of the imagination. Indeed, it is what greater Pittsburgh has conspicuously lacked and is only now beginning to establish. Such a forum, while plodding in some respects and very dependent on effective leadership to overcome apprehension, has been a real source of "soft power" (Nye 2004) for tackling shared problems in the heart of industrial Brazil. Rather, the problem-solving perspective on democracy highlights the importance of regularly renewing a community's mechanisms for collective action. This is essential for partnering, and it helps distinguish truly innovative economic milieus from those that merely claim the label, adopting the ubiquitous language of "knowledge economy" and "technology-led future."

This may mean rethinking the heavy focus on consensus-oriented decisionmaking in regional action. Learning-oriented dialogue aimed at consensus has a prominent place over the long run. But effective bargaining and risk-taking mechanisms are likely to deliver many of the breakthroughs when bold decisions are needed, as they are in the ABC and other industrial regions worldwide. This suggests a key reason why broad-based civic capacity may reproduce itself: where deliberative learning makes it more likely that the right goods will (eventually) be delivered, bargaining is crucial to getting them delivered, and with those deliverables, young institutions are much more likely to win the support they need to become durable. Conversely, a civic life rich in dialogue or deal-making capacity but not both does little to build confidence in trying out new institutional approaches—or sustaining the trials beyond some initial phase.

IV

Investing in the Next Generation

9

Leading Change in Child and Youth Well-Being

Politics is [seen as] a direct threat when it takes power out of the hands of the experts who, presumably, are in the best position to recognize a superior technology. Or it is a necessary evil—the distasteful course that must be taken to get the proper policies and programs into place—to be banished as quickly and completely as possible once that goal has been accomplished.
—Stone et al., *Building Civic Capacity* (2001)

The previous two parts of this book examined urban growth and economic restructuring as tests of a community's civic capacity. This final part focuses on the most fundamental resource—and a crucial target for collective work—in any community: the next generation. An earlier era might have classified this work simply as redistributive social policy, whereby wealthier households are taxed to benefit the children of poorer ones, and public goods provision, in which education and other services are ensured for all. But a growing focus worldwide on developing high skills, the shared benefits of a healthy population, and other imperatives makes it possible to tie the well-being of a community's children and youth to its economic competitiveness and "quality of life." Outcomes for the next generation are much more than a welfare concern, narrowly defined.

Analogous to the prior section, where I distinguished between the work of operating a viable local economy and that of transforming a nonviable or noncompetitive one (through restructuring), my focus here is on leading *change* in the sets of arrangements that shape the well-being of young people. The focus is on nonroutine collective action to significantly improve opportunities and outcomes, with a particular concern for disadvantaged young people. While reforming systems of public schooling around the world has rightly received great attention, I focus mainly on the vital out-of-school systems, formal and informal, that also affect children and youth in significant ways: systems of health promotion, tutoring, violence prevention, leadership development, job training, and even the basic community development—secure housing in communities with healthy supports—that provides the foundation for healthy individual development.

In America in recent years, the African proverb "it takes a village to raise a child" has become a catchphrase for those who advocate approaches to young people's well-being that are founded on communitywide commitment and action; the proverb also has storied connections to the concept of social capital, which I described in chapter 1 as an ingredient of civic capacity that has frequently been confused for the whole.[1] Perhaps broad engagement seems so vital to us in America because our political commitment to high-quality, publicly guaranteed services for all young people and their families has been so limited, at least when compared to other wealthy societies. Whatever the case, it seems fitting that the two chapters that follow present revealing cases of leading change in America and South Africa, respectively.

Below, I characterize the task of leading change in the well-being of children and youth, including important civic features of this domain, and I overview the landscape of players who have a clear stake in that change. I then discuss the distinction between broad "systems change" and best-practice (or model) projects, as well as the tensions between building broader social movements and getting things done—or between the logic of changing politics and political relationships (to create the *will* to act) on one hand and producing measurable change in social outcomes (by finding effective *ways* to act) on the other.

That dual agenda of problem solving, which I outlined in chapters 1 and 2, often defines what policy advocates and service providers in America have come to label "community building" (Briggs 2007; Gibson, Kingsley, McNeely 1997; Walsh 1997). But it also reflects the twin influences, worldwide, of participatory democracy or "participatory development" on one hand and efficiency-focused "new public management" on the other. Those influences create major challenges for change agents in complex young democracies, such as South Africa (Pieterse 2002b), and complex older ones, too.

What Is the Work?

Local efforts to improve the well-being of the next generation have four crucial features as tests of a community's civic capacity. The first is about the overall strategies or "theories of change" that determine more specific tasks of problem solving. In terms of goals, these efforts target either the scale or effectiveness of action to serve young people. That is, the efforts are about expanding resources and implementing capacity (if there is some agreement on what works but too little of it happening), about discovering more effective interventions (what works best), or both. Efforts focused on expanding resources often take the form of broad-based campaigns, with public education, budget advocacy, and other strategies (Scott et al. 2006). At the global level, the Millennium Development Goals, for example, include reducing child mortality by two-thirds and ensuring universal access to primary education for all the world's children by 2015. Locally, strategies to define and pursue such goals by expanding resource commitments may combine professionalized advocacy with grassroots political organizing, including savvy coalition building to shift policy decisions (Briggs 2001; Scott et al. 2006).

In wealthier nations, the public mobilization in this kind of problem solving is often cyclical, driven by budget and election calendars. In America, well-publicized landmark reports, such as the Carnegie Corporation's *Starting Points* (on meeting the needs of young children) or the Annie E. Casey Foundation's annual *Kids Count Databook* (of key indicators), become focal points in efforts to focus more attention on, and win larger social investments in, young people. United Ways, community foundations, and other intermediaries act as local champions. But the aim, typically, is to expand the resources available in systems that reach everyone or to complete that coverage.

In developing countries, debating the allocation of resources to child investment versus, say, military expenditure or economic development incentives, takes on a different level of urgency. Crisis-level needs are many, reliable and up-to-date data on service provision and outcomes are harder to come by, and formal systems of human services, healthcare, subsidized housing, and schooling may not reach the entire population (at *any* scale), particularly in the poorest and most remote rural areas or in urban slums. While recent decades have seen a number of actions within the community of nations to affirm human rights, including every nation's special obligations to meet the needs of children, there is a chasm between aspiration and resources, between rhetoric and reality. In South Africa, which has an unusually ambitious constitution of social and economic rights, the debate is whether those rights, such as the child's right to shelter, are mostly aspirational as opposed to "justiciable" by courts and realizable by government and others. Advocates and scholars wonder: is "right-based development" more than a mantra in the quest to expand vital investments in the next generation?

Enhancing the *effectiveness* of formal or informal programs serving young people is the other major change strategy at the local level. One approach is focusing on a single program that needs overhaul, and the other approach is "systems change." Systems change refers to structural reforms to make better use of resources already allocated, but it may be part of a campaign to expand resource commitments as well (Fulbright-Anderson, Kubisch, and Auspos 2003). Systems change is messy and slow, more "muddling through" than campaignlike (Brown 2006), though short-run campaigns may be one element.

Why is it necessary? The structure of institutions and programs serving young people and their families is famously entrenched and fragmented in many countries, meaning that significant improvements in child and youth outcomes could be gained by restructuring the system, not just running best-practice projects that succeed at highly focused objectives (a new after-school curriculum, a child vaccination initiative, and so on). A large literature documents the fragmentation in human service delivery that generally follows from bureaucratic specialization and a layering on of programs by lawmakers, over time, to meet particular needs, and more recently from outsourcing services to nonprofit organizations (Kagan 1996; Moore, Longo, and Palmer 1999; Schorr 1988, 1997). Cross-functional teaming up is often at the heart of systems change efforts (Ostroff 1999), many of which have inherited the service integration goals of an earlier wave of reforms, dating at least to the 1970s—the original "new" public management.

The second feature that shapes the civics of problem solving in this area reflects the distinction between alliances that do work (produce services or other outputs) and coalitions that influence decisions (about resources or policy). This feature is the tension between *collective action as pressure politics*, for example holding public agencies or elected officials accountable for better child and youth outcomes, and *collective action as coproduction*. The former emphasizes core political values such as citizen participation in decision making, and it often includes public education, media outreach, policy research, and other traditional advocacy tactics focused on senior decision makers. It draws on the strategies and tactics of value-driven social movements that organize actors to make political claims of decision makers (reviews in Briggs 2001; Oldfield and Stokke 2006; Scott et al. 2006).[2]

As a target of collective action, coproduction is a very different game, and it can also emerge from political organizing, as was the case for India's slum dwellers in chapter 5. The leverage points for coproduction strategies are often internal: shifting the attitudes and behaviors of regulators or service-providing professionals but also of parents and community members whose practices shape the lives of young people in the most immediate ways; and developing and implementing better processes for coordinating work and measuring its impact. Improving child health or preventing youth violence are just two examples of the kinds of multidimensional challenges that call for coproduction by parents, teachers, health workers, community elders, and others. "Community-driven" housing development in poor nations is another domain in which local knowledge together with external resources and approvals can yield terrific results, as the chapters on India and South Africa make clear. Smart interventions leverage key elements of "community," such as information and referral networks, accepted norms that regulate behavior informally, and feelings of solidarity and mutuality. In the shorthand of management, coproduction may call on stakeholders to shift the content of labor (what their practices are), the division of that labor (who does what), and the ways labor is coordinated (how actors work together and hold each other accountable for results). The risk for civil society, though, is being co-opted by government or other players who expect partners to refrain from criticism. Too many "partners" are contractors with a glorified label.

Two final, interrelated features shape the civics of improving child and youth outcomes. Both are about the importance of framing and perception (Schön and Rein 1994). First, in the form of a strategic question: Are young people, as a group, framed as a resource or asset to be protected and cultivated or as a problem and source of risk for the wider community to curb? Child and youth advocates emphasize the former, and at least in America, a well-defined school of thought—"positive youth development," focused on enrichment and opportunity and defined by a canon of core principles—has worked to shape policy discussions, and displace negative imagery focused on deviance and control, over the past decade (Pittman and Irby 1998; review in Scott et al. 2006). But problems of youth homicide, robbery, vandalism, and other behaviors invariably compete with that asset-building perspective—particularly where adolescents and young adults are the focus rather than infants and young children. The former are typically more "blameworthy" in the public arena, and security concerns are a potent force in the politics of any community, most of all in cities where crime problems are highly visible or where the perception of decline is strong.

The second framing issue is about whether a "community" effort to improve youth outcomes is thought to benefit the entire community (a win-win prospect) or to provide benefits to a select subgroup through a (zero-sum) transfer of resources. Here again, advocates typically emphasize the broad-based benefits of a healthy, safe, well-educated next generation. And, as I will explore, South Africa's progressive postapartheid constitution provided new legal and political means by which to define what society owes the most disadvantaged children as a cornerstone of democratic transformation. But where the efficacy of programs to serve young people and their families is in doubt, as it often is, and where racial or other boundaries create important political divides, voters, taxpayers, policy makers, organized interest groups, and the media may treat child well-being as one of a series of special-interest policy goals. In the near term, it is one that cannot help but compete for resources with other priorities. Historically, much local government spending on social programs has been treated this way by the body politic (Peterson 1981), with cash-strapped municipalities promising to tackle poverty and other problems but finding that major drivers of those problems are structural economic change, national wage policy, and other factors that are not decided locally. Investing in young people too often becomes a fight over the fiscal scraps in this too-little-too-late debate.

Stakeholders

What stakeholders become involved in the tasks I have outlined? First, *policy advocates* who specialize in the needs of children, youth, and their families monitor budgets, cultivate knowledge about effective interventions, and sometimes organize other stakeholders in common cause—or try to act as good-faith mediators of policy agreements.

Second, organized *parents* and, in some cases, *young people* themselves, act as the primary grassroots constituency for change (Ginwright and James 2002; Oldfield and Stokke 2006; Scott et al. 2006).

Third, organized *service providers*, sometimes as unionized professionals (for example, school teachers) and sometimes in looser coalitions, often weigh in on proposed change.

Fourth, *public managers* and *elected officials*, whether legislators or executives, are often important. The former run or staff agencies that allocate budgets, provide service delivery or monitor that delivery by other agencies, and disseminate indicators of child and youth well-being. As the quote atop this chapter outlines, the professionals often feel a distinct ownership as the "experts," and this category includes law enforcement officials who endorse approaches such as "fight crime, invest in kids." For their part, elected officials, who may have begun their civic careers as advocates outside of government, may campaign on children's issues—whether under the "positive youth development" or "curb delinquency" or other story frames—and also develop and oversee policies and mobilize constituents. They may commission studies or otherwise seek to expand policy knowledge about the issues affecting young people and their families.

A fifth group of stakeholders—*business*—has become increasingly vocal in recent decades, whether under the broad mantle of social responsibility or as interest-group advocates who define the well-being of young people as an investment in a community's prosperity and economic competitiveness or who mobilize to curb youth crime. Business leaders want children to become skilled workers and want to attract high-skill workers and their families to an economic region with quality schools and services.

Finally, the *media* play a significant attention-shaping role: helping to place or keep issues on the public agenda, portraying young people and families and the programs that serve them in a positive or negative light, monitoring follow-through on promises—more often exposing failures than highlighting what works, some complain—and more.

How Does Politics Matter? Working against the Odds for Significant Change

As seen in the epigraph to this chapter, a number of observers of policy making and politics have noted the preference for "managerialist" language, and for consensus themes and win-win solutions, over suggestions of give-and-take political contests. Stone (1988) highlights this efficiency-focused managerialism as a staple of persuasion in American politics, and Heller (2001) has underlined its prevalence in emerging democracies, even those that define policy making, at least rhetorically, as part of broad social transformation (as in the case of South Africa). The turn in this direction seems particularly pronounced following peak periods of popular mobilization, such as in America after the movements of the 1960s, after India's independence movement gave way to large government-run programs for social welfare in the 1950s, after South Africa's transition to nonracial democracy in 1994 (with one dominant party), and to a lesser extent, after Brazil's transition from dictatorship to democracy in the late 1980s.

Some of this may reflect healthy pragmatism and the recognition that winning support for principles is one thing and acting on them effectively—accomplishing things—quite another. But as Stone (1988, 305) warns about politics in America, "Inspired by a vague sense that reason is clean and politics is dirty, Americans yearn to replace politics with rational decision making." The same could be said anywhere that rational planners hope to supplant politics with evidence-based decision making that is "above" the give-and-take—that is, decision making that operates independent of political process.

In this vein, the standard advice to child advocates is to appeal to enlightened self-interest and to sell results and efficiency. One is told to emphasize the positive potential roles of stakeholders, instead of harping on grievances or highlighting differences in power and influence. But again, beyond adhering to the old advice to "catch flies with honey," it appears in some instances as though politics—that vital arena in which we deliberate important purposes and values and make difficult decisions that derive from the same—has been trimmed from the picture altogether. More specifically, great faith is placed in the notions that evidence-backed ideas promising better results will persuade, as long as they are sold effectively to the right players, and that such persuasion will shift the key decisions on which new outcomes for kids depend, even where sacrifices to existing interests are involved.

The flaws in this apolitical notion are several, and these flaws underscore the importance of building a constituency that supports change, even pressures for it, against considerable resistance. First, achieving better outcomes for young people comes at some opportunity cost in terms of alternative investments of time, money, and attention, so "better" overall is in the eye of the beholder, at least in the short term. If helping children and youth indeed helps everyone in the medium to long term—from those who want safer streets to business and government leaders who want a more competitive economy—it is nevertheless the case that many political decisions are driven by a fairly short-term calculus of losses and gains to specific agendas. Understanding stakeholder values, interests, and perceived trade-offs, therefore, and knowing how to negotiate those effectively turns out to be as important as being clear and "data-driven" about one's own interests and action agenda.

Second, significant and durable change in the way a system works typically involves leaving behind much that is known for beliefs and habits that are unknown, and this poses risks. As behavioral scientists have documented time and time again, most human beings do not reason well in the face of risk and uncertainty, and most find change to be fraught with uncertainties and loss—and therefore anxiety-producing— as the old proverb about "the devil you don't know" instructs (Anderson and Anderson 2001).

Third, and in part because change often has a limited appeal, "buy-in" by political elites and senior agency decision-makers is one thing, support by staff implementers and by client-citizens quite another. In large public systems in particular, but in nonprofits and private firms as well, middle managers and line staff have considerable latitude to informally "veto" unattractive or threatening expectations perceived as imposed from above (Bardach 1998; Pressman and Wildavsky 1973). As I explored in the chapter on economic restructuring in Pittsburgh, systems change thus includes an important "inside game" of organizational support building, risk taking, peer-to-peer encouragement, and new rewards for new behavior, alongside the "outside game" of sustaining political pressure and expanding public and private resources for change. In addition, grassroots participants, including families and informal community leaders, may veto change efforts if they perceive a threat to traditional perks, attacks on traditional allies, or business as usual in top-down decision-making. Stone (2001) has chronicled the latter reaction as part of the political legacy of elite-led school reform in Atlanta, for example.

Summary and Preview

Building political will and operational "way" in support of a significant change agenda to benefit the next generation turns out, like the other tests of civic capacity, to demand much more than advocacy of "smart" policy. Particularly where government-provided resources are scarce, problem solving calls for strategies of civic engagement developed over time and at several levels, from grassroots to grasstops and from pivotal service-provider agencies to the children and families themselves, who are not only citizen-stakeholders and clients but potential coproducers of change. It often includes the civics of pressure politics but also the different, and typically slower-moving, civics of coproduction.

In the San Francisco case in the next chapter, which features America's first "Children's Budget" for a local government, building will called for mastering the ins and outs of California-style direct democracy, in which voters make policy at the ballot box, as well as the labyrinth of municipal budget making. It also meant finding ways to enhance the accountability of programs for children and youth through both learning and bargaining across the government-nonprofit divide. It is this search for cross-sector accountability, not the ballot-box clout that is in some ways special to progressive San Francisco, that makes the case a revelatory one for other communities and for students of democratic problem solving (on case study logic, see Yin 1994).

In the case of South Africa, the civic work includes varied mobilization and litigation strategies to press claims about new social and economic rights, including children's rights, and also to coproduce change with technocratic and often unpopular public agencies. This is in a climate of one-party rule unfriendly to political pressure by civil society groups, in a nation reeling under rapid economic change and the backlog of apartheid-era social disparities. It is also where institutions of local governance have undergone massive reorganization as a central feature of the transition from white minority rule to multiracial democracy. Those features define the context for developing vital civic capacity in the face of government's inability to meet social needs. These features make the South Africa case an important source of lessons for the developing world as a whole—and perhaps beyond it as well.

10

From the Ballot Box to Better Results: Cross-Sector Accountability in the San Francisco Children's Movement

Depending on one's perspective, San Francisco is a free space or a decadent place, a melting pot of cultures or Pandemonium itself.
—Richard DeLeon, *Left Coast City* (1992)

You move to San Francisco to be a part of progressive paradise . . . and compassion starts with those least able to protect themselves.
—California political consultant

It is a bit like watching a sophisticated public policy debate unfold at a large family gathering. How can public funds leverage private ones most effectively? Should scarce funds target the greatest need or the greatest potential impact? What does each area of the city deserve, given the range of family resources and needs from one neighborhood to another? It is July 2003, and I am in a meeting room at city hall in San Francisco, alongside two dozen service providers and child advocates who are meeting with city government staff from the Department of Children, Youth, and Families. At issue is how the city should allocate some $30 million set aside in the municipal budget for children's programs, through a charter amendment that was pioneered in this city by the Bay a dozen years earlier.

The participants' comments reflect a wealth of knowledge about children's programs and city budgeting—and also a familiarity and trust born of frequent interaction over years of advocacy and planning together. Staff members distribute tables showing the number of children served, by zip code, by the city-funded programs that are delivered by the large network of nonprofit service providers represented in this room. Input on official priorities is laced with insider jokes about veteran advocates in the room and the reputational quirks of the city's neighborhoods: the director of a respected, school-based youth center in one of the city's higher income neighborhoods receives a playful jab about working in an "overserved" area.

This is one of a series of "community stakeholder meetings" the city will hold before announcing the annual budget. Minutes earlier, Margaret Brodkin, executive director of Coleman Advocates for Children and Youth, handed out flyers advertising a strategy meeting to "discuss children's issues and the mayor's race." It was Coleman that spearheaded the country's first-ever ballot initiative to create a "children's budget" at the local level, in the form of an amendment to the San Francisco city charter, and then to renew and enhance that set-aside a decade later. It is Coleman that will organize the city's extraordinarily politicized voters and advocacy groups to secure specific commitments for children from the mayoral candidates in the upcoming election; the election is a kind of political crossroads after eight years under the charismatic and controversial Mayor Willie Brown. And a year from now, Brodkin, after twenty-six years in nonprofit advocacy, will be named by the new mayor to run this department.

Now it is November 2003, and the subject is the salary levels and other operating expenses of the city's fire department. What does this have to do with the well-being of young people? "We found $45 million in waste in the fire department this year," Brodkin told me earlier in the week. Coleman more or less invented the practice, among advocates in the city, of identifying budget savings (or "offsets") to go with each of its budget requests. So I look on as one more seventeen-year-old activist learns just how fast those sergeant's salaries add up for one of the city's most political powerful blocs: the unionized firefighters. We are in a retreat space in Golden Gate Park, near the city's western edge. I am at an "all-agency" Coleman meeting on a Saturday, not to be confused with the all-staff retreats that many professional advocacy organizations might convene. This is a meeting for and with constituents, too. Activists are here, from Youth Making a Change, an independent group which Coleman started up in 1991, and Parent Advocates for Youth, launched in 1994. Board members have come from other cities in the San Francisco Bay Area, and Coleman's full-time staff of seven are here as well, sitting in on small groups discussing everything from the campaign to win a new school bond to juvenile justice policy in the city and how to work effectively with the newly elected mayor, Gavin Newsom.

Experts argue that no discernible movement to define and protect the rights of children, as distinct from the well-being of their parents, existed in America until the early twentieth century, and that a clear focus on youth policy came much later, in the 1960s (Scott et al. 2006). Since then, many professional advocacy organizations have sprung up to monitor indicators of child well-being and disadvantage, analyze government budgets, file lawsuits to protect or advance child rights, and lobby for new policies and for policy reform. Many of these advocates are highly dedicated, but most remain marginal to the politics of their cities and states, part of a struggling group of social welfare advocates who deploy the media to shame a wealthy nation into doing more for those who lack political influence, including the poorest children. It is rare when an organization that represents a nonvoting constituency—children, in this case—commands significant clout, such that candidates for office clamor to appear at its events and declare themselves the "child-friendly" candidate in the race.

This is a story about developing clout as well as civic capacity in a political centrifuge, in a city where progressive factions fight over uncompromised visions of the Good City. In global perspective, it is not so much remarkable for the financial resources mobilized—San Francisco is a wealthy city, after all—or for the level of activism on behalf of children's issues—San Franciscans are willing to be activist about almost everything, the record shows. Rather, the case holds lessons about how political actors create a shared sense of purpose, and institutionalize accountability in policy making and outcomes, in the context of contentious "hyperpluralism." This is how political scientist Richard DeLeon (1992), a longtime student of San Francisco politics, labels the city's propensity to adopt myriad causes. Hammering out effective roles for government and the nonprofit sector is a worldwide challenge. It means forging meaningful, two-way accountability for results, not the don't-ask-don't-tell politics that is content simply to allocate more money to children's needs (or any other worthy cause, for that matter). San Francisco insiders are divided as to how far the city has actually progressed on this point—freeing critical children's services from nonprofit patronage politics, for example—but this chapter unpacks the civics of tackling the issue, which is rarely documented anywhere. Finally, as a case of civic capacity in the making and using, this chapter holds lessons about yet another kind of intermediary: a civil society organization that is not a mass membership group and not merely a professional advocacy outfit either but—as a hybrid—a significant catalyst for both the learning and the bargaining that contribute to problem solving. To appreciate these lessons, one needs, first and foremost, to understand what is and is not special about the context.

The Capital of Progressivism and Dissent

In the early 1980s, Congresswoman Nancy Pelosi, now the nation's first female Speaker of the House of Representatives, famously declared San Francisco "the capital of the progressive movement" in America.[1] The statistics support her claim, both the notion of a strongly progressive bent and the movement element as well. Using survey data on dozens of U.S. cities, DeLeon (2002) identifies San Francisco as a clear outlier in its voters' progressive ideology as well as their levels of political engagement and literacy. Progressives are many and, not surprisingly, quite differentiated: At least three overlapping "lefts" are discernible in voting patterns, according to DeLeon (1992), including *liberals* who favor government redistribution and intervention in the economy, *populists* who emphasize protection of communal traditions, and *environmentalists* who want to limit economic growth and safeguard quality of life. A respected political consultant and pollster explained it to me more simply: "small city, many factions."

San Franciscans are also more likely to act on their political beliefs than people in other American cities. Even noncitizens in this city get informed and mobilize more often: their knowledge of elected officials and levels of activism are comparable to citizens in other parts of the country (DeLeon 2002). In an age renowned for citizen apathy and for mistrust of both politics and government in America, San Franciscans are, comparatively speaking, highly engaged as well as highly tolerant culturally. A gay mecca, the city was the first to financially protect domestic partnerships, for example. There are no majority blocs; every group is a minority and so must forge coalitions (DeLeon 1992). Moreover, the political culture of the city favors protest and other forms of direct-action politics far more than do other parts of the country (DeLeon and Naff 2004).

But as Gabriel Metcalfe, senior analyst for a good-government think tank in the city, observes, the clear implication for this left-dominated city is that, unusual for America, the left must actually *govern* in San Francisco, and create the conditions for economic prosperity and a healthy society, not merely dissent or "speak truth to power."[2] It must also find appropriate political spaces, he argues, for negotiating or otherwise managing the trade-offs that cities confront, between growth and preservation, between market mechanisms and social protection.[3]

This is no small thing in a city where progressives spent decades organizing opposition to a pro-growth coalition of big businesses and politicians, largely through voter mobilization and California's direct democracy provisions—the initiative, referendum, and recall—and not through legislative or bureaucratic compromise. The citizen initiative, in particular, favors a winner-take-all approach: policy making via the ballot box. It often reflects voters' mistrust of elected officials, the desire to create what historian Peter Schrag (1998) terms "the clockwork state": a government operating with only the most limited discretion left to those elected to govern.

Broader economic and social changes shape this political appetite. Famously an epicenter of the 1960s counterculture, San Francisco became, in the final decades of the twentieth century, a high-skill hub of the expanding Pacific Rim economy, a postindustrial center of finance, management services, and tourism (Hartman 1984; Mollenkopf 1983). The city's postwar economic success, and perhaps its reputation for tolerance as well, drew Asian and Latin American immigrants as well as black migrants and progressive whites. The 1980s saw a downtown building boom under Mayor Dianne Feinstein, as well as sharp increases in homelessness, child poverty, substance abuse, and street crime.

By the early 1990s, reacting to market-driven redevelopment of their city, San Francisco progressives had created what DeLeon (1992) calls an "antiregime"—reactive, wary of power, and skilled at erecting restrictions on business-led urban development, not articulating a positive, majoritarian program for the city that reflected economic realities. Mayor Art Agnos had been elected in 1987 on a slow-growth, focus-on-the-neighborhoods platform. Business became politically reactive, too, fighting off new taxes and perennially warning that the San Francisco Left's idealism and mistrust of the market threatened to choke off prosperity. Says a former member of the Board of Supervisors (city council), "When I was in office, the business community only showed up to say 'no' to things . . . they weren't a part of problem-solving."

When the late 1990s brought the unprecedented dot-com boom—the explosive growth in wealth and income produced by the nearby Silicon Valley tech cluster, as the first wave of Internet companies hit the stock market—there was a new round of political, ideological, and material dilemmas to confront. On one hand, there was a larger economic pie to tax for improvements to public services and infrastructure. The city's coffers were full, and the Children's Fund grew in nominal as well as inflation-adjusted terms. The city expanded commitments to innovative youth programs, as well as protections for children in healthcare, childcare, and other vital domains. It also approved new school spending to tackle persistently high dropout rates and prevent violence.

On the other hand, housing prices skyrocketed in the late 1990s and early 2000s. Red-hot demand met highly constrained supply: San Francisco is a small, built-up, physically attractive city with extensive restrictions on new construction, thanks in part to its progressive politics but also to the general trend in that direction in local land use planning in America. Mayor Willie Brown oversaw ambitious physical revitalization, more of what has sometimes been labeled the "Manhattanization" of San Francisco. The city gentrified rapidly, leaving pockets of poverty and social distress amidst enormous affluence (figure 10.1). Two-thirds of the households that left the city in the 1990s were low or middle income, according to the Census Bureau, and leavers were disproportionately families with children. By 2000, the share of households with children had dropped to 19 percent, the lowest of any major U.S. city. The African-American population, concentrated in the city's lower-wage service jobs, was particularly hard hit, losing 15,000 residents between 1990 and 2000; the share of black families with children declined a dramatic 45 percent in that decade. The long-run decline in the presence of children was also substantial: the city's population under age eighteen declined from 25 percent to 15 percent of total population between 1960 and 2000.[4]

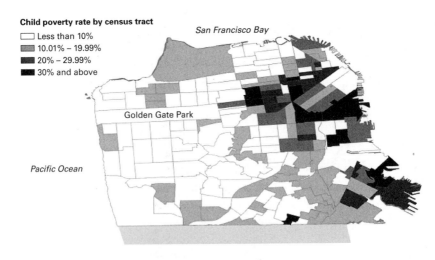

Figure 10.1
Child poverty in San Francisco, by neighborhood, 2000. *Source*: U.S. Census Bureau.

San Francisco's pragmatic children's movement, and its unique budget amendment to the city charter, was born in this heady mix of inequality, affluence, political contention, and dramatic economic restructuring and demographic change. Its evolution traced a path from administrative reform to city budgeting and ambitious new program design. This institutional path explains much about how advocates built a cohesive, consistently influential movement, both inside and outside of government, in such a contentious polity. It also helps explain the political salience of accountability in a context that might otherwise have produced *bigger* government expenditures on behalf of children but not necessarily more *effective* ones.

Child Advocacy and the First Children's Amendment

As students of social movements have long recognized, the story of movements is bound up with the life cycles of lead organizations in complex ways. There was child advocacy in San Francisco before the Coleman Advocates but nothing approaching an organized, sustained movement. Coleman was born in 1975 through the bequest of a wealthy donor to a local philanthropic foundation. Coleman's first phase was defined by citizen activists' outrage over a very specific injustice: the failure to handle juvenile status offenders and children in foster care humanely, through effective care rather than institutionalized isolation. Coleman's formative years, then, were defined by the complexities of system reform. It was a slog through the service-providing bureaucracies and also through the judicial system. "It was a huge learning experience for me," remembers Margaret Brodkin, "dealing with the courts, state law, and more. It took us seven years to deal with the status offender issue."

These reform efforts evolved into a broader focus on the institutions that served, or failed to serve, children in San Francisco (Gardner Center 2005). In the early 1980s, as the organization began to learn more from child advocacy groups elsewhere, Coleman organized a network of emergency services for homeless youth and a successful initiative to expand and improve playground space throughout the city. It began to convene an annual conference of education and social service providers in the city. These moves led Coleman to target the electoral process, convening the first-ever candidate's forum—it turned out to be the largest crowd assembled for the local elections in 1987—plus an annual, highly visible Speak Up For Kids Day at City Hall.

The press began to regularly cover the organization's rallies, report releases, and other events, describing Coleman in these early years simply as a "respected youth advocacy group" and "child welfare organization."[5] Service providers around the city, and even critics of Coleman's approach, acknowledge the significance of the organization's decision to focus on citywide advocacy on budget and elections. Coleman began to issue report cards rating local elected officials' decisions on policy issues affecting children and youth. This led to annual assessments of the city's proposed budget as it affected children and to lobbying against the major budget cuts that marked the late 1980s. Coleman's reports highlighted growing child poverty and abuse in the city, as well as a staggering dropout rate of one-third of public school children and an estimated 5,000 youth among the city's growing homeless population.[6]

Coleman had evolved from a primary focus on administrative reform to become a respected and strategic lobbyist, developing an expertise in municipal budget assessment that was rare among child advocacy organizations in America at the time while retaining an orientation to the implementation side of policy as well. Coleman avoided competing for political resources with those who provided services to children and youth, acting as a policy research and advocacy organization, organizing providers and citizen advocates through mailings, rallies, and other tactics. Beyond not competing, however, Coleman's relationship with the largely neighborhood-based, service-providing nonprofit organizations around the city was symbiotic and fluid. The providers gave Coleman eyes and ears on the ground and a staff and volunteer infrastructure for publicizing key events. Coleman provided access to elected supervisors, senior agency staff, and other influentials at city hall—at least for the providers Coleman's staff respected and wanted to strengthen. But sometimes, the providers parted ways with the lead advocate. "We don't get too close," one told me, citing a discomfort with Coleman's characterization of public safety officers in municipal budget battles, "but we try to go to all their events . . . [and] they can say things we can't, since we rely on government contracts."

Coleman was skilled at attracting media attention, and it consistently looked for ways to institutionalize change (Gardner Center for Youth and Their Communities 2005; Scott et al. 2006). The election cycle provided a natural device to strengthen the accountability of local politicians for protecting children, and the city's annual budget process created a very immediate, tangible structure within which to confront political actors in the city, including the voters, about priorities and prior commitments.

In 1987, Coleman proposed that the city create a standing commission on meeting the needs of children and their families, to "coordinate $575 million worth of publicly financed programs that are now administered by a maze of a half-dozen city departments and hundreds of private agencies and organizations," as the press reported.[7] Newly elected Mayor Art Agnos had come to office backed by a progressive coalition bent on redirecting the focus on downtown real estate development that had defined the 1980s (DeLeon 1992). The Coleman proposal led to a new Mayor's Office on Children, Youth, and Families. It was a sign of the times, the press reported:

In the six months since Agnos has been mayor of San Francisco, he has slowly and systematically turned over the keys of City Hall to people who in the past often had the door slammed in their face. . . . Margaret Brodkin, executive director of Coleman Advocates for Children and Youth, said this was the first year in the 14-year history of her group that she has been invited to meet with the mayor's staff to discuss how the budget will affect children. "I think he dramatically changed the budget process by making it much more open, making fundamental changes for the good," Brodkin said. "Before, the mayor used to unveil the budget June 1 and no one outside the City [government] had much input until it was too late.

In 1989, Coleman presented the first Children's Budget, a comprehensive spending proposal with proposed offsets in the larger city budget; the proposal garnered wide endorsements and invited some criticism as well, for example from police and healthcare professionals who considered some of the proposed offsets unrealistic or imprudent.[8] The *Chronicle* reported:

In making its detailed requests, the 83-page Coleman report uses an unusual tactic. Instead of simply pleading for more money, the group has gone a step further by identifying specific reductions in the current budget to pay for the children's programs it seeks. . . . All told, Coleman is asking the mayor to cut $5.6 million in seven departments. . . . Coleman is also trying to get a quick start on a looming budget battle over how Agnos will erase a $72 million projected deficit for fiscal year 1989–90.[9]

By 1990, Coleman's staff and board leadership concluded that conventional lobbying on the city budget—the key to matching public resources to policy commitments—had hit the point of diminishing returns. Sophisticated budget analysis and effective mobilization had worked to stave off deeper cuts in public funding for children's programs, and budgeting itself had become a somewhat more transparent process in the city's politics. When Coleman hosted a national conference of child advocates, the press emphasized "mastering the political process" as the defining challenge for advocates nationwide—and lauded Coleman.[10] But overall funding had declined as the City focused, in lean-budget years, on other needs. The evolving movement of advocates and service providers needed a way to guarantee basic funding levels for key services in a political context that would always be pressured to cut children's programs in order to fund something backed by more political muscle, as Brodkin recalls the rationale.

And so the campaign for the landmark Children's Amendment to the city charter was born: the strategy to use a citizen initiative, whereby a proposal with sufficient voter support can be put on the ballot and, if approved on election day, become public policy, to create a set aside in the budget that would guarantee a "floor" of funding for children's services. The focus would be on preventive services, not law enforcement or crisis management. The provision would be funded by a phased-in set aside of property taxes collected for the next decade; it included features to discourage fiscal substitution. The amendment would create a "fiscal bill of rights for children," Margaret Brodkin told the press, "Children can't vote. They can't participate in the city's budget battles."[11]

Though Coleman and its supporters had secured significant access at city hall, the creation of the Children's Amendment was entirely an advocate's affair. City officials, while publicly supportive of Coleman's advocacy, were wary of "special interest" budget restrictions. The city attorney's office consulted on the wording of the measure, and the controller's office provided data on tax revenues and projections. But the core proposal was designed by the small group of advocates convened by Coleman—in sharp contrast to close give-and-take with government insiders a decade later, when the measure would reappear on the ballot. The advocates hammered out basic agreements on fund targeting and eligibility.

In July 1991, Coleman and its network of supporters delivered 67,000 voter petitions to city hall, in bright red children's wagons led by 150 children carrying balloons, as the cameras snapped—half again more than the 41,000 required. The measure, now added to the ballot as Proposition J, won wide endorsement in the months leading up to the November vote. "A group of advocates, frustrated and despairing, have decided to bet everything on the hope that the public is miles ahead of the politicians," wrote the *Chronicle*.[12] A city supervisor called Proposition J a "motherhood and apple pie issue."[13] There was no organized opposition, though a few elected officials warned that the measure would unduly restrict budgeting flexibility.

The victory of the Children's Amendment, which passed with just under 55 percent of the vote on November 5, 1991, was a watershed for the children's movement in San Francisco and for the Coleman Advocates. Core supporters, campaign insiders, and more detached observers alike, including leading political consultants, identify a wide range of effects. By restructuring the city budget to protect children's needs, the win put Coleman in a new league, among the city's most effective political organizations. Additional ballot initiatives proposing budget set-asides would be modeled directly on the Children's Amendment in the years to come. As the first of its kind in America, the victory also put Coleman in the national spotlight, extending its access to philanthropic funding, media, information and informal support networks, and other resources vital for advocacy. The concept of a children's fund would be successfully emulated by child advocates in a handful of other U.S. cities in the years that followed—and envied by many more (Gardner Center for Youth and Their Communities 2005).

These gains aside, municipal budgeting, a process of mind-numbing detail and fiscal sleight of hand, had provided the crucial institutional machinery that focused the maturing children's movement. It provided specific, winnable targets. It gave advocates in a hypercontentious city an institutional space to focus disparate concerns and face up to real trade-offs while developing bargaining relationships with the city's political establishment. Coleman, in particular, had demonstrated the art of carefully applied political pressure founded on a firm foundation of mobilized voters and favorable media. The larger opening in the Agnos years reflects the progressive tide that overturned the elite, pro-growth coalition that had dominated the city's politics and public policy for over a decade. But progressive sentiment and access alone do not explain how advocates developed a focused agenda for children or began to transform local government budgeting. Those achievements reflect specific decisions by advocates who organized and sustained a new movement with and on behalf of young people.

Still, there was nothing in the ballot measure to guarantee that the new money would produce results. It might be diverted in spite of the guidelines on eligible use. It might be spent on poorly run children's programs. It might go only to established, tradition-bound programs and fail to address the changing needs of young people. The collective effort, inside and outside of government, to act more effectively and accountably had only begun. Given the complexity of this next phase and the fact that other researchers have investigated the civics of another vital "policy system" for children and youth—public education improvement in San Francisco in the 1980s and 1990s (see Stone et al. 2001)—I will continue to focus primarily on the landmark Children's Fund.

Clear Direction and Better Results: Implementing the Fund

The children's movement had turned a page, and now began the slow work, across the divide between public and nonprofit sectors, out of the headlines, of developing accountability mechanisms, designing better interventions, making hard choices about priorities for funding, and building new schemes of cooperation among nonprofit advocates, nonprofit service providers, the city's many private philanthropic funders, and city government.

The City had to rush to meet Proposition J's mandated deadline to issue a Children's Services Plan for using the new fund, so in 1992, the office of newly elected Mayor Frank Jordan hastily appointed a forty-five-member citizen advisory board and competitive bidding process for nonprofit service providers seeking funds. At the end of year one, once funding had been announced, Coleman sent the mayor a report that was largely critical of the City's implementation, calling it a "piecemeal list of services rather than a comprehensive strategy to address well-defined and carefully prioritized needs" (p. 2).[14] While praising some of the initiatives funded, most of the report was a litany of public sector failures: unqualified staff in the mayor's Office of Children, Youth, and Families; diffuse targeting of the funds ("filling a gap here and there"); evidence of a political "backdoor" or mayoral "slush fund" for service providers who wanted to avoid competing for the new funds; and poorly organized community input into the allocation plan, with the result that some members of the quickly assembled advisory board resigned while others disengaged. Other problems included slow funding of vital public agencies, such as parks and libraries; vaguely defined requirements of collaboration that produced inefficient "shotgun marriage" proposals by nonprofits; and the failure to approve an independent evaluation of the fund, one that would not be controlled by the mayor's office—among other problems.

In 1995, following an implementation survey of providers, Coleman issued similar findings. Many funded programs appeared to be making a difference for children and youth in the city, and certainly many programs were popular with children and their parents, but no independent evaluation had been conducted to rigorously assess strengths and weaknesses. Monitoring was limited to counting up units of service delivered and basic indicators of compliance with program rules. The allocation of funds remained relatively technocratic and politicized; hearings before the Board of Supervisors provided the only forum for public oversight. Goals for the fund were overly broad. One-year contracts undermined program quality and long-range planning, while matching funds from private, philanthropic organizations were limited. Capacity building, for example through technical assistance to nonprofit service providers, was limited and ineffective, so the annual allocation favored the most established providers, leaving innovative, fledgling agencies stuck on the margins.

From the standpoint of political influence, these considerations are secondary, and this distinction is crucial for the treatment I offer, in this book, of civic capacity as a resource for problem solving and not just policy agenda setting. The children's movement, as I outlined above, had mastered the electoral process and the yearly municipal budget cycle. The sophisticated network of child advocates garnered significant clout, as well as much-needed focus, in the process. It was not a question of dominating the political big league. San Francisco's major urban development and transportation conflicts, such as waterfront megaprojects and transit overhaul, the perennials of crime control and homelessness, and the local interest-group elite—big business, the municipal unions, environmentalists—continued to dominate the local agenda and the headlines. But child advocates had won themselves a rare seat at the bargaining table.

But the point now was impact on social conditions—that is, on outcomes for young people—and the strategies that led to influence on policy could not guarantee that impact. Arguably, in fact, the twin goals were in tension. With funding levels essentially guaranteed for a decade, limited scrutiny of children's programs—flying "below the radar" politically—was useful for the obvious reasons. Why threaten the public's sense that Proposition J was working as planned? Why risk giving city officials incentive to focus elsewhere or undermine the fund? Why make enemies at city hall and in the neighborhoods by de-funding a nonprofit service provider with strong political connections? The problem with this play-it-safe approach was that a decade of child advocacy had emphasized accountability—made it a defining goal from the start, in fact—and so the relationships among public agencies that provided services, nonprofit advocates, and nonprofit service providers would need to evolve.

Since the local children's movement had entered a new phase with the implementation of the Children's Amendment, and since the now-established rituals of the advocacy network continued on schedule each year with Coleman Advocates as lead strategist, entrepreneurship *within* government—proactive rather than reactive strategy, and political risk taking, by city officials—assumed greater importance. This shift in the center of gravity picked up steam with the election of Mayor Willie Brown, San Francisco's first black mayor and one of its most controversial, in 1995. Born poor in rural Texas, Brown had risen to the pinnacle of political power in the state of California, representing San Francisco in the state assembly for thirty years and eventually serving as its all-powerful Speaker. Renowned for cultivating favors, brokering huge political deals, and rewarding loyalists, Brown easily defeated Frank Jordan to become mayor and launch a new chapter in the city's civic life. Along the way, he enthusiastically endorsed the child advocacy agenda and promised strong support of the Children's Fund. The mayor would court controversy and butt heads constantly with the Board of Supervisors for the next eight years, as the tech boom pulled the region out of recession, big real estate projects picked up steam, and allegations of political favoritism multiplied.[15] But Brown's political appointments would also take the children's movement to the next level.

In 1996, Brown's first year in office, Youth Making a Change, the semi-independent youth organizing network seeded by Coleman, convened the city first-ever "youth summit," billed as a dialogue between young people and the city's political leadership—with Coleman's visible support. At the event, youth activists criticized the mayor as the press looked on. Caught off guard, Brown was furious. "He never forgave Coleman," says a political insider. Brown quickly replaced the head of his Office of Children, Youth, and Families with a political ally, Jeff Mori, who had run a youth agency in the Japantown neighborhood and rallied voters for Brown during the campaign.

"He really wanted me to clean up the house," Mori recalls, "and I terminated a lot of contracts in those first two years—bad contracts, where there had been no audit in 4 or 5 years. I was called a racist. . . . We then had to go find agencies in those neighborhoods so that services would continue." In some cases, Mori notes, these were nonperforming contracts, not just contracts that lacked financial integrity and transparency. The sweep included public and nonprofit agencies. "In some cases," adds Mori, "the community would say 'before you do anything in this neighborhood, you have to de-fund this program.' I had never heard that before." Brown also encouraged Mori to aggressively pursue matching funding from philanthropies. And the mayor emphasized these changes over community input in the allocation of funds. "It wasn't that [Brown] was against it," argues Mori, "He just felt we should be spending our political capital elsewhere. And he thought we [in government] would make the right decisions."

The focus on a more accountable, strategic, and highly leveraged Children's Fund—accountable in terms of credible outcomes, that is, if not the most participatory decision making—expanded under Deborah Alvarez-Rodriguez, who replaced Mori in 1998. Alvarez-Rodriguez brought a strong background in the political management of public agencies, having staffed the San Francisco Superintendent of Schools, as well as management consulting. The reauthorization of the Children's Amendment was now just three years away, and Mayor Brown agreed to make his Office on Children, Youth, and Families, the decade-old unit that implemented the Children's Fund, a full department. Alvarez-Rodriguez stressed the importance of a visibly independent unit that could lift the Children's Fund above the appearance of patronage, of a "fake" process of competing for public monies. She recalls,

I worried that [the Amendment] would not pass again. . . . It had passed [in 1991] by a slim margin, and business support was lukewarm. . . . There was no real plan, no strong story about results, no citizen oversight. I saw [the Fund] as vulnerable. And I didn't want victory at the ballot box with a slim margin. I wanted a mandate, a vote that showed a real commitment to children and families. . . . With an advocacy base made up of service providers, there was the appearance of self-interest [in their pushing for the Amendment].

Alvarez-Rodriguez also regarded the limited evaluation completed so far as "soft." After canvassing service providers throughout the city, she decided to focus on contracting, "something that would touch the organizations very directly . . . and I had had a contract [with the Fund] while working in the public schools. So I knew it from the other side." She offered longer contracts and simpler applications in exchange for an agreement to apply with more focused plans, specific program goals, and appropriate, measurable results and also to help "design an evaluation process that makes sense." In my interviews with veteran managers, nonprofit agencies confirm that these steps built significantly on Mori's effort to up performance on both ends of the contractual relationship. For example, Alvarez-Rodriguez accelerated payment turnaround as well, a boon to nonprofits that often waited months for bureaucratic wheels to produce vital cash flow—and an exemplar of the "accountability compacts" (quid pro quos) that performance management gurus endorse more and more (see Behn 2001).

Alvarez-Rodriguez also defunded more programs and replaced numerous staff under her management. "I defunded the oldest, Latino-serving agency in the city. It was very politically contentious." Coleman, she recalls, "stayed on the sidelines. It was their way of being supportive."

But the department also began the practice of collaborating with private funders to figure out which service providers could be turned around, through intensive restructuring or capacity building, rather than defunded. Nonprofit social service agencies typically rely on a revolving cast of funders with distinct requirements and ever-changing program priorities, making strategic planning and coherent management a constant struggle (Smith and Lipsky 1993). The city had never before worked with private funders to organize a turnaround (where possible) and make the tough decision to defund otherwise. "This way, no one funder took all the heat," argues Alvarez-Rodriguez, "and it discouraged agencies from playing off one funder against another." Says a respected longtime provider, "This was new—not just defunding a group but finding a way to improve them."

The long-awaited, comprehensive evaluation of programs funded by the Children's Fund was also launched, with much broader stakeholder participation than the city had welcomed or expected to date. The Department of Children, Youth, and Families organized service agencies into clusters by specialty area and invited them to identify leading approaches to service delivery and then design the criteria by which their programs could be fairly assessed. "We also insisted that young people themselves be part of the process," says Alvarez-Rodriguez. When the Department bid the evaluation contract, she pressured the evaluation team to take the idea of a central role for young people seriously. "It was very contentious," she recalls. But before long, youth evaluators were training adults on how to visit and understand youth-serving programs. The adults were practitioner peers, largely from outside the city, not funded by the department. As Alvarez-Rodriguez observes,

It changes the dynamics when your agency gets visited by a 12-year-old and a 35-year-old using very strict protocols. And we invited the evaluators to coach and respond [to what they saw] if they liked, to act as peer resources. Then we used this when we went to the Board [of Supervisors] and the Mayor to get more money. Service providers at the hearing said, "I want to be held accountable.

This is an important way to use our money. For the first time, people know the value of what I do."

Other insiders are more skeptical that this is, or was ever, the reigning view among service providers seeking government funding, a point to which I return below. But the focus on negotiating support for a more demanding kind of accountability—accountability for credibly demonstrated accomplishment—extended to a jewel in the crown: the Beacon Schools. This multiyear initiative, a revealing case within the case, established round-the-clock community centers housed in selected San Francisco public schools, open after school, on the weekends and in the summer, for free, serving children, youth, and their parents. The Beacon School concept was pioneered by youth development advocates in New York City and became one of the most widely admired and discussed models in the field of youth development in the 1990s, when focus intensified on engaging young people productively in the out-of-school hours.[16]

With encouragement from the Coleman Advocates, San Francisco had developed four Beacon Schools under Mayor Jordan by 1995. But it was Willie Brown who recognized the political potential in serving a wider array of San Francisco neighborhoods with well-funded Beacon Centers. Not only were the centers popular with parents, but the fiscally frugal business lobby liked the idea of making better use of public buildings (the schools). The number of Beacons doubled under Brown, reaching beyond the city's poor and minority neighborhoods, with Jeff Mori leading the challenging negotiations with San Francisco schools in 1996 and 1997.

As the number of centers expanded rapidly, so did the variation in performance. Deborah Alvarez-Rodriguez, by the time she assumed office in 1998, turned to the Haas Fund, a major local philanthropy, to help lead a credible process to set priorities and hold the centers accountable. Pressure and financial support from the private, philanthropic funders helped. Where the early Beacons had no strategic, evidence-based plans for achieving specific outcomes for young people, the collaborative three-year process provided a framework for such plans: a clear logic model or "theory of change" that left room for flexibility. Carefully designed technical assistance followed, not just compliance requirements. Like the Heinz Endowment role I analyzed in the Pittsburgh chapter, the role played by key San Francisco philanthropies created political space for the pubic and nonprofit sectors to negotiate a well-informed, more legitimate framework of accountability.

To illustrate the point, "We ranked low on leadership development," recalls one Beacon director, "and that led to a real dialogue with the kids and parents . . . and also with other Beacons about what we wanted to focus on and take credit for."

Results to Show: Accountability and the Reauthorization of the Children's Fund

The Children's Amendment would be back on the ballot for voter approval in November 2000, and so would Mayor Brown, whose appointees had fundamentally restructured the use of funds and the way government collaborated with private, nonprofit service providers. In 1999, Coleman Advocates organized a working group to prepare the new Children's Amendment. Made up primarily of advocates and service providers, the group also included several government staff acting ex officio. There were few big controversies. The new Children's Amendment would retain key features of the original: a fixed percentage of the city's property tax valuation (which virtually ensured a growing fund even during economic downturns); a baseline budget (to prevent city officials from using the Children's Fund to meet other expenses rather than add to the total spent on children and youth); and recognition, as one advocate put it, of "the dual-delivery" structure for meeting young people's needs (with public and nonprofit agencies, and joint efforts by both, eligible for funding). Other features would be adjusted. The provision would "sunset" (terminate) in fifteen years, rather than ten, this time, to allow for longer-range planning and improvements. The text provided for evaluation, and mandated, in general terms, public involvement in that evaluation.

But advocates wanted two new features, which led to some tense negotiation with the mayor's staff. First, the set-aside would be raised from 2.5 percent to 3 percent of tax revenues. Second, the amendment would call for a new approach to citizen oversight, which had been, advocates and service providers agreed, a contentious, often disappointing feature of the fund for a decade. Some believed a formal commission, reporting to the Board of Supervisors, would create more room for oversight, while others felt it would further politicize the process of allocating the fund. "Sometimes, it's those political appointees that make a commission useless," concedes one advocate who was involved in the debate. Clearly, Mayor Willie Brown's ongoing feud with the Board of Supervisors shaped this short-term standoff. Did citizens and the service provider community need a check on mayoral power, or would involving parents and agencies—perhaps too closely—in funding decisions generate basic conflicts of interest in the use of public funds?

The mayor's office ceded the rate increase but insisted on an advisory committee of mayoral appointees as a condition for his endorsement of the amendment. "We had already stripped a lot of the mayor's power by turning [the unit implementing the fund] into a city department," argues Deborah Alvarez-Rodriguez. "I was back and forth on the phone with the mayor, and I said [to the advocates] 'we won't sign, we won't endorse.' Literally twenty-four hours before the amendment had to be filed, it got rewritten. . . . The mayor's office could be a tremendous ally in the future. Why cut us out?"

Wary of Brown's muscular political style, some advocates were furious at the outcome, but now there was more success than ever to "sell" to the electorate, and the network of advocates that had driven San Francisco's children's movement quickly closed ranks behind the amendment. The unproven set-aside launched in 1991 had produced a decade of investments throughout a small and generally progressive city. Though agency staff could not officially campaign, in the months leading up to the November election, the city's Department of Children, Youth, and Families released a detailed and compelling portrait of the impact of the amendment's decade in use, including the first part of *Youth Impact*, the fruit of the intensive, innovative, peer-based assessment process the department had managed. It found a large majority of parents and youth supportive and satisfied with child services funded by the city and highlighted specific areas for improvement, such as a wider range of programs to serve youth, the need for more culturally competent staff, and getting the basics right (convenient locations and hours of operation, food, supports for less stable families).[17]

Meanwhile, with the amendment on the ballot as Proposition D, Margaret Brodkin and the Coleman Advocates spearheaded another time-tested, citywide drive to stir the voters and engage the media. The process was "masterful," says one veteran political observer. The generally skeptical *Chronicle* weighed in:

It is generally expected that, in government or politics, nothing ever functions nearly as well as promised. But the San Francisco Children's Amendment has proved to be one of those public policy oddities that has exceeded general expectations, even surpassing what supporters once claimed it would. That's why passage of Proposition D, extending the amendment beyond its 2001 expiration date, is a must.[18]

Support was nearly universal. "The city's power structure has united behind the measure," reported the *Chronicle*, "with support from [Mayor] Brown, all 11 supervisors, the Board of Education, the local PTA, the League of Women Voters, the Democratic and Republican parties and many others." Contributing to this broad base was the political tidal wave generated by a return to district voting in the city, approved by voters in 1996 and put into effect with the 2000 election. Based on returns, many San Franciscans, resentful of gentrification and the pro-business Willie Brown political machine, voted in progressive supervisors, for the second time in two decades, to refocus city hall on the neighborhoods.[19]

The lone public critic appeared to be a voice in the wilderness. A tax watchdog group, the Good Government Alliance, said $107 million had been "diverted" from the city's general fund since the Children's Amendment went into effect and argued that much of the money, while "outwardly appealing," had gone for "a bureaucracy of paper-pushers" and significant duplication of effort. It was not clear how the group had determined this, and the voters clearly felt otherwise. On November 7, 2000, Proposition D passed with nearly 74 percent of the vote, ensuring another fifteen years for the Children's Fund.

In the years after reauthorization, accountability continued to be an important source of learning as well as conflict—beneath the umbrella of a broad consensus on values, that is, that defines San Francisco's remarkable children's movement. The city required service agencies to do more detailed tracking of clients and outcomes, a labor-intensive task the agencies often resisted, but government provided more in the way of technical assistance and training to help agencies adapt, too. To some knowledgeable insiders, too many funding decisions are still made on the basis of ethnic group served and the strength of a service provider's city hall connections rather than demonstrated performance, and not enough providers are defunded for nonperformance. To critics who hold this view, the 1990s made the process *less* politicized and *more* performance-focused—but not nearly enough.[20] By some measures, moreover, not enough funding from the Children's Budget has reached the city's worst-off children, who are African-American, in part because of the policy decision to focus on prevention—which is "always hard to accomplish or measure," says Michael Wald, a veteran analyst of child welfare nationwide who is active in San Francisco policy making—rather than crisis intervention for very needy children and families.

Youth Impact gave providers a host of specific insights, many from children and youth themselves, to apply to improve the programs, and the evaluation's findings would come up again and again in planning and funding meetings in subsequent years. But the evaluation did not and could not definitively answer the million-dollar question about any program: Is this intervention, apart from all confounding factors, improving a child's health, school achievement, emotional resilience, or other important outcomes? Reviews of the community advisory committee overseeing the Children's Fund were predictably mixed. Some, including city officials, felt it met the basic test of ensuring a diverse array of public perspectives on priorities and tradeoffs, while critics complained that committee members were too ill-informed about programs to provide meaningful guidance. Coleman secured philanthropic funding to study options for restructuring the committee.

The local children's movement contributed to other victories, adding to the list of progressive accomplishments that set San Francisco apart from most, if not all, major American cities: universal preschool, a city-wide minimum wage for childcare workers, and universal health coverage for children and young adults. These initiatives got crucial early backing from progressive and reform-minded Supervisors such as Tom Ammiano, Matt Gonzalez, and Chris Daly. By the early 2000s, the Children's Amendment was generating $35 to $40 million per year for the public and nonprofit agencies that served young people in the city.

The 2003 election brought the Willie Brown era to an end and certified the arrival of a bright young political star at the forefront of San Francisco politics. Gavin Newsom, a wealthy, thirty-seven-year-old restaurant owner who Brown had named to a vacant supervisor's seat, was elected mayor. Newsom had gained visibility with a campaign to tackle the city's perennially hot-button homelessness problem with "care, not cash"—that is, with well-delivered services rather than handouts to panhandlers on the street. The concept seemed to embody perfectly the resolution of San Francisco's political idealism with a pragmatism focused on changing a social outcome. Newsom moved quickly to fill his administration with strong, capable department heads, and to head child and youth services, he chose Margaret Brodkin. "Margaret has been a pioneer in developing the theory and practice of local child advocacy," Newsom told the press, which called her "a high-profile fixture," and the Coleman Advocates "a powerful force," at city hall.[21] The children's movement had turned another page.

Summary and Implications

As a case of developing and using civic capacity to address a communitywide concern, the San Francisco children's movement holds important lessons about (1) the conditions for setting the local policy agenda when community sentiment is balkanized; (2) mechanisms for developing accountability between government and the voters (in the classic sense of democratic politics) and also between government and the many private and nonprofit agencies with which government must coproduce important policy outcomes; and (3) the role of nongovernmental organizations that do not fit neatly in the professional advocacy or mass membership categories but represent hybrids with significant civic roles. The case also offers a reminder of how much more there is to an effective movement—one that delivers the goods, not just the votes—than pressure politics or adversarial relationships between civil society and government.

First, even in a progressive city that favors public investment, a culture of factionalized politics, hyperplural and perhaps hyperdissenting as well, can lead to mobilization without impact, heat without light. Child advocates settled brilliantly on the local budget process as an annual ritual, largely opaque to voters generally and even more so to the poorest parents, that focuses a very public confrontation with policy priorities and the trade-offs they force—and that puts an easily grasped "sticker price" on citizen outrage about injustices done to children. The local children's movement chose this road and not the more traveled one of crafting a "consensus-based" vision for children, or perhaps a strategic plan, that would be coupled loosely, if at all, with public spending decisions. Echoing prior research on civic capacity and school reform (Stone 2001), this study suggests that choosing and mastering specific institutional arenas, such as local budgeting, goes a long way toward using preexisting civic capacity effectively while extending it through new practices and accomplishments.

Together with well-organized candidate forums, report cards on elected officials, and other savvy tactics for voter education, the budget-focused strategy spearheaded by Coleman Advocates made child advocacy a well-targeted niche issue in a city more occupied, like most American cities, with crime, jobs, aging transportation and infrastructure, the nuisances that irritate the middle class, and other headline grabbers.

The focus on pressure politics around the budget and the opportunity for ballot-box policy making led, in turn, to the successful Children's

Amendment. (This does not settle the question of whether budget set-asides represent prudent public policy, but that debate is secondary for my purposes.) And that success set the stage for something more than pressure politics, for the children's movement came to include senior government insiders, several of whom described to me at length how they managed the tensions of a dual role: responsible public official and committed child advocate. The tension was especially serious, and the leadership challenges many, when the role holder was not a midlevel "guerrilla in the bureaucracy" but rather the boss.

Second, following that thread, the creation of a high-profile investment vehicle for public spending on children created the need for a new sequence of learning and bargaining, one focused on multiple dimensions of accountability. On the one hand, broad public purposes, such as meeting the needs of the next generation, embody multiple objectives, which compete with each other for scarce resources and sometimes motivate interventions that function at cross-purposes. Legitimacy demands some deliberation with policy makers and public managers to discuss those trade offs and dilemmas, a practice that some forms of popular mobilization forgo (Fung 2004).

On the other hand, implementing chosen strategies effectively demands accountability for results that cannot stop at the mayor's office or public agencies. It must include the private, nonprofit actors that receive public funds and that often operate with weak indicators of their own effectiveness. In the case of the San Francisco Children's Fund, this included the large network of nonprofit service providers who had played a central role in mobilizing support for the special set-aside of funds. In this chapter, I examined a process defined by *political management* as well as *operations management*, whereby public agencies offered greater flexibility and responsiveness to nonprofit contractors in exchange for more rigorous, field-tested evaluation schemes and self-monitoring designed in part by the contractors themselves. Grounded, then, in the kind of accountability "compacts" that performance management experts recommend (Behn 2001), the system has introduced more marketlike competition for services. But for now, funding decisions may be as performance-based as the system of mutual accommodation will permit: not as much as evaluators or the most critical child advocates might like but more so than a new spigot of public funding, focused only on units of service delivered, would be. As Richard DeLeon (1992) shows in his study of San Francisco's fractious politics and exceptionally high rates of citizen activism, neighborhood-based nonprofits are important centers of power and often defenders of ethnic turf in a city where those interests must be delicately balanced by political decision makers. "Providers" are rarely just contractors to be fired for dropping the ball.

But viewed in sequence, the children's movement's focus on public spending priorities (making claims of elected officials and the taxpayer) and then accountable use of funds (making claims of nonprofit agencies as well as public ones) helped to elevate child advocacy beyond self-serving patronage demands. It set problem solving on a higher ground than the alternative of building a public or nonprofit empire of child bureaucracies, flush with more funding, that would not be called to perform *or* reflect any meaningful community mandate. According to key insiders, it is simply that some nonprofit agencies, and their backers in government, still have a long way to go to walk that higher road consistently.

Third, there is the Coleman Advocates, the nonprofit organization at the forefront of the advocacy movement and—often—the public-non-profit interaction, which longtime Coleman head Margaret Brodkin defines as a "hybrid" group—not a stand-alone, "professionalized" advocacy organization and not a traditional membership organization either. Scholars in the United States have chronicled a general decline in mass membership political organizations, over the last half century, and a shift toward professionalized advocacy, a trend sociologist Theda Skocpol captures in her aptly titled book *Diminished Democracy: From Membership to Management in American Civic Life* (2003). But while Coleman maintains the professionalized policy research and media operations of some "memberless" advocacy groups, it has steadfastly maintained a program of creative constituency building as well. The maturing early focus on voter education and mobilization may be cause and effect of that constituency building, which took on new complexity in the early 1990s when Coleman seeded youth and parent organizing networks that would function autonomously (in the sense of being self-governing) but in close exchange with Coleman's board and core staff. While service providers and other Coleman constituents part ways with the organization on some issues, Coleman has managed to maintain, over many bruising political fights, a reputation for being in touch with its base, not committed to parochial agendas.

Pinning down the essential organizational determinants of such hybrids is beyond the scope of this study of long-run civic process. But those factors appear to include effective board governance to support the best of both models (membership, professional advocate) and face up to tensions between them; stable staff leadership allowing for institutional memory, learning, and effective political networking citywide (the relational work of civic life); and a management style at the top that balances high-advocacy pressure with "high" (consistent) listening and a deliberative approach to strategy. To focus on the last point, Coleman and its network fight hard for young people once they close ranks, but based on multiple interviews and observations among insiders, they are willing to argue amongst themselves—to "have a good fight" within the ranks, to use the concept from chapter 2—before that point.

This hybrid capacity, which SPARC-India built up through its alliance with the slum dwellers and women's savings groups in Mumbai (chapter 5), lends Coleman some of the legitimacy of the membership-for-mobilization model and much of the agility and policy design strength of the (typically) less constituency-driven professional advocacy model.

I leave the intraorganizational determinants as well as the civic-contextual ones on the agenda of much-needed future research, along with comparative study of the politics of public-private accountability for child outcomes in other U.S. cities. I do not wish to oversell San Francisco's accomplishments on that dimension. But the broader final point is this: without a grasp of Coleman's hybrid function in the context of fractious interest-group activism in a very activist city, it is impossible to understand the vibrant and effective San Francisco children's movement of the past two decades and counting.

11

Rights, Conflict, and Civic Capacity: Meeting the Needs of Poor Children and Families in Postapartheid Cape Town

South African cities, and the politics that keeps them afloat, are caught in a strange contradiction. On the one hand, enormous effort is exacted to create a post-apartheid identity and form through a plethora of legislation, policies, and plans. On the other hand, the more the state acts on the city with all of its "good" intentions, the more it seemingly stays trapped in its apartheid form, if not identity. Eleven years after political liberation, there is an undeniable gap between policy intent and outcome.

—Edgar Pieterse (2006a, 286)

In my vote, I am going to be thanking the government because we have a house now. Then maybe I'll ask God if he can help us with jobs.

—Alpha Lupuzi, former shackdweller in the Cape Flats, Cape Town[1]

The woman, who is on top of a shiny new car, seems completely at ease. Lying on her stomach, casually dressed, with her knees bent and a smile on her face, she is carefree. The green countryside opens around her. The day is sunny. It is an image of leisure, conveying perfect security—or so we are meant to conclude. Above the woman, a banner reads, "My bank is my freedom." In a globalized age, this is a ubiquitous marketing message aimed at middle- and upper-income adults, a message linking financial services, and the flexibility that wealth and disposable income afford, to a secure and happy life. But this particular woman is black, and in South Africa, the message—at least to well-off blacks in a majority-black society—is also *you have arrived*. It is June 2005, and I am in the Johannesburg airport, staring at the screen of an automated teller machine. Whether on tiny ATM screens or in newspapers or billboards that ring the highways, I will see messages just like this one time and time again on this visit to South Africa, which, over the past decade, has expanded the black middle class and also the class of millionaires that make up a black elite, faster than any nation on earth. There have been tremendous changes in the meaning of citizenship, and also in wealth and poverty, since the dual transition that is still poorly understood outside the country. One was a transition from white-dominated apartheid rule to a multiracial democracy buttressed by a remarkable array of economic and social rights. The other was a jarring, and far more controversial, shift from protectionist isolation to an open, "liberalized" economy—the largest and most stable economy on the world's poorest continent but also an economy marked by extreme inequality.

A week later, I am in Khayelitsha, the largest township in Cape Town, at a Youth Day gathering. Under apartheid, the townships were established as segregated "group areas" along the urban periphery, with black workers and their families in one set of areas, coloreds (mixed-race people of mostly South Asian and Malaysian descent) in others. Strictly segregating townships was part of a divide-and-rule strategy employed by the white minority. And after apartheid, the townships remain largely isolated, in many dimensions, from the country's economic gains; indeed, they bore the brunt of its major job losses, especially in textiles and other hard-hit manufacturing sectors. Not surprisingly, moreover, the townships continue to shape the country's social and political fault lines. Though analysts debate the measures, some 46 percent of Khayelitsha's adults, and over half its youth, are unemployed. Many others work insecurely, and for low wages, in the informal sector—as street vendors or day laborers, for example—and a large majority are poor.[2] According to grimly reliable police statistics, the homicide and assault rates are much higher than the national average (in one of the highest-crime nations on earth). In effect, I am now on the other end of the two transitions—the bottom end.

Khayelitsha sits on the wide plain dominated by the Cape Flats, in the southeast sector of the city, behind the picturesque, flat-topped mountain that dramatically frames a compact city center where Cape Town's more affluent neighborhoods lie. The mountains help divide that "city bowl" so popular with foreign visitors from the city of townships and informal settlements that are home to most of the city's poor children and families (figures 11.1 and 11.2). These geographic divides reflect social and political ones in South Africa's most contested city. Though Cape Town is far more colored than South Africa's other big cities—48 percent of the city's population of 3.2 million is colored, 32 percent black, and 19 percent white—and though a major opposition party has controlled local government here for most of the postapartheid period, Khayelitsha is a largely black township and, as such, a stronghold of the African National Congress (ANC).

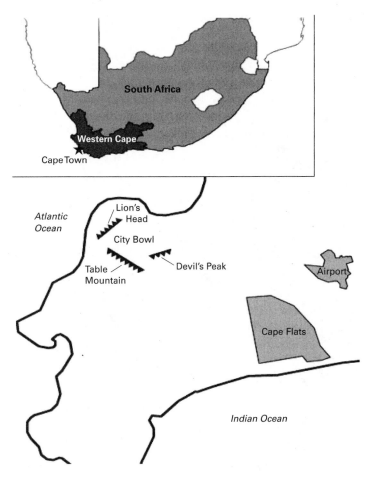

Figure 11.1
Cape Town (showing the Cape Flats), Western Cape Province, South Africa.
Sources: 2000 Landsat, MACON AG, 2005.

The ANC is the party of liberation from apartheid rule, of the often deadly struggle that culminated in a remarkably peaceful transfer of power in 1994, and the nation's highly dominant ruling party. It is the party of the one-time insurgent and political prisoner and later president Nelson Mandela, a statesman admired throughout the country and indeed throughout the world, and also the party of his controversial but powerful successor, Thabo Mbeki.

Yet today, in Khayelitsha, this community rally holds little praise for the ruling party. By custom, speeches punctuate the music and dancing held in a plain concrete plaza. There are no billboards here pitching the latest

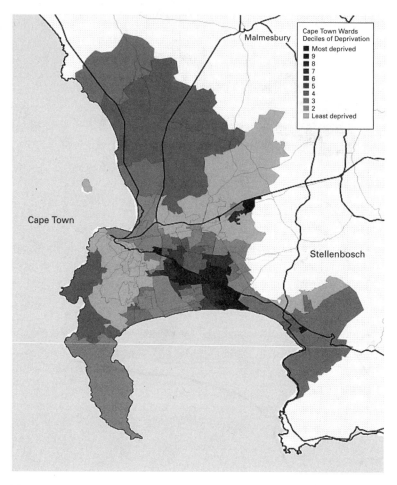

Figure 11.2
City of Cape Town, Western Cape Index of Multiple Deprivation, 2001.
Source: Centre for the Analysis of South African Social Policy, Oxford University,
using South African National Census, 2001.

consumer goods or financial services, but there is a mural with the familiar
face of that global revolutionary icon, Ché Guevara. With fists in the air,
adults at the rally wear t-shirts that convey the urgent, basic needs that
drive their activism: *Stop evictions! Stop water cuts! Scrap Arrears! Adequate public housing! Stop privatizing municipal services!* The speeches,
mostly by representatives of leftist movements that are on the political
margins in South Africa, echo steady themes for the crowd: *You are not
being treated fairly, the government talks a good line but does not deliver,
and*—perhaps most seriously—*the ANC has forgotten you.*

I am here with organizers from the Western Cape Anti-Eviction Campaign, a loose confederation of community-based organizations and activist networks that blend "pro-poor" legal advocacy, demonstrations, community self-help, and civil disobedience, including the illegal "invasion" of public and private land. The Campaign employs that range of tactics to press for improvements in basic water, sanitation, and electricity delivery, as well as the provision of housing, in the city's townships (made up of regular housing) as well as its informal settlements, where children and their families live in shacks. The Campaign is focused on this region's share of what low-income housing expert Marie Huchzermeyer (2004) estimates to be three million homeless families and perhaps twenty million more who live in underserved poor communities in South Africa.

The Campaign is part of a rapidly evolving resurgence of urban activists willing to contend with the ANC-led government—this after years of "collegiate" interaction between a progressive public sector and civil society organizations (Habib 2005). In a country with no meaningful electoral opposition to the ANC, the Campaign is part of an evolving landscape of learning and bargaining, some informal and some highly structured and institutionalized, to address the staggering and persistent inequalities and service backlogs that are a key legacy of apartheid. The gaps are especially serious in the housing and basic services that provide the foundation for healthy child and youth development.

After a decade spent developing a complex array of planning and decision-making institutions at the local level—many of them unevenly implemented, with an alphabet soup of technocratic jargon to match—South African activists, organizers, legal advocates, public servants, and others are trying in new ways to make governance and development more accountable and more effective. Apropos the focus of this book, it was only a few years after the fall of apartheid that influential players in South Africa, and especially in its government, began to wonder aloud whether stronger democracy, far from being a key to collective accomplishment, might be at odds with getting things done (Gumede 2005; Heller 2001).

The barriers to civic capacity, from mistrust to institutional complexity, from ethnic rivalry to entrenched bureaucratic culture, make this case an important source of lessons about how government planning and reform, progressive rights, and civil society organizing can combine to address serious social and economic problems at the local level. But less optimistically, the case is also a source of lessons on common myths about those instruments: about the power of government to centralize and lead "development," about the magic of rights as guarantees, and about the potential of political organizing as a source of meaningful pressure for change. In this chapter, with a focus on events in Cape Town, I use the case of basic community development needs to examine these lessons, looking across the institutions of government and civil society to build on prior research, which has focused, for the most part, on other measures of democratic vitality in South Africa, including the shortcomings of elected government and the reemergence of organized dissent in civil society.

I begin with a look at the big project of nation building and the evolution of relationships between government and civil society in South Africa. The chapter turns next to the question of why urban governance, in particular, is so vital, so complicated, and so highly contested. This sets the stage for a close look at how efforts to change outcomes for young people in Cape Town include developing more civic capacity and also deploying it more effectively.

Institutionalizing Democracy and Driving Economic Change

A large body of research and commentary has analyzed South Africa's progress at nation building, broadly defined as creating and advancing stable, inclusive democratic institutions as well as a sustainable basis for economic growth and human development. After the fall of apartheid in 1994, many elements of South African society worked together to accelerate the nation-building work that had begun with local community-development forums in the 1980s and led to the intensive, behind-the-scenes negotiations that enabled a peaceful transition of power. But as numerous histories and insider commentaries have documented, that was largely bargaining among elites (Gumede 2005). The institutions and policy agendas needed to turn a hugely unequal nation around and set it on a new course, and the work of incorporating everyday people into those institutions and agendas, had barely been outlined. Likewise, the development of inclusive citizenship and democratic participation would need to happen alongside aggressive reforms to an outdated economy. A new and much more ethnically diverse group of policy makers, working with industry leaders who were overwhelmingly white, would need to address the anemic economic growth and staggering unemployment that apartheid had produced since the 1970s. This included the task of making South Africa's major city-regions—in particular, Cape Town,

Johannesburg, and Durban—more competitive in a rapidly changing global economy (Boraine et al. 2006).

There is broad consensus that South Africa's trajectory since apartheid has been defined by an assertive, government-led development strategy that is highly centralized and often technocratic and inflexible. That strategy is shaped in the upper ranks of the ANC, a dominant, historically hierarchical ruling party—not a "movement" party like Brazil's Workers' Party—that retains a loyal supermajority as its electoral base in spite of growing criticism from the party's coalition partners and smaller opposition parties (Gumede 2005; Heller 2001). The lack of electoral threat, together with the ANC's strict norms against public dissent, even led Nobel Peace Prize winner Desmond Tutu to warn publicly of a "culture of sycophantic, obsequious conformity" emerging under President Mbeki.[3]

Since 1996, the ANC development strategy has largely emphasized the neoliberal approach to economic growth—with low trade barriers, deregulation, privatization, and fiscal conservatism, together with some redistribution through income transfers and other social programs—as the key to South Africa's progress (Marais 1998). Politically, this has required a "talk Left, act Right" strategy, as a prominent journalist I interviewed characterized popular perception, and encouraged a relentless rhetoric focused on "delivery" rather than political deliberation (Gumede 2005).

The twin projects of institutionalizing democracy and driving equitable economic change were subjected to renewed scrutiny, both inside and outside South Africa, at the tenth anniversary of the democratic transition, in 2004. There was stock taking on the accomplishments and shortcomings of a remarkable decade. Observers widely agree, for example, that South Africa has been heavily influenced by the global drive for public-private partnerships, government decentralization, and the "new public management," which promises efficiency and measurable results (Heller 2001; Miraftab 2004; Pieterse 2002b).

But analysts also recount intensive efforts to adapt these broader influences, to create models of governance and a "developmental state" that suit the country's special history and challenges. This includes a more activist and perhaps ambiguous role for local governments, which have gained responsibility and authority, but unfortunately lost significant fiscal strength, since the end of apartheid (Parnell and Pieterse 2002). The effort to give democratic institutions a firm foundation in a society with long history of inequality and repressive government also includes a progressive constitution, enacted in 1996, with a charter of extraordinary social and economic rights touted by many observers worldwide (Roux 2002, 2003); toward the end of the chapter, I turn to the particular question of rights as a resource for problem solving.

But the South African government has projected so much ambition and so many new requirements—the "plethora of legislation, policies, and plans" that Pieterse identifies atop this chapter—that governing through any of them amounts to chasing moving targets, constantly learning new rules, socializing an entire population in a much more fluid and confusing political context than the repressive apartheid government had ever sought or permitted (Parnell and Robinson 2006; Pieterse 2006a). At the risk of understatement, apartheid was awful, yet awfully clear as to roles and responsibilities. What followed it has unfolded, of course, very differently and with fewer signposts.

The Evolution of Government/Civil-Society Relations

Among longtime observers, there is ever-more consensus, too, about the evolution of government/civil society roles and interactions, in three broad phases, over the past two decades. In the first phase (1982–1994), the dominant elements of organized civil society, taking advantage of modest openings permitted by apartheid reformers, focused their energies on thwarting and delegitimating the apartheid state (Habib 2005). These elements included local civic associations ("civics") and umbrella groups that brought together progressive civics, churches, students, and others. The focus was political change, and not surprisingly, community development (broadly defined) was limited to modest grassroots self-help efforts and programs funded by foreign donors.

After 1994, government/civil-society relationships became overwhelmingly "collegiate," part of a compact for building a new nation with consensus-oriented decision making (Gumede 2005; Heller 2001). First under President Nelson Mandela (1994–1999) and then Thabo Mbeki (1999–present), the leftist electoral coalition led by the ANC, which includes the Congress of South African Trade Unions and the South African Communist Party, spurred the creation of a South African National Civic Organization to formalize and regularize policy development and implementation with civil society. This drew formerly contentious groups in close to support the ruling party, not to sway it (Gumede 2005; Habib 2005).

After 1994, government also replaced the nongovernmental sector as the principal recipient of foreign aid and philanthropic funding and as the principal driver of social initiatives. Hundreds of activist associations became service-providing contractors for government, as privatization swept both social policy and municipal service delivery (Miraftab 2004; Swilling and Russell 2002). Since a strong national government had promulgated only interim rules and powers for local governments, civil society players bargained and planned with uncertainty about the local government role—this although ambitious new planning requirements generated new waves of "stakeholder" meetings and community consultations, along with new demand for planning consultants to help structure those gatherings (Lemon 2002; Parnell and Pieterse 2002; Wilkinson 2004).

The beginning of the third era, the current one, is roughly marked by the 2000 elections, when two important things happened. First, local governments—newly consolidated into metropolitan units and reorganized as to functions and revenue sources—took a "permanent" form;[4] and second, civil society activists began to show a new willingness to confront and sharply criticize the government and the ANC party. Some argue that a resurgent, contentious bloc of civil society, sometimes in the form of social movement organizations and sometimes not, must now be counted alongside the large number of nongovernmental organizations (NGOs) and community-based organizations (CBOs) that receive government contracts to provide services. That is, government/civil society interactions have assumed a new pluralism that some see as vital to the continued strengthening of democracy in South Africa (Dykes 2004; Habib 2005; Oldfield 2006). In particular, with no meaningful electoral competition for the ANC, and no organized party to the left of it at all, emerging social movements represent an important, contentious force and one focused largely on the needs of the poor (Ballard et al. 2005).[5] But for now, much of this new vigor on the left is limited to pro-poor pressure politics. In the language of my earlier chapters, without a more focused agenda of change, sustained coalitions, and flexible engagement with government, the risk is that that new pressure will be heat without light.

Economic and Social Progress

As for driving economic change, affirmative action and "black economic empowerment" policies have spurred rapid growth in the black middle class and elite (Boraine et al. 2006; Gumede 2005). There is also a general consensus that while more a more inclusive government has made important commitments to the poor and previously excluded racial groups—in the form of child support grants, school integration,

subsidized housing for 1.6 million households, and more—massive economic restructuring, including a huge loss of heavy industry, has led to
an increase in poverty, unemployment, and economic inequality since
1994 (Boraine et al. 2006). With strict apartheid-era controls on relocation gone, rapid migration from rural areas has compounded the challenges facing urban areas, which are much more socially diverse and
politically contentious than rural towns.

In the nine cities that propel the South African economy and that host
a growing share of its population, unemployment jumped 59 percent,
adding a million people to the queues, between 1996 and the latest census,
2001. Violent crime, while down from the mid-1990s peak, remained
high in all of the big cities. Only 27 percent of working-age adults in these
cities had completed high school and only 12 percent reported any higher
education (South African Cities Network 2004). With few exceptions,
the years since apartheid appear to have reproduced the "jobless growth"
trend of the 1970s and 1980s (Boraine et al. 2006). And the full impacts
of the HIV/AIDS pandemic have yet to be felt.

Moreover, thanks to growth in both population and households, the
housing backlog (shortage) has not been reduced in spite of the addition
of some 321,000 housing units, in the top nine cities, between 1996 and
2001. Nationally, government reports a shortage of 2.5 million units, a
rate that grows by about 250,000 annually[6] in spite of very large-scale
production of social housing: government has subsidized the production
of some 189,000 new units per year, on average (against an original,
post-1994 target of twice that rate) or nearly two million units between
1994 and 2005.[7] In Cape Town, about 250,000 families, many of them
rural migrants, are "homeless" (housed only in shacks or on pavements),
and according to housing policy insiders, the growth in backlog outpaces
new production there by an estimated 10,000 units per year. Access to
basic services has increased dramatically in the past decade—school
enrollment from 70 to 85 percent, homes with electricity from 40 to
70 percent—but remains out of reach for many of the poor and
ill-housed.

The Role of Local Governance in South Africa's Progress

South African researchers and advocates have argued persuasively that
the nation's changing cities, not its poorer and more tradition-bound
rural areas, best illustrate the enormous challenges of expanding democratic citizenship and effective governance in the context of deeply rooted

ethnic divisions and some of the world's most extreme material inequalities (Beall, Crankshaw, and Parnell 2002; Bond 2000; Pieterse 2006a). Given that cities are center stage in the struggle to build a new society, that needs and opportunities vary widely in a society that is still highly segregated at the local level, and also that the project of development has been largely top-down and growth oriented, the *effectiveness* of local governance, above and beyond its formal shape or official aspirations, is a major factor in the country's progress (Boraine et al. 2006; Parnell and Pieterse 2002; South African Cities Network 2004).

Government decentralization was a key aim in South Africa's democratic transition, since local government had been relegated, in the apartheid era, to maintaining law and order and providing basic services in ways that favored white residential areas (Heller 2001; Parnell and Pieterse 2002). The "one-city-one-tax-base" principle, moreover, was central to the urban movements that attacked apartheid and, with it, the system of Black Local Authorities renowned for "inefficiency, graft, and collaboration with White interests" (Pieterse 2002a, 13; also see Wilkinson 2004). In 1993, a Local Government Negotiation Forum was established at the national level to build consensus on the transition from an apartheid form of urban management to an inclusive future form.

In the early postapartheid years, not only did a new vision of local government include an ambitious, if ambiguous, "developmental" role, but it clearly signaled an interest in *governance* with "partners" outside of government. Drawing on reviews of government reform and citizen participation around the world, and also on renewed attention to local governance and city-level strategic planning by the World Bank and other global players,[8] the national government's seminal White Paper on Local Government called for a new form of planning, for example—Integrated Development Planning—as a framework through which local governments might "understand the various dynamics operating within their area, develop a concrete vision for the area, and [formulate] strategies *for realizing and financing that vision in partnership with other stakeholders*" (emphasis added).[9] As Wilkinson (2004, 218) observes, the White Paper further called for "continuous engagement" with citizens, business, and community groups on four levels: as voters, as stakeholders in policy development, as consumers of municipal services, and as "organized partners involved in the mobilization of resources for development." Simplified a bit, the vision, then, treated nongovernmental players as citizens (through the vote as well as more direct participation in policy making), consumers, and also coproducers of change. Finally, the White

Paper called for a significant push to integrate the traditionally fragmented or "stovepiped" functions of comprehensive spatial planning,
government budgeting, and the delivery of services by public agencies
and private contractors.

Given such a vision, how are things working out? To date, researchers
have produced two kinds of analyses specifically focused on governance
in South Africa's cities (i.e., apart from relevant research that is more
broadly about the country's politics and legal institutions). While the
boundaries blur, the first kind is about the effort to democratize local
government and how those efforts should be judged.[10] The focus of these
analyses is on whether reformist government, with its metropolitan councils and sublocal ward councilors, operating via the formal instruments
of planning and implementation, is working—against new, higher standards—or even likely to work, given the context in which it must
operate.[11] Often with a deep insider knowledge of the institutional
reforms, and sometimes as direct participants in those reforms, South
African scholars have examined changes in local government vis-à-vis a
changing market, civil society, and what management gurus call the "task
environment" (Moore 1995)—that is, the varied operational contexts of
the work that needs doing (building or repairing roads, delivering power
to homes, preparing budgets, acquiring land for housing, finding and
supervising skilled staff to run youth programs, and so on).

Analyses in this vein have produced cautiously optimistic conclusions
so far: that South Africa's new local government institutions hold promise
but also that an entrenched culture of bureaucracy and control in the
public sector has not changed enough since apartheid to match new
hopes and on-paper requirements (so the rhetoric of responsive,
democratic institutions gives way, say critics, to "bean counting," ill-
considered mandates, and turf battles); and that early efforts at broader
civic participation in planning were poorly structured and so reinforced
a bureaucratic mindset ("government and the experts have the answers"
and "too much democracy is bad for development"). Other conclusions
are that the public sector lacks the skill to engage civil society and
business more productively in many important tasks (South Africa's
human capital shortages are well documented); that this downward
spiral has only reinforced popular distrust of government and its ability
to deliver (so the ruling *party* may be trusted but not government as an
apparatus); and that beyond the lack of trust or confidence, the eagerness
to reform and the lack of accountability and monitoring while reforming
have created enormous complexity, which is daunting and baffling to

citizens—most of all to poor people living in poor and isolated communities.[12] South Africa's progressive constitution of social and economic rights adds to this complexity, as I explore in the case of homeless children and families below. And until recently, when public hearings were launched to evaluate results achieved by the Integrated Development Plans, there was no mechanism for public accountability and only limited empirical assessment of the shortcomings and accomplishments of the IDPs or other reforms.

Summing up a decade of persistence and change, in 2004, the South African Cities Network, an alliance of government and civil society analysts, highlighted these challenges to the "well-governed city" in the nation's first-ever "state of the cities" report: "Bad relations between communities and municipalities, poor public participation, discord between and within communities, and high levels of crime and violence. Also financially and administratively weak institutions of government" (p. 9).

These assessments call into question recent promises by the ANC government to rely less strictly on "developmental" government as the director of innovation and progress (Boraine et al. 2006). But leaving that aside, with few exceptions, these broad, structural analyses, which draw on vibrant global debates about urban governance and often summarize or extrapolate from many cases of institutional function and dysfunction, stay at the level of summary narrative. These accounts offer relatively little from the political actors themselves, in their own words, about strategies they have developed and barriers they have encountered. (Conversely, as in other countries, vivid, street-level accounts tend to be advocacy driven and descriptive, rather than analytic.) Given a rich portrait of political, economic, and operational context, we learn too little about the agents of change and their actions in that context. This is unfortunate, since civic capacity is not only reflected in structural contexts and the outcomes of action. Many important lessons about building and deploying more civic capacity are about effort, roads foregone, and mental models that prevent the needed learning and change from happening.

If the first type of governance assessment is from the "inside" (reformist government) looking out on the challenges, then, the second type offers a view from the outside in. That is, the second type has centered on civil society, and work in this vein tends to emphasize the failures of government's rigid, technocratic approach and the variation in "community capacity" to effectively engage government. In the area of community development to serve poor children and families, for example, analysts have identified a failure to value and build on resourceful patterns of informality in South Africa's townships and settlements (Harrison 2006; Huchzermeyer 2004). This critique highlights the modernizing ideology that imposes on community life a strict conception of the good city and its form and function (Scott 1998). It is a critique reminiscent of the attacks on top-down "urban renewal" in America in the 1950s and 1960s—attacks that accompanied popular resistance to government-led redevelopment in cities and that helped bring an end to the "golden era" of expert-led planning and policy making in America (Friedmann 1987).

Other analysts, mining case studies rich in the texture of specific local actors and their actions, have focused on variation in community capacity. Oldfield's (2000) comparative study of one colored and one black township in Cape Town, for example, defines this as the capacity to access and use government resources as part of larger, community-based strategies of change. Finally, some case-study research emphasizes how these communities *experience* ANC-driven public policies that advertise empowerment and participation, or perhaps coproduction through "partnership," but emphasize trimming government expenditures and privatizing public services in ways that further isolate and alienate the urban poor (e.g., Miraftab 2004).

No study of governance can be all-inclusive, of course. Nor should new research merely straddle the two types of governance analysis for the sake of synthesis. With this case of civic capacity, and how it is both developed and deployed, I try to build on prior work on urban governance in South Africa by focusing very explicitly on how actors inside and outside of government work to drive change. Again, structural context matters and so do the "end" outcomes that motivate the public to engage in problem solving in the first place: getting children to complete school, expanding employment, protecting the environment, and so on. But South Africa is something of a governance morass. There is so much hope alongside so much division and complexity. The analysis below, like the others in this book, centers on action (how the players choose to play) as much as the structural barriers to action—and therefore on where the prospects for change may lie. Following a brief overview of the Cape Town context, I examine a multidimensional effort to tackle the huge problem of insecure housing and under-served communities, a problem that powerfully shapes the well-being of South Africa's most disadvantaged young people.

Cape Town: Governing the Fragmented City

At the outset of this chapter, I described Cape Town as a city that is both unusually fractious politically and unusually diverse ethnically—that is, relative to other South African cities. Social, political, and economic divisions among the colored half (48 percent of population) and the sizeable white (19 percent) and black (32 percent) minorities are rooted in the long history of European colonization of the Western Cape, over three centuries, and the decades of apartheid rule, from the 1920s to the 1990s (Watson 2002). But the city is also exceptionally competitive in its electoral politics. The ANC and the Democratic Alliance, a center-right opposition party supported mainly by whites and coloreds, have traded control of local government several times since 1994, and the DA has governed since the March 2006 elections (whereas the ANC consistently dominates elections in other major cities, as it does the national elections).

One reason for this successful challenge to the ANC in Cape Town and the larger Western Cape province is quite simple: coloreds, who were disadvantaged in one way under white rule, now fear being second-class citizens (in a new way) under a dominant, black-led party. And white politicians have responded to that fear, as well as public concern about corruption and incompetence in the ANC's government appointments.[13] The ANC, in turn, has warned of a rollback to the apartheid era if its political competitors gain strength. In October 2006, for example, the party attacked a call by Mayor Helen Zille, of the DA, to the public to "take back your city" as an "arrogant message" aimed at "white, leafy suburbs." The ANC also attacked her restructuring of electoral boundaries and government contracting as an effort to "roll back key elements of our national agenda."[14]

In 2006, no party secured a clear majority—or mandate—in the Cape Town elections. The DA won 42 percent of the vote, marginally higher than the ANC's 38 percent, and successfully formed a coalition government with several small parties; the Independent Democrats, with 11 percent of the vote, sided with the ANC, thus leaving the DA-led coalition a razor-thin majority. This lack of an electoral majority is all the more important since the formal structure of Cape Town's municipal government favors party discretion over strong executive authority.[15] As a longtime activist who helped design the local government reforms observes, the theme of division, and of needing to bridge differences and fragmentation, is a constant in the area's politics:

This uncertainty, this deep set of unresolved issues that move in the body politic and the psyche of this city has its reflection in the fact that whenever you come to a vision statement . . . or anything like that for [Cape Town] government, "for all" is always the word [sic] that's used, way back from '94. You know, "the city that works for all" or "one city, one future" and now "a home for all" [provincial campaign] . . . as opposed to Joburg's "a world-class African city." Two very different understandings. . . . This is a very important dynamic to Cape Town, the fact that you can't point to a dominant, hegemonic "vault," which you could probably do in Joburg . . . [where] you could actually say, "There's an informal power bloc." Cape Town, [it's] much more fragmented, much more disconnected, much more trying to find a way in the context of a lot of contestation and an inability of leadership to emerge that can hold the whole city and forge a strong and determined agenda.

This postapartheid fragmentation has robbed the city of the optimism and success that marked the years leading up to the first democratic elections in 1996. For example, the Western Cape Economic Development ment Forum, an umbrella body of businesses, unions, civic associations, political parties, and other civil society organizations played a major consensus-building role, acting as a "mediated forum" to shape transitional local government arrangements in significant ways (Wilkinson 2000; Pieterse 2002a). The city's white political elite welcomed this "corporatist" approach, which gave traditionally excluded groups their first seat at the table but not through direct consultation in diverse community settings. That process led, in 1993, to a formal Metropolitan Negotiation Forum, also corporatist, which appointed an interim council to manage the city until the first democratic elections in 1996, and a successor Unicity Commission, the multistakeholder group that planned the transition to permanent local government status. But since then, no body or process appears to have managed the same broad consensus building, and some insiders highlight the hard-fought campaigning and jockeying for position in a no-majority electoral context as reasons that trust eroded rapidly. As Pieterse (2002a, 25) concludes, "This renders an inclusive and broad-based consensus-based model of city politics unviable in the short term."

As I also previewed at the outset, social and political divisions in Cape Town are reflected in, and compounded by, sharp *spatial* ones. The new metropolitan "unicity" government consolidated in December 2000 encompasses an affluent and historically significant city center that is home to businesses and professional households as well as tourist facilities, similarly high-priced waterfront communities to the west and southwest, prosperous growing suburbs and "edge cities" (with more and more office space) to the north, and the large flats of the southeast, where the poor, overwhelmingly black and colored townships and informal settlements are concentrated (figure 11.2). The more affluent and white communities, and some poor and working-class colored ones, tend to support the Democratic Alliance, poor and working-class black communities the ANC.

As Wilkinson (2004) observes, Cape Town thus represents a particularly extreme version of the opportunities and tensions, after apartheid, in pursuing both inclusive democracy and economic revitalization, in reconciling "pro-growth" and "pro-poor" strategies. Wilkinson argues, furthermore that the pro-growth white coalition of city councilors and business owners that governed the city under apartheid—that is, the regime of that era—has been undermined but not replaced with a robust, broad-based coalition willing and able to reconcile the dueling agendas. And newer political actors, especially those with a pro-poor focus, such as social movement activists and their networks, exert pressure but are not incorporated into wider coalitions with the resources sufficient to govern such a fragmented place.

The result, he concludes, is not just electoral swings and erratic shifts in policy priorities but bureaucratic resistance, since public managers perceive political mandates to be slim and temporary. Add to that opposition to needed management reforms by unionized civil servants who fear that significant restructuring is a prelude to privatizing their jobs away or opposition by managers whose political patrons are eager to protect service levels for the white, middle-class communities that elect them (Pieterse 2002a). Not surprisingly perhaps, there is little evidence thus far that Cape Town's Integrated Development Plan is significantly reshaping service delivery and coordinating public investment in ways that the 1998 White Paper on Local Government, and many activists and observers, had hoped.

As if these serious barriers were not enough, Cape Town is infamous for gangsterism and widespread patterns of law-breaking informality in poor communities. Drug gangs and informal "survivalist" networks in poor and working-class areas "present a formidable challenge to the credibility and authority of local government largely because they are impervious to [government's] disciplinary and regulatory efforts," observes Pieterse (2002a, 29). And he adds, "They can render entire communities inaccessible and out-of-reach if they perceive a municipal intervention to counteract their interest and livelihood." But as Pieterse also reminds, these informal systems are, nevertheless, forms of governance, and they compete with the formal systems for legitimacy, resources, and control. Finally, the high rate of crime and violence, much of it concentrated in homes and neighborhoods, acts as a barrier to positive engagement in collective action to improve community life. The new movements to challenge evictions and obtain land, housing, and basic services have emerged, as I examine below, in this inhospitable soil.

The changing physical form of Cape Town is a sobering barometer of what these multiple, competing systems of governance will contend with for the foreseeable future. In a pattern of "persistent polarization" (Turok 2001), government proposals to develop a major job center in the poor southeast of the city have gone nowhere in a decade, and market trends continue to favor tourist-oriented development in the city center, plus growth in both housing and jobs in the north. The Cape Town government's need to quickly plan and build a major new stadium in time to host games for the soccer World Cup in 2010 appears to be reinforcing this uneven development trend.

Are there *any* prospects for significant progress on the needs of the city's most disadvantaged children and their families? The next section examines strategies of collaboration and contention and what they suggest about how to develop and use civic capacity in such an extremely challenging setting.

Tackling Homelessness in Cape Town: Collaboration, Protest, and the Courts

As I outlined above, under apartheid, South Africa accrued enormous shortages of housing suitable for the lowest-income families. After apartheid, with strict racial restrictions on relocation gone, significant migration from the countryside to cities—where even low-wage jobs in the informal sector mean much higher average incomes than irregular work in the countryside—added to local shortages, including Cape Town's. The transition to democracy also brought substantial new investments in housing and basic services, strategies to break down segregated spatial planning, and a new constitution with remarkable social and economic rights. But by the early 2000s, protests were growing against service cutoffs and the scarcity of land and subsidy to ensure adequate shelter for homeless families, especially in black and colored townships and informal settlements. It was clear that the hoped-for partnership of government, business, and civil society groups had fallen far short of the need and expectations. Metropolitan Cape Town was losing ground on the severe backlog of basic needs, and bureaucratic delays, as well as conflict over who should be targeted first to receive new homes, only fueled these fires. By 2005, media accounts of "alleged irregularities in the allocation of houses," complaints of graft, the vandalization of empty homes, and land invasions to secure somewhere to build were almost daily fare.[16]

In Cape Town, efforts to address these needs have tracked the broad categories of government/civil-society engagement that I reviewed early in the chapter: *collaborating* directly with government, through consultation and negotiation, and combining government resources as well as "community" resources with the support of nongovernmental developers and service providers staffed by professionals; *contending* with government, in particular through demonstrations, resistance to evictions and service cutoffs, and other forms of civil opposition, and through court interdicts and litigation aimed at policy and program reform (leveraging rights on paper to create meaningful changes in policy or practice); and *blending* contention with basic forms of collaboration—a pattern seen in a number of grassroots efforts in poor communities in Cape Town and elsewhere in the Western Cape (Oldfield and Stokke 2006). Next, I examine these approaches in turn.

Collaborating with Government: The Homeless People's Federation

In 1991, with support from professionals, hundreds of low-income shack dwellers in several South African cities, including Cape Town, formed the Homeless People's Federation and a supporting nongovernmental organization (NGO), the People's Dialogue on Land and Shelter (Huchzermeyer 2004). The Federation linked itself to nascent savings clubs, a form of rotating credit association, based in poor communities. The Federation would mobilize members and enable them to negotiate with government for themselves; the NGO would provide technical assistance and help secure and manage external funds, including aid from international donors; and the clubs would mobilize capital saved by poor people themselves, meet vital credit needs for those not served by mainstream financial institutions, and in the process strengthen bonds of reciprocity and mutual reliance (Baumann, Boelnick, and Mitlin 2002). Modeled in key respects after the innovative Alliance in India that I examined in chapter 5, and recognized as the most important housing production movement in South Africa, this Federation-led, tripartite alliance of interdependent civil society organizations (hereafter, "The

Alliance") exemplifies the power and limits of the collaborative approach in the Cape Town context.

By 2002, the Federation had over 80,000 members, at least 2,000 affiliated, community-level savings clubs, and city-level federations throughout the country. These city-level groups engaged local government, while the national network engaged the provincial and national governments. The Alliance had also launched the uTshani Fund, a revolving loan and "bridge finance" fund able to blend monies from multiple sources to speed up and scale up new construction. Yet only 1 percent of government subsidies had gone to poor households directly. Under South Africa's initial housing policy, almost all subsidies went to for-profit real estate developers (tied to the unit, not a household), who often built shoddy homes on the only land readily available: out on the urban periphery, isolated from transportation networks, reliable services (power, water, waste collection, and sanitation), and most job growth (Huchzermeyer 2004). But the Alliance had shown that with training and support, Federation members were capable of building higher quality housing units better suited to their everyday needs; 8,000 were completed by 2002, roughly half of those with uTshani funds alone and another 1,250 with the unit-based government subsidy. Could the Alliance now get government to respond?

As former staff of the now-disbanded People's Dialogue emphasize, the Alliance's process-oriented approach departs from the narrow focus on "delivery" that marks many community development interventions worldwide, but it also departs from traditional approaches to making claims of government (Baumann, Bolnick, and Mitlin 2002, 21–22):

The major focus of the [claim-making] process is on acquiring what is needed from the state, either through the use of existing legislation or the enactment of new rights. . . . The emphasis within their campaigns is on ensuring that formal conventional approaches to urban development are accessible by the poor. However, in many cases, these do not work for the poor, especially for the lowest income families . . . often even success does not support community activities. . . . This is not to say that the state does not have responsibilities . . . [but] the federation seeks to use processes that enable the poor to be involved in designing solutions that work for them, and then to negotiate with the state to obtain support where this is applicable.

Along with Alliance counterparts in Asia, Latin America, and other parts of Africa, the South African Alliance began to attract attention worldwide for combining "community" capacity with professional expertise, private capital, financial creativity, and government resources.

Yet understandably, the Alliance's material output paled against the national housing shortage, the Alliance labored on the margins of technocrat-driven national housing policy in South Africa, and a number of municipalities—Cape Town, in particular—strongly resisted the expansion of community-driven housing development. Public officials regularly preached the virtues of the private building industry as the key to achieving the required scale of low-income housing supply.

In spite of these limits, argues Joel Bolnick, founding director of People's Dialogue and a new support NGO, becoming a mainly oppositional movement—"fighting over entitlements and rights," beyond "brokering deals"—makes little sense for the Alliance, given the setting:

Clearly, there is a need that is not being addressed by the state. But I think [those who take a more contentious approach] have misread the moment. You have a highly legitimate state. You have a developmentally virile state. It's not even just a developmentally strong state. It believes that elections are the point of contact between the government and the poor and that there are no other actors that need to be in the picture. Thereafter, the poor are beneficiaries, and the state has the capacity to deliver all the entitlements. I don't think this state responds very positively, at this moment in time, to confrontational strategies. . . . It makes much more sense, and you are much more likely to secure entitlements, if you "play chess" with them.

Whether Bolnick is right or wrong about this, the best strategy, he concludes, must also reflect the root problem that undercuts "delivery":

There is a very high level of political will to deliver to the poor. And at the local government and community levels, there is sufficient capacity to implement delivery mechanisms that can scale up. . . . But in between . . . there's a whole new genre of [national] government officials who are preoccupied with policy frameworks and legislative arrangements . . . who use those, what they regard as preconditions, to short circuit the scaling up.

In Durban, local government has committed a share of its own tax and fee revenue to support flexible, community-driven housing development, generating what the Homeless People's Federation, newly reconstituted after a membership crisis as the Federation for the Urban Poor, considers a significant impact on scale and speed of delivery. By contrast, in Cape Town and other South African cities, local governments tend to be implementation agencies for inflexible national housing policies and the funds that come with them—a top-down, technocratic pattern long-time observers consider a legacy of "apartheid urban management" (Parnell 2004) and a pattern that makes local public managers resistant to community-driven approaches.

The Cape Town exemplar, for better or worse, is a project known as N2 Gateway. Designed to upgrade major shackdweller settlements along the airport highway in time for Cape Town to host international visitors for the soccer World Cup in 2010, the Gateway project was to be the yardstick for a renewed national housing program, providing new homes to over 22,000 and beautifying the visitor's "gateway" to the city at the same time. As of 2005, however, the project was severely behind schedule, beset with political conflicts over which groups of families would be given priority for new housing and, despite the contentiousness of that targeting issue, unable to count on a reliable census of families in the existing settlements.

Initially, fearing delays in a process-driven "community approach," national government refused the Federation's request to implement a community-based "enumeration" exercise pioneered in India in the 1980s—something Durban officials, using their own resources, agreed to support after visiting a model site in India. Back in Cape Town, government hired a private consultancy to do the N2 Gateway census work. When the end product turned out to be unreliable and utterly inadequate, government went back to the Federation to ask for the enumeration, which is one key to resolving targeting disputes between migrant families who are relative newcomers to Cape Town and longtime residents who languish five or ten years or more, in many cases, on the waiting list for decent, subsidized housing.

And there were other major problems with the Gateway project. Both newcomers and longtimers were resisting government's relocation and resettlement policy—another crucial feature of community upgrading that the Alliance in India helped pioneer in negotiations with the World Bank and Indian government officials, as I explored in chapter 5—and the dense and unfamiliar housing type (of three- to five-story buildings) proposed by the project architects. "They've run into all the trouble we predicted," said the Alliance's Joel Bolnick at the time. By early 2007, over a year into construction, the project was still plagued with contention and delay, which centered on the targeting dispute.[17]

The Federation, on behalf of its Alliance partners, redoubled efforts to cultivate networks of key national government officials. In the Indian case, SPARC and its Alliance partners won crucial allies "on the inside" early on, in the 1980s, specifically among government officials frustrated with decades of failure and deep public mistrust of public agencies—insiders willing to commit to something new. The Indian Alliance made a "huge, long-term commitment" to that approach, says Bolnick. That was markedly different from the South African context dominated by a still young and confident ANC-led government. But there, the Federation's hope was to build awareness at the top and through it constructive pressure on local governments to be more welcoming of tested community-driven approaches.

The past decade has taught civil society innovators some hard lessons about working with a confident developmental state that is propelled by a dominant electoral force—and about the risk of being co-opted by that state to defend failed policy (Khan and Pieterse 2006). Bolnick, for example, compares SPARC's patient approach to the South African Federation's different approach, and his sense of its strategic error, after the fall of apartheid:

In South Africa, we were cursed by our successes . . . were able to secure huge amounts of external resources very quickly and move rapidly [away] from slowly but surely building long-time relationships with officials and getting local government, right at the ward councilor level and then at the city level and then at the province level and national level to begin to understand what we were doing and how we were doing it and why. We just went straight from savings into building houses, and the institutional awareness of what we did and why we did it and who we were was very, very superficial. And when the virile, developmental state was able to finally consolidate itself, it was able to just swat us out of the way.

Contending with Government: The Western Cape Anti-Eviction Campaign

At the beginning of this chapter, I described a Youth Day gathering in Khayelitsha, which I attended with organizers from the Western Cape Anti-Eviction Campaign (AEC). The AEC, an umbrella group that includes a youth-focused member organization in Khayelitsha township and more than a dozen other poor communities, is part of the surge in civil society contention with government, and sometimes with the ruling ANC party as well as its opponents on the right, since 2000 (Habib 2005; Dykes 2004). Most of that surge has focused on service gaps in black and colored communities, including the enormous range of problems facing homeless (shack dweller) families and the service cutoffs and evictions that threaten even those with regular, if modest, homes.

The youth day gathering in Khayelitsha offered a glimpse of the harsh criticism that political parties and government have received from increasingly frustrated poor communities concentrated in the southeastern sector of Cape Town (figure 11.2). But such legal demonstrations, say researchers Oldfield and Stokke (2002,38), are just the tip of the iceberg:

The modes of protest vary considerably among the organizations within the Western Cape Anti-Eviction Campaign. The present repertoire of protest ranges from strategies that are compatible with the rules and procedures of the formal political system (e.g., community meetings, [legal] petitions, negotiations, and legal demonstrations) to practices that are more confrontational and unlawful (e.g., illegal reconnections [of utility services], occupations of houses, forceful block of evictions, and sit-ins). Many of the organizations combine these kinds of protests and only employ the more radical tactics when negotiations and legal demonstrations fail to yield acceptable outcomes.

Some clashes with government, whether at group rallies or individual sites of eviction, have turned violent. Policing is federalized in South Africa, a structure rooted in apartheid-era control strategies, and frustrated communities likewise retain a repertoire of protest from that era that includes blocking roads and illegal occupation, as noted above. The interplay has invited hotly debated comparisons, in recent years, of government "repression" of civil society, and in particular of groups based in the poorest urban communities, in the apartheid and postapartheid periods. The publication of scholar-advocate Ashwin Desai's impassioned *We Are the Poors* (2002) both reflected and shaped such critical comparisons, which were taboo, and perhaps unimagined, in the early years of relatively consensual and "collegiate" transition from white minority rule.

In contrast to "positive" collaborating civil-society organizations, as of this writing, insurgent groups have been dismissed and denounced frequently by the ANC leadership as disruptive "ultra-revolutionaries" (Gumede 2005; Oldfield and Stokke 2006). But revolutionary says little about the aims and means of these groups, and even "insurgent" vastly oversimplifies their stance and approach. Oldfield and Stokke emphasize the risk of a false dichotomy between "adversarial" and "cooperative" groups. The member groups of the AEC, for example, vary widely in the quality of their access to public officials, including Cape Town's elected councilors and sublocal ward councilors. So some AEC groups, as Oldfield and Stokke have documented, pursue close engagement with public officials while others disengage: At the extreme, the mostly colored Tafelsig township had, by July 2002, established territorial control through its nonelected community organization, in effect refusing to recognize the authority of Cape Town's elected government within the community's boundaries. Also, some AEC member groups are registered as civic associations (formally recognized by government) and function as formal membership organizations while others, such as the Tafelsig Anti-Eviction Campaign, "operate on the basis of a more informal mandate" (Oldfield and Stokke 2002, 39). Given perennially scarce funding, some of the groups actively pursue strategic alliances with NGOs and larger networks, while others deem such close relations unacceptable—too politically compromising. Leaders in some community groups have loyal ties to the ANC, while others have long resisted it. As explained above, poor and working-class colored communities frequently vote for conservative parties in Cape Town, in part because they promise a check on black political power and perceived favoritism toward blacks.

Particular community groups may thus be cooperative one day and adversarial the next, and networks of these groups can pursue a particularly wide range of strategies to engage government, from the electoral end of politics to policy making and implementation (table 11.1). I return to this range, and what it implies about civic capacity, below.

Amidst this diversity—and sometimes fragmentation—say Oldfield and Stokke, the umbrella AEC seeks unity in major campaigns. Despite consistently poor funding, the AEC also seeks to offer multifunctional support to communities, with a legal coordinating committee (that assists in filing legal petitions to slow down evictions and cut-offs and thus to "clog the system"), a media unit to project a consistent public face for the movement's goals, and a community research group developed in partnership with local university researchers. Based on media and AEC internal accounts, the network has so far been able to raise public awareness and "contain the damage" (limit government action) but not transform government's approach to basic needs in poor communities.

Some observers have emphasized that AEC and similar social movement actors generate "invented" spaces of citizenship that are crucial for planning in the context of unequal power and resources—this in contrast to government's "invited" spaces for consultation with citizens, which is the traditional realm of "participatory planning" (Miraftab and Wills 2005). This is a particularly important perspective given the enormous influence of the consultative frame of mind in "new public management" around the globe (what Americans know as "reinventing government") and the frequent inclination in expert-led bureaucracies—whether public, private, or nongovernmental—to view nonprofessionals, in particular, as disengaged, inexpert, parochial, and even disingenuous. But this perspective has special relevance in South Africa, given (1) the lack of electoral opposition at the national level, and (2) the enormous proliferation of official planning and decision-making concepts and procedures, resulting in great technocratic complexity and bureaucratic proceduralism, over the past decade.

Table 11.1
Government–civil society engagement and civic capacity in South African governance

	Arena		
	Electoral politics	Policy making	Implementation
Main function of domain	Agenda setting (problem setting)	Problem setting and direction setting	Political management of implementation design and operations
Character of engagement	Vote-based mandate	Range: Consultative (advisory) to "empowered" direction setting	Range: From noncooperative "foiling" to bounded cooperation to "deep" coproduction
Citizen role	Voter	Stakeholder and expert (source of "local knowledge")	Client and coproducer of change
Source(s) of civic capacity	Defined agenda with broad-based electoral support	Relatively stable strategies with broad-based stakeholder support	Legitimacy and productive capacity required for synergy, learning and adaptation, and operational accountability between implementers
Context and dynamics	National: Dominant center-left party with coalition partners, modest opposition from the right, none from the left Local: Iteration in governing coalition, no electoral majority	Legislative and executive: Integrated Development Planning, council and ward councilor system of consultation; civil society organizations as expert sources, allies, critics Judicial: Litigating through the Constitutional Courts, advancing or challenging justiciable rights, major claims	Executive: "Developmental" government (directive, subsidy providing, extensive outsourcing, increasingly consolidated since 2000), civil society organizations as partners or mobilizers of foiling Judicial: Court interdicts, dispute resolution, major to minor claims

The larger issue, from a civic capacity perspective, is not whether there is *room* to contend and to employ pressure politics on behalf of change or whether there is *value* to such contention, which is an important ingredient in any democratic society. Having room, whether through "invitation" by government or "invention" outside its sanctioned spaces, is necessary but not sufficient. The larger question is whether that contention leads, over time, to continued standoff and a shortage of the incremental trust, or "studied" trust in Sabel's (1992) terms, required to transform dysfunction for the better—that is, to do more than decry it with moral authority. As Oldfield and Stokke (2006, 31) caution,

The present period seems . . . to be marked by a growing mistrust between civil society organizations and actors from the state. On the one hand, state officials and politicians interpret activities by organization like [the AEC] as by definition adversarial. On the other hand, activists and organizations interpret state actions as, by definition, neo-liberal and therefore counter to the interests of the poor and progressive politics.

The question for civic capacity is whether and how pressure is applied in a way that helps lead change—that is, whether contention, in addition to being legitimate, is also *effective* beyond a short-run, thwart-the-opposition level. This is not a criticism of the most oppositional and confrontational tactics in Cape Town or any other corner of the globe. Indeed, civic capacity assumes no one legitimate authority and therefore no "automatic" respect due to authority figures. Legitimacy is something to be earned and reearned. But Bolnick's observation about the choice to "play chess" or not with a strong government, and if so when and how, begs exactly this question about the effectiveness of confrontation. AEC's work focuses on government's failure to do what it presumably can and should, while the Federation of the Urban Poor focuses on government's inability to get the job done without the creative collaboration of poor communities themselves.

To sharpen this contrast, I look, finally, at the effort to contend with government by leveraging the South African constitution's extraordinary charter of social and economic rights, including the child's right to shelter.

Leveraging New Rights through the Courts: The *Grootboom* Case and beyond

The past few decades have brought a dramatic increase in worldwide attention to human rights, but until recently, observers note, "with only a handful of exceptions, the human rights community has ignored socio-economic rights" (Jones and Stokke 2005, 1). That is, advocates, legal scholars, governments, and others focused largely on what have been called "negative" rights, such as bans on illegal search and seizure, disenfranchisement, or press censorship by government. As *limits on government authority*, these negative rights protect vital civil and political liberties but do not guarantee social and economic basics, such as access to healthcare, education, water, and shelter. These are keys to human development that rest in part on what society provides or enables, not just on individual effort. "Positive" social and economic rights address those basics. Positive rights imply *obligations for government to act* and, as such, they have major implications for resource allocation and priority setting that negative rights typically do not have.

As of 2000, most nations (144) were parties to the International Covenants on Civil and Political Rights and a similarly high number (142) to the International Covenant on Economic, Social, and Cultural Rights. But as Schneider and Ignatieff (2001) note, very few had taken any steps to realize social and economic rights in law or to provide individuals or groups with opportunities to redress alleged violations of those rights (see Steiner and Alston 2000).

It is the surge in interest in the fuller conception of rights—and vigorous debates over what that conception means in practice—that defines the evolving framework of "rights-based development." As a major United Nations report argues, "development" (the pursuit of social and economic progress) adds much to the conversation about rights, including practical concerns about how to measure change, how to decide on trade-offs and priorities (which is crucial whenever resources are limited and need is great), and how to create the "enabling environment" needed to realize rights (United Nations Development Program 2001). Otherwise, debates over rights can become narrowly philosophical and legalistic.

But conversely, the discourse of rights, and the active use or "leveraging" of rights through judicial and other institutions, adds much to the conversation about development and human progress as well. First and perhaps most importantly, rights and the institutions that help adjudicate them locate accountability: "It links the human development approach to the idea that others have duties to facilitate and enhance human development" (United Nations Development Program 2001, 91). Second, rights help regulate the process of social and economic change, setting boundaries, for example, on how much particular individuals or groups should have to sacrifice in the name, say, of "national progress." In lieu of such boundaries, ideologies and processes of development can create very selective benefits and exact an enormous cost on human dignity, livelihood, and cultural identity, as well-intended "planning disasters" around the world have shown (Scott 1998).

The question for now is what social and economic rights add to South Africa's progress—in the context of young democratic institutions, limited resources, and the tension between pro-growth and pro-poor policy making—on urgent social needs. In the past decade, South Africa has arguably done more than any nation on earth to pursue the idea that social and economic rights are not merely aspirational but imply real duties for the government and wider society, particularly vis-à-vis the poor. This effort has also sparked debate on the limits of the judiciary and the need to combine litigation strategies—the formal route to adjudicating rights but a narrow route—with political mobilization, community-driven interventions, and other strategies for leading change in tangible "conditions on the ground" (Gloppen 2005a). Here, I review the highlights of these events and debates and examine their relationship to civic capacity for local problem solving.

In 1996, the new South African Constitution articulated rights to housing, healthcare, food, water, social security, and education, with special provision of these rights for children (Gloppen 2005b, 154).[18] As insider accounts make clear, these rights were to be more than utopian "directive principles" of the kind articulated by newly independent India in the transition from British rule a half century ago—that is, more than broad aspirations to inform policy making by the legislative and executive branches of government (Sachs 2005; Steiner and Alston 2000). As De Vos (2001, 260) observes, "The constitution explicitly rejects the social and economic status quo and sets as one of its primary aims the transformation of society into a more equitable place." But it would be up to a transformed Constitutional Court to decide just what the newly codified rights would mean, if more than "symbolic resources" for bargaining in the political arena. More precisely, since courts are reactive institutions, it would depend on the interests and capacity of claimants (who bring cases forward), the court's decision outcomes, and the impacts of those decisions in the world beyond the judicial system (Gloppen 2005a). Since courts have no capacity to *directly* implement the remedies they order, the impacts would depend, in turn, on a host of political, institutional, and market factors.

As of this writing, several landmark cases have addressed the basic shelter and service needs of the poorest children and families in South Africa (Huchzermeyer 2003; Roux 2002), and more "public-impact litigation" is emerging each year. In the first and most famous of the major cases, *Grootboom*, shack dwellers who illegally occupied land, represented by the Legal Resource Centre, a public interest law organization, sought funding for emergency housing from the Western Cape's provincial government and secure land rights from the Oostenberg municipal government. A cornerstone of the plaintiff's case was the children's right to shelter.[19] After the provincial High Court ruled in the tenants' favor, ordering government to provide for their needs, provincial government appealed the decision to the Constitutional Court, which found that the government had not fulfilled its responsibilities under the constitution to address the needs of such families and also that this did extend to providing the plaintiffs with shelter.[20]

The outcome showed that South Africa's highest court was willing to treat rights as "justiciable" and not merely as directive principles, but the ruling was narrow: Government was ordered to create a program of emergency housing, where there had been none at all previously, as part of its obligation to "progressively" realize families' rights to "adequate housing." The court did not address the controversies over targeting outlined earlier in this chapter or how much government should devote (in the way of resources) and how quickly. Furthermore, it left monitoring of the remedy to the South African Human Rights Commission, a reporting agency without direct authority (Roux 2002).

Provincial government moved to create an emergency housing program, and national government likewise developed one a few years later (Huchzermeyer 2006). But government insiders claimed that the nation's severe resource gap, along with conflicts over targeting and other features of social policy implementation, not political will, persisted as the real barriers to progress on the ground (Schneider and Ignatieff 2001). Later cases provided rights advocates with even less reason to hope; the *Bredell* decision and *Alexandra* out-of-court settlement supported forceful evictions by government where homeless families had occupied land on the urban periphery, although protections from such evictions was an early pillar of postapartheid law (Huchzermeyer 2003).

Hailed by international observers as a breakthrough, *Grootboom* has been received much more skeptically within South Africa. For example, Roux (2002, 51) calls it a "remedy without a sanction," highlighting the absence of any enforcement mechanism beyond monitoring by the Commission. Roux and others have criticized the court's choice, as a matter of "judicial restraint," to forgo bolder options, such as requiring the public agency at fault to return to the court with a plan for review as well as a timeline for its implementation, since the stated aim was to serve people with "no access to land, no roof over their heads, and who are living in intolerable conditions or crisis situations."[21] In an interview, Judge Richard Goldstone of the Constitutional Court told me, "We had no capacity and no authority to get into policy making. That wasn't our role." While crediting *Grootboom* as a catalyst for critical policy development, including policies supporting wider participation by civil society groups in housing and community development "delivery," analysts of the case and later cases have also highlighted ambiguous and complicating elements of the judiciary's rulings (McLean 2006).

Although the legal and policy landscape continues to evolve, for several reasons, the scope of the *Grootboom* decision in particular, and the limited role assumed by the court in making that decision, is relevant to the question of how civic capacity gets developed and used to solve public problems in a changing society. First, in a politically fragmented and extremely unequal context, elected officials may not be willing *or* able to forge and pursue agendas of change that adequately respect important human rights. The most disadvantaged persons and groups may be asked to bear unacceptable burdens, and be treated inhumanely by stubborn bureaucracies, as they wait for changes to "trickle down" and benefit them.[22] The dominant national party has labeled its most frustrated grassroots critics "disruptive ultrarevolutionaries," and the more conservative parties in the Western Cape—sometimes in opposition and sometimes ruling—have resisted redistribution of land and resources to meet the urgent needs of the urban poor. Without giving core concepts such as "reasonable attention" to basic housing needs some teeth, the judiciary has failed to supply the policy making *and* implementation processes with critical safeguards. Problem solving in lieu of such safeguards may be participatory, but it can hardly be democratic in the way the transformative South African constitution hoped.

Second, because impasses over targeting and other complexities of policy design and implementation act to thwart the realization of rights, it seems perfectly reasonable for the courts to make government implementers submit plans and implementation timelines for review and also for the courts to offer interpretations of competing responsibilities, for example the responsibility to respect years-long waiting lists for "regular" housing on one hand and to meet immediate basic needs of the homeless on the other (typically through "emergency" housing). Adjudicating this, minimally by defining which trade-offs are unacceptable, has been an important contribution of courts to the progressive realization of rights

in politically contested domains, such as in fair housing and equal-oppor-
tunity education in America.

Third and finally, as a particularly challenging, nonroutine form of
governance, collective problem solving for significant social progress
calls for extraordinarily robust accountability, which, as I have shown
in other chapters, may call for new institutions to handle learning and
bargaining, new roles for existing institutions, new relationships among
them, or all of these. Such accountability rarely follows from more information alone, for example through official reporting.[23] And without
robust accountability, there can be little legitimacy or trust—and thus
little to build the momentum for broad-based investment in change by
government actors together with nongovernmental ones. Yet the Constitutional Court of South Africa has thus far foregone the use of court-
appointed "masters" or other mechanisms for implementing remedies
with sanctions, as well as the use of official "experts" to inform remedies
beyond whatever facts lawyers and plaintiffs can muster to inform
complex policy disputes. Without such mechanisms or bolder forays into
the politics of policy and implementation, one wonders if social and
economic rights will, in fact, be more than directive principles.

Separate from this is the important question I turn to next: which civil
society strategies are likely to pay off most if rights *are* a key resource.

The Housing Crisis versus the AIDS Crisis, Public-Impact Litigation versus "Organizing"

The movement to tackle the basic community development needs of poor
children and their families—whether through "partnership," contentious
pressure politics, or *Grootboom*-type public-impact litigation—differs
dramatically, in course and outcomes so far, from the movement to
ensure treatment of HIV/AIDS in South Africa, which has one of the
highest prevalence rates in the world. This contrast sheds light on the
role of varied political strategies, and patterns of government/civil society
interaction, as determinants of civic capacity for change. Broadly, this
contrast reinforces the classic insight that contrary to what "cause
lawyers" and their clients may hope, the courts tend to have a limited
direct impact on social conditions; they are more usefully thought of as
sources of leverage on important public attitudes and the options considered by policy makers (Scheingold 1974; Sarat and Scheingold 1998,
2001; Gloppen 2005b).

The Treatment Action Campaign (TAC), propelled mainly by middle-
class professionals with roots in the gay rights movement, has success-

fully used South Africa's Constitutional Court to force government to offer subsidized retroviral treatment to prevent mother-to-child transmission of HIV—this after President Thabo Mbeki and his health minister steadfastly maintained, to world astonishment, that HIV had not been proven to cause AIDS (Power 2003). TAC is a membership organization that seeks victories for an entire class of people (those affected by HIV/AIDS) and not its members alone—a feature that distinguishes TAC from the Federation and its approach.

Founded in Cape Town in 1998 by Zackie Achmat, an HIV-positive activist, TAC became world renowned when Achmat publicly refused to buy treatment drugs until they were provided by government. But what casual observers miss, in focusing on TAC's landmark courtroom victory on the right to healthcare, which began to put retroviral drugs in public clinics throughout the country, is the fact that that public-impact litigation strategy has complemented a skillful blend of media education, grassroots mobilization for protest and civil disobedience, and also mobilization for self-help in many HIV-affected communities (Heywood 2005). Grassroots organizing broadened TAC beyond a small group of activist professionals to embrace the mostly poor black and colored communities where the AIDS pandemic hits hardest.

Through a "sophisticated engagement with government," as a former government insider described it to me, TAC has maintained an exceptionally broad but coherent approach to its target problem. This includes strategies aimed at sustaining a broad constituency, shifting public attitudes, compelling public agencies to enforce the court ruling and also building the capacity of those agencies to learn and improve delivery, compelling government to allocate resources, and more. To make a difference, litigation strategies do not simply need social movements "on the outside" to apply pressure, as scholars are contending worldwide (e.g., Gloppen 2005a). Policy itself can be a limited instrument, so the focus on making claims of government captures a necessary but insufficient condition for changing important social outcomes.

By comparison, though, South Africa's community development "movement," broadly defined, has remained much more fragmented and poorly resourced. Collaborative groups such as the Federation of the Urban Poor build needed capacity at the community level and model innovation on the ground—acting as coproducers of change with government—but they must avoid the pressure-politics strategies that might sour their relationship with government resource providers. They negotiate, rather than litigate, for government action. The Western Cape

Anti-Eviction Campaign, a resourceful umbrella group, manages small-scale self-help efforts, protests, and acts of civil disobedience, as well as the routine litigation of evictions and service cut-offs that "clogs" the system. And the public-impact litigation seen through the mid-2000s, *Grootboom* most famously, has not been connected to broader organizing or program innovation strategies. It does appear to represent the start of a road that has brought South Africa's Constitutional Court further into the politics of resource allocation, which is crucial for the country's continued transformation (Roux 2003).

We have seen these outcomes before, at least in a broad sense. Soon after the high water mark of civil rights reforms and progressive social policy making that defined America in the 1960s, Scheingold (1974, 5–6), in a major assessment of resistance to court-ordered change and of the use of rights as resources for political mobilization, contrasted "the myth of rights" with a more complex "politics of rights":

The myth of rights is . . . premised on a direct linking of litigation, rights, and remedies with social change. . . . The political approach thus prompts us to approach rights as skeptics. Instead of thinking of judicially asserted rights as accomplished social facts or as moral imperatives, they must be thought of, on the one hand, as authoritatively articulated goals of public policy and, on the other, as political resources of unknown value in the hands of those who want to alter the course of public policy.

This still useful formulation falls short in at least one major respect, though, as the concept of civic capacity makes clear. Altering "the course of public policy" does not directly change conditions on the ground, as Scheingold later acknowledged. Where the capacity and legitimate authority to act on social problems is fragmented, and where policy interventions alone are necessary but insufficient to change those conditions, rights are seen, more properly, as political resources that can help redirect attention, money, and other kinds of resources, including resources for coproduction. As I reviewed above, rights can "locate" accountability—especially if the adjudication of rights is more enforceable than *Grootboom*—and this is no small thing in loosely coupled systems wherein much important action must be negotiated. And more recent developments point to shack dwellers' movement organizations allying with housing rights activists around public-impact litigation strategy in a way that *Grootboom* lacked. But codified rights guarantee nothing, and as analysts of cause lawyering note, they may, in some instances, distract from the work of building coherent, broad-based strategies of change beyond the narrow courtroom win. Even in the "success" case of TAC, for example, the fight continues to get AIDS medicine properly supplied to public clinics and to mobilize patients to utilize the drugs effectively as well as prevent the spread of the disease through unsafe sex.

The larger point is that rights add something potentially powerful to the effort to build and deploy civic capacity on behalf of problem solving. Conversely, in a world of fragmented governance, civic capacity offers a useful lens for analyzing the politics of rights as resources for real change.

Summary, Implications, and Comparison

When South Africa emerged, in 1994, from decades of apartheid rule to become a multiracial democracy, its dreams were much like those of newly independent African nations a half century earlier. But across the continent, too many of those dreams led to nightmares of political repression, mismanagement, and institutionalized corruption. By comparison, South Africa navigated an extraordinarily peaceful transition—violence now behind it, in the struggle to end apartheid—and propelled itself into a new century with a bold vision of reformed governance and comparatively big investments in human development.

Yet inequality remains severe—among the world's worst—and South Africa's ability to make significant progress hinges to an important degree on how well it can consolidate new democratic institutions, whether reformed government, transforming civil-society organizations, or mechanisms that productively link the two. More than anything, given the pace of change, "consolidate" means learning how to put those institutions to work to get things done. This is the challenge of civic capacity. It is more than the capacity to formulate procedures, let alone defend bureaucratic turf. It is also more than the capacity to contend, since political pressure alone does not ensure change or direct it sensibly.

A confident, some say vastly overconfident, government led by a dominant political party (the ANC) represents the "dance partner" for a civil society that has become increasingly radicalized in many quarters. The severe lack of electoral competition at the national government level, which is highly directive in spite of decentralization reforms, makes this a very different context for collective problem solving than the one I examined in the San Francisco case. Yet there are lessons in the parallels.

First, only time will tell whether South Africa will develop India's fatigue with bureaucratically directed development (see chapter 5). The former has taken a much more neoliberal approach to the economy than India did, of course, in the decades after its independence. But bureaucratic culture, including some vestiges of "apartheid urban management," have clearly persisted in South Africa. It may be that a coalition of the willing, inside and outside government as in San Francisco, can find a way to outgrow the bureaucratic blinders and avoid a costly impasse with angry grassroots groups, especially in the poor townships and informal settlements where most of the country's disadvantaged children and their families live.

Second, organizational forms and political strategies are much more varied in Cape Town than in San Francisco, which is both good and bad from a civic capacity standpoint. On the community development front, the Federation of the Urban Poor, a membership organization, represents the leading embodiment of what Appadurai, addressing slum redevelopment in Mumbai, called "the politics of patience" (chapter 5). It is not passive, nor does it naively expect the best of government agencies or businesses—or civil society groups for that matter. But it ultimately views development as hinging on a partnership of government with the wider community and views the latter as an important *coproducer* of change— not just a *stakeholder* in policy making, a *client* for public service entitlements, or an object for "empowerment" by outsiders.

Such pragmatism clearly drives the work of the highly effective Treatment Action Campaign, a membership organization that targets victories for the entire class of people affected by HIV/AIDS and not just its members. TAC has redirected the country's approach to the AIDS crisis. But in Cape Town and other cities, no broadly supported intermediary analogous to the Coleman Advocates in San Francisco has been able to focus civil society advocates and nongovernmental service providers on an agenda of change and a core set of political strategies to serve the neediest children and their families. Only recently has a movement organization in the TAC mold—Abahlali, founded in Durban, with support from international agencies—emerged. It may be the first group in South Africa to create both a broad agenda and a blend of mobilization and litigation strategies to shift the approach to basic housing and community development needs of the poor.

The up side of all this variety and fragmentation is a much wider debate about stakes and best-strategies-for-change than San Francisco, or any other American city for that matter, has seen since the 1960s.

From this standpoint, there is the possibility of broader social transformation. But on the down side, it has become very difficult to organize, or even recognize, broadly shared agendas of change. In this chapter, I set this problem in key nationwide developments but also looked in depth at Cape Town's particularly extreme social and political divides. The civic capacity tests are enormous, and the directive national government still drives so many rules and resources that matter for children and their families. This is a daunting combination.

Third and finally, South Africa's remarkable effort, through the 1996 constitution, to articulate realizable, and not merely aspirational, social and economic rights is relevant to the development and use of civic capacity. And there is a direct parallel here to San Francisco advocates' use of the ballot box to guarantee a level of government spending on young people in the form of the Children's Budget. By locating accountability—pinning down the obligations of government, in particular, more fully—rights are important resources in a world of fluid commitments and disparate expectations about responsibility for public problems.

Rights might indeed prove crucial as safeguards in the South African context. But for that to prove true, several conditions, not yet secured on the community development front in Cape Town or other South African cities, are key. Those who bring legal cases will have to work harder at integrating litigation strategies with broader strategies of mobilization, and the judiciary will need to encourage policy learning, for example on which trade-offs are acceptable when public policy is stymied with competing objectives, resources are tight, and political bargaining may not protect the most disadvantaged. The judiciary will likewise need more enforcement leverage, which could be factored into the design of remedies and ongoing monitoring of their implementation. And finally, those who mobilize civil society, along with their allies, will have to sustain pressure for change inside *and* outside of government—a tall order that the civic capacity perspective clarifies—since judicial mandates have long proven to be such limited tools for resolving complex social problems.

V

Lessons

12

Conclusion

Unless local communal life can be restored, the public cannot adequately resolve its most urgent problem: to find and identify itself. But if it be re-established. . . . it will be alive and flexible as well as stable, responsive to the complex and worldwide scene in which it is enmeshed. While local, it will not be isolated.
—John Dewey, *The Public and Its Problems* (1927, 216)

In the broad sweep of history, the transformation in collective action on local challenges from that rooted in small-town communal life in agrarian societies to the institutionally complex, city-led democracies of today's global age has been remarkably quick. But as I reviewed in chapter 2, so was the emergence of deep disaffection with a model of public problem solving resting on broad mandates from voters linked to "expert" planning, regulation, and service delivery by professionalized bureaucracies. Along with that disaffection came a debate between those who see democracy functioning—in practice, if not in principle—as a contest for influence and those who seek to expand deliberation, broaden our conceptions of self-interest to include collective values and interests, and make us better citizens—as part of a public that thinks of itself as a public—and not just craftier competitors, in the process. Yet many ideas about making democracy work stop at asking the question: how might we improve the relationship between citizens and their government? That is an important question, but I have pursued a broader one: how might we improve the relationships among citizens, government, and private parties (including businesses and unelected interest-group advocates and philanthropies that bring vital resources and capacity) *in relation to important public problems?*

The most pressing problems of our day call for collective learning and bargaining, as well as mechanisms of accountability, that go well beyond the recipe of free and competitive elections through which citizens in democratic societies are supposed to "steer" government. That global influences can make it very challenging for local leaders and institutions to steer change in desired directions does not alter the fact that a wide array of urgent problems—from health and environmental sustainability to education, economic competitiveness, and more—require broad-based community action *with and beyond government*, that is, across the public, private, and nongovernmental sectors. At the same time, too many hopes for making democracy a stronger recipe for solving problems mistake trusting interpersonal bonds, or the usefulness of specific procedures and institutional designs for consensus-building or deliberation (mechanisms or tools), for the more complex and elusive resource of civic capacity. Conversely, some pessimists have concluded—despite scholars' efforts to stress the contrary—that some places are destined to be effectively "civic," and other places not, for all time.

In this chapter, I discuss six major lessons of the study and then return to the broader question of how we define democracy or, more precisely, of what makes particular approaches to collective problem solving worthy of the label "democratic."

Six Lessons

1. History is not a curse: civic capacity is producible, even against the odds, and transformable.

The first lesson of this inquiry is that is possible to construct effective forms of civic capacity, under particular conditions outlined below and at the end of each case chapter, even where history has not endowed a place with a tradition of civic cooperation, trust in public institutions, and a widely shared sense of *being* a public with common concerns and a collective ability to tackle them. Indeed, in communities across the globe, significant and precious forms of civic capacity, including institutional space to name problems and devise better approaches to them, mechanisms for organizing disengaged or disenfranchised stakeholders, and more can be built even where history has not endowed a place with those valuable starting points and "stocks" of social capital. Civic capacity can be built in spite of such deficits, against the odds so to speak.

Yet as I stressed in the introduction, there is everything to confirm, Robert Putnam's (1993, 183) claim that "the civic community has deep historical roots." To cite two brief examples, Envision Utah invoked

Mormon settler roots, not only to help a public define itself vis-à-vis the issue of rapid urban growth but even to remind Utahns of the early commitments that shaped their century-and-a-half history in the American West. In Mumbai, the slum dwellers movement draws on the shared traditions of rural migrants to that megacity and the patterns of cooperation that reflect their shared struggle for survival and livelihood in the city's slums. The effort to redevelop the slums physically, while also developing new civic capacity to make that possible, meanwhile, has inherited the government structures and gradual reforms that followed Indian independence half a century ago, plus the deep reservoir of mistrust slum dwellers have for government, based on decades of abuse, corruption, incompetence, and neglect. But in both places, creative action transformed the limited ingredients of civic capacity into more robust and visible forms that invited wider cooperation and bolder risk taking over time. In those cases and the others, creative action also focused preexisting social capital on specific problems and built new relationships and social capital, across stubborn old divides, in a gradual process of risk sharing, trial-and-error, and confidence building. The lessons that follow offer a partial roadmap to that process.

In sum, history matters, and for a variety of reasons, context indeed structures the effort to build and use civic capacity, but the past is not a curse. We need to learn more about the types of contexts and historical moments in which particular civic approaches, such as politically savvy visioning exercises (the Utah case), ballot box initiatives that trigger new performance commitments by public and nonprofit agencies (the San Francisco case), and pragmatic policy innovation grounded in vibrant social movements and government reform (the India case), can contribute most to civic capacity and to the resolution of important public problems.

2. Civic capacity is important for implementing change, beyond forging and supporting a shared agenda of change, and it need not take the form of a governing regime.

It is not uncommon, especially among agents of change, to associate civic impact with "running the show." But the second lesson of this study is that many demonstrably valuable forms of civic capacity lie between the one extreme of the muscular governing coalition (or local regime), which runs the proverbial show on matters of citywide import, and the other extreme of the innovative but isolated partnership project. The former, the evidence is clear, is particularly difficult to construct or reconstruct as a force for change (Stone 2004), and even revolutions that transform regimes may not produce effective ones. If regimes were the only form of civic capacity, problem solving would indeed be mostly about who has resources rather than who can be resourceful. As for partnerships between organizations, isolated ones function without substantial civic support and thus without much potential for social impact. Partnership projects may be exemplars of collaborative process and the basic unit of coproduction—getting results, not just setting agendas, through joint action—but they often begin, and sometimes endure, as appealing miniatures. They cannot do much without a broader civic strategy, and this is a major reason why social capital on the small scale may not add up to larger change, which inevitably entails confronting conflict, trade-offs, and loss. It is also a reason why so many funder hopes, grounded in a sort of "demonstration theory of social change"—build it small, and if it "works," the political and financial support will come to scale it up—go unrealized.

If, on the other hand, partnerships come to embody broader civic "schemes of cooperation" (Stone 2004), they give major interest groups new options for deploying resources to accomplish purposes of communitywide importance, such as improving the skills of the workforce, modernizing transportation infrastructure, promoting environmentally sustainable development, and more. This kind of hard-won alignment would not appear to transfer directly from one problem to another, though this is not something my study was designed to examine directly and though some of the civic insights, bonds of trust, and institutional mechanisms for nonroutine problem solving certainly could be transferred. Some useful transfer from one problem domain to another may happen inadvertently. Becoming more purposeful about it would require recognizing what, specifically, is worth transferring, why, and how. And sadly, the surplus of elastic buzzwords for collective action—partnership, collaboration, community building, grassroots leadership, and so on—and of pet formulas for pursuing those things does not help us much.

The test of civic capacity, then, is constructing the schemes and mobilizing significant resources—that is, beyond a microlevel transaction between organizations—without necessarily reorienting the dominant governing agenda of a community. Of the cases I examined, the remarkable Alliance in Mumbai, India, with its "politics of patience," captures the robust civic approach to partnering particularly well. But so does the San Francisco children's movement, inside and outside of government, since investing in child well-being has become a politically potent cause without becoming a top citywide agenda item for a governing coalition in that city.

The two core *structures* for building and deploying civic capacity are stable coalitions, not political marriages of convenience, for broad-based support, developed together with pragmatic, implementation-focused alliances. Coalitions authorize things, and alliance or partnership arrangements get them done. It is in this sense that much joint action on community problems remains civic even when it seems mostly operational. Winning a wider commitment to changing "conditions on the ground" hinges on using implementation to enhance one's reputation for being legitimate to act on a problem, capable of engaging a variety of participants and resources over time, and also capable of orchestrating productive activity that gets tangible results. These twin structures help reconcile the two pervasive and sometimes competing logics that I discussed in chapter 2: the logic of *empowerment* (which emphasizes changing political and social relationships and access to influence) and the logic of *efficiency* (which emphasizes securing measurable results).

Except for playing the "palace politics" of narrowly serving political patrons or, more generously, of vetting one's actions with executive and legislative authority figures as part of the politics of public management, traditional bureaucratic approaches to public problem solving divorce legitimacy and support winning from operational effectiveness. This is especially true when insular bureaucracies confront the kinds of public problems I have focused on in this book, where the legitimate authority and the resources required are widely dispersed and not centrally controlled or confined to the machinery of government. Such problems require more complex learning, bargaining, and accountability developed through community stakeholders' evolving participation, as I explore below. The travails of South Africa's confident postapartheid government, led by a dominant political party, illustrate these limits of government-led problem solving especially well. Brazil's democratic transition, which yielded much more political competition and patient institution building at the local level, has taken a very different course. This is a telling contrast since both countries, like many others around the world, embrace the rhetoric of democratic participation and working in partnership.

3. Civil society intermediaries can be vital cultivators and deployers of civic capacity—yet go unrecognized and undervalued.

The third lesson is that an important, largely unrecognized role of non-governmental or civil-society organizations in community life is that of intermediary, broker, or go-between. Most research and commentary on the role of civil society organizations or the "third sector" fail to capture these go-between roles well, focused as they are on interest-group advocacy (including the role of associations that "intermediate" between citizens and government) or service delivery roles. Civic intermediaries compensate in specific ways for a lack of civic capacity because of what government, business, or civil society organizations are not able, or not trusted, to do, and also—along a more temporal dimension—for process breakdowns, such as impasse, polarization, and avoidance, that thwart collective problem solving. The roles of a given intermediary can change dramatically over time, even short periods of time, as a process of significant problem solving unfolds (see table 4.1). Examples of intermediary roles include the following: developing space for informal bargaining or conflict resolution, blending service delivery and policy enforcement (the latter being a role more typical of government), blending and disseminating various types of knowledge (professional and "local" or craft knowledge) to improve decisions and implementation, building constituencies and coalitions for a civic approach rather than a policy position, organizing the disenfranchised to have a voice in decisions and also to coproduce change that is in their interests, and developing adjuncts to formal policy processes to compensate for bureaucratic blinders or political constraints on public officials.

Civic brokers and their fluid interactions with business, government, and civil society were evident in every case, from the philanthropies and the Allegheny Conference in greater Pittsburgh and the constantly evolving Envision Utah to the cross-sector civic forums that, sadly, did not long endure in transition from apartheid to multiracial democracy in Cape Town, South Africa. So were healthy questions about whether such players constitute unaccountable "third-party government."[1] In the cases, I emphasized the electoral processes, rule of law, and other mechanisms that held these groups in check—for example, as influences on agenda setting and implementation—and also emphasized that intermediaries can arise to fill a civic vacuum precisely because electoral politics and professionalized bureaucracies are limited as tools for collective action on big, contested problems. We all know reasons why politicians and public managers alike can become risk averse, turf-minded, blinded by outdated rules and frames of reference, responsive largely to powerful minority interests, and more—even when they sincerely believe they are doing the public's work.

Working to shore up the twin ingredients of legitimacy and productive capacity, often where capacity is outdated and trust is threadbare, the go-betweens are sometimes "interested facilitators." This is significantly different from, and no substitute for, the role of "true neutrals" recommended by advocates of formal, facilitated consensus building or dispute resolution (e.g., Susskind and Cruikshank 1987). That is, some of these actors—SPARC in Mumbai, for example—have interests in specific *outcomes* (unlike professional mediators or other true neutrals), but they invest significant resources—time, money, talent, reputation, and more—in improving decision-making *process* (the classic role of the facilitator), too. That investment in process is an investment in better governance, not just winning a particular outcome. This contributes to community life by bridging otherwise isolated "pockets" of social capital to enable civic cooperation between them.[2]

Even the classic definition of nongovernmental groups as associations that mediate between citizens and government—checking the power of government, enhancing representation, sometimes facilitating deliberation, and so on (Cohen and Rogers 1995; Fung 2003)—fails to capture important dimensions of the go-between role I have in mind. This is not an argument against the performance of those other roles or against the claim that more traditional associations matter to democracy, as observers from Tocqueville to Putnam have argued persuasively. Rather, it is an argument about how we have understood the kinds of value that civil society organizations may create, the range of ways they interact with government and with other nongovernmental organizations, and therefore the range of ways they may contribute to public problem solving.

Cohen and Rogers (1995) have proposed a restructuring of both government and civil society organizations to enable more effective teamwork (in plain terms) at the task of governing, with civil society groups enriching the information that drives decision making and aiding in policy enforcement and other traditionally governmental aspects of implementation. As recapped above, the cases in this book suggest what forms that teamwork can take and do so beyond the realm of economic policy making on which Cohen and Rogers have focused. But we need to know more about the multiple ways that intermediaries are held accountable both for fair play and for "creating public value" (Moore 1995), how they evolve as the roles of other actors also evolve, and what kinds of capacities and networks they survive or thrive on.

4. Combining learning and bargaining is an ongoing, not one-time, requirement, for which formal as well as informal civic space matters.

Another lesson is that building and using civic capacity in democratic societies that disperse power to get things done hinges on developing durable routines and institutions that combine learning and bargaining—not just over the long haul but in nimble mechanisms that let committed players switch back and forth in real time. This is a practical rejoinder to the contending models of democracy—competitive contest or school for producing deliberative citizens focused on the public good—which, taken narrowly, distort what problem solving actually entails.

Many civic prescriptions, which understand "engagement" to be either consensus-oriented partnership and citizen input or adversarial pressure politics, fail to recognize how central this range and nimbleness are. While they rightly emphasize the value of learning and relationship building, hopes for participatory democracy and planning grounded mainly in better, more inclusive dialogue, for example, often downplay or fail to adequately account (1) for the important place of bargaining, which, to many, connotes "adversary" democracy, egos, and myopic outcomes, or (2) for the ways in which learning and bargaining need to be sequenced.

Mumbai's cross-sector effort to develop bold new agreements and cooperative implementation mechanisms for resettling and relocating thousands of slum dwellers—a contentious challenge with huge humanitarian, economic, and environmental implications in many Third World cities—is a case in point. Traditional conceptions of policy advocacy through pressure politics "from below" miss the mark, because official policy making held so little legitimacy in the eyes of slum dwellers and because so many of the fundamentals—the issue agenda, space for dialogue, bargaining stakes and leverage for the urban poor and other stakeholders, and promising practices for getting results—were invented as the players interacted with each other. There was no single instance wherein a multistakeholder "table" of consensus building produced a grand design for problem solving. Multiple decision points, connected by pressing concerns, the institutions that evolved to address them, and informal as well as formal bargaining, defined progress.

The Mumbai case illustrated all three forms of social learning I have addressed in this inquiry, and the other cases reflect at least one of the forms: the *distribution of policy-relevant beliefs*, or beliefs about the problem itself, held by those who act in a particular field or domain (Jenkins-Smith and Sabatier 1993); the *insight into counterparts' interests and values* that is crucial to pragmatic and principled bargaining, as well as evolving innovations in the field of facilitated consensus building (Fisher and Ury 1981; Susskind and Cruikshank 1987, 2006a); and the *assumptions and practices related to how engagement in collective problem solving should happen (assumed rules of the game)*—"transgressive politics," in the terms employed by students of social movements (McAdam, Tarrow, and Tilly 2001).

All three forms are part of "becoming a public," in Dewey's terms. In terms of contributing to public problem solving, learning unveils new definitions of problems, new or once-obscured preferences, and better options for action. Learning can also transform relationships and take civic action well beyond horse trading. But bargaining still matters: both informal, on-the-fly, behind-the-scenes bargaining that authorizes the little steps that big breakthroughs require and formal bargaining over major decisions that call for more structured interactions among parties, formalized commitments, writing things down, and often going public with the outcomes and enforcement mechanisms.

In local civic life, where repeat encounters and not one-time transactions are the rule, several other features of bargaining are particularly important: reputations become a vital, intangible asset, rapidly communicated along local networks; players "trade on the future," linking one bargain to another with promises to do X down the line in exchange for Y today (which adds another dimension of efficiency from the bargaining standpoint but invites resentment about "politicizing" today's agreements, too); and multilevel strategies add complexity and opportunities for civic entrepreneurship. To elaborate on the last point, with constituents "end running" the agents who represent them and vice versa, and with imperfect communication and knowledge at all levels, the agents' authorization to act is fluid and sometimes fragile, and since constituents have incentives to insist their agents "hold tough" to positions they have articulated, the risk of costly impasse is great.[3]

Regardless of the form bargaining takes, without adequate space for it and skill for doing it, civic capacity stops at "assembling resources" and "developing an understanding" (Stone 2001)—that is, without the

means of advancing that understanding in the form of a wisely implemented program of change.

*5.   Multiple forms of accountability are needed to connect "top-
down" and "bottom-up" contributions to public problem solving.*

All the rest is process and plan without meaningful mechanisms of
accountability, but these need to cross the ideological lines that are so
sharply drawn in discussions of how to promote both "democracy"
(defined minimally as inclusive and transparent decision making) and
"development" (defined broadly as economic and social progress). And
there is the problem that relatively few players in any one sector or interest group are accountable for building the *community's* capacity to solve
problems (Stone 2001). Rather, they have more specific duties to their
clients, political constituents, donors, and others (Brown and Moore
2001), and to be fair, a myopic focus on accountability can drive out
learning and innovating (Ebrahim 2005).

But as instances of civic capacity in the making and in use, the cases
in this book show why multiple mechanisms and logics of accountability
matter—they win support from different actors and generate different
kinds of information—and more specifically how they combine over
time. The mechanisms, each with its own logic, include: *pressure politics*,
from voters or from social-movement-type organizations or from elite
ones, which, when constructive, acts as a check on government, business,
or civil-society action (enhancing transparency, spotlighting specific successes and failures, curbing abuse); *informal authorization* (or legitimation) to act, such as that given to nonelected civil society organizations
by constituents (in the form of prestige, money, favors, time), often to
learn and innovate beyond the "delivery" expectations of the moment,[4]
market rules and incentives that exert a different kind of pressure—for
efficient and consistent allocation of resources beyond claims or promises, tapping consumer demand but also highlighting crucial contributions by civil society groups and government that can facilitate economic
transactions (for example by mitigating the risk faced by private lenders
in community development investments) and also project shared community values into those transactions (for example, by certifying to
consumers that products are consistent with their values, such as fair
trade or environmental sustainability); and codified *rights*, which embody
a set of formally authorized, fundamental social standards and, as such,
may delineate a societal obligation to invest significant public resources
or otherwise act to change a social condition.

I have focused on types and sources of accountability more than on mechanisms for generating it, which, beyond transparent elections and markets, include well-structured and "empowered" citizen participation in governance functions usually monopolized by government (Ackerman 2003; Fung 2004); organized civil-society monitoring of the functions performed by public and private organizations (O'Rourke 2004; Weber 2003); publicly disclosed compacts developed among stakeholders (Behn 2001; Brown and Moore 2001; Weber 2003); elections and performance reviews, formal and informal, within member-based civil society organizations (Skocpol 2003; Warren 2001); and more. Whatever the mechanism, observers agree that the model of the professional bureaucrat "insulated" from politics—in any sector, whether public, private, or nongovernmental—is a recipe for disaster. What matters is not the presence of political pressure but the form it takes and the specific ways it influences behavior. The conventional accountability package—the popular vote, together with government-enforced rules for procedural compliance—is inadequate. The issue is how to induce responsiveness, not rule abidance per se.

The need for accountability of several kinds, operating in several directions, is one reason that policy reform "menus" and calls for community-driven development do not spur more change: there is very little here to suggest a simple transfer of decision-making responsibility, resources, or influence (power). There are multiple transfers—up, down, and across—and multiple checks in place. *Accountability can only be meaningfully defined in a system of relationships* (see Ebrahim 2005).

Furthermore, sweeping changes over the past three decades have triggered vital debates about what ideologies and assumptions are shaping our lives in a market-driven, "postwelfare" age. But approaching accountability from the perspective of civic capacity and effective problem solving suggests that each logic of accountability has a role to play if sustainable solutions to public problems are the end goal. None of these logics is merely a fig leaf for ideological takeover.

6. *Broad calls for "participation" aside, either the grassroots or the grasstops can initiate or lead, and the lead can shift over time.*

The final lesson responds to a grand shift, in debates about democracy and public problems over the past generation, toward "bottom-up" approaches. As previewed above, the shift includes a well-founded skepticism about the quality and the legitimacy of solutions proposed by trained experts, higher-status groups, or those with special access to power, such as bureaucratic insiders in government, business, or nongovernmental organizations. But this study suggests a useful distinction between who *initiates* action and who *participates*, in other ways, over time.

In particular places and times, efforts to lead significant change can be either "top-led" or "bottom-led," and both can achieve defensibly democratic results, as long as leaders on either end focus fairly consistently and pragmatically on the other's motivations to achieve purpose. "Bottom-led" slum redevelopment in Mumbai and the "top-led" quality growth movement in Salt Lake City illustrate this contrast. But the "top" was far more important to the former, and the "bottom" to the latter, than appealingly simple labels or stories would suggest. Moreover, as San Francisco's children's movement and the movement to improve the lives of South Africa's urban poor so richly illustrate, the lead role can shift over time without any of the players leaving the ring, so to speak. This question of who is propelling change most at any given moment does not settle the question that motivated my study: whether there are productive routines for getting things done together across the sectors and across levels of decision making and power.

The tension between the bottom and top is central to the evolution of modern planning, policy making and policy analysis, and public management—and of their discontents (Friedmann 1987; Healey 1996). But a great deal of rhetoric and ideology have obscured things, too, as though interests and legitimacy lined up neatly with government-versus-"community," powerful-versus-powerless, us-versus-them, distinctions. We have a rich, international body of commentary on which to build, commentary on "tyranny from below"—highlighting the risk of parochial decision making when control is shifted downward, factions within communities that complicate efforts to understand who is representing what to whom, "ritual" versus meaningful participation, and the gap between developing a legitimate mandate to act (which includes a mandate from "below") and developing the capacity to act on that mandate and get things done (Arnstein 1969; Briggs 2001; Cooke and Kothari 2001; Fung 2004; Piven and Cloward 1977). Yet decades of such critical thinking about bottom-up approaches does not seem to have dimmed or sufficiently enriched a rather unexamined enthusiasm for "community-driven" approaches.

This is not an indictment of the ideal of participatory democracy, participatory planning, or participatory development—related strains of this inclusionary ideal—but rather an observation that too little of the critical reflection seems to diffuse in common practice. We rely on simplistic labels, and we make the same old mistakes, rather than new ones, from context to context. One reason for this, perhaps, is that examples of top-down, exclusionary planning and decision making still abound, distracting us from the need to get more specific about how alternative approaches could function effectively. But worldwide, our problems demand the attention and the continuous learning of policy makers, resource providers, opinion leaders, and other influentials ("grasstops") as well as "grassroots" stakeholders. And many grasstops actors are not political or economic elites in the traditional sense; they are simply well positioned to influence others and to mobilize resources. Surely some of the most important tasks ahead include developing a range of recipes, not one best mousetrap, for mobilizing the roots *and* the tops in ways that enable them to problem-solve together. Effective civic intermediaries, a pragmatic willingness to lead or follow at any given stage of problem solving, and a richer appreciation of accountability's varied and worthy forms all play a role in that.

This is not a dream of easy consensus or inappropriate conformity, of problem solving as getting along well with new ideas in play. Productive conflict and pressure politics can play important roles, such as mobilizing participation, clarifying stakes, and getting more options for action considered, as all of the cases showed. Furthermore, significant transformation includes change that provokes conflict and with it competition. But the need for bridging institutions and routines in diverse and fragmented societies is one reason that go-between roles, as distinct from traditional interest-group advocacy or service delivery, are so important for entrepreneurial civic organizations. This is also why savvy iterations of learning and bargaining, plus multiple forms of accountability that are widely recognized and sustained, are so crucial. Without them, a pluralism of mobilized interest groups leads to a Tower of Babel marked by polarized debate, impasse, domination, and—as a by-product—by disengagement as well, since those who see no payoff to participating have every reason to stay out of politics. But together, the positive ingredients can make democracy a more effective recipe for problem solving. They could also define a new generation of civics education across the life course.

These observations leave unanswered, however, the question of what makes collective problem solving democratic and what the trade offs between core democratic values, such as liberty and equality, and "getting things done" really are. Autocrats, after all, can get certain things done much more efficiently than democrats. And trade-offs must often be faced when the stakes are high, resources are limited, capacity to solve problems is widely dispersed, and indicators of progress are contested.

On Democracy: How *Should* It Work?

In chapter 2, I juxtaposed two very broad notions of how democratic politics can function: as a contest for influence and control of resources or as a deliberative exercise that helps the public define itself, discover shared interests, and explore a better future even in the face of deep disagreement. My focus thus far in the book has been instrumental and empirical: how things *do* work, not how they *should* work. I have briefly addressed the obvious concerns about unelected leaders driving the show and vigorous popular movements threatening deliberation. But in deferring the normative question of should, I did not indicate what tests a process might have to meet in order to be called "democratic" and not merely collectively efficacious in the narrow sense: tackling a social condition, through joint action, in a promising way.

Since dictators can spur collective efforts to clean up the environment, curb runaway urban growth, eradicate disease, get most students in a society to complete secondary school, restructure outdated economies, and "solve" other complex problems, there is obviously nothing in efficacy as to task (alone) that suggests a democratic problem-solving process accomplished it. With such risk of abuse and subterfuge, and there being so many ways for the players in collective problem solving to interpret what is fair, the normative questions cannot be avoided for long.

Yet there are many ways to define democracy, and important debates about what is essential, as opposed to desirable, to the definition rage on (reviews in Held 2006; Shapiro 2003). This is especially true for the kinds of democratic societies profiled in this book, all of which tolerate extreme economic inequality and also show many deeply rooted political inequalities. But as a process recipe, we expect that democracy requires that the people in those problem-solving scenarios above, and not some strongman as master planner, be sovereign. *This means that those with stakes in key decisions have some nontrivial opportunity to influence those decisions* (Cohen and Rogers 1995). Robert Dahl has added that this includes not only "effective participation" in ways that help set agendas and form preferences but "enlightened understanding" and voting equality (Dahl 1989).

Other leading political theorists, drawing on forebears from ancient Athens to eighteenth-century Europe to the modern day, add that *democ-*

racy is a set of arrangements for structuring relationships of power in ways that avoid domination of some groups by others (Shapiro 2003). This is not to say, of course, that everyone can win all the time. But it requires that no one lose out consistently because their interests are systematically excluded or denied—for example, through biased rules or such extreme inequality that many are effectively rendered voiceless and invisible. Representative government has been the core design in liberal democracies, since the late eighteenth century, for meeting these tests, and yet it often falls short.

As David Held (2006, 275) observes, "None of the models of liberal democracy is able to specify adequately the conditions for the possibility of a structure of common political action, on the one hand, and the set of governing institutions capable of regulating the forces which actually shape everyday life, on the other." In other words, the formal models provide neither adequate designs for collective problem solving *as legitimate process* nor adequate means of handling the substantive challenges in our lives—crime, war, economic decline, illness, environmental degradation, and more—so as to produce outcomes that would satisfy us. The extreme inequalities I highlighted above exacerbate both shortcomings.

The tests advocated by respected observers of democracy, not to mention the specific requirement that democracy show tangible results on public problems, become so much trickier when our gaze is focused, as it has been in this book, on efforts with and beyond government. Now citizens are not merely voters forming and expressing preferences—to agents who steer government on their behalf—but experts with distinctive knowledge, association builders promoting particular interests, and sometimes coproducers of change who engage in the operational work— the collective "barn raising"—that change requires, through their behavior as consumers, parents, peer advisers, and so on. Because "joint action" can include so many stages and levels, the key decision makers, decisions, and opportunities for influence multiply exponentially. But so do the opportunities for deception, exclusion, forced impasse, and violations of what we consider fair, democratic rules of engagement. Scholars have highlighted these reasons why a brave new world of governance beyond government make accountability so tricky (e.g., Stoker 2002). Yet we must be able to hope for something better than a massive codex of new procedural rules—the kinds that encourage fair treatment and punish abuse in the sphere of government action—to handle this wider orbit.

At the heart of this, I argue, are two questions: What makes action on public problems *legitimate* in the democratic sense? And since inclusion and the avoidance of domination are surely a part of that legitimacy, must there be *trade offs* between those core democratic values and the instrumental value that motivated this book to begin with: progress on public problems? To address both concisely, I will venture a definition and then briefly derive it:

Democracy is a recipe for structuring the participation of stakeholders in solving problems that confront them collectively in a way that (1) makes significant decisions as accessible and inclusive as possible and (2) avoids patterns of domination, subject to the aim of (3) producing outcomes that are recognized as promoting legitimate interests and values.

Dissecting that paragraph could fill another volume—and indeed has filled many, if we consider the debates on the component parts. But the essentials are straightforward: democracy is a particular recipe for structuring participation in problem solving. As a general matter, that participation is important for getting results, for reasons I discussed in chapter 2: better learning, pragmatic accountability in the form of a truly public mandate to act, and fostering the commitment to act in support of the decisions taken. Participation can have all three of those important effects. But too much participation of the wrong kinds, under ambiguous rules, can have exactly the opposite effects. And pervasive disengagement (nonparticipation) creates its own problems: undermining the legitimacy of public action, thwarting learning, encouraging inequality, and more.

That democracy structures power relations, too, by making significant decisions as accessible and inclusive as possible and also by using various mechanisms to avoid domination (civil liberties, distribution of powers, and so on), only follows from a conception that democracy's task is to enable participation that resolves collective problems by structuring the way stakeholders in those problems relate to each other and the problem before them. This is more specific and more demanding than the classic observation that it is the people, in a democratic society, who invent government to serve them, voluntarily binding each other to it—again, because the definition above envisions a role for a variety of structures of collective action beyond government. Also, by creating cross-checks, the recipe generates some of the very fragmentation of power that makes collective problem solving so difficult. Yet the more democratic a process, the more people will be treated as equals in that process (Dahl 1989; Fung 2006b; Shapiro 2003), which does not require that they play equal or uniform roles or that equal treatment define every stage of an extended process with public stakes. The latter idea is a practical impossibility but also, I think, excessive in principle.

Moreover, judgments about how much inclusion is possible and when, while they may often follow templates (institutional designs) that are replicated from place to place and that persist over time, must suit a place and a time—in the sense of "era"—because problems change, conceptions of success change, and so do social judgments about how to pursue successful outcomes in ways that are fair. Such judgments must be adaptable, or the stakeholders and their representatives will get hung up on procedure—democracy by fixed formula, not democracy as an adaptive recipe—with defenders of the rules winning out over those whose creativity and commitment could make vital contributions to human progress. As Fung (2006b, 2–3) puts it,

Some problems are best solved by experts who do their work largely untethered by tight chains of popular accountability while other issues and contexts call for widespread and empowered citizen engagement. A workable understanding of democracy should account for these two modalities and many others as well. Because our social and political worlds—and the problems in it—are so varied and complex, democrats should resist constructing premature institutional blueprints.

More pointedly, though, the first-order test in my definition, that democracy must enable us to make a collective impact on the state of the world, acts as an appropriate limit on inclusion and even on mechanisms crafted to protect against domination. I am not arguing that some forms of domination are ever acceptable, only that one can thwart democracy's basic purpose—to help us act collectively to improve our lives and not merely protect individual interests or referee among them—with a rigid attachment to well-intended protections. There become too many veto junctures, too many opportunities for parochial interests to undermine vital collective ones.

Finally, it is only in the public square, as deliberative democrats have argued, that we discover which interests and values are legitimate as guides for collective action, which are legitimate but private concerns, and which are illegitimate (uncivil or domineering, threatening to the common good).

There is a long history to many of these ideas. Many scholars have offered and reviewed rich arguments about the risks of tyrannies of the majority or the minority, for example (Shapiro 2003), and how much the effects of particular rules for decision making depend on the nature

Table 12.1
Inclusiveness versus efficacy: Types of governance

Efficacy as to task (public problems)	Inclusiveness in public decision making	
	High	Low
High	**Type 1 Effective democracy** (institutions and norms for prudent collective direction-setting and regular accomplishment of significant public goals, subject to legitimate protections)	**Type 3 Effective autocracy** (institutions and norms for directing centralized public authority to accomplish significant goals, without protection against domination)
Low	**Type 2 Incompetent democracy** (stalled or imprudent collective direction-setting, limited accomplishment of significant goals, subject to legitimate protections).	**Type 4 Incompetent autocracy** (institutions and norms for strong centralization of authority without the means of accomplishing significant public goals, without protection against domination)
	Type 2a Disengaged formalism (minimal participation, pervasive miustrust).	
	Type 2b Activist impasse (scarcity of shared agendas, agreements and schemes of cooperation for implementation)	

of the political community's interests in an issue: Are they largely shared or in conflict (Innes and Booher 2004; Mansbridge 1980)? Furthermore, astute observers are rapidly expanding our understanding of the dimensions along which participation can be structured, particularly in collaborative public management—dimensions such as who participates, via what modes of communication or exchange, and with what scope of authorization to drive action (e.g., Fung 2006c; Held 2006). My modest aim has been to trace out some implications of rethinking democracy as problem solving *for* the essential values of liberty (exercising choice), which demands access and some form of inclusion, and equality, which specifically calls for measures to avoid domination. A major reason to do this, as the cases made plain, is that much effective action that has public consequences is carried out by unelected parties, some of whom bargain, formally or informally, out of the public eye—though not to say out of its reach. But the other reason is that the popular vote has proven to be a limited device in democracies both young and old.

Table 12.1 highlights a set of ideal types to illustrate these points at four extremes (the quadrants). In particular, it is a vision of effective versus ineffective democracy. It recognizes that there can be a trade-off between inclusiveness and effectively accomplishing tasks (Type 2b) or a failure to engage the public in participating enough (Type 2a), but that these challenges can be managed better to create democracies that structure participation to accomplish more in the way of solving public problems (Type 1). There is no roadmap here to particular procedures for enhancing effectiveness, such as devolution of authority to citizen councils or supplementing legislative and agency decision making with ad hoc, facilitated consensus-building groups of stakeholders. There is room for a variety of these innovations if they help a society better meet the multiple tests.

But the table has a broader purpose, too, for it implies that human progress is not only about moving societies from the right to the left of the table, because we value people's sovereignty and their right to key freedoms, but also from Type 2 to Type 1, because we value recipes for collective action insofar as they accomplish things that make our lives better. With cultural diversity and concerns about the unprecedented challenge of the climate crisis on the rise in many communities worldwide, with global forces impinging on our local lives and livelihoods, and with the complexity of public problems ever more apparent, it will be very difficult to sustain or recover civic institutions and habits of community—the sense of consciously being a public, with shared stakes, in Dewey's terms—without such accomplishment. This is the civic capacity imperative, and it is urgent.

Notes

Chapter 1

1. Not all of these are formal, testable hypotheses. I return to this point in the discussion of method later in the chapter.

2. See Giddens 1984 on the broad theory of *structuration*, in which action is structured as well as structure making (or "structuring") over time. For application to collaborative planning as a form of "governance of place," see Healey 2003.

3. Such an outcome focus and explanatory aim would add another key condition for case selection: the need to avoid "selecting on the dependent variable" (Denters and Mossberger 2006; King, Keohane, and Verba 1994; Ragin 1987).

4. Snowballing and other network sampling methods tend to enhance access, which is especially important in research on "hidden populations" or political insiders who tend to refuse cold calling (Goldman 1961). But since it is nonrandom, sampling along referral chains also generates the risk of selection bias. Unless asked to name divergent thinkers, for example, and sometimes even when asked to do so, sources may recommend others who tend to share their views, resources, identities, and more. On compensating for biases, see Erickson 1979; Heckathorn 2002; King, Keohane, and Verba 1994.

5. I made two or three trips to each site, typically getting a range of perspectives on agenda setting and stakes, as well as learning the landscape of players, on the first trip and then conducting the focused, in-depth interviews with a focused selection of key informants on the subsequent trips. Except for Brazil, where I conducted all interviews in Portuguese, most interviews were conducted in English. In India, a translator helped me interview slum dwellers in Marathi.

Chapter 2

1. Stoker (2002, 38) identifies a similar set of factors as "tensions" inherent in contemporary hopes for effective local governance, including how to give legitimacy to leadership, how to ensure wide participation, and "the need to rethink accountability relationships in the context of community leadership."

2. Though beyond my focus here, the role of storytelling and persuasive framing about complex issues is important in democratic life, and it has received growing attention over the past two decades, in the planning, policy analysis, and public management literatures (Moore 1990; Roe 1994; Schön 1979; Schön and Rein 1994; Throgmorton 1996).

3. Behn (2001) provides an in-depth review of the rise of two bureaucratic foci of accountability, with a focus on accounting for *use of the public's money* and *fair use of power*, and later of watchdog authorities, such as inspectors general, who tend to follow what he calls the "accountability bias"—pressure to focus on compliance monitoring over the third focus: *performance* (getting results that the public values).

4. Social capital became a hot idea inside and outside of academia, beginning in the mid-1990s, thanks largely to Robert Putnam's widely cited book, *Making Democracy Work* (1993), which focused on regional differences in associational life and governance outcomes in Italy, and *Bowling Alone* (2000), his encyclopedic analysis of declining civic engagement and its implications in America. Unfortunately, too many treatments of the impact of collective action on public problems have used social capital as a synonym, in effect, for civic capacity, or attacked the useful concept of social capital as though it included an intrinsically antigovernment political agenda: "More community, less government." For review and discussion of these critiques and counterarguments, as well as an intellectual history of the slippery concept, see Foley and Edwards 1999; Woolcock and Narayan 2000; Warren 2001; Briggs 1997, 2004; Portes 1998; Putnam 2000.

5. As Woolcock and Narayan (2000, 239) helpfully summarize, "The challenge is to transform situations where a community's social capital substitutes for weak, hostile, or indifferent formal institutions into ones in which both realms complement one another."

6. "Neighborliness," a particular form of solidarity, captures the disposition beneath the norm of reciprocity, which in turn underlies community self-help (see Kadushin et al. 2005; Putnam 1993).

7. The environmental justice field has likewise highlighted the importance of civil-society organization before, during, and after litigation, formal consensus building, and other common elements of resolving serious environmental problems (Consensus Building Institute 2003).

8. Fifty years ago, an early academic treatment of this idea examined "the local community as an ecology of games" (Long 1958)—a view at odds with the prevailing treatment of community as social cohesion, attachment, or solidarity within groups.

9. An early usage is in the public relations field, see Gabriel 1992.

10. For critical discussion of the politics and institutional roles that help define local community development in the United States, which is replete with civic capacity hopes, gains, and losses, see Halpern 1995, Keyes et al. 1996, and Marwell 2004.

Chapter 3

1. Attacking the claim that urbanization in the developing world is "unprecedented" in its pace, Satterthwaite (2002) notes that rates of urbanization in low- and middle-income nations in 1975–2000 were roughly equal to those in Europe and North America a century earlier. He also warns that much popular depiction of Third World cities assumes, inaccurately that they are growing rapidly everywhere and also lurching toward chaos.

2. Alex Perry, "Bombay's Boom," Time, June 26, 2006. Massive growth in India's stock market, its red-hot IT economy, and the nation's identity as the world's largest democracy have drawn growing attention from Western political leaders, businesspeople, and the press.

Chapter 4

1. Quoted in Kemmis 1990, 69.

2. A multistate region, centered on the Rocky Mountains, that includes Colorado, Idaho, Montana, Nevada, Utah, and Wyoming.

3. Both Utah senators, and two of its three representatives in the House, are small-government Republicans whose voting records receive very high ratings from conservative watchdog groups, and 71 percent of the state's vote went to George W. Bush, the Republican candidate in the 2004 presidential election. In 2005, the American Conservative Union gave House Representatives Bishop and Cannon "perfect scores" (100 percent) and Senators Bennett and Hatch very high ratings (90, 87 respectively). See www.conservative.org. On the history of politics and government in Utah, including Mormon influence, see Campbell 1989, Larson 1989, May 1987, and Peterson 1989. May emphasizes that the state's electoral history is not dominated by any one party, but its post-1960s history reflects America's conservative swing (Poll 1989), a swing that has been particularly pronounced in the Mountain West. On the influence of Mormonism and the Mormon Church, see note 7.

4. Although knowledgeable observers confirmed that the church rarely takes public stands on political issues, historical analysis of LDS and my interview data as well suggest multiple influences of the church on civic life. First, Mormonism is a relatively hierarchical religion, founded on and still governed by appointed "elders" who set policy (Hill 1989; Larson 1989). Its quiet approval of important civic efforts, such as Envision Utah, thus carries weight. Second, it is, in the shorthand of sociology, a "social site" through which civic leaders build and sustain vital informal networks through exchanges and reputations for trustworthiness. Third, it is a large landowner and has faced the real estate development challenges and neighborly responsibilities typical of other large "anchor institutions," such as universities and hospitals.

5. In its first seven years, Envision Utah raised about $7 million, or 80 percent of its cash support, from private, philanthropic foundations and additional support from local government, special congressional appropriations requested

by Senator Bennett, and competitive grants from federal environment and transportation agencies. See Envision Utah, *The History of Envision Utah* (Salt Lake City: Envision Utah 2003).

6. McKinney and Harmon (2004, 19–20) observe that natural resource disputes in the American West frequently involve the invocation of values *as* rights, with competing ideals about private ownership versus the public trust, for example, or about the primacy of economic or consumptive value versus religious, cultural, scientific, aesthetic, and other values. Others have suggested reframing problems to make value conflicts more tractable (e.g., Schön and Rein 1994; cf. Forester 1999).

7. Susan Snyder, "Blame Babies, Not Transplants, for Growth in Utah," *Salt Lake Tribune*, May 11, 1998. The twin notion framing Envision Utah's planning effort—that growth is a given but how to accommodate it is not—has been criticized, in Utah and elsewhere, by some environmentalists, who cite the risk of overpopulation. Knowing that local Mormon tradition favors large families, Envision Utah and its supporters chose not to place on the public agenda the notion of limiting natural increase. Furthermore, in the nineteenth century, the LDS Church directly encouraged Mormon migration to the region, through missionary work and relocation assistance and other means, grounded in the vision of founding an "earthly Kingdom of God" in the Salt Lake basin (Larson 1989). In recent years, the missionary element has led to a rapid growth in non-European immigration to the region, for example by Pacific Islanders.

8. Bob Mims, "Bonneville Shoreline Disappearing, Giving Way to New Homes," *Salt Lake Tribune*, May 18, 1998. And see Linda Fantin, "Workshops Give Utahns Say in How Growth Can Be Managed," *Salt lake Tribune*, May 11, 1998.

9. Snyder 1998.

10. Brandon Loomis, "Wasatch Front May Need to Shrink in Order to Grow," *Salt lake Tribune*, May 17, 1998.

11. Brandon Loomis, "Neighbors Persuade Framington Developer to Enlarge Lots," *Salt Lake Tribune*, August 26, 1998.

12. "Reconsidering Growth," Opinion, *Salt Lake Tribune*, August 30, 1998.

13. Linda Fantin, "Envision Utah Will Debut Four Scenarios for Growth," *Salt Lake Tribune*, September 20, 1998.

14. Contrast Lofgren's observation with Kemmis's (1990, 66–67) recollection of a public hearing on a contested real estate development proposal in small-town Montana: "The rural residents spoke passionately of their property rights and of their undying opposition to the urban arrogance which would presume to limit those rights in any way. The city dwellers who supported the plan spoke just as passionately of the quality of life which was so important to them and of the need they felt for some regulation to protect that quality of life against developments which threatened it. . . . I heard, that evening, almost no expression of that mutual stake in the shape of one another's lives. . . . People in this

situation do not speak of what they have in common or of how the common good might be guarded and enhanced."

15. While systematic research on the civics of long-range regional growth planning and implementation remains oddly rare given the growing popularity of this approach, action-oriented publications by well-respected local and national groups compare various regional visioning efforts and offer key principles for effectively implementing them, including means to broaden constituent support and manage conflict. See, for example, Cartwright and Wilbur (2005). On visioning process generally, see Moore, Longo, and Palmer (1999).

16. Linda Fantin, "Is 'Envision Utah' All Talk?: Some Fear Planning Exercise Will Produce Nothing Concrete," *Salt Lake Tribune*, December 13, 1998.

17. Brandon Loomis, "Envision Utah Feels Suburban Backlash," *Salt Lake Tribune*, January 30, 1999.

18. Brandon Loomis, "Gore's 'Smart Growth' Plan Could Benefit Utah," *Salt Lake Tribune*, January 12, 1999. The federal proposal, and a range of similar proposals by national interest groups, came on the heels of the November 1998 elections, in which over 240 local ballot-box initiatives reflected voter concerns about growth-related issues, including traffic congestion, loss of open space and farmland, and overcrowding in suburban schools.

19. Envision Utah reported that approximately 6,270 filled out the survey online, 11,210 mailed them in, and 2,000 people attended community meetings. Source: *History of Envision Utah*, 38.

20. Brandon Loomis, "Utahns Spurn Sprawl," *Salt Lake Tribune*, March 12, 1999.

21. Envision Utah hired professional survey researchers to construct and analyze the survey, using weighted results to enhance its validity. As I mention briefly in the text, 3 percent is not unusually low for mail-in surveys or combined mail-in and online surveys. Phone surveys and face-to-face interviewing garner higher response rates but are much more costly.

22. Brandon Loomis, "Utah in Spotlight as Congress Ponders Nation's Sprawl Fixation," *Salt Lake Tribune*, March 20, 1999.

23. Brandon Loomis, "Planned Development Takes Look at Sprawl, Open Space and Transit Planning," *Salt Lake Tribune*, March 28, 1999.

24. Brandon Loomis, "New Envision Utah Boss, Jon Huntsman Jr., Sees Growth as State's Most Pressing Issue," *Salt lake Tribune*, April 10, 1999.

25. Utah Foundation, *An Analysis of the Envision Utah Process*, Report 626 (Salt Lake City: Utah Foundation, July/August 1999). The Foundation noted: "Though there is strong support for Envision Utah, there is also strong criticism . . . [We] grouped these criticisms into three general categories: (1) urban planning versus market solutions; (2) flawed data in the analysis of Utah's growth; and (3) bias in the Envision Utah public participation process" (p. 94). The report underscored that urban growth had long occurred in "an already heavily regulated environment" (p. 94) and that the scenarios were "educated guesses backed by a substantial amount of work" (p. 95). As for leading

participants toward a "predetermined" decision, the report found little evidence to support the critics' claim.

26. *Quality Growth Act of 1999* (HB 119). www.utah.gov.

27. "Enact Growth Bills," Opinion, *Salt Lake Tribune*, February 25, 1999.

28. Brandon Loomis, "A New Emphasis at Envision Utah," *Salt Lake Tribune*, June 16, 2001.

29. Paul Foy, "Utah Mining Company Building a New City," *Washington Post*, April 7, 2006.

30. Joe Baird, "Envision Utah Lacking Identity," *Salt Lake Tribune*, May 16, 2003.

31. Kemmis highlights a wider trend toward collaborative stewardship of land in the West, and tracing the history of federal bureaucratic mismanagement alongside nonpartisan local activism, he makes a pointed case for granting Westerners extensive sovereignty, as part of the project of "becoming a public" in a shared place. In *This Sovereign Land* (2001, 232–233), he writes, "If there was a time when national control of most of the West was the most democratic and ecologically sound approach, there is also a time when that approach must give way to a more vital, more human-scale, more grounded form of democracy . . . and now the Rocky Mountain West, for reasons largely beyond itself, may finally be prepared to help recall the nation to its deepest democratic roots."

Chapter 5

1. See, for example, "The Tiger in Front: A Survey of India and China," *The Economist*, March 5, 2005; "India's Shining Hopes: A Survey of India," *The Economist*, February 21, 2004.

2. See "India: The Next Wave," *The Economist*, December 17, 2005; Amy Waldman, "In Today's India, Status Comes with Four Wheels," "India Accelerating" series, *New York Times*, December 5, 2005; and Alex Perry, "Bombay's Boom," *Time*, June 26, 2006.

3. Bombay First and McKinsey and Company, *Vision Mumbai: Transforming Mumbai into a World-Class City* (Mumbai: Bombay First and McKinsey and Company, 2003). See also "Mumbai Urban Renewal Business Plan," Draft aide-mémoire, World Bank mission, March 22–28, 2005.

4. "Inside the Slums," *The Economist*, January 27, 2005.

5. As noted later in the chapter, government was initially unwilling and is still, to some extent, unable, to generate reliable population estimates and maps of urban slums—a circumstance that the Alliance has creatively exploited with its trademark enumeration and mapping. The figure of one-half is the best estimate across a range of sources, including demographic specialists based in the region. See, for example, D. P. Singh, "Slum Population in Mumbai," Indian Institute of Population Sciences, *ENVIS Bulletin* 3(1), Mumbai, March 2006.

6. The U.S. media has compared the scale of India's massive national investments in roadway expansion and upgrading to Britain's landmark construction of railways across the subcontinent in the nineteenth century. "Mile by mile," writes one reporter, "India is struggling to modernize its highway system, and in the process, itself." Better roads lower shipping costs and also make it easier for migrants to reach cities, accelerating the process of change. See Amy Waldman, "Mile by Mile, India Paves a Way to Its Future," *New York Times*, December 4, 2005.

7. Sanjay Sharma, "Task Force Urges CR to Break Stalemate with Encroachers," *The Times of India*, February 5, 1998.

8. Amy Waldman, "All Roads Lead to Cities, Transforming India," *New York Times*, December 7, 2005.

9. Radha Rajadhyaksha, "All I Want Is a Room Somewhere," *The Times of India*, September 5, 1999.

10. For a detailed history, see Mukhija (2003).

11. See Appadurai 2001 and SPARC, "Enumeration as a Toll for Mobilization," (Mumbai: SPARC, no date). www.sparcindia.org.

12. See Charities Aid Foundation, *Dimensions of the Voluntary Sector in India* (New Delhi: Charities Aid Foundation, 2000); Appadurai 2001; Patel, d'Cruz, and Burra 2002; Mukhija 2003.

13. This tension appears to be "rediscovered" from time to time in community development work (broadly defined) around the world. Analyzing America's Community Action Program in the 1960s, for example, Marris and Rein (1967) treated this tension as a core dilemma of social reform. A decade later, also in the United States, Berndt (1977) attacked "community" development corporations as out-of-touch bureaucrats with little accountability to their base ("new rulers in the ghetto"). Chaskin (2005) observed the tension in the philanthropically funded "community-building" initiatives that multiplied in a variety of American cities in the 1990s. And Sanyal (1994) provides indirect analysis of the same problem when he notes that some nongovernmental organizations active in developing countries have been inappropriately treated, by aid donors and others, as poor people's organizations—when in fact they are staff-dominated, or dominated by elites on their board, and lack such accountability.

14. The corresponding 73rd Amendment gave new powers to local assemblies in rural areas. Democratic decentralization in rural India, and in particular the village-level *panchayat* assemblies, have received considerable scholarly attention worldwide in recent years. See, for example, Isaac and Heller 2003.

15. Because these groups are identified on a government schedule, they are commonly referred to as "scheduled castes and tribes."

16. Tracking and cultivating local democracy and governance reforms triggered by the 74th amendment has been a major project of the Institute of Social Sciences, New Delhi. Those reforms, along with participatory development and governance more broadly, define the work of Participatory Research in Asia

(PRIA). LogoLink, a global network based at the University of Sussex, links PRIA to similar institutions in Latin America and Africa.

17. Shiv Sena formed a governing coalition with the Bharatiya Janata Party (BJP). For media commentary on the sequence of housing schemes, see Nauzer Bharucha, "Government's Slum Policy Ineffective—Experts," *The Times of India*, April 1, 2002.

18. Based on a review of *The Times of India*, the English-language newspaper favored by the city's middle and upper classes, from 1997 forward, as well as interviews with government insiders and third-party sources, including World Bank staff.

19. This section draws on my interviews, as well as a SPARC report. See Sundar Burra, *Resettlement and Rehabilitation of the Urban Poor: The Story of Kanjur Marg* (Mumbai: SPARC, no date) and Cheryl Young, "Shaping Their Own Destinies: Railway Slum Resettlement Negotiations in Mumbai," unpublished student paper, John F. Kennedy School of Government, Harvard University, November 2004. See also World Bank reports, *Mumbai Urban Transportation Project: Environmental Impact Assessment* (Washington, DC: World Bank, 2002) and *Inspection Panel Progress Report* (Washington, DC: World Bank, 2007).

20. On the role of career cycles, volunteers who "cross over," shared board members, and other sources of *interlock* (in the shorthand of network analysis), see Keyes et al. 1996, which analyzes the forms and consequences of social capital in a local community-development system—or "institutional support networks"—made up of government, business, and nongovernmental organizations that back nonprofit housing sponsors tied to a community base.

21. The Bank developed the policy after harsh criticism of its approach to major infrastructure projects, such as dams, and the accompanying displacement of "project-affected persons." See World Bank, *Involuntary Resettlement Sourcebook* (Washington, DC: World Bank, 2004).

22. Young 2004 (see note 19).

23. Anil Singh and Nauzer Bharucha, "Rehab Schemes Have Low-Rises Looking Up," *The Times of India*, March 25, 2002.

24. "Financing Slum Rehabilitation in Mumbai: A Nonprofit Caught in the Middle," Case Program, John F. Kennedy School of Government, Harvard University, Cambridge, Massachusetts, 2003.

25. Bharucha 2002 (see note 17).

26. The Government of Maharashtra's (GOM's) response to Vision Mumbai included a planned Citizen Action Group, for example, but failed to specify its role clearly or define firm timelines for establishing the body. See GOM, *Transforming Mumbai into a World-Class City: First Report of the Chief Minister's Task Force* (Mumbai: GOM, 2004).

27. See, for example, "How Mumbai Is Being Shanghaied," Editorial, *The Times of India*, October 13, 2004.

28. "India's Horror," *The Economist*, July 15, 2006.

Chapter 6

1. In a review of research on the politics of local economic development, Wolman and Spitzley (1996) observe that the term *economic development* is frequently left undefined in the literature or is treated as generating business activity (which may be redistributive). Drawing on multiple sources, they distinguish development that fosters activity from growth more specifically (which grows the value "pie"). For reasons stated in text, I rely on another distinction, between growth-oriented strategies (anywhere) and the range of challenges and opportunities associated with *restructuring* specifically—that is, transformation from an old competitive base to a new one.

2. Using the understated shorthand of economics, Giarratani and Houston (1989, 555) conclude that the benefits alleged to accrue from development projects "may well contain substantial, upwardly-biased errors." The authors emphasize that the mismatch between mobile financial capital and immobile political authority may force public-sector officials to enroll private support "at a high price in terms of public subsidy." Scholars have also used principal-agent theory to analyze this behavior: firms seek windfall benefits (rents), and public agents (elected officials) have their own interests to look after, leading to collusion between firms and agents and a corresponding loss for the political principals (voters).

3. Austin (2000) considers degree of integration in the business-nonprofit alliances, while Kanter (1994) offers some attention to this in the context of business-to-business alliances.

4. An important, newer body of work focuses on the evolution of strategy—that is, according to game dynamics (review in Axelrod 1997). In addition, fruitful efforts to integrate game theory and cognitive psychology have produced much more realistic assessments of how human actors process information and come to decisions—beyond the image of perfectly rational, flawless information processors who are unencumbered by past losses (the decision makers of classic game theory). One result is the field of behavioral economics.

Chapter 7

1. Steve Massey, " 'Outside' CEOs Arrive," *Pittsburgh Post-Gazette*, August 1, 1993.

2. Tom Barnes, "County Sales Tax May Be Seven Percent by July," *Pittsburgh Post-Gazette*, February 23, 1994.

3. Steve Massey, "Reviving Region's Economy," *Pittsburgh Post-Gazette*, November 7, 1993.

4. Massey 1993.

5. Steve Massey, "Developing a Unified Approach: New Regional Alliance to Coordinate Work of Four Agencies," *Pittsburgh Post-Gazette*, November 8, 1995.

6. Clarke Thomas, "Untangling the Global Thing," *Pittsburgh Post-Gazette*, December 6, 1995.

7. Henry Stoffer, "Group Takes Regional Agenda to Washington," *Pittsburgh Post-Gazette*, June 30, 1993.

8. Dennis Roddy, "A Tax Drive That Upended Politics," *Pittsburgh Post-Gazette*, November 6, 1997.

9. Tom Barnes, "Growth Alliance Unites 10 Counties," *Pittsburgh Post-Gazette*, April 9, 1998.

10. "Working Smart: The Allegheny Conference Retools for the Future," editorial, *Pittsburgh Post-Gazette*, December 27, 2002.

11. Corilyn Shropshire, "Then . . . and Now: The Allegheny Conference Public Policy Group Grows in Diversity," *Pittsburgh Post-Gazette*, November 11, 2004.

12. Steve Massey, "100-Day Plan Spells Out Steps to Rev Up Region's Economy," *Pittsburgh Post-Gazette*, November 18, 1994.

13. Massey 1994.

14. Steve Massey, "In Search of a New Pittsburgh, Leaders Gear Up to Push for Jobs," *Pittsburgh Post-Gazette*, April 13, 1995.

15. Corilyn Shropshire, "CMU Says Researchers Spawned Record Number of Start-Ups in '06," *Pittsburgh Post-Gazette*, August 17, 2006; Harold Miller, "Job Creation in the Pittsburgh Region" (Pittsburgh: Pittsburgh's Future, 2006), www.pittsburghfuture.com.

16. Robert Lowe, Center for Technology Transfer, Carnegie Mellon University, personal communication May 2, 2006.

17. Carey Durkin Treado, "The Pittsburgh Cluster of Suppliers to the Steel Industry," *Pittsburgh Economic Quarterly* (Pittsburgh: University of Pittsburgh, June 2005).

18. The government-can-invest-smarter message was covered in all major media markets in the state. See, for example, Ed Blazina, "State Development Spending Driving Migration from City," *Pittsburgh Post-Gazette*, December 7, 2003; "Think Tank Gives Us a Stern Talking To," editorial, *Philadelphia Inquirer*, December 7, 2003.

19. And see Myron Orfield, *Pittsburgh Metropolitics: A Regional Agenda for Community and Stability* (Pittsburgh: Heinz Endowments, 1999).

20. Stephanie Strom, "Private Groups in Pittsburgh Halt Millions in School Aid," *New York Times*, July 16, 2002; also see Carmen J. Lee and Jane Elizabeth, "Foundations Yank City School Grants," *Pittsburgh Post-Gazette*, July 10, 2002).

21. Court Gould, "A Plea for Regional Leadership: The Southwestern Pennsylvania Commission Must Change Its Focus," *Pittsburgh Post-Gazette*, October 11, 2000.

22. See Robert Lurcott, *Regional Visioning Public Participation: Best Practices* (Pittsburgh: Sustainable Pittsburgh, 2005).

23. Insiders emphasize that fledging earlier attempts to create an umbrella institution lacked the financing and staffing to be viable—that is, beyond ad hoc mobilization. On the historical absence of a coordinating and bargaining mechanism to represent the nonprofit sector, see Sbragia 1990.

24. *Community Threads: The Nonprofit Sector of Southwestern Pennsylvania, Leading the Region's Next Renaissance* (Pittsburgh: Forbes Funds and Pittsburgh Foundation, 2006).

25. On the multiple important roles of state government, see Jennifer Vey, *Restoring Prosperity: The State Role in Revitalizing America's Older Industrial Cities* (Washington, DC: Brookings Institution, 2007).

Chapter 8

1. Barry Bearak, "Poor Man's Burden," *New York Times Magazine*, June 27, 2004.

2. Larry Rohter, "Brazil's Presidential Election Reflects the Power of São Paulo," *New York Times*, October 20, 2002.

3. Yet few rigorous studies of the impact of state or local economic development programs have yet been conducted in Brazil (Barberia and Biderman 2006).

4. On the evolution of participatory institutions, see Baiocchi 2003a, 2003b, for an overview. Also see Spink, Bava, and Paulics 2002; Benevides, Vannuchi, and Kerche 2003; Carmo, Carvalho, and Teixeira 2000.

5. "Make or break," In "A Survey of Brazil," *The Economist*, February 22, 2003.

6. "Lula's Midterm Blues," *The Economist*, June 4, 2005.

7. For a detailed history focused on the all-important automotive industry in the region, see Humphrey 1992.

8. This and other translations are mine, from Brazilian Portuguese. This forum, for example, has been described, in several English-language publications, as the "Citizenship Forum" (Boniface 2001) or "Forum on the Issues of Citizenship" (Rodriguez-Posé, Tomaney, and Klink 2001). But in English, *citizenship* generally connotes a legal status vis-à-vis the nation-state, not engaged citizenry or membership in an active civic community. It is these latter themes that that the Greater ABC Forum emphasized—and that the Portuguese word *cidadania* encompasses.

9. Though the state and federal police concluded their investigations in 2002 and charged several young men with the murder, state prosecutors pursued their own, lengthier investigation, with one indictment returned, as of September 2006, and no one convicted of the crime. Those prosecutors suspected that Daniel knew of a multimillion-dollar fund, based on kickbacks, to finance Workers' Party campaigns. Daniel's family has accused high-ranking members of the party of involvement in the crime and/or cover-up. See Larry Rohter, "Corruption Accusations Rise from Brazil Mayor's Death," *New York Times*,

February 1, 2004; "Testemunha do caso Celso Daniel complica ainda mais situa-ção de Sombra," *Folha de São Paulo*, September 6, 2006.

10. Câmara ABC, *A Região Encontra Soluções: Planejamento Regional Estratégico* (Santo André, Brazil: Câmara ABC, 2000).

11. Pressures center on the ongoing struggle to make the region's old auto assembly plants competitive as demand fluctuates in the domestic and international markets for autos. See Patrícia Zimmerman and Andreza Matais, "Dilma diz que 'não vê com bons olhos' fechamento da Volks no ABC," *Folha de São Paulo*, August 30, 2006.

12. Leone Farias, "Polietilenos União cresce em tamanho e produção," *Diário do Grande ABC*, September 7, 2006.

13. Agência de Desenvolvimento Econômico Grande ABC, *A Atividade Econômica nos Anos 90 no Grande ABC: Cadernos de Pesquisa* 2, 3, and 4, (Santo André: Agência de Desenvolvimento Econômico Grande ABC, 2000, 2001, 2002).

14. The regional daily, *Diário do Grande ABC*, covered many of these developments, from the technical aspects of environmental risks to institutional conflicts and civil society dynamics. See, for example, Márcia Pinna Raspanti, "Mauá discute termelétrica nesta quarta," February 13, 2001; "Santo André cria comissão para acompanhar instalação de termelétrica," March 29, 2001. I am grateful to Ana Cristina Martes for her generous insights into this case.

Chapter 9

1. The saying has been attributed to West Africa. Among scholars, the benefits of collective approaches to childrearing were central to sociologist James Coleman's (1988) influential theoretical work on the meanings and value of social capital in urban environments. Likewise, Sampson, Raudenbush, and Earls (1997) develop a construct for measuring social capital as "goal-oriented" collective efficacy, which I outlined in chapter 1, specifically in terms of its childrearing benefits.

2. Major philanthropic efforts in America have adopted this movement-building frame. See, for example, the Annie E. Casey Foundation's Making Connections initiative.

Chapter 10

1. Quoted in DeLeon 1992, 2.

2. Gabriel Metcalfe, "Open Letter to the Left," San Francisco Planning and Urban Research Association, February 1, 2003.

3. Gabriel Metcalfe, "Democracy and Planning," San Francisco Planning and Urban Research Association, July 1, 2003.

4. Coleman Advocates for Children and Youth, *Families Struggling to Stay: Why Families Are Leaving San Francisco and What Can Be Done* (San Francisco: Coleman Advocates for Children and Youth, March 2006).

5. Bill Wallace and Ann Stone, "State's System for Adoptions Breaking Down," *San Francisco Chronicle*, July 21, 1986.

6. "The Sad State of Our Children," editorial, *San Francisco Chronicle*, February 16, 1989.

7. Jerry Roberts, "S.F. Youth Commission to Be Proposed at Meeting," *San Francisco Chronicle*, June 2, 1987.

8. This section draws on interviews and on the report, *From Sand Boxes to Ballot Boxes: San Francisco's Landmark Campaign to Fund Children's Services* (San Francisco: Margaret Brodkin and Coleman Advocates for Children and Youth, 1994).

9. Thomas J. Keane, "Group Tells Agnos How to Cut Budget and Give Kids More," *San Francisco Chronicle*, February 8, 1989.

10. Susan Sward, "Child Advocacy Groups Gathering in S.F. to Devise Strategy," *San Francisco Chronicle*, October 25, 1990.

11. Jack Viets, "Plan to Protect Services for S.F. Kids," *San Francisco Chronicle*, April 20, 1991.

12. Ellen Goodman, "A Ballot Experiment On Behalf of Kids," *San Francisco Chronicle*, October 22, 1991.

13. Elaine Herscher, "Proposition J Would Aid S.F. Children," *San Francisco Chronicle*, October 31, 1991.

14. *The Children's Amendment: Issues and Problems in Year 1, A Report to Mayor Jordan* (San Francisco: Coleman Advocates for Children and Youth, December 1992).

15. Lance Williams and Chuck Finnie, "Mayor's Patronage Army, Brown Fattens Payroll with Loyalists, Colleagues, Friends," *San Francisco Chronicle*, April 30, 2001.

16. Karen Walker and Amy J. A. Arbreton with the Stanford School of Education Research Team, *After-School Pursuits: An Examination of Outcomes in the San Francisco Beacon Initiative* (Philadelphia: Public/Private Ventures, March 2004).

17. See evaluation report, *Youth Voices Inspiring Change* (San Francisco: Department of Children, Youth, and Families, July 2001).

18. *San Francisco Chronicle*, editorial, October 9, 2000. The effort included 800 questionnaires of parents, staff, and youth, 35 structured site visits, and 33 focus groups. The youth participated in designing the instruments, collecting the data, and analyzing it as well.

19. Data not shown, provided by Richard DeLeon, who has studied election returns closely in San Francisco over many cycles (see DeLeon 1992, 2002).

20. The same criticism was made of San Francisco's allocation of funds under the federal Empowerment Zones/Enterprise Communities program in the 1990s. Researchers reported little scrutiny of programs run by well-established, well-connected nonprofit agencies. See Richard DeLeon and Lisel Bash, *San Francisco EZ/EC Interim Outcomes Assessment, Quarterly Report July 1999*, prepared for Abt Associates (Cambridge, MA, February 2000).

21. Rachel Gordon, "Mayor Names Kids' Advocate to Run Department on Youth, Brodkin Gives Up Activist Role to Become an Insider," *San Francisco Chronicle*, September 14, 2004.

Chapter 11

1. John Donnelly, "Joy, Worry in South Africa Housing Spree," *Boston Globe*, April 12, 2004.

2. Southern Africa Labor Development Research Unit, *Khayelitsha/Mitchell's Plain Survey 2000* (Cape Town: University of Cape Town, 2003). Also see Helmo Preuss, "52 Percent of Youth Unemployed," iAfrica.com, November 18, 2005.

3. "A Man of Two Faces," *The Economist*, February 22, 2005. A detailed look at the political culture of South Africa's ruling party is beyond my scope, but for a critical discussion of its historical roots, see Marx 2002.

4. Via the Local Government: Municipal Systems Act, signed into law in November 2000 (see Wilkinson 2004).

5. Other civil society analysts emphasize the divide between highly organized civil society organizations on the one hand (whether NGOs dominated by professionals or CBOs with stronger grassroots ties to the poor) and the thousands of informal community groups, with the least funding and capacity and yet the strongest focus on the disadvantaged, on the other (Swilling and Russell 2002).

6. Donwald Pressly, "Housing Needs Fast-Tracking," *Sunday Times,* February 15, 2007.

7. Government of South Africa, *Breaking New Ground* (Pretoria: Department of Housing, 2004).

8. For a review of the South African debates vis-à-vis a global discourse on good governance at the local level, see Pieterse 2002b.

9. Ministry for Provincial Affairs and Constitutional Development, *White Paper on Local Government* (Pretoria: Ministry for Provincial Affairs and Constitutional Development, 1998, 27), cited in Wilkinson 2004, 216–217.

10. See Parnell and Pieterse2002, for example, for both prospective assessments (institutions in flux) and studies of operating planning and development institutions. Also see Bond 2000; Beall, Crankshaw, and Parnell 2002; Boraine et al. 2006; Heller 2001; Wilkinson 2004; Watson 2002]. This section also draws on a variety of interviews with public officials, planning consultants, civil society activists, journalists, and researchers in Cape Town and Johannesburg.

11. For a concise overview of the transition from provisional to permanent structures (1993–2000), the nature of those structures, and the variation in practice across cities, see Pieterse's (2002a) account of the effort to establish effective metropolitan governance in Cape Town.

12. These complaints are especially evident for the most carefully studied mechanisms of postapartheid local planning and management: the (home-grown) five-year *Integrated Development Plans* (IDPs), which were implemented nationwide (Boraine et al. 2006; Harrison 2006; Wilkinson 2004), and the growth-driven, twenty-year *City Development Strategies* (CDS), one of several large-scale, institutionally complex planning efforts in Cape Town (Pieterse 2002a) and Johannesburg in the late 1990s and early 2000s, patterned after long-range strategic planning in Barcelona, Toronto, and other cities and encouraged by the World Bank and international consulting firms (Parnell and Robinson 2006). But there is more to the alphabet soup of South African local-governance reforms, as these authors recount: a Metropolitan Spatial Development Framework (MSDF), Urban Development Framework (UDF), Urban Renewal Strategy, and more.

13. See Wisani wa ka Ngobeni and Dumisane Lubisi, "ANC Ministers for Sale," *Sunday Times*, February 18, 2007; "ANC Has Lost the Plot, Says DA," *Sunday Times*, November 20, 2006.

14. Mcebisi Skwatsha, "Zille Needs to Be Mayor of Entire Cape Town, Not Just a DA Enclave," op-ed, *Sunday Times*, October 29, 2006.

15. The 210-member city council reports to a 28-member executive council, which is managed by an executive mayor (elected by the council) and city manager. Half of the large council is elected directly by the voters, through a system of 105 sublocal wards, and half by party-list proportional representation. Each ward also elects a ward councilor, who has no decision-making authority.

16. See, for example, Babalo Ndezne, "High Court Overturns 'Illegal' City Bid to Remove Homeless," *Cape Times*, June 16, 2005; Thulani Magazi, "Anger over Empty Crossroad Houses," *Independent Newspapers*, date unknown; Ashley Smith, "And the Gateway Houses will go to . . .," *Cape Argus*, March 22, 2005; Vusumuzi ka Nzapheza, "N2 Gateway Tainted with Grafts, Sisulu Told," *Cape Times*, October 30, 2006.

17. Bobby Jordan, "Anger as Only 11 Make First Cut for State Housing," *Sunday Times*, February 21, 2007.

18. Republic of South Africa, *The Constitution of the Republic of South Africa, 1996* (Act No.108 of 1996).

19. For details on the case content and precipitating context, see Schneider and Ignatieff 2001 as well as Huchzermeyer 2003.

20. Constitutional Court of South Africa, *Grootboom and Others v. Oostenberg Municipality and Others* 2000(3) 277 BCLR (C).

21. *Grootboom*, paragraph 99, cited in Roux 2002, 51.

22. As Judge Albie Sachs (2005, 141) of the Constitutional Court emphasizes, "Bureaucratic authoritarianism was intrinsic to apartheid. People simply did not count as human beings."

23. McLean (2006) highlights the "systemic weakness" entailed in the court requiring the executive branch to merely report on its obligation and planning, notably in the *Rudolph* case that followed *Grootboom*.

Chapter 12

1. Lester Salomon, "The Rise of Third-Party Government," *Washington Post,* June 29, 1980.

2. Sociologists have labeled this feature of social capital *bounded solidarity* in that trust, mutual identification, and other features of solidarity operate most effectively within distinct social boundaries, not across them (Portes 1998).

3. The strategic implications and common outcomes of multilevel bargaining "games" have been best developed in the field of international diplomacy (see Evans, Jacobson, and Putnam 1993; Fisher 1989; also see Raiffa, Richardson, and Metcalfe 2002).

4. On formal versus informal authorization, see Berrien and Winship 1999; Heymann 1987; Johnson, Dowd, and Ridgeway 2006. The latter use experimental evidence from social psychology as well as longitudinal organizational studies of ideas and practices in context to consider how "social facts" come to be validated. They emphasize particularly powerful roles for status beliefs and cultural capital in the reproduction of inequality and inefficiency, as some practices are legitimated and others not.

References

Abers, Rebecca. 2000. *Inventing Local Democracy: Grassroots Politics in Brazil.* Boulder, CO: Lynne Rienner.

Ackerman, John. 2003. Co-Governance for Accountability: Beyond "Exit" and "Voice." *World Development* 32(3):447–463.

Adams, James L. 1979. *Conceptual Blockbusting.* New York: Norton.

Allen, James B. 1989. Religion in Twentieth Century Utah. In *Utah's History*, eds. Richard D. Poll, Thomas G. Alexander, Eugene E. Campbell, and David E. Miller, 609–628. Logan, UT: Utah State University Press.

Altenburg, Tilman, and Jörg Meyer-Stamer. 1999. How to Promote Clusters: Experiences from Latin America. *World Development* 27(9):1693–1713.

Altshuler, Alan. 1965. *The City Planning Process.* Ithaca, NY: Cornell University Press.

———. 1999. The Ideo-logics of Urban Land-Use Politics. In *Dilemmas of Scale in America's Federal Democracy*, ed. Martha Derthick, 189–226. Cambridge: Cambridge University Press.

Altshuler, Alan, and David Luberoff. 2003. *Mega-Projects: The Changing Politics of Urban Public Investment.* Washington, DC: Brookings Institution Press.

Amabile, Theresa. 1996. *Creativity in Context.* Boulder, CO: Westview Press.

Amsden, Alice. 1989. *Asia's Next Giant: South Korea and Late Industrialization.* New York: Oxford University Press.

Anderson, Dean and Linda S. Ackerman Anderson. 2001. *Beyond Change Management.* San Francisco: Jossey-Bass.

Andrews, Clinton J. 2002. *Humble Analysis: The Practice of Joint Fact Finding.* Westport, CT: Praeger.

Appadurai, Arjun. 2001. Deep Democracy. *Environment and Urbanization* 13(2):23–43.

Argyris, Chris. 1985. *Strategy, Change, and Defensive Routines.* Boston: Pittman.

Arnstein, Sherry. 1969. A Ladder of Citizen Participation. *Journal of the American Institute of Planners* 35(4):216–224.

Austin, James. 1998. Business Leadership Lessons from the Cleveland Turnaround. *California Management Review* 41:1–21.

———. 2000. *The Collaboration Challenge*. San Francisco: Jossey-Bass.

Austin, James, and Arthur McCaffrey. 2002. Business Leadership Coalitions and Public-Private Partnerships in American Cities: A Business Perspective on Regime Theory. *Urban Affairs Review* 24(1):35–54.

Axelrod, Robert M. 1984. *The Evolution of Cooperation*. New York: Basic Books.

———. 1997. *The Complexity of Cooperation: Agent-Based Models of Competition and Collaboration*. Princeton, NJ: Princeton University Press.

———. 2004. The Theoretical Foundations of Partnerships for Economic Development. In *Evaluation and Development: The Partnership Dimension*, ed. Andres Liebenthal, Osvaldo Feinstein, and Gregory Ingram, 9–20. New Brunswick, NJ: Transaction.

Baiocchi, Gianpaolo. 2003a. The Long March Through Institutions: Lessons from the PT in Power. In *Radicals in Power: The Workers' Party and Experiments in Urban Democracy in Brazil*, ed. Gianpaolo Baiocchi, 207–226. London: Zed Books.

Baiocchi, Gianpaolo, ed. 2003b. *Radicals in Power: The Workers' Party and Experiments in Urban Democracy in Brazil*. London: Zed Books.

Ballard, Richard, Adam Habib, Imraan Valodia, and Elke Zuern. 2005. Globalization, Marginalization, and Contemporary Social Movements in South Africa. *African Affairs* 104:615–634.

Barber, Benjamin. 1984. *Strong Democracy: Participatory Politics for a New Age*. Berkeley: University of California Press.

Barberia, Lorena, and Ciro Biderman. 2006. Local Economic Development Policy in Brazil: Theory, Evidence, and Implications for Policy. Unpublished paper, Fundação Getulio Vargas, São Paulo, August.

Bardach, Eugene. 1998. *Getting Agencies to Work Together*. Washington, DC: Brookings Institution Press.

Baum, Howell. 1997. *The Organization of Hope: Communities Planning Themselves*. Albany: State University of New York Press.

Baumann, Ted, Joel Boelnick, and Diana Mitlin. 2002. *The Age of Cities and the Organizations of the Urban Poor: The Work of the South African Homeless People's Federation and the People's Dialogue on Land and Shelter*. Working paper 2, Poverty Reduction in Urban Areas Series. London: International Institute for Environment and Development, London.

Baxter, Christie, and Peter Tyler. 2007. Facilitating Enterprising Places: The Role of Intermediaries in the United States and United Kingdom. In *The Economic Geography of Innovation*, ed. Karen R. Polenske, 261–288. Cambridge: Cambridge University Press.

Beall, Jo, Owen Crankshaw, and Susan Parnell. 2002. *Uniting a Divided City: Governance and Social Exclusion in Johannesburg*. London: Earthscan.

Beauregard, Robert A. 1989. Space, Time, and Economic Restructuring. In *Economic Restructuring and Political Response*, ed. Robert A. Beauregard, 209–240. Thousand Oaks, CA: Sage.

Beauregard, Robert A., Paul Lawless, and Sabina Deitrick. 1992. Collaborative Strategies for Reindustrialization: Sheffield and Pittsburgh. *Economic Development Quarterly* 6(4):418–430.

Behn, Robert D. 2001. *Rethinking Democratic Accountability*. Washington, DC: Brookings Institution Press.

Benevides, Maria Victoria, Paulo Vannuchi, and Fábio Kerche, eds. 2003. *Reforma Política e Cidadania*. São Paulo: Instituto Cidadania and Editora Fundação Perseu Abramo.

Berndt, Harry Edward. 1977. *New Rulers in the Ghetto: The Community Development Corporation and Urban Poverty*. Westport, CT: Greenwood.

Berrien, Jenny, and Christopher Winship. 1999. Boston Cops and Black Churches. *Public Interest* 136:52–68.

Bhowmik, Sharit. 2003. National Policy for Street Vendors. *Economic and Political Weekly* 38(16):1543–1546.

Bolan, Richard S. 1969. Community Decision Behavior: The Culture of Planning. *Journal of the American Institute of Planners* 35(5):301–310.

Bond, Patrick. 2000. *Cities of Gold, Townships of Coal*. Trenton, NJ: Africa World Press.

Boniface, Dexter S. 2001. Post-Statist Development Initiatives in Greater "ABC" São Paulo: A Case Study in Innovation. Paper presented at the annual meetings of the Latin American Studies Association, Washington, DC, September 6–8.

———. 2002 Governor's Games: The Emerging Development Model in Brazil. Paper presented at the annual meetings of the Midwest Political Science Association, Chicago, April 24–28.

———. 2003. The Rise of the Pragmatic Left: Brazil in Comparative Perspective. Paper presented at the annual meetings of the Latin American Studies Association, Dallas, TX, March 27–29.

Boraine, Andrew, Owen Crankshaw, Carien Engelbrecht, Graeme Gotz, Sithole Mbanga, Monty Narsoo, and Susan Parnell. 2006. The State of South African Cities a Decade after Democracy. *Urban Studies* 43(2):259–284.

Bowman, James, and William Rehg. 2000. *Deliberative Democracy: Essays on Reason and Politics*. Cambridge, MA: MIT Press.

Briggs, Xavier de Souza. 1997. Social Capital and the Cities: Advice to Change Agents. *National Civic Review* 86(2):111–118.

———. 1998. Doing Democracy Up Close: Culture, Power, and Communication in Community Building. *Journal of Planning Education and Research* 18:1–13.

———. 2001. *The Will and the Way: Local Partnerships, Political Strategy, and the Well-Being of America's Children and Youth*. Faculty Research Working Paper RWP01-050. Cambridge, MA: John F. Kennedy School of Government, Harvard University.

———. 2003a. Community Building. In *Encyclopedia of Community: From the Village to the Virtual World*, ed. Karen Christensen and David Levinson. Thousand Oaks, CA: Sage.

———. 2003b. *Perfect Fit or Shotgun Marriage?: The Power and Pitfalls in Partnerships*. The Community Problem-Solving Project @ MIT, Massachusetts Institute of Technology, Cambridge, MA. *www.community-problem-solving.net*.

———. 2004. Social Capital: Easy Beauty or Meaningful Resource? *Journal of the American Planning Association* 70(2):151–158.

———. 2005. More *Pluribus*, Less *Unum*?: The Changing Geography of Race and Opportunity in America. In *The Geography of Opportunity: Race and Housing Choice in Metropolitan America*, ed. Xavier de Souza Briggs, 17–41. Washington, DC: Brookings Institution Press.

———. 2007. *Networks, Power, and a Dual Agenda: New Lessons and Strategies for Old Community Building Dilemmas*. Working Smarter in Community Development, Massachusetts Institute of Technology, Cambridge, MA. *web.mit. edu/workingsmarter*.

Brookings Institution. 2003. *Back to Prosperity: A Competitive Agenda for Renewing Pennsylvania*. Washington, DC: Brookings Institution.

Brown, Lawrence D. 2006. *Developing Local Infrastructure: The Salience of Muddling Through*. Lessons from the Urban Health Initiative, Occasional Paper Series. Seattle: Urban Health Initiative.

Brown, L. David, and Darcy Ashman. 1999. Social Capital, Mutual Influence, and Social Learning in Intersectoral Problem-Solving in Africa and Asia. In *Organizational Dimensions of Global Change*, ed. David Cooperrider and Jane E. Dutton, 139–167. Thousand Oaks, CA: Sage.

Brown, L. David, and David C. Korten. 1991. Working More Effectively with Nongovernmental Organizations. In *Nongovernmental Organizations and the World Bank*, ed. S. Paul and A. Israel, 44–93. Washington, DC: World Bank.

Brown, L. David, and Mark Moore. 2001. Accountability, Strategy, and International Nongovernmental Organizations. *Nonprofit and Voluntary Sector Quarterly* 30(3):569–587.

Campbell, Eugene E. 1989. Governmental Beginnings. In *Utah's History*, ed. Richard D. Poll, Thomas G. Alexander, Eugene E. Campbell, and David E. Miller, 153–174. Logan: Utah State University Press.

Campbell, Timothy. 2003. *The Quiet Revolution: Decentralization and the Rise of Political Participation in Latin American Cities*. Pittsburgh: University of Pittsburgh Press.

Cardoso, Eliana. 2004. Monetary and Fiscal Reforms. In *Reforming Brazil*, ed. Mauricio Font and Anthony Peter Spanakos, 29–52. New York: Lexington.

Carmo, Maria do, A. A. Carvalho, and Ana Claudia C. Teixeira, eds. 2000. *Conselhos Gestores de Política Públicas*. São Paulo: Polis.

Carpenter, Susan. 1999. Choosing Appropriate Consensus Building Techniques and Strategies. In *The Consensus Building Handbook*, ed. Lawrence Susskind, S. McKearnan, and J. Thomas-Learner, 61–97. Thousand Oaks, CA: Sage.

Cartwright, Suzanne D., and Citoria R. Wilbur. 2005. *Translating a Regional Vision into Action.* Washington, DC: Urban Land Institute.

Carvalho, José Murilo de. 2000. Dreams Come Untrue. *Daedalus* 129(2): 57–82.

Chaskin, Robert J. 2005. Democracy and Bureaucracy in a Community Planning Process. *Journal of Planning Education and Research* 24:408–419.

Chaskin, Robert J., Prudence Brown, Sudhir Venkatesh, and Avis Vidal. 2001. *Building Community Capacity.* New York: Aldine de Gruyter.

Clark, Gordon L. 1989. Pittsburgh in Transition: Consolidation of Prosperity in an Era of Economic Restructuring. In *Economic Restructuring and Political Response,* ed. Robert A. Beauregard, 41–67. Thousand Oaks, CA: Sage.

Cleverley, J. Michael. 1989. The Development of an Urban Pattern. In *Utah's History,* ed. Richard D. Poll, Thomas G. Alexander, Eugene E. Campbell, and David E. Miller, 545–562. Logan: Utah State University Press.

Cohen, Joshua, and Joel Rogers. 1995. *Associations and Democracy.* London: Verso.

Coleman, James S. 1988. Social Capital in the Creation of Human Capital. *American Journal of Sociology* 94 (summer): S95–S120.

———. 1990. Rational Action, Social Networks, and the Emergence of Norms. In *Structures of Power and Constraint,* eds. Craig Calhoun, Marshall W. Meyer, and W. Richard Scott, 91–112. Cambridge: Cambridge University Press.

Consensus Building Institute. 2003. *Using Dispute Resolution Techniques to Address Environmental Justice Concerns: Case Studies.* Washington, DC: Environmental Protection Agency.

Cooke, Bill, and Uma Kothari, eds. 2001. *Participation: The New Tyranny.* London: Zed.

Corburn, Jason. 2005. *Street Science: Community Knowledge and Environmental Justice.* Cambridge, MA: MIT Press.

Cornwall, Andrea, and John Gaventa. 2001. *From Users and Choosers to Makers and Shapers: Repositioning Participation in Social Policy.* Brighton, UK: Institute for Development Studies.

Coser, Lewis. 1956. *The Functions of Social Conflict.* New York: Free Press.

Dahl, Robert A. 1961. *Who Governs?* New Haven, CT: Yale University Press.

———. 1989. *Democracy and Its Critics.* New Haven, CT: Yale University Press.

Daniel, Celso. 2001. Uma Experiência de Desenvolvimento Econômico Local: A Câmara Regional do Grande ABC. In *Competitividade e Desenvolvimento: Atores e Instituições Locais,* ed. Nadya Araujo Guimarães and Scott Martin, 449–468. São Paulo: Editora SENAC.

Davis, Mike. 2006. *Planet of Slums.* New York: Verso.

DeGrove, John M. 2005. *Planning Policy and Politics: Smart Growth and the States.* Cambridge: Lincoln Institute for Land Policy.

Deitrick, Sabina. 1999. Multi-layered Restructuring in an Old Industrial Region: The Pittsburgh Transition. *Great Lakes Geographer* 6(1 and 2):12–28.

DeLeon, Richard Edward. 1992. *Left Coast City: Progressive Politics in San Francisco, 1975–1991.* Lawrence: University Press of Kansas.

———. 2002. *Only in San Francisco?: The City's Political Culture in Comparative Perspective.* Report 411. San Francisco: San Francisco Planning and Urban Research Association.

DeLeon, Richard Edward, and Katherine C. Naff. 2004. Identity Politics and Local Political Culture. *Urban Affairs Review* 39(6):689–719.

Deming, W. Edward. 2000. *Out of the Crisis.* Cambridge, MA: MIT Press.

Denters, Bas, and Karen Mossberger. 2006. Building Blocks for a Methodology for Comparative Urban Political Research. *Urban Affairs Review* 41(4): 550–571.

Desai, Ashwin. 2002. *We Are the Poors: Community Struggles in Post-Apartheid South Africa.* New York: Monthly Review Press.

De Tocqueville, Alexis. [1835] 2004. *Democracy in America*, vol. 1, translated by Arthur Goldhammer. New York: Penguin Putnam.

Deutsch, Morton. 2000. Justice and Conflict. In *The Handbook of Conflict Resolution*, ed. Morton Deutsch and Peter T. Coleman, 43–68. San Francisco: Jossey-Bass.

De Vos, Pierre. 2001. Grootboom, the Right to Access to Housing and Substantive Equality as Contextual Fairness. *South African Journal on Human Rights* 17(2):258–276.

Dewey, John. 1927. *The Public and Its Problems.* New York: H. Holt and Company.

Dykes, Kevin. 2004. New Urban Social Movements in Cape Town and Johannesburg. *Urban Forum* 15(2):162–179.

Ebrahim, Alnoor. 2005. Accountability Myopia: Losing Sight of Organizational Learning. *Nonprofit and Voluntary Sector Quarterly* 34(1):56–87.

Ehrman, John R., and Barbara L. Stinson. 1999. Joint Fact-Finding and the Use of Technical Experts. In *The Consensus Building Handbook*, eds. Lawrence Susskind, S. McKearnan, and J. Thomas-Learner, 375–399. Thousand Oaks, CA: Sage.

Eisenhardt, Kathleen. 2002. Building Theory from Case Study Research. In *The Qualitative Researcher's Companion*, eds. A. Michael Huberman and Matthew B. Miles, 5–35. Thousand Oaks, CA: Sage.

Eisenhardt, Kathleen, Jean Kahwajy, and L. J. Bourgeois III. 1997. How Management Teams Can Have a Good Fight." *Harvard Business Review* 75(4):77–87.

Elazar, Daniel. 1966. *American Federalism: A View from the States.* New York: Crowell.

Envision Utah. no date. *The History of Envision Utah.* Salt Lake City: Envision Utah.

Erickson, Bonnie H. 1979. Some Problems of Inference from Chain Data. *Sociological Methodology* 10:276–302.

Evans, Peter. 1995. *Embedded Autonomy: States and Industrial Transformation.* Princeton, NJ: Princeton University Press.

———. 1996 Government Action, Social Capital, and Development: Reviewing the Evidence on Synergy. *World Development* 24(6):1119–1132.

Evans, Peter, Harold K. Jacobson, and Robert D. Putnam, eds. 1993. *Double-Edged Diplomacy.* Berkeley: University of California Press.

Fainstein, Susan S. 2000. New Directions in Planning Theory. *Urban Affairs Review* 35(4):451–478.

Fainstein, Susan S., and Norman I. Fainstein. 1979. New Debates in Urban Planning: The Impact of Marxist Theory in the United States. *International Journal of Urban and Regional Research* 3:381–403.

———. 1989. Technology, the New International Division of Labor, and Location: Continuities and Disjunctures. In *Economic Restructuring and Political Response*, ed. Robert A. Beauregard, 17–39. Thousand Oaks, CA: Sage.

Fainstein, Susan S., Norman I. Fainstein, Richard Child Hill, Dennis R. Judd, and Michael Peter Smith. 1983. *Restructuring the City: The Political Economy of Urban Development.* New York: Longman.

Fainstein, Susan S., and Clifford Hirst. 1995. Urban Social Movements. In *Theories of Urban Politics*, ed. David Judge, Gerry Stoker, and Harold Wolman, 181–204. Thousand Oaks, CA: Sage.

Fisher, Roger. 1989. Negotiating Inside Out. *Negotiation Journal* 5(1):33–41.

Fisher, Roger, and William Ury. 1981. *Getting to Yes: Negotiating Agreement without Giving In.* Boston: Houghton Mifflin.

Fishkin, James. 1991. *Democracy and Deliberation.* New Haven, CT: Yale University Press.

Fishlow, Albert. 2000. Brazil and Economic Realities. *Daedalus* 129(2):339–357.

Flint, Anthony. 2006. *The Land: The Battle over Sprawl and the Future of America.* Baltimore: Johns Hopkins University Press.

Florida, Richard. 2000. *Cities and the Creative Class.* New York: Routledge.

Foley, Michael W., and Bob Edwards. 1999. Is It Time to Disinvest in Social Capital? *Journal of Public Policy* 19(2):199–231.

Forester, John. 1999. Dealing with Deep Value Differences. In *The Consensus Building Handbook*, ed. Lawrence Susskind, S. McKearnan, and J. Thomas-Learner, 463–479. Thousand Oaks, CA: Sage.

Friedmann, John. 1987. *Planning in the Public Domain.* Princeton, NJ: Princeton University Press.

Fulbright-Anderson, Karen, Anne Kubisch, and Pat Auspos. 2003. *Reforming Public Youth Service Systems: Can Youth Employment, Public Education, Child Welfare, and Juvenile Justice Be Improved So That They Do a Better Job of*

Promoting Youth Development? Report on the Forum on Reforming Publicly Funded Youth Systems. Aspen Institute Roundtable on Comprehensive Community Initiatives, New York.

Fung, Archon. 2003. Associations and Democracy: Theories, Hopes, and Realities. *Annual Review of Sociology* 29:515–539.

———. 2004. *Empowered Participation.* Princeton, NJ: Princeton University Press.

Fung, Archon. 2006a. Democratizing the Policy Process. In *The Oxford Handbook of Public Policy*, ed. Michael Moran, Martin Rein, and Robert E. Goodin, 667–683. New York: Oxford University Press.

———. 2006b. Pragmatic Democracy. In *Democracy Unbound: Solving Dilemmas of Modern Governance.* Unpublished book manuscript, Harvard University, Cambridge, MA.

———. 2006c. Varieties of Participation in Complex Governance. *Public Administration Review* 66 (December):66–76.

Fung, Archon, and Erik Olin Wright. 2003. Thinking about Empowered Participatory Governance. In *Deepening Democracy*, ed. Archon Fung and Erik Olin Wright, 3–42. New York: Verso.

Furdell, Kimberly, Harold Wolman, and Edward W. Hill. 2005. Did Central Cities Come Back? Which Ones, How Far, and Why? *Journal of Urban Affairs* 27(3):283–305.

Gabriel, Edward M. 1992. The Changing Face of Public Affairs in Washington. *Public Relations Quarterly* 37.

Gamson, William. 1966. Reputations and Resources in Community Politics. *American Journal of Sociology* 72(2):121–131.

Ganz, Marshall. 2000. Resources and Resourcefulness: Strategic Capacity in the Unionization of California Agriculture, 1959–1966. *American Journal of Sociology* 4:1003–1062.

Gardner Center for Youth and Their Communities. 2005. *Coleman Advocates for Children and Youth: Advocating to Institutionalize Children's Rights.* Palo Alto, CA: School of Education, Stanford University.

Gaventa, John. 1980. *Power and Powerlessness.* Urbana: University of Illinois Press.

Gendron, Richard. 2006. Forging Collective Capacity for Urban Redevelopment: Power To, Power Over, or Both? *City & Community* 5(1):5–22.

Giarratani, Frank, and David B. Houston. 1989. Structural Change and Economic Policy in a Declining Metropolitan Region: Implications of the Pittsburgh Experience. *Urban Studies* 26:549–558.

Gibson, James O., G. Thomas Kingsley, and Joseph B. McNeely. 1997. *Community Building: Coming of Age.* Washington, DC: The Urban Institute and Development Training Institute.

Giddens, Anthony. 1984. *The Constitution of Society.* New York: Cambridge University Press.

Giloth, Robert P., and Robert Mier. 1989. Spatial Change and Social Justice: Alternative Economic Development in Chicago. In *Economic Restructuring and Political Response*, ed. Robert A. Beauregard, 181–208. Newbury Park, CA: Sage.

Ginwright, Shawn, and Taj James. 2002. From Assets to Agents of Change: Social Justice, Organizing, and Youth Development. In *New Directions for Youth Development*, ed. Benjamin Kirshner, Jennifer L. O'Donoghue, and Milbrey McLaughlin, 27–46. San Francisco: Jossey-Bass.

Gittell, Ross, and Avis C. Vidal. 1998. *Community Organizing: Social Capital as a Development Strategy*. Thousand Oaks, CA: Sage.

Glaser, Barney. 1998. *Doing Grounded Theory*. Mill Valley, CA: Sociology Press.

Glaser, Barney, and Anselm Strauss. 1967. *The Discovery of Grounded Theory: Strategies for Qualitative Research*. Chicago: Aldine.

Gloppen, Siri. 2005a. Public Interest Litigation, Social Rights, and Social Policy. Paper presented at The World Bank conference, New Frontiers in Social Policy: Development in a Globalizing World, Arusha, Tanzania, December 12–15.

———. 2005b. Social Rights Litigation as Transformation. In *Democratizing Development: The Politics of Socio-Economic Rights in South Africa*, eds. Peris Jones and Kristian Stokke, 153–179. Boston: Martinus Nijhoff.

Goldfrank, Benjamin. 2003. Making Participation Work in Porto Alegre. In *Radicals in Power: The Workers' Party and Experiments in Urban Democracy in Brazil*, ed. Gianpaolo Baiocchi, 27–52. London: Zed Books.

Goldman, Loe A. 1961. Snow-ball Sampling. *Annals of Mathematical Statistics* 32:148–170.

Gomes, Eduardo Rodrigues and Fabrícia C. Guimarães. 2004. Entrepreneurs: The PNBE. In *Reforming Brazil*, ed. Mauricio Font and Anthony Peter Spanakos, 177–194. New York: Lexington.

Granovetter, Mark. 1985. Economic Action and Social Structure: The Problem of Embeddedness. *American Journal of Sociology* 91(3):481–510.

Gray, Barbara. 1989. *Collaborating*. San Francisco: Jossey-Bass.

Grindle, Merilee S. 2004. *Despite the Odds: The Contentious Politics of Education Reform*. Princeton, NJ: Princeton University Press.

———. 2007. *Going Local: Decentralization, Democratization, and the Promise of Good Governance*. Princeton, NJ: Princeton University Press.

Guimarães, Nadya Araujo, Álvaro A. Comin, and Márcia Paula de Leite. 2001. Por um Jogo de Soma Positiva: Conciliando Competitividade e Proteção ao Emprego em Experiências Inovadoras de Negociação no Brasil. In *Competitividade e Desenvolvimento: Atores e Instituições Locais*, ed. Nadya Araujo Guimarães and Scott Martin, 417–448. São Paulo: Editora SENAC.

Guimarães, Nadya Araujo, and Scott Martin. 2001. Decentralização, Equidade, e Desenvolvimento: Atores e Instituições Locais. In *Competitividade e Desenvolvimento: Atores e Instituições Locais*, ed. Nadya Araujo Guimarães and Scott Martin, 13–29. São Paulo: Editora SENAC.

Gumede, William Mervin. 2005. *Thabo Mbeki and the Battle for the Soul of the ANC.* Cape Town: Zebra.

Gutmann, Amy, and Dennis Thompson. 1996. *Democracy and Disagreement.* Cambridge, MA: Harvard University Press.

Habib, Adam. 2005. State–Civil Society Relations in Post-Apartheid South Africa. *Social Research* 72(3):671–692.

Halpern, Robert. 1995. *Rebuilding the Inner City: The History of Neighborhood Initiatives to Address Poverty in the United States.* New York: Columbia University Press.

Hamilton, David K., David Y. Miller, and Jerry Paytas. 2004. Exploring the Horizontal and Vertical Dimensions of the Governing of Metropolitan Regions. *Urban Affairs Review* 40(2):147–182.

Harding, Alan. 1995. Elite Theory and Growth Machines. In *Theories of Urban Politics*, ed. David Judge. Gerry Stoker, and Harold Wolman, 35–53. Thousand Oaks, CA: Sage.

Harrison, Philip. 2006. On the Edge of Reason: Planning and Urban Futures in Africa. *Urban Studies* 43(2):319–335.

Hartman, Chester. 1984. *The Transformation of San Francisco.* Totowa, NY: Rowman and Allanheld.

Healey, Patsy. 1996. The Communicative Turn in Planning Theory and Its Implications for Spatial Strategy Formation. *Environment and Planning B: Planning and Design* 23(2):217–234.

———. 1997. *Collaborative Planning: Shaping Places in Fragmented Societies.* New York: Palgrave Macmillan.

———. 2003. *Collaborative Planning* in Perspective. *Planning Theory* 2(2):101–123.

Heckathorn, Douglas D. 2002. Respondent-Driven Sampling II: Deriving Valid Estimates from Chain-Referral Samples of Hidden Populations. *Social Problems* 49(1):11–34.

Heifetz, Ronald A. 1994. *Leadership without Easy Answers.* Cambridge, MA: Harvard University Press.

Held, David. 2006. *Models of Democracy.* 3rd ed. Stanford, CA: Stanford University Press.

Heller, Patrick. 2001. Moving the State: The Politics of Democratic Decentralization in Kerala, South Africa, and Porto Alegre. *Politics and Society* 29(1):129–162.

———. 2003. Reclaiming Democratic Spaces: Civics and Politics in Post-Transition Johannesburg. In *Emerging Johannesburg*, ed. Richard Tomlinson, Robert Beauregard, Lindsay Bremner, and Xolela Mangcu, 155–184. New York: Routledge.

Henig, Jeffrey. 2002. Equity and the Future Politics of Growth. In *Urban Sprawl: Causes, Consequences, and Policy Responses*, ed. Gregory D. Squires, 325–350. Washington, DC: Urban Institute Press.

Heymann, Philip B. 1987. *The Politics of Public Management*. New Haven, CT: Yale University Press.

Heywood, Mark. 2005. Shaping, Making and Breaking the Law in the Campaign for a National HIV/AIDS Treatment Plan. In *Democratising Development: The Politics of Socio-Economic Rights in South Africa*, ed. Peris Jones and Kristian Stokke, 181–211. Boston: Martinus Nijhoff.

Hill, Marvin S. 1989. The Rise of the Mormon Kingdom of God. In *Utah's History*, ed. Richard D. Poll, Thomas G. Alexander, Eugene E. Campbell, and David E. Miller, 97–112. Logan: Utah State University Press.

Holland, John. 1995. *Hidden Order: How Adaptation Builds Complexity*. Reading, MA: Addison-Wesley.

Huchzermeyer, Marie. 2003. Housing Rights in South Africa: Invasions, Evictions, the Media and the Courts in the Cases of Grootboom, Alexandra, and Bredell. *Urban Forum* 14(1):80–107.

———. 2004. *Unlawful Occupation: Informal Settlements and Urban Policy in South Africa and Brazil*. Trenton, NJ: Africa World Press.

———. 2006. The New Instrument for Upgrading Informal Settlements in South Africa: Contributions and Constraints. In *Informal Settlements: A Perpetual Challenge?*, ed. Marie Huchzermeyer and M. Karam, 43–61. Cape Town: University of Cape Town Press.

Humphrey, John. 1982. *Capitalist Control and Workers' Struggle in the Brazilian Auto Industry*. Princeton, NJ: Princeton University Press.

Humphrey, John, and Hubert Schmitz. 2001. Governance in Global Value Chains. *IDS Bulletin* 32(3):1–14.

Innes, Judith. 1996. Planning through Consensus Building. *Journal of the American Planning Association* 62(4):460–473.

———. 2004. Consensus Building: Clarifications for the Critics. *Planning Theory* 3(1):5–20.

Innes, Judith, and David Booher. 2004. Reframing Public Participation for the Twenty-First Century. *Planning Theory and Practice* 5(4):419–436.

Innes, Judith and Judith Gruber. 1994. *Coordinating Growth and Environmental Management through Consensus Building*. Working paper, California Policy Seminar, Berkeley, CA.

Isaac, Thomas, and Patrick Heller. 2003. Democracy and Development: Decentralized Planning in Kerala. In *Deepening Democracy: Institutional Innovations in Empowered Participatory Governance*, ed. Archon Fung and Erik Olin Wright, 77–110. New York: Verso.

Jenkins-Smith, Hank C., and Paul A. Sabatier. 1993. The Dynamics of Policy-Oriented Learning. In *Policy Change and Learning: An Advocacy Coalition Approach*, ed. Paul A. Sabatier and Hank C. Jenkins-Smith, 41–56. Boulder, CO: Westview Press.

John, DeWitt. 1994. *Civic Environmentalism: Alternatives to Regulation in States and Communities*. Washington, DC: CQ Press.

Johnson, Cathryn, Timothy J. Dowd, and Cecilia Ridgeway. 2006. Legitimacy as a Social Process. *Annual Review of Sociology* 32:53–78.

Jones, Peris, and Kristian Stokke. 2005. Introduction. In *Democratizing Development: The Politics of Socio-Economic Rights in South Africa*, ed. Peris Jones and Kristian Stokke, 1–37. Boston: Martinus Nijhoff.

Judd, Dennis. 2006. The Several Faces of Civic Capacity. *City & Community* 5(1):43–46.

Judge, David. 1995. Pluralism. In *Theories of Urban Politics*, ed. David Judge, Gerry Stoker, and Harold Wolman, 13–34. Thousand Oaks, CA: Sage.

Kadushin, Charles, Mathew Lindholm, Dan Ryan, Archie Brodsky, and Leonard Saxe. 2005. Why Is It So Difficult to Form Effective Community Coalitions? *City & Community* 4(3): 255–275.

Kagan, Sharon Lynn. 1996. Linking Services for Children and Families: Past Legacy, Future Possibilities. In *Children, Families and Government: Preparing for the Twenty-First Century*, ed. Edward F. Zigler, Sharon Lynn Kagan, and Nancy W. Hall, 378–393. Cambridge: Cambridge University Press.

Kanter, Rossabeth Moss. 1994. Collaborative Advantage: The Art of Alliances. *Harvard Business Review* 13:96–108.

Kantor, Paul, H. L. Savitch, and Serena Vicari Haddock. 1997. The Political Economy of Urban Regimes: A Comparative Perspective. *Urban Affairs Review* 32(3):348–377.

Kaplan, Robert S., and David P. Norton. 2000. *The Strategy-Focused Organization*. Boston: Harvard Business School Press.

Katz, Bruce, and Roberto Puentes, eds. 2005. *Taking the High Road: A Metropolitan Agenda for Transportation Reform*. Washington, DC: Brookings Institution Press.

Kearns, Kevin. 1996. *Managing for Accountability: Preserving the Public Trust in Public and Nonprofit Organizations*. San Francisco: Jossey-Bass.

Keck, Margaret. 1992. *The Workers' Party and Democratization in Brazil*. New Haven, CT: Yale University Press.

Kemmis, Daniel. 1990. *Community and the Politics of Place*. Norman: University of Oklahoma Press.

———. 2001. *This Sovereign Land: A New Vision for Governing the West*. Washington, DC: Island Press.

Kerstein, Robert. 1993. Suburban Growth Politics in Hillsborough County: Growth Management and Political Regimes. *Social Science Quarterly* 74(3):615–630.

Kettl, Donald F. 2000. *The Global Public Management Revolution*. Washington, DC: Brookings Institution Press.

Keyes, Langley, Alex Schwartz, Avis C. Vidal, and Rachel Bratt. 1996. Networks and Nonprofits: Opportunities and Challenges in an Era of Devolution. *Housing Policy Debate* 7(2):201–229.

Khan, Firoz, and Peter Cranko. 2002. Municipal-Community Partnerships. In *Democratising Local Government: The South African Experiment*, ed. Susan Parnell, Edgar Pieterse, Mark Swilling, and Dominique Wooldridge, 262–275. Cape Town: University of Cape Town Press.

Khan, Firoz, and Edgar Pieterse. 2006. The Homeless People's Alliance: Purposive Creation and Ambiguated Realities. In *Voices of Protest: Social Movements in Post-Apartheid South Africa*, ed. Richard Ballard, Adam Habib, and Imraan Valodia. Pietermaritzburg: University of Kwazulu-Natal Press.

King, Gary, Robert O. Keohane, and Sidney Verba. 1994. *Designing Social Inquiry: Scientific Inference in Qualitative Research*. Princeton, NJ: Princeton University Press.

Kingdon, John. 1984. *Agendas, Alternatives, and Public Policies*. Boston: Little, Brown.

Kingstone, Peter. 2004. Industrialists and Liberalization. In *Reforming Brazil*, ed. Mauricio Font and Anthony Peter Spanakos, 161–176. New York: Lexington.

Klink, Jeroen Johannes. 2001. *A Cidade-Região: Regionalismo e Reestructuração no Grande ABC Paulista*. Rio de Janeiro: DP&A Editora.

Knoke, David. 1990. *Political Networks*. New York: Cambridge University Press.

Krumholz, Norm. 1999. Equitable Approaches to Local Economic Development. *Policy Studies Journal* 27(1):83–95.

Larson, Gustave O. 1989. The Mormon Gathering. In *Utah's History*, ed. Richard D. Poll, Thomas G. Alexander, Eugene E. Campbell, and David E. Miller, 113–132. Logan: Utah State University Press.

Laws, David, Lawrence Susskind, James Abrams, Jonna Anderson, Ginette Chapman, Emily Rubenstein, and Jaisel Vadgama. 2001. *Public Entrepreneurship Networks*. Cambridge, MA: Environmental Technology and Public Policy Program, Department of Urban Studies and Planning, Massachusetts Institute of Technology.

Leite, Marcia de Paula. 2002. *The Struggle to Develop Regional Industry Policy: The Role of the Plastics and Auto Sectors in the Regional Chamber of ABC, São Paulo*. Working Paper 154. Sussex, England: Institute for Development Studies, University of Sussex, March.

Lemon, Anthony. 2002. The Role of Local Government. In *Democratising Local Government: The South African Experiment*, ed. Susan Parnell, Edgar Pieterse, Mark Swilling, and Dominique Wooldridge, 18–30. Cape Town: University of Cape Town Press.

Letts, Christine, William Ryan, and Allen Grossman. 1999. *High Performance Nonprofit Organizations: Managing Upstream for Greater Impact*. New York: Wiley.

Lipset, Seymour Martin. 1994. The Social Requisites of Democracy Revisited. *American Sociological Review* 59:1–22.

Logan, John R., and Harvey L. Molotch. 1987. *Urban Fortunes: The Political Economy of Place*. Berkeley: University of California Press.

Logan, John R., and Min Zhou. 1989. Do Suburban Growth Controls Control Growth? *American Sociological Review* 54(June):461–471.

Long, Norton. 1958. The Local Community as an Ecology of Games. *American Journal of Sociology* 64(1):251–261.

Lubove, Roy. 1996. *Twentieth Century Pittsburgh*. Pittsburgh: University of Pittsburgh Press.

Lurcott, Robert H., and Jane A. Downing 1987. A Public-Private Support System for Community-Based Organizations in Pittsburgh. *Journal of the American Planning Association* 53:459–468.

Mahoney, James. 1999. Nominal, Ordinal, and Narrative Appraisal in Macro-causal Analysis. *American Journal of Sociology* 104(4):1154–1196.

Mansbridge, Jane. 1980. *Beyond Adversary Democracy*. Chicago: University of Chicago Press.

Marais, Hein. 1998. *South Africa: Limits to Change*. Cape Town: University of Cape Town Press.

March, James, and Johan P. Olsen. 1996. Institutional Perspectives on Political Institutions. *Governance* 9(3):247–264.

Markusen, Ann R. 1989. Industrial Restructuring and Regional Politics. In *Economic Restructuring and Political Response*, ed. Robert A. Beauregard, 115–147. Newbury Park, CA: Sage.

Marris, Peter, and Martin Rein. 1967. *Dilemmas of Social Reform*. New York: Asherton.

Martes, Ana Cristina Braga, and Ronaldo Porto Macedo. 2004. Entrepreneurship and Strategic Cooperation among Companies, Government, and the Community: The Case of the Negotiation for Setting Up a Thermo-Electric Power Generating Plant in Santo André, Brazil. Paper presented at the BALAS Conference, Babson College, Wellesley, Massachusetts, May 19–21.

Martin, Ron, and Peter Sunley. 2002. Deconstructing Clusters: Chaotic Concept or Policy Panacea? *Journal of Economic Geography* 3:5–35.

Martin, Scott B. 1997. Beyond Corporatism: New Patterns of Representation in the Brazilian Auto Industry. In *The New Politics of Inequality in Latin America*, ed. Douglas A. Chalmers, Carlos M. Vilas, Katherin Hite, Scott B. Martin, Kerianne Piester, and Monique Segarra. New York: Oxford University Press.

Marwell, Nicole. 2004. Privatizing the Welfare State: Nonprofit Community-Based Organizations as Political Actors. *American Sociological Review* 69:265–291.

Marx, Christoph. 2002. Ubu and Ubuntu: On the Dialectics of Apartheid and National Building. *Politikon* 29(1):49–69.

May, Dean. 1987. *Utah: A People's History*. Salt Lake City: University of Utah Press.

McAdam, Doug, Sidney Tarrow, and Charles Tilly. 2001. *The Dynamics of Contention*. New York: Cambridge University Press.

McFarland, Andrew S. 2004. *Neopluralism: The Evolution of Political Process Theory*. Lawrence: University Press of Kansas.

———. 2006. Comment: Power—Over, To, With. *City & Community* 5(1):39–41.

McKinney, Matthew, and William Harmon. 2004. *The Western Confluence*. Washington, DC: Island Press.

McLean, Kirsty. 2006. Housing. In Stuart Woolman, Theunis Roux, Jonathan Klaaren, Anthony Stein, Matthew Chasklason, and Michael Bishop, eds. *Constitutional Law of South Africa*, 2nd ed., 55.1–55.57. Cape Town: Juta.

Mehta, Suketu. 2004. *Maximum City: Bombay Lost and Found*. New York: Knopf.

Mershon, Sherie. 2000. *Corporate Social Responsibility and Urban Revitalization: The Allegheny Conference on Community Development, 1943–1968*. Unpublished doctoral dissertation, Carnegie Mellon University, Pittsburgh, PA.

Meyer-Stamer, Jörg. 2003. *Why Is Local Economic Development So Difficult, and What Can We Do to Make It More Effective?* Working paper. Duisburg, Germany: Mesopartner.

Mills, C. Wright. 1956. *The Power Elite*. New York: Oxford University Press.

Miraftab, Faranak. 2004. Public-Private Partnerships: The Trojan Horse of Neoliberal Development? *Journal of Planning Education and Research* 24:89–101.

Miraftab, Faranak, and Shana Wills. 2005. Insurgency and Spaces of Active Citizenship: The Story of the Western Cape Anti-Eviction Campaign in South Africa. *Journal of Planning Education and Research* 25:200–217.

Mitchell-Weaver, Clyde. 1992. Public-Private Partnerships, Innovation Networks, and Regional Development in Southwestern Pennsylvania. *Canadian Journal of Regional Science* 15(2):273–288.

Mitchell-Weaver, Clyde, Sabina Deitrick, and Aspasia Rigopoulou. 1999. Linkages between Reconversion of Old Industrial Milieux, Intra-Regional Dynamics, and Continentalization of the Economy: The Case of Pittsburgh. In *Entre la Metropolisation et le Village Global: Les Scenes Territoriales de la Reconversion*. Montreal: Presses de l'Université du Quebec.

Mohan, Sudha. 2001. Vitalising Urban Local Democratic Governance. In *Revitalising Indian Democracy*, ed. Nawaz Mody, Kanamma S. Raman, and Louis D'Silva, 205–215. Mumbai: Allied Publishers.

Mollenkopf, John. 1981. Neighborhood Political Development and the Politics of Urban Growth: Boston and San Francisco. *International Journal of Urban and Regional Research* 5(1):15–39.

———. 1983. *The Contested City*. Princeton, NJ: Princeton University Press.

Molotch, Harvey L. 1976. The City as a Growth Machine. *American Journal of Sociology* 82(2):309–333.

Montero, Alfred P. 2000. Devolving Democracy?: Political Decentralization and the New Brazilian Federalism. In *Democratic Brazil: Actors, Institutions, and Processes*, ed. Peter R. Kingstone and Timothy J. Power, 58–76. Pittsburgh: University of Pittsburgh Press.

———. 2001. Making and Remaking "Good Government" in Brazil: Subnational Industrial Policy in Minas Gerais. *Latin American Politics and Society* 43(2):49–80.

Moore, Carl N., Gianni Longo, and Patsy Palmer. 1999. Visioning. In *The Consensus Building Handbook*, ed. Lawrence Susskind, Sarah McKearnan, and Jennifer Thomas-Larmer, 557–590. Thousand Oaks, CA: Sage.

Moore, Mark. 1995. *Creating Public Value*. Cambridge, MA: Harvard University Press.

———. 1999. Creating and Exploiting Networks of Capacity. Unpublished paper, John F. Kennedy School of Government, Harvard University, Cambridge, Massachusetts, January.

Mukhija, Vinit. 2001. Enabling Slum Redevelopment in Mumbai: Policy Paradox in Practice. *Housing Studies* 16(6):791–806.

———. 2003. *Squatters as Developers: Slum Redevelopment in Mumbai*. Burlington, VT: Ashgate.

Muller, E. K. 1988. Historical Aspects of Regional Structural Change in the Pittsburgh Region. In *Regional Structural Change and Industrial Policy in International Perspective*, ed. J. J. Hesse, 17–48. Baden-Baden: Nomos Verlag.

Neuwirth, Robert. 2004. *Shadow Cities: A Billion Squatters, a New Urban World*. New York: Routledge.

Nivola, Pietro S. 1999. *Laws of the Landscape: How Policies Shape Cities in Europe and America*. Washington, DC: Brookings Institution Press.

Nye, Joseph, Jr. 2004. *Soft Power: The Means to Success in World Politics*. New York: Public Affairs.

Nylen, William R. 2003. An Enduring Legacy? Popular Participation in the Aftermath of the Participatory Budgets of João Monlevade and Betim. In *Radicals in Power: The Workers' Party and Experiments in Urban Democracy in Brazil*, ed. Gianpaolo Baiocchi, 91–112. London: Zed Books.

Olberding, Julia Cencula. 2002. Diving into the "Third Waves" of Regional Governance and Economic Development Strategies. *Economic Development Quarterly* 16(3):251–272.

Oldfield, Sophie. 2000. The Centrality of Community Capacity in State Low-Income Housing Provision in Cape Town, South Africa. *International Journal of Urban and Regional Research* 24(4):858–872.

Oldfield, Sophie, and Kristian Stokke. 2002. *Western Cape Anti-Eviction Campaign Report*. Mimeograph, Western Cape Anti-Eviction Campaign, Cape Town, July.

———. 2006. Building Unity in Diversity: Social Movement Activism in the Western Cape Anti-Eviction Campaign. In *Voices of Protest: Social Movements in Post-Apartheid South Africa*, ed. Richard Ballard, Adam Habib, and Imraan Valodia, eds., 25–49. Pietermaritzburg: University of Kwazulu-Natal Press.

Olson, Mancur. 1965. *The Logic of Collective Action*. Cambridge, MA: Harvard University Press.

O'Rourke, Dara. 2004. *Community-Driven Regulation*. Cambridge, MA: MIT Press.

Ostroff, Frank. 1999. *The Horizontal Organization*. New York: Public Affairs.

Ostrom, Elinor. 1996. Crossing the Great Divide: Coproduction, Synergy, and Development. *World Development* 24(6):1073–1087.

Parnell, Susan. 2004. Constructing a Developmental Nation: The Challenge of Including the Poor in the Post-Apartheid City. Paper presented at the conference "Overcoming Underdevelopment in South Africa's Second Economy," Development Bank of South Africa, Midrand, October 28–29.

Parnell, Susan, and Edgar Pieterse. 2002. Developmental Local Government. In *Democratising Local Government: The South African Experiment*, ed. Susan Parnell, Edgar Pieterse, Mark Swilling, and Dominique Wooldridge, 79–91. Cape Town: University of Cape Town Press.

Parnell, Susan, and Jenny Robinson. 2006. Development and Urban Policy: Johannesburg's City Development Strategy. *Urban Studies* 43(2):337–355.

Patel, Sheela, Sundar Burra, and Celine d'Cruz. 2001. Slum/Shack Dwellers International: Foundations to Treetops. *Environment and Urbanization* 13(2):45–59.

Patel, Sheela, Celine d'Cruz , and Sundar Burra. 2002. Beyond Evictions in a Global City: People-Managed Resettlement in Mumbai. *Environment and Urbanization* 14(1):159–172.

Peterson, F. Ross. 1989. Utah Politics Since 1945. In *Utah's History*, ed. Richard D. Poll, Thomas G. Alexander, Eugene E. Campbell, and David E. Miller, 515–530. Logan: Utah State University Press.

Peterson, Paul. 1981. *City Limits*. Chicago: University of Chicago Press.

Pettigrew, Andrew M. 1990. Longitudinal Field Research on Change: Theory and Practice. *Organizational Science* 1(3):267–292.

Pierre, Jon. 1999. Models of Urban Governance: The Institutional Dimension of Urban Politics. *Urban Affairs Review* 34(3):372–396.

Pieterse, Edgar. 2002a. From Divided to Integrated City?: Critical Overview of the Emerging Governance System in Cape Town. *Urban Forum* 13(1):3–37.

———. 2002b. Participatory Local Governance in the Making. In *Democratising Local Government: The South African Experiment*, ed. Susan Parnell, Edgar Pieterse, Mark Swilling, and Dominique Wooldridge, 1–17. Cape Town: University of Cape Town Press.

Pieterse, Edgar. 2006a. Building with Ruins and Dreams: Some Thoughts on Realizing Integrated Urban Development in South Africa through Crisis. *Urban Studies* 43(2):285–304.

———. 2006b. *Rebuilding amongst Ruins: The Pursuit of Urban Integration in South Africa, 1994–2001.* Doctoral dissertation, London School of Economics and Political Science.

Piore, Michael, and Charles F. Sabel. 1984. *The Second Industrial Divide.* New York: Basic Books.

Pittman, Karen, and Merita Irby. 1998. Reflections on a Decade of Promoting Youth Development. In *The Forgotten Half Revisited,* ed. Samuel Halperin, 159–169. Washington, DC: American Youth Policy Forum.

Piven, Frances Fox, and Richard Cloward. 1977. *Poor People's Movements: Why They Succeed, How They Fail.* New York: Pantheon.

Poll, Richard D. 1989. An American Commonwealth. In *Utah's History,* ed. Richard D. Poll, Thomas G. Alexander, Eugene E. Campbell, and David E. Miller, 669–682. Logan: Utah State University Press.

Polletta, Francesca. 2002. *Freedom Is an Endless Meeting: Democracy in American Social Movements.* Chicago: University of Chicago.

Polodny, Joel and Karen L. Page. 1998. Network Forms of Organization. *Annual Review of Sociology* 24:57–76.

Porter, Michael E. 2000. Location, Competition, and Economic Development: Local Clusters in a Global Economy. *Economic Development Quarterly* 14(1):15–34.

Portes, Alejandro. 1998. Social Capital: Its Origins and Applications in Modern Sociology. *Annual Review of Sociology* 24:1–24.

Power, Samantha. 2003. The AIDS Rebel. *New Yorker,* May 19.

Power, Timothy J., 2000. Political Institutions in Democratic Brazil: Politics as a Permanent Constitutional Convention. In *Democratic Brazil: Actors, Institutions, and Processes,* ed. Peter R. Kingstone and Timothy J. Power, 17–35. Pittsburgh: University of Pittsburgh Press.

Power, Timothy J., and J. Timmons Roberts. 2000. A New Brazil?: The Changing Sociodemographic Context of Brazilian Democracy. In *Democratic Brazil: Actors, Institutions, and Processes,* ed. Peter R. Kingstone and Timothy J. Power, 236–262. Pittsburgh: University of Pittsburgh Press.

Pressman, Jeffrey L., and Aaron Wildavsky. 1973. *Implementation.* Berkeley: University of California Press.

Pritchett, Lant, and Michael Woolcock. 2004. Solutions When *the* Solution is the Problem: Arraying the Disarray in Development. *World Development* 32(2):191–212.

Putnam, Robert. 1993. *Making Democracy Work.* Princeton, NJ: Princeton University Press.

———. 2000. *Bowling Alone: The Collapse and Revival of Community in America.* New York: Simon & Schuster.

Ragin, Charles C. 1987. *The Comparative Method.* Berkeley: University of California Press.

————. 2000. *Fuzzy-Set Social Science*. Chicago: University of Chicago Press.

Raiffa, Howard. 1982. *The Art and Science of Negotiation*. Cambridge, MA: Harvard University Press.

Raiffa, Howard, with John Richardson and David Metcalfe. 2002. *Negotiation Analysis: The Science and Art of Collaborative Decisionmaking*. Cambridge, MA: Harvard University Press.

Reese, Laura A. 1997. *Local Economic Development Policy: The United States and Canada*. New York: Garland.

Reese, Laura A., and Raymond A. Rosenfeld. 2002. *The Civic Culture of Local Economic Development*. Thousand Oaks, CA: Sage.

Richmond, Henry R. 2000. Metropolitan Land-Use Reform: The Promise and Challenge of Majority Consensus. In *Reflections on Regionalism*, ed. Bruce Katz, 9–39. Washington, DC: Brookings Institution Press.

Rodriguez-Posé, Andrés, and John Tomaney. 1999. Industrial Crisis in the Centre of the Periphery: Stabilisation, Economic Restructuring and Policy Responses in the São Paulo Metropolitan Region. *Urban Studies* 36(3):479–498.

Rodriguez-Posé, Andrés, John Tomaney, and Jeroen Klink. 2001. Local Empowerment through Economic Restructuring in Brazil: The Case of the Greater ABC Region. *Geoforum* 32:459–469.

Rodrik, Dani. 2004. *Industrial Policy for the Twenty-First Century*. Working paper RWP 04-047. Cambridge, MA: John F. Kennedy School of Government, Harvard University.

Roe, Emery. 1994. *Narrative Policy Analysis*. Durham, NC: Duke University Press.

Roux, Theunis. 2002. Understanding Grootboom: A Response to Cass R. Sunstein. *Constitutional Forum* 12(2):41–51.

————. 2003. Legitimating Transformation: Political Resource Allocation in the South African Constitutional Court. *Democratization* 10(4):92–111.

Rubin, Herbert J. 1988. Shoot Anything That Flies, Claim Anything That Falls: Conversations with Economic Development Practitioners. *Economic Development Quarterly* 2(3):263–277.

Rusk, David. 1999. *Inside Game/Outside Game: Winning Strategies for Saving Urban America*. Washington, DC: Brookings Institution Press.

Sabatier, Paul A. 1993. Policy Change over a Decade or More. In *Policy Change and Learning: An Advocacy Coalition Approach*, ed. Paul A. Sabatier and Hank C. Jenkins-Smith, 13–40. Boulder, CO: Westview Press.

Sabel, Charles A. 1992. Studied Trust: Building New Forms of Cooperation in a Volatile Economy. In *Industrial Districts and Local Economic Regeneration*, eds. Frank Pyke and Werner Sengenberger, 215–250. Geneva: International Institute for Labor Studies.

————. 2004. Beyond Principal-Agent Governance: Experimentalist Organizations, Learning and Accountability. In *De Staat van de Democratie: Democratie voorbij de Staat*, ed. Ewald Engelen and Monika Sie Dhian Ho, 173–195. Amsterdam: Amsterdam University Press.

Sachs, Albie. 2005. The Judicial Enforcement of Socio-Economic Rights: The Grootboom Case. In *Democratizing Development: The Politics of Socio-Economic Rights in South Africa*, ed. Peris Jones and Kristian Stokke, 131–151. Boston: Martinus Nijhoff.

Sahlman, William, Howard H. Stevenson, Michael J. Roberts, and Amar V. Bhide. 1999. *The Entrepreneurial Venture*. 2nd ed. Boston: Harvard Business School Press.

Sampson, Robert. 1999. What Community Supplies. In *Urban Problems and Community Development*, ed. Ronald Ferguson and William Dickens, 241–292. Washington, DC: Brookings Institution Press.

Sampson, Robert, Stephen Raudenbush, and Felton Earls. 1997. Neighborhoods and Violent Crime: A Multi-Level Study of Collective Efficacy. *Science* 277(5328):918–924.

Sandercock, Leonie. 1998. *Making the Invisible Visible: A Multicultural Planning History*. Berkeley: University of California Press.

Sandoval, Salvador. 2004. Working-Class Contention. In *Reforming Brazil*, ed. Mauricio Font and Anthony Peter Spanakos, 217–230. New York: Lexington.

Sanoff, Henry. 1999. *Community Participation Methods in Design and Planning*. New York: Wiley.

Sanyal, Bishwarpriya. 1994. *Cooperative Autonomy: The Dialectic of State-NGOs Relationship in Developing Countries*. Geneva: International Institute for Labor Studies.

Sanyal, Bishwarpriya, and Vinit Mukhija. 2001. Institutional Pluralism and Housing Delivery: A Case of Unforeseen Conflicts in Mumbai, India. *World Development* 29(12):2043–2057.

Sarat, Austin, and Stuart Scheingold. 1998. *Cause Lawyering: Political Commitments and Professional Responsibilities*. New York: Oxford University Press.

———. 2001. *Cause Lawyering and the State in a Global Era*. New York: Oxford University Press.

Sassen, Saskia. 1989. New Trends in the Sociospatial Organization of the New York City Economy. In *Economic Restructuring and Political Response*, ed. Robert A. Beauregard, 69–113. Thousand Oaks, CA: Sage.

———. 1991. *The Global City: New York, London, Tokyo*. Princeton, NJ: Princeton University Press.

Satterthwaite, David. 2002. *The Ten and a Half Myths That May Distort the Urban Policies of Governments and International Agencies*. London: Human Settlements Program, International Institute for Environment and Development.

———. 2005. The Scale of Urban Change Worldwide, 1950–2000, and Its Underpinnings. Human Settlements Discussion Paper. London: International Institute for Environment and Development.

Savitch, H .L., and Paul Kantor. 2004. *Cities in the International Marketplace: The Political Economy of Urban Development in North America and Europe.* Princeton, NJ: Princeton University Press.

Saxenian, AnnaLee. 1994. *Regional Advantage: Culture and Competition in Silicon Valley and Route 128.* Cambridge, MA: Harvard University Press.

Sbragia, Alberta M. 1990. Pittsburgh's "Third Way": The Nonprofit Sector as a Key to Urban Regeneration. In *Leadership and Urban Regeneration: Cities in North America and Europe*, ed. Dennis Judd and Michael Parkinson, 51–68. Newbury Park, CA: Sage.

Schattschneider, Elmer E. 1960. *The Semisovereign People: A Realist's View of Democracy in America.* New York: Reinhart and Winston.

Scheingold, Stuart. 1974. *The Politics of Rights: Lawyers, Public Policy, and Political Change.* New Haven, CT: Yale University Press.

Schmidtz, David. 2006. *Elements of Justice.* New York: Cambridge University Press.

Schneider, Daniel, and Michael Ignatieff. 2001. The Constitutional Right to Housing in South Africa: The Government of the Republic of South Africa vs. Irene Grootboom. Case 1627.0 and 1627.1. Cambridge, MA: Kennedy School of Government Case Program, Harvard University.

Schön, Donald. 1979. Generative Metaphor: A Perspective on Problem-Setting in Social Policy. In *Metaphor and Thoughts*, ed. Andrew Ortony, 254–283. New York: Cambridge University Press.

Schön, Donald, and Martin Rein. 1994. *Frame Reflection: Toward the Resolution of Intractable Policy Controversies.* New York: Basic Books.

Schorr, Lisbeth B. 1988. *Within Our Reach: Breaking the Cycle of Disadvantage.* New York: Anchor Books.

———. 1997. *Common Purpose: Strengthening Families and Neighborhoods to Rebuild America.* New York: Anchor Books.

Schrag, Peter. 1998. *Paradise Lost: California's Experience, America's Future.* New York: New Press.

Scott, Allen J. 1999. Industrial Revitalization in the ABC Municipalities, São Paulo: Diagnostic Analysis and Strategic Recommendations for a New Economy and a New Regionalism. *Regional Development Studies* 7:1–32.

Scott, James. 1998. *Seeing Like a State: How Certain Schemes to Improve the Human Condition Have Failed.* New Haven, CT: Yale University Press.

Scott, W. Richard, Sarah Deschenes, Kathryn Hopkins, Anne Newman, and Milbrey McLaughlin. 2006. Advocacy Organizations and the Field of Youth Services: Ongoing Efforts to Restructure a Field. *Nonprofit and Voluntary Sector Quarterly* 35(4):691–714.

Senge, Peter. 1990. *The Fifth Discipline: The Art and Practice of the Learning Organization.* New York: Doubleday/Currency.

Shapiro, Ian. 2003. *The State of Democratic Theory.* Princeton, NJ: Princeton University Press.

Shutkin, William A. 2001. *The Land That Could Be: Environmentalism and Democracy in the Twenty-First Century.* Cambridge, MA: MIT Press.

Silva, Marcelo Kunrath. 2003. Participation by Design. In *Radicals in Power: The Workers' Party and Experiments in Urban Democracy in Brazil,* ed. Gianpaolo Baiocchi, 113–130. London: Zed Books.

Skidmore, Thomas E. 1999. *Brazil: Five Centuries of Change.* New York: Oxford University Press.

Skocpol, Theda. 2003. *Diminished Democracy: From Membership to Management in American Civic Life.* Norman: University of Oklahoma Press.

Skocpol, Theda, and Margaret Somers. 1980. The Uses of Comparative History in Macrosocial Inquiry. *Comparative Studies in Society and History* 22:174–197.

Smilor, Raymond, Niall O'Donnell, Gregory Stein, and Robert S. Welborn III. 2007. The Research University and the Development of High-Technology Centers in the United States. *Economic Development Quarterly* 21(3):203–222.

Smith, Steven Rathgeb. and Michael Lipsky. 1993. *Nonprofits for Hire: The Welfare State in the Age of Contracting.* Cambridge, MA: Harvard University Press.

Snyder, William. 2002. *Organizing for Economic Development in Chicago: A Case Study of Strategy, Structure, and Leadership Practices.* Report for CEOs for Cities, New York, March.

Snyder, William, and Xavier de Souza Briggs. 2003. *Communities of Practice: A New Tool for Government Managers.* Washington, DC: IBM Center for the Business of Government.

Somekh, Nádia, and Jeroen Klink. 2001. The Future Is Coming: Economic Restructuring and Local Governance, The Case of Santo André, Metropolitan Region of São Paulo, Brazil. Mimeo. Municipality of Santo André, Brazil, September.

South African Cities Network (SACN). 2004. *State of the Cities Report 2004.* Johannesburg: South African Cities Network.

Sparrow, Malcolm. 2000. *The Regulatory Craft.* Washington, DC: Brookings Institution Press.

Spink, Peter, Silvio Caccia Bava, and Veronika Paulics, eds. 2002. *Novos Contornos da Gestão Local.* São Paulo: Polis.

Squires, Gregory D., ed. 1989. *Unequal Partnerships: The Political Economy of Urban Development in Postwar America.* New Brunswick, NJ: Rutgers University Press.

Squires, Gregory D. 2002. Urban Sprawl and the Uneven Development of Metropolitan America. In *Urban Sprawl: Causes, Consequences, and Policy Responses,* ed. Gregory D. Squires, 1–22. Washington: Urban Institute Press.

Steiner, Henry, and Philip Alston. 2000. *International Human Rights in Context.* New York: Oxford University Press.

Stepan, Alfred. 2000. Brazil's Decentralized Federalism: Bringing Government Closer to the Citizens? *Daedalus* 129(2):145–170.

Stiglitz, Joseph, and Andrew Charlton. 2005. *Fair Trade for All: How Trade Can Promote Development*. New York: Oxford University Press.

Stoker, Gerry. 1995. Regime Theory and Urban Politics. In *Theories of Urban Politics*, ed. David Judge, Gerry Stoker, and Harold Wolman, 54–71. London: Sage.

———. 1998. Public-Private Partnerships and Urban Governance. In *Public-Private Partnerships in Urban Governance*, ed. Jon Pierre, 34–51. New York: St. Martin's.

———. 2002. International Trends in Local Government Transformation. In *Democratising Local Government: The South African Experiment*, ed. Susan Parnell, Edgar Pieterse, Mark Swilling, and Dominique Wooldridge, 31–39. Cape Town: University of Cape Town Press.

Stone, Clarence N. 1989. *Regime Politics: Governing Atlanta, 1946–1988*. Lawrence: University Press of Kansas.

———. 2001. Civic Capacity and Urban Education. *Urban Affairs Review* 36(5):595–619.

Stone, Clarence N. 2004. Rejoinder: Multiple Imperatives, or Some Thoughts about Governance in a Loosely Coupled but Stratified Society. *Journal of Urban Affairs* 26(1):35–42.

———. 2005. Looking Back to Look Forward: Reflections on Urban Regime Analysis. *Urban Affairs Review* 40(3):309–341.

———. 2006. Power, Reform and Urban Regime Analysis. *City & Community* 5(1):23–38.

Stone, Clarence, Jeffrey Henig, Bryan D. Jones, and Carol Pierannunzi. 2001. *Building Civic Capacity: The Politics of Reforming Urban Schools*. Lawrence: University Press of Kansas.

Stone, Deborah A. 1988. *Policy Paradox and Political Reason*. New York: HarperCollins.

Storper, Michael. 1997. *The Regional World: Territorial Development in a Global Economy*. New York: Guilford.

Surowiecki, James. 2004. *The Wisdom of Crowds: Why the Many Are Smarter Than the Few and How Collective Wisdom Shapes Business, Economies, Societies, and Nations*. New York: Doubleday.

Susskind, Lawrence, and Catherine Ashcraft. 2007. How to Negotiate Fairer and More Sustainable Water Agreements. Unpublished manuscript, Department of Urban Studies and Planning, Massachusetts Institute of Technology, Cambridge, MA.

Susskind, Lawrence, and Jeffrey Cruikshank. 1987. *Breaking the Impasse*. New York: Basic Books.

———. 2006a. *Breaking Robert's Rules*. New York: Oxford University Press.

———. 2006b. Can Public Policy Dispute Resolution Meet the Challenges Set by Deliberative Democracy? *Dispute Resolution Magazine* (winter): 5–6.

Susskind, Lawrence, and Alexis Gensberg. 2002. *The Important Role of Consensus Building in Planning for Smart Growth.* Working paper. Washington, DC: George Washington University Center for Smart Growth.

Susskind, Lawrence, and Merrick Hoben. 2004. Making Regional Policy Dialogues Work: A Credo for Metro-Scale Consensus Building. *Temple Environmental Law Journal* 22(2): 123–140.

Susskind, Lawrence, Sarah McKearnan, and Jennifer Thomas-Larmer, eds. 1999. *The Consensus Building Handbook.* Thousand Oaks, CA: Sage.

Swilling, Mark, and Bev Russell. 2002. *The Size and Scope of the Nonprofit Sector in South Africa.* University of Witswatersrand and University of Kwazulu-Natal, Johannesburg and Durban.

Tauxe, Caroline. 1995. Marginalizing Public Participation in Planning. *Journal of the American Planning Association* 61(4):471–482.

Tendler, Judith. 1997. *Good Government in the Tropics.* Baltimore: Johns Hopkins University Press.

———. 2000. *The Economic Wars between the States.* Report for the Organization for Economic Cooperation and Development and the Bank of the Northeast, Massachusetts Institute of Technology, Cambridge, MA, September.

Throgmorton, James. 1996. *Planning as Persuasive Storytelling.* Chicago: University of Chicago Press.

Turok, Ivan. 2001. Persistent Polarization Post-Apartheid?: Progress Towards Urban Integration in Cape Town. *Urban Studies* 38(1):2349–2377.

United Nations Development Program. 2001. *Human Rights and Human Development: The Human Development Report, 2000.* New York: Oxford University Press.

United Nations Human Settlements Programme (UN-Habitat). 2005. *Financing Urban Shelter: Global Report on Human Settlements.* London: Earthscan.

United Nations Millennium Project. 2005. *A Home in the City: Improving the Lives of Slumdwellers.* Sterling, VA: Earthscan.

Wade, Robert. 1990. *Governing the Market.* Princeton, NJ: Princeton University Press.

Waddell, Steve, and L. David Brown. 1997. *Fostering Inter-Sectoral Partnerships.* IDR Report 13. Boston: Institute for Development Research.

Walsh, Joan. 1997. *Stories of Renewal: Community Building in America.* New York: Rockefeller Foundation.

Warren, Mark. 2001. *Dry Bones Rattling: Community Building to Revitalize American Democracy.* Princeton, NJ: Princeton University Press.

Watson, Vanessa. 2002. *Change and Continuity in Spatial Planning in Cape Town under Political Transition.* London: Routledge.

Weber, Edward P. 2003. *Bring Society Back In: Grassroots Ecosystem Management, Accountability, and Sustainable Communities.* Cambridge, MA: MIT Press.

Weber, Michael P. 1988. *Don't Call Me Boss, David L. Lawrence: Pittsburgh's Renaissance Mayor.* Pittsburgh: University of Pittsburgh Press.

Weir, Margaret. 2000. Coalition Building for Regionalism. In *Reflections on Regionalism*, ed. Bruce Katz, 127–153. Washington, DC: Brookings Institution Press.

Weir, Margaret, Harold Wolman, and Todd Swanstrom. 2005. The Calculus of Coalitions: Cities, Suburbs, and the Metropolitan Agenda. *Urban Affairs Review* 40(6):730–760.

Wenger, Etienne. 1998. *Communities of Practice.* New York: Cambridge University Press.

Wilkinson, Peter. 2000. City Profile: Cape Town. *Cities* 17(3):195–205.

———. 2004. Renegotiating Local Governance in a Post-Apartheid City: The Case of Cape Town. *Urban Forum* 15(3):213–230.

Williamson, Abby, and Archon Fung. 2005. Public Deliberation: Where Are We? Where Can We Go? *National Civic Review* 93(4):3–15.

Wolman, Harold. 1995. Local Government Institutions and Democratic Governance. In *Theories of Urban Politics*, ed. David Judge, Gerry Stoker, and Harold Wolman, 135–159. Thousand Oaks, CA: Sage.

Wolman, Harold, with David Spitzley. 1996. The Politics of Local Economic Development. *Economic Development Quarterly* 10(2):225–262.

Wood, Donna J., and Barbara Gray. 1991. Toward a Comprehensive Theory of Collaboration. *Journal of Applied Behavioral Science* 27(2):139–162.

Woolcock, Michael, and Deepa Narayan. 2000. Social Capital: Its Significance for Development Theory, Research, and Policy. *World Bank Research Observer* 15(2):225–249.

World Bank. 1997. *The State in a Changing World: The World Development Report 1997.* New York: Oxford University Press.

———. 2000. *Entering the 21st Century: The World Development Report 1999/2000.* New York: Oxford University Press.

Yin, Robert K. 1994. *Case Study Research: Design and Methods.* Thousand Oaks, CA: Sage.

Yusuf, Shahid, Simon Evenett, and Weiping Wu. 2000. Local Dynamics in a Globalizing World: 21st Century Catalysts for Development. In *Local Dynamics in an Era of Globalization*, ed. Shahid Yusuf, Weiping Wu, and Simon Evenett, 2–8. New York: Oxford University Press and The World Bank.

Index